# LLOYD'S OF LONDON

Lloyd's New Building; an impression from Lime Street by Sydney R. Jones
(October, 1956).

# Lloyd's of London

## *A Study in Individualism*

BY

### D. E. W. GIBB
*Member of Lloyd's*

LONDON
MACMILLAN & CO LTD
NEW YORK · ST MARTIN'S PRESS
1957

MACMILLAN AND COMPANY LIMITED
*London Bombay Calcutta Madras Melbourne*

THE MACMILLAN COMPANY OF CANADA LIMITED
*Toronto*

ST MARTIN'S PRESS INC
*New York*

*First edition 1957*
*Reprinted 1957*

Printed in Great Britain by
W. S. Cowell Ltd, at the Butter Market, Ipswich

# ACKNOWLEDGEMENTS

My thanks are due to several Chairmen and Committees of Lloyd's for the great help they have given me in the work of writing this history. They have put all their records at my disposal and have never refused any assistance that I asked. But they are not responsible for anything that appears in the book – whether fact, opinion or inaccuracy.

Members of the Committee's staff have put me under a great debt of gratitude, particularly those of the Information Department, who have done a good deal of work that ought to have been done by me. Particularly I must thank them for their energy in collecting photographs to lighten the printed word.

My special thanks go to Mr Boxford, former Principal Clerk, who owed his appointment on the staff of Lloyd's to his precocious knowledge of geography (*see* chapter 8); and to Mr Chapman, one of the present Clerks to the Committee, who has been a constant stand-by. I cannot say how grateful I am both to Mr Boxford and to Mr Chapman for their never-failing advice and encouragement.

Thanks are also due to the Leathersellers' Company for permission to reproduce their portrait of Richard Thornton, and to the Herron Art Museum of the Art Association of Indianapolis for permission to reproduce J. S. Copley's painting of Sir Brook Watson; also to Mr George MacBeath (Curator of the Department of Canadian History, New Brunswick Museum, St John, N.B.), Mr B. C. Norton of the Norton Galleries, New York, and the staff of the Guildhall Library, London, for their willing help and co-operation.

No mention by name of any living member of Lloyd's has been made in this book. While it was being written Sir Percy MacKinnon was still alive and his name will not be found in it. Last month he died and a reference to his great work at Lloyd's is now possible. He was a member of Lloyd's for sixty-two years and for five years he was its Chairman. He played a great part in shaping the modern Lloyd's and in fostering the corporate spirit which is the theme of the book's later chapters. His name would certainly have appeared in the last chapter of all.

A last acknowledgement: it is fifty-two years since I was first connected with Lloyd's, and, like most people who have spent their working lives there, I keep in my heart a very warm corner for the Room.

*December*, 1956.                                                         D.E.W.G.

v

# CONTENTS

# LIST OF PLATES

# 1

## THE ORIGIN OF LLOYD'S

*Coffee and Coffee Houses – Edward Lloyd – Shipping – Lloyd's News – Contemporary Journalism – White servitude – Edward Lloyd's ambition*

---

AS THE SOCIETY OF LLOYD'S has a pedigree that goes back to a seventeenth-century coffee-house it is natural for any history of Lloyd's to begin with the first introduction of coffee to England – that odd episode in English social history when coffee drinking became a fashion and the fashion swept London like an epidemic.

England owes the introduction of coffee to Archbishop Laud.[1] He was interested in the welfare of Christian refugees who sometimes came here escaping from Mohammedan rule in the Eastern Mediterranean. One of his protégés was a Cretan scholar named Canopis who was brought by the Archbishop to Balliol College, Oxford, and there 'desseminated his grave learning and amused his colleagues' by brewing 'a drink of a soote colour dryed in a furnace and that they drink as hot as can be endured.' He seems to have communicated the taste quickly to a number of people both in Oxford and in Cambridge. An apothecary started selling coffee publicly in his house 'against All Soules College', and within a few years under-graduates in both Universities were spending so much time in the coffee-houses that the practice was denounced by some of the more serious-minded dons. In our own day the head of an Oxford College once spoke regretfully of the 'time-wasting habit of morning coffee' and in saying that (whether he knew it or not) he was only repeating the complaint of a Cambridge don nearly three centuries before him. 'Why,' cried the Cambridge don in 1677 'why doth solid and serious learning decline and few or none now follow it in the University? Answer: because of coffee-houses where they spend all their time.'

London kept pace with the University towns and in 1652 an English merchant in the Levantine trade, who had acquired the habit abroad, began making coffee in his English home. Immediately he found that he

[1] C. V. Wedgwood: *The King's Peace*.

was a far more popular person than he had ever before realized. Friends and acquaintances gathered at his house every morning to enjoy his conversation, until they became an unbearable nuisance and he a most reluctant host. Suspecting at last that the attraction lay less in his personality than in the 'new kind of black liquor his servant was in the habit of preparing every morning,' he suggested to his servant that he should set up professionally as a coffee-man in St Michael's Alley, Cornhill. The servant agreed and the first of London's coffee-houses was opened.

The earliest advertisements put out by this servant made the most remarkable claims for coffee, emphasizing rather its medical than its social advantages, and putting it forward almost as a panacea for the maladies of mankind. 'It so incloseth', the servant's advertisement ran ,'the orifice of the stomach, and fortifies the heat within, that it is very good to help digestion; and therefore of great use to be taken about three or four o'clock afternoon as well as in the morning. It much quickens the spirits and makes the heart lightsome; it is good against sore eyes and the better if you can hold your head over it and take in the steam that way. It suppresseth the fumes exceedingly and therefore it is good against the headache and will very much stop any deflexion of rheums, that distill from the head upon the stomach, and so prevent and help consumptions and the cough of the lungs. It is excellent to prevent and cure the dropsy, gout and scurvy. It is known by experience to be better than any other drying drink for people in years or children that have any running tumours upon them, as the King's Evil, etc. It is a most excellent remedy against the spleen, hypochondriac winds and the like. . . . It is neither laxative nor restringent.'[1] That was a telling advertisement; but when the public had once tasted the black drink it was not its therapeutic value that drew them back to it. It was the new delicious flavour of it and the social pleasure of sipping it in company with one's friends, the charm of friendly conversation in familiar surroundings, the break in the monotonous routine of the daily round.

It is significant, perhaps, that the habit started between 1650 and 1660, the heyday of the Puritans, when Englishmen were living under strange new conditions, cut off from many of the pleasures with which they had been accustomed to fill their leisure time. Whether he liked it or not the citizen of London had at that time to subordinate his habits to the Puritan way of life. His pastimes must conform to the Puritan doctrine and pass the Puritan tests of conduct and morality. He might no longer pay for a seat in the theatre or go bear-baiting in the environs of the town. The stages

[1] Warren R. Dawson, F.R.S.L.: *The London Coffee-Houses and the Beginnings of Lloyd's.*

were closed and bear-baiting prohibited – 'not', as Macaulay said, 'because it gave pain to the bear, but because it gave pleasure to the spectators'. Cockfighting and dancing were taboo; May-day festivities round that 'stynking idoll' the maypole were suppressed; and the Christmas dinner itself was robbed by law of all the things that made it a Christmas dinner. To the gay cheery sociable type of man, whatever his politics, life in the 1650's must have been abominably drab and austere; and he had to bear the austerity, not for economic reasons which he might have respected, but in the cause of a theology with which he did not necessarily agree.

To such a man the coffee-house, indifferent substitute though he might think it for the theatre and the bear pit, could still do something to pierce the gloom. He could at least go to his club, and what club could be cheaper or more handy than a neighbouring coffee-house where for three halfpence he could meet his friends and dawdle away an hour or two in talk? So the club-habit fastened itself on London, and when the Puritan rule collapsed the habit was passed on to the livelier existence of the Restoration, which adopted and fostered it till it grew so strong as to leave its mark on English commerce and English politics up to our own day.

Indeed Green in his *History of the English People* saw in those early coffee-houses the birthplace of modern English prose. It was in them that men learnt 'the new-found pleasure of talk'; and the habit of conversation they encouraged led to the natural easy style of the eighteenth-century essayists, which fixed for two centuries and more the standard of writing in English books and English newspapers. If that theory of Green's is correct, then every book and article written today owes something of its shape and form to the coffee-houses of the seventeenth century; and we may claim that Lloyd's and the modern English language have a common ancestor in the London of William and Mary.

How many of these coffee-houses there were in the City we do not know; but in 1708 the number was guessed by contemporaries as three thousand. That must be a gross exaggeration, but, in a contemporary picture of the life our forerunners lived, even a gross exaggeration may have some value for us as we try to reconstruct the scene. And the figure of three thousand could never have been suggested unless there was a coffee-house or two in every street and the houses had in fact become one of the chief features of the City. So we may assume that from 1700 onwards these places had a very important niche in the Londoner's life; that City men passed much of their time in them; and that many hours which might have been given to industrious toil were spent there in idle desultory conversation. How sharp is the contrast between that daily routine of 1700 and its counterpart in the City of 1956.

Of those old coffee-houses the greater part died long ago and are finished as though they had never been, leaving no memorial. But one or two of them laid an egg before they died, and so their stock was carried on to later generations, the line surviving (though in barely recognizable form) until today. The present Stock Exchange is the lineal descendant of Jonathan's, and the Shipping Exchange of the Baltic Coffee-House; while Lloyd's (internationally perhaps the best known of them all) still bears the surname of the man who started the house and for more than twenty years owned and controlled it. He was Edward Lloyd, and his shop was situated in Tower Street at the eastern end of the City. He himself was certainly an able, industrious and enterprising man and within his own sphere he achieved a certain amount of distinction.

But although many hours have been spent by antiquarians in poring over parish registers, rating books, old newspapers and other City records, and in searching out every crumb of information to be found about his origin, life and death, no one has been able to collect information enough even for a brief biography. We are told that he was born in or about 1648; that he was three times married; that he was a member of the Framework Knitters' Company; that he opened his first coffee-house not later than 1688-9; that within a few years his business was large enough to support a staff of two men and three maids; that he was a Churchwarden; that he tried to run a newspaper which did not prosper though his coffee-house did; that he left his business to a son-in-law; that his clientèle probably included (as well it might in Tower Street) a number of shipowners and captains; that he was about sixty-five when he died; that he was buried in St Mary Woolnoth's in Lombard Street; that his remains were dug up and reburied; that there is no separate tombstone to mark the place of his burial. Beyond these facts we really know very little about him.

As the Coffee-House was in existence in 1688 and the Bank of England was not created until 1694, Lloyd's may claim to be senior by at least six years to its august neighbour in Threadneedle Street. But though Lloyd's and the Bank were so close to each other in the dates of their birth, there is a great difference between them in the matter of early records and ascertainable facts. And the difference does not favour Lloyd's. When Sir John Clapham began in 1938 to write the history of the Bank of England, and was concerned with its origin and early life, he had ready to hand a great deal of contemporary evidence – Parliamentary journals, books of subscriptions, minutes, Governors' memoranda, ledgers, day journals, note journals and other documents which by themselves made up a detailed and comprehensive history.

On the other hand when Wright and Fayle set out to write their great history of Lloyd's they lacked for at least its first century all such aids as these. With admirable industry they collected scraps and pieces of information which, by deduction or direct evidence, proved that this thing or that happened to the infant Lloyd's; but the table was not laid and spread for them as it was for the historian of the Bank. Theirs was a very different task from his, and the reason for the difference is obvious. The Bank was born to greatness and Lloyd's achieved it only after eighty years of life and struggle. From the first, everybody was interested in the Bank. Nobody cared much about the Coffee-House. A baby born heir to a throne is surrounded from the beginning by attendants watching and noting every step in its progress, jotting down many things that its future biographer will be glad to have when he begins his task. But when beggars are born no comets are seen. A baby born in a log cabin in the Middle West may be destined to become President of the United States but he is not watched and publicized at birth; nobody bothers to make notes about his infancy; and a generation later his biographer, if he wants to know anything of what happened, will have to scrape the bottom of the barrel for hints, deductions and half-forgotten memories. In 1694 the Bank of England was the infant Prince and Lloyd's the Middle West baby. No one had cause to think that the little coffee-house, started in an unfashionable corner of the City, would become great and famous – so why trouble to describe it or locate it or leave any record of its activities and growth?

This distinction between the fullness of information about the young Bank of England and the scarcity of information about the young Lloyd's may seem unimportant and irrelevant, but in fact it is not. The contrast between an institution which was equipped originally for one kind of business, and has stuck to the same business for two and a half centuries, and an institution that has changed by slow degrees from a small shop to a great insurance market, moving along an unforeseeable path to an unpredictable destiny – that contrast is the key to the history of Lloyd's.

Even the date when Edward Lloyd started his own business is uncertain, and the question is not likely ever to be definitely settled. Official returns of 'victuallers' in the City of London for the year 1687/8 contain the name of Lloyd, frame-work knitter.[1] That entry is proof enough that Lloyd was then engaged in the victualling business, but the first printed reference to his coffee-house is dated February 1688/9 and occurs in an advertisement which appeared in the *London Gazette*. The advertiser, a Mr Edward Bransby of Derby, had been robbed and he wanted publicly to offer a reward for the recovery of his goods. Five watches belonging to him had been stolen, and the suspect was described as a middle-sized man with black curled hair and pockholes in his face, wearing a beaver hat and a brown riding coat. The watches, by the description in the advertisement, must have been of considerable value. They were all decorated well up to the limits of good taste, and Mr Bransby offered to anybody who gave notice of them the handsome reward of one guinea, the notice to be sent either to Mr Bransby's own address in Derby or to Mr Edward Lloyd's Coffee-House in Tower Street.

That is Lloyd's first appearance in English history, and it is strangely appropriate. Two hundred years or so later Lloyd's underwriters were to originate an insurance policy, of a sort never known before, to cover jewellery against all risks. And now scarcely a day passes without advertisements appearing in the London papers of jewellery lost or stolen, for the recovery of which underwriters will gladly pay a reward up to ten per cent of the value. But the main interest of the 1688 advertisement is the light it throws on the position of the coffee-house at that time. When a watchmaker in Derby, more than a day's journey from London, chooses this coffee-house out of all the coffee-houses he might have selected, one may conclude that its name is already reasonably well known in the City and not quite unknown in the Midlands; and it is a fair guess that Edward Lloyd as a coffee-man was already a local success and, in the City itself at any rate, a fairly familiar figure.

Where exactly in Tower Street the coffee-house stood has long been a matter of debate, but it seems certain that the official address was Salutation Precinct and is now identified with a small area at the western end of Great Tower Street. But wherever it was, Lloyd was not there very long. In 1691 – only three years after the *Gazette* had printed the stray advertisement which proves his occupancy – he left the house and went to a place in Lombard Street in which he and his successors plied their trade for the next eighty years.

It has always been assumed – and there is no reason to doubt the assumption – that Lloyd took with him from Tower Street to Lombard Street a

[1] Warren R. Dawson.

rich Gold Lace, and Furred with *Ermin*, as also with the Collar of the Order of the *Garter*; And as soon as the Crown was put upon His Head, the Officers of Arms and Sergeants at Arms Entred the House of Lords; and the Noblemen who preceded His Majesty, having placed themselves on each side of the Throne, as usually, and His Majesty (whose Train was borne by Noblemens Eldest Sons) being seated on the Throne, Sir *Thomas Duppa*, Gentleman Usher of the Black Rod, was Commanded to summon up the Commons, who being accordingly introduced into the House of Peers, and their Speaker Conducted to the Bar with the usual Formalities, the Lords being in their Robes, His Majesty made a most Gracious Speech to the Lords and Commons, relating to the present Circumstances of Affairs; After which His Majesty departed, and having Disrobed Himself, was Attended down to the Water-side, with the like Ceremony as before.

*Whitehall*, Febr. 20. The Right Honourable *Thomas Wharton* Esq; Comptroller of His

ing, 14 hands high, with white hairs in his forehead, and a black spot on his near Buttock. Whoever can give notice of them at the Lord Colchester's House in Lichfield-street in Soho, shall have two Guinea's Reward.

LOst the 15th Instant, between Arlington-street and Lincoln-inn-fields, a Diamond Ring with four large Rosset Diamonds, set square in Gold, with black Enamel. Whoever shall bring the said Ring to Mr *Philip Werker* at the Countess of Northampton's House in Lincoln-inn-fields, shall have five Guinea's Reward.

STolen the 30th Instant, from *Edward Bransby* in Darby, five Watches; one was a Pin Case, and a Silver Box, with a Silver Dyal Plate, hours cut upon Harris, it was a fine Wheel Chain, the watch Makers Name was *William* of Leicester; The second was a plain Silver Box, with a close Silver Case, a Pearl Dyal Plate, with Glass, the Dyal had a Pot of Flowers, the Makers Name was *William Corder* in Darby; The third had a Silver Box with a close Silver Case, a Pearl Dyal Plate, with the day of the Month; The fourth had a Silver Box and Pin Case, many of the Pins being come out, so that the Brass was seen, The fifth Watch had a Silver Box and Pin Case, long hours of the Dyal Plate, and fronted, it was a Wheel Chain Watch: supposed to be taken by a middle sized Man, having black curled Hair, Pockholes in his Face, wearing an old brown Riding Coat, and a black Bever Hat. Whoever gives notice of them at Mr. *Edward Bransby* in Darby as above, shall have 3 Guinea's Reward, or to Mr. *Edward Loyd's* Coffee-House in Tower-street, or to Mr. *Edward*

LOst the 16th instant, from the Right Honourable the Lord Viscount Cholmondeley's House by St James's, a little Italian Bitch, with a white Ring round her Neck, white under her Belly, white on the end of her Tail, her Body toward a dumbish Whoever will bring her into the above-mentioned House, shall have a Guinea Reward.

Printed by *Edw. Jones* in the *Savoy*, 1688.

Part of the *London Gazette* of February 18–21, 1688–9, showing, in the right-hand column, the advertisement about stolen watches in which occurs the earliest printed reference to Lloyd's Coffee-House.

connection among shipping men; and it is possible that this connection was the mainstay of his business, bringing him the prosperity that justified a move to the larger premises in 1691. Anyhow, it is beyond doubt that a year after the move he was beginning (as they say of rising young barristers in the Temple) to get into the heavy commercial work. When some shipowner or auctioneer had three boats to sell down at 'Plimouth' and wanted to give London owners the chance of buying them, he sent an inventory to Lloyd's and published an advertisement telling prospective buyers to go to 'Lloyd's Coffee House in Lombard Street London' where full particulars could be had. The place was clearly frequented already by shipping and commercial people, and Lloyd was cutting into the business of his older competitors in the better class of City trade.

Fifteen years later, but still during the lifetime of Lloyd, a queer person called Ned Ward was dividing his time between keeping a public house and writing a vast number of racy books under such titles as *The Northern Cuckold or the Garden House Intrigue*, exporting (as Pope said of him) vile rhymes to the Colonies in exchange for bad tobacco. This author published among his many books a work called *The Wealthy Shopkeeper* which described a normal working day in an active merchant's life. And Lloyd comes into the description. The shopkeeper worked in his counting-house till 8 a.m.; breakfasted on toast and Cheshire cheese; spent two hours in his shop; went to a coffee-house for news; dined on a thundering joint; looked in on 'change; went to Lloyd's Coffee-House for business; moved on to a different coffee-house for recreation, and then to a sack-shop to drink with acquaintances.[1] From this summary of a City man's routine it is clear that Edward Lloyd had now got what he was after – a solid connection among business men who came to him when they wanted to work, and went elsewhere to frivol, drink, and make merry. How Lloyd prospered and made money out of it all is something of a mystery, for his customers seem to have reserved their serious drinking for other places and (as one would imagine) drank but little in his shop. But prosper he did, and when he died in 1713 he left a substantial estate to his family and dependants.

.        .        .        .        .

As early as the year 1696, Lloyd had tried to cultivate the mercantile seafaring type of customer by breaking into the newspaper industry, which had had a great revival when the licence and the imprimatur were allowed to lapse in 1693. He published the first number of *Lloyd's News*.

[1] G. M. Trevelyan: *English Social History*.

But several London newspapers had already come into existence under such titles as *The Flying Post* and *The Protestant Mercury*, and their competition proved to be too strong for Lloyd, partly because they had two or three years' start of him, and partly because they made a much wider appeal. *Lloyd's News* in fact lasted only for five months and petered out without a word of printed explanation from its proprietor. We should have known nothing about its death but for a fluke – a short news item in *The Protestant Mercury* to the effect that Lloyd had made a mistake in his general news and (rather than 'rectifie' it) had decided to cease publication. The inaccurate piece of news had (Lloyd explained) 'been added by the printer'. It was a trifling error, but Lloyd was probably glad of an excuse to jettison the paper because he knew by this time that it was not likely to be a success. And you have only to study it side by side with its rivals to understand why it was not.

By good luck there is preserved at the Bodleian Library a file of *Lloyd's News* from the third copy to the last, bound with four contemporary papers, so that the student gets at one sitting a view of the London Press as it was in 1696. And when he has gone through the file he can have no doubt that Lloyd's paper failed because it was not at all a good paper, while the others survived because they were (considering their age and inexperience) very bright indeed. Edward Lloyd's method (to judge by internal evidence) was to scrape together all the information he could get about ships' movements, hand it on to his printer and tell him – if it was not enough – to fill up the chinks with whatever general news might come to hand. The amount of shipping news varied a good deal from day to day. Sometimes the printer would have three-quarters of his space given over to shipping and a quarter to general matters, while on other days ships' movements would take only a third of the paper and the open spaces were padded out with the odds and ends. Nor was the padding of a good quality. As you read it, issue by issue, you can almost see the printer, on a night when shipping news was short, grabbing at a handful of miscellaneous copy and slinging it *en masse* on to the front page.

The shipping news came mostly from English ports and was usually more naval than commercial. The most frequent reports were from Falmouth, Plymouth, Portsmouth and Yarmouth; but there were occasional messages from Harwich, Deal, Liverpool, Shields, Guernsey, and 'Middleburgh'; and once in every few weeks, when an Irish mail came in, there was a batch of messages from Dublin, Dungarvan, and Galway. From foreign ports the service was irregular and fragmentary, with an occasional report from Amsterdam, Lisbon, Cadiz or Toulon (though we were at war with France), and even from far-off Alexandria. But it is difficult to believe that the skimpy overseas news could have had much value for merchants or owners, and it is probable that the shipping news was read more for the movements of convoys up and down the Channel than for anything else it could provide. That would account for the very large number of messages from the West Country ports.

When we turn from *Lloyd's News* to the other papers, we find a difference that accounts at once for the failure of Lloyd's experiment. All the papers – Lloyd's and the others – were printed on a single sheet on both sides; but the other sheets were all larger than those of *Lloyd's News* and far more matter was compressed into them than Lloyd ever had to offer. The ambit of their interest, too, was remarkably wide. They dealt generously in home and foreign intelligence, in war news, social chit-chat, and crime. Indeed, they needed only a sports' section to make them the match of a twentieth-century daily. But it was in their foreign news that they were most remarkable; and if only half of the messages they printed were genuine, they had certainly built up in a few years an astonishing foreign organization.

*The Flying Post*, for example, in one issue had despatches from Pignerol, Warsaw, Turin, Venice, Strasbourg, Copenhagen, Namur, Ghent, Hague, and Amsterdam, with quotations from 'divers eminent merchants in the City' repeating their private news from abroad. And although we were at war with France it published fairly regular reports from Paris. It claimed, indeed, to be in touch with a man in Paris whom it called a Faithful Hand, whom we should now call a well-informed correspondent, and this hand got for his paper what must be the biggest scoop in the history of English journalism. A rumour had run through London that the French King was dead. *The Flying Post* mentioned the rumour, but valued its good name for accuracy too highly to endorse what it could not report as a fact. It suspended judgment. But happily the Faithful Hand had just sent it exclusive news about the French King's health, and his private bulletin could safely be published. He had actually had an interview in Paris with His French Majesty's Chief Chirurgion, who had kindly given him exact details of the exalted patient's present indisposition. This is what he said in the issue of 12th September, 1696:

His Majesty's distemper is that of virulency and one of the seven boils on his shoulder has turned to an antrax or pestilential bubo which cannot be brought to suppuration and though lanced to the quick, there proceeds nothing from it but livid and thin matter which will ne'er come to a head but putrifie and occasions that intolerable pain that His Majesty cannot dispose himself to any rest or ease but upon his face a posture that he has been too much addicted to and most people conclude that the malady is natural to him because his mother died of the same kind of cancerous tumours which the chirurgions could never bring to digestion or keep from breeding of worms or rather lice in the body of the sore which was then looked on as the effect of Divine Vengeance on her for though she was Louis the fourteenth's certain mother yet is he *dubio genitore creatus*: so that if the King falls by the like distemper we may justly attribute it to that same Hand which brought Herod to be eaten up of worms.

Against authentic news of that quality, innocent-minded Edward Lloyd and his printer stood no chance, and it is not surprising that while the other papers got advertisements in fair quantities, Lloyd got almost none. In *The Flying Post* all sorts of worthy people advertised. An eye surgeon bought space whenever he did a successful operation for the black cataract, and the headmaster of Felsted School advertised in Latin the merits of an anthology (recently compiled by him) of Greek epigrams suitable for schoolboys. But *Lloyd's News* in its whole career only advertised about six articles – the sale of furniture in Crooked Lane – a lost note case in a public house at Deal – and a parcel of canaries for sale at 'Black Joe's, the German bird man next the Church in Crooked Lane, the choicest singing birds both white and gray, also hens; also if any desire birds taught with the Flageolet he can furnish them with those that are very well taught.'

That does not read like a very highly paid insertion nor do any other of Lloyd's open advertisements. But in one issue Lloyd or his printer rather suspiciously gave up the whole front page to what purports to be a piece of general news – of all queer things a verbatim reproduction of an ordinance recently published in the Island of Barbados. It ordained that if anyone brought into the Island a Christian servant, aged between sixteen and forty in a physical state that satisfied the Treasurer, indentured for at least four years and of English, Welsh or Scottish nationality, then the importer should get a lump sum payment of £18. The Christian servant should get food, three pairs of drawers a year, two jackets, four pairs of shoes and (in cash) an annual salary of one pound five shillings. Eighteen pounds down for the man who brought the Christian in, and twenty-five shillings at the end of a year for the Christian himself.

What Lloyd was doing when he published this document was to lend a hand to the trade known sometimes as Indentured Labour, sometimes as Christian Servants, and sometimes as White Servitude.[1] It flourished in the second half of the seventeenth century and continued up to the time when it was replaced by negro slavery which the planters found more satisfactory. It was carried on between the British Isles and the West Indies and, to a smaller extent, with Virginia and New England; and in the sixty years 1640 to 1700 the numbers so transported were considerable, and the quality and nature of the persons shipped very various. Several thousand political prisoners were exported to the plantations during the civil war; men and women of dissolute and disorderly character were sent out by order of the magistrates; waifs and strays, swept up in the streets of London, were herded on board ship at the instance of the Mayor and were carried across the Atlantic to be indentured as plantation workers. Other children whose parents wished to get rid of them met the same fate, and a certain number of adult men and women, who genuinely wanted to emigrate, selected this as the cheapest method of getting a passage. But others went because they were shanghaied – escaping the Government Press Gang to fall into the clutches of a merchant captain.

This kidnapping trade was well organized and was technically known as 'spiriting', the spirits being the agents scattered about the town and adjacent country, who made a living by enticing the victims and handing them over to the ship. So hated was the trade that a bystander in a London street could at any moment raise a disturbance by pointing to a woman and calling her a 'common spirit'. Considerable riots were produced in this way, and the Government, under pressure of public opinion, started a system of registration to make kidnapping impossible. But the attempt at reform must have been a failure for in 1670 the legal punishment was raised from a fine of £20 to the death penalty without benefit of clergy – sure sign that the law was ineffective. And indeed how could a magistrate distinguish in Court between the man who had promised to indenture himself and then repented, and the man who had been inveigled by a prostitute and had his drink doctored? Exactly at what stage of inebriation did the Christian servant pass from the voluntary class, which was permitted, to the involuntary class which involved a capital sentence?

When the exported men, women and children reached their destination they were technically servants under contract, but in at least one of the Colonies they became chattels that passed from owner to owner for a cash

[1] B. M. Ballagh: *Indentured Servitude in Virginia.*

payment. For laziness and bad discipline they could be flogged naked by the Master. In some Colonies they could be put in irons for years, hanged, shot, broken on the wheel, and even (it is said) burnt alive. In Virginia for a Christian servant to get married without permission from his Master was a serious crime punished by an extension of his period of bound labour; and even the minor offence of extra-marital intercourse was officially frowned on. But if an illegitimate child were born it could straightway be indentured for twenty-one years, and the parents' period of indenture was extended beyond its former limit. And this arrangement sometimes paid the masters so well that they would lower the working costs of their plantations by encouraging immorality among their Christian servants. There was, however, a better and a brighter side to the picture. Deeper matters were not neglected. Attendance at Church was compulsory, and before evening prayers on Sundays the servants were bound by law to receive sound instruction from the Minister of the Parish.

The key-men in this kidnapping trade were the master-mariners; and there can be no doubt that the new Barbadian law was published in *Lloyd's News* to remind the seafaring customers of the Coffee-House how money could still be made from the shipment of Englishmen, Scotsmen, and Welshmen to the Colonies. Now that over two centuries have passed since that quasi-slavery came to an end, the whole business looks unspeakably revolting – a piece of wickedness that no decent man could ever have touched. But in matters of cruelty it is dangerous to apply twentieth-century standards to seventeenth-century conduct; and if Edward Lloyd and his printer felt no qualm about advertising the traffic to Barbados, we must remember that the Royal Navy lived by the Press Gang; that Privateers (often indistinguishable from pirates) were an essential part of naval warfare; that transportation of criminals under the most horrible conditions was to continue for another century and more; that British statesmen in the War of American Independence allowed Red Indians to be used for scalping our kindred in America; and that the wealth of the first British Empire grew largely from the trade in negro slaves.

. . . . . .

It was on 23rd February, 1696/7, that *Lloyd's News* appeared for the last time. And Edward Lloyd was doubtless wise in his decision to throw in the sponge. The truth is that the paper fell between two stools. As a general newspaper it was behind the times, and as a shipping journal it was ahead of them. There was not yet enough shipping intelligence to feed a journal that had to come out two or three times every week; and what shipping news could be had was too uncertain and irregular to make any paper – what every trade paper must claim to be – indispensable. But from time to time, not apparently very often, Lloyd, even after the collapse of *Lloyd's News*, published and sold fly sheets in which the movements of shipping were recorded. He seems to have made up his mind that he had not got enough shipping news to feed a paper appearing at regular intervals, but that he could usefully issue shipping lists at odd times when information enough had been accumulated. We have to remember that when he started dabbling in journalism Lloyd had been established as a coffee-house keeper only for eight years, and in the new grandeur of Lombard Street only five.

But the paper is, nevertheless, an important landmark in Lloyd's history, because it proves that from the early days of the Coffee-House the proprietor's ambition had run in a particular direction; that he set out of purpose to attract the custom of merchants and shipowners; that the link between his rooms and the overseas trade of England was not fortuitous, but planned. And as the insurance business of Lloyd's grew out of this connection with shipping, it is not a mistake for underwriters in the twentieth century to look back to Edward Lloyd as, in a sense, the founder of their market. But for his deliberate policy in 1690, the work done by his successors would not have been possible, and the history of British insurance, both marine and non-marine, would have taken a very different course. And *Lloyd's News* – failure though it was – may well have helped him in getting together the connection that he had always wanted, the connection that before his death he achieved.

On the standing and reputation of Lloyd as a shipping expert at this period of his career, we have a curious piece of evidence in a letter written in 1697 by a Government official to the English plenipotentiary in Holland. The object of the letter was to keep our plenipotentiary informed of the movements of the English fleets, and it ran as follows:

> The homeward bound Straits' fleet which has so long been coming about from Milford Haven has at last arrived in the Downs. There is a report in London that the Virginia fleet has arrived in Ireland. This comes from Lloyd who keeps a coffee-house and pretends to have an account of it but will not tell me how it came to him. The last letters from Dublin say nothing of it.[1]

From this it is clear that Edward Lloyd already claimed to be particularly

[1] C.S.P. Dom. 1697.

well-informed on shipping, and was not anxious to disclose the names of his correspondents. His name, however, was not yet completely familiar in Government circles (or he would scarcely have been described as 'Lloyd who keeps a coffee-house') and in Westminster his news was not accepted without confirmation. But the letter does not affect his standing within the four walls of his own premises, and before the end of the century his reliable shipping news was undoubtedly one of the things for which his customers valued him.

Apart from the supply of news, he gave to his customers the advantages of a business address at which they might send and receive letters; and City men were not above using the Coffee-House as a place for anonymous correspondence. One anonymous letter that has survived was signed 'R.S.' and addressed from Lloyd's Coffee-House to the Admiralty. It was written in 1703 when the Grand Alliance was at war with France, and the Allies were struggling with the difficulties of co-ordinating a joint commercial and military policy. We had persuaded Holland to cut all communications with France and 'R.S.' thought that in this matter we were not playing straight ourselves.

> It is very strange (he wrote) that after persuading Holland to forbid all commerce with France one Gipson should come upon the Exchange and tell the Merchants there that he is going to France and desire their commissions at letters that he shall keep a public office in Waghorn's Coffee-House to receive all people that hath any commission to give him and that this place should in the face of a Government be crowded with people sending messages and letters thither. It is stranger that when we desire the Dutch not to exchange prisoners taken at sea but in concert with us this Gipson shall declare instructions to treat for a general exchange.[1]

It is a pity that we do not know who 'R.S.' was. The motive behind his letter may not have been altogether patriotic or impersonal. Perhaps he resented the increase of trade that this Gipson was bringing to Waghorn's instead of to Lloyd's.

Anyhow, there is good reason to believe that Lloyd, among his other activities, acted as agent and adviser to people who were travelling abroad. As we were then at war a passport was necessary before you could leave the country, and every applicant for a pass had to be recommended to the passport authority. There is extant a list of travellers who were granted

[1] C.S.P. Dom. 1702/3.

leave and the names of their recommendors.[1] Most of the travellers were Dutchmen going home, and generally they were recommended by their own ambassador or a Lutheran Minister. But other people so regularly backed the applications that the service must have been part of their ordinary business. And no name appears more often than Edward Lloyd's. From March to December it pops up fifteen times, recommending over thirty voyages – Germans off to Bremen and Danzig, Englishmen bound for Portugal or setting out via Falmouth for the West Indies, and a Mr Sedgwick leaving for an unnamed destination. All these men and women got their passes on the word of Edward Lloyd, and though we cannot be absolutely certain that he was Edward Lloyd of the Coffee-House, the balance of probability tilts very strongly indeed in his direction. No other man of the same name is known to have been engaged directly or indirectly in foreign trade; and what could be more natural than that our Lloyd, with all his overseas connections and his daily intercourse with shipowners and ship captains, should oblige the customers by helping them with the formalities of travel? In addition to his other activities, Lloyd seems to have run an embryo travel agency.

And he was not only a travel agent. He went in for other business, some of it rather mysterious, connected with shipping. The Committee of Lloyd's has a mass of papers that came to them in 1931, left by a Captain Bowrey who was a London merchant and shipowner in Lloyd's time. In 1703, when England was at war with France, Bowrey went to Edward Lloyd for 'protection' for one of his ships – the *Riseing Sun* – at the moment when she was on the point of sailing for the East Indies. Lloyd got for Bowrey what he wanted and sent in the following invoice:

1703  Cpt Bowrey in debit

| | | | | | | | |
|---|---|---|---|---|---|---|---|
| Octo. 5 | A protection for a Mate and Boatswaine for | | | | | | |
| | Cpt Wyborg | .. | .. | .. | .. | .. | 00 10 00 |
| 11 | for a letter of Mart | .. | .. | .. | .. | 11 00 00 |
| | a protection for all his men | .. | .. | .. | 03 04 06 |
| | | | | | | | 14 14 06 |

The account was paid on 10th November:

> Received Nob[r] 10[th] 1703
> fourteen pounds four shill
> in full          Edw Lloyd

[1] C.S.P. Dom. 1703/4.

This transaction chimes in with the business of the passports and indicates a man ready and able to give any kind of help to anyone making arrangements for a sea voyage, including protection against the press gang.

From all this scattered casual information can we piece together some kind of portrait of the man? Let us try. A good man of business, ambitious, active, energetic, successful, restless and, perhaps, impatient; always looking out for new openings and quick to seize an opportunity when it was offered; a good mixer to whom strangers found it easy to talk, with a flair for collecting news and assessing its value, but too closely concerned with shipping to make a good general journalist; determined above all else to make his house the favourite meeting place of shipping men and to give them whatever help he could in the management of their business. All this he was, and all this he planned. But man's prayers are not always answered exactly as he presents them; and if Edward Lloyd, as he worshipped in St Mary Woolnoth's, ever prayed for the fulfilment of his earthly ambitions, we may be certain that he was not asking to be known as the founder of the world's most famous place of insurance.

# 2

## EIGHTEENTH–CENTURY UNDERWRITING

*Brokers and Underwriters – Dangers of Fraud – Campaign for Companies – South Sea Bubble – The Bubble Act – The 'Monopoly'*

EDWARD LLOYD lived till the year 1713 and the last few months of his life were full of incident. In October, he lost his second wife – Elizabeth. In November, he married his third – Martha. In January, he saw his daughter married to his head waiter William Newton. In February, he died himself. In the following year Newton (who had become owner of the Coffee-House on Lloyd's death) followed his old chief; and the widowed Mrs Newton, true to the family form, quickly married again – this time to a man named Sheppard – so making in the Lloyd family three marriages and two transfers of the business in two and a half years. Indeed, the business changed hands three times in fourteen years and the transferee always got it through a lucky marriage. Newton and Sheppard got it by marrying Lloyd's daughter; Jemson (who followed Sheppard) by marrying Sheppard's sister; and later on, Baker through being the nephew of another Miss Sheppard. The movement was always lateral not direct, and the property was rather like a piece of territory in medieval times, passing from hand to hand in the dowry of a royal bride. There seems to be no doubt that from the first it was well worth having, for the founder had built up a goodwill that was not to be shaken by repeated changes of ownership and management.

From the very slight records we have, it looks as though the prosperity of the place in Lloyd's lifetime had grown most quickly from 1706 to 1711, the evidence for that guess being found in a table that Frederick Martin compiled for his *History of Lloyd's*. He went through the *London Gazette* and other newspapers of the period from 1698 to 1712, looking for advertisements of auction sales at Lloyd's. He found that in the year 1700 there were two such advertisements; that in 1706 there was only one; that in 1710 there were forty-four; and in 1711 there were thirty-five. Not all by any means were sales of ships. One was a sale of shares in the Lustring

17

Company; one of a farm, and another of two estates; but mostly they were of wine and brandy, which were sold at Lloyd's while they were actually lying at Wapping Old Stairs, at Fresh Wharf near London Bridge, and at Sir Theodore Janssen's house in Bucklersbury. The Coffee-House was obviously a great spot for selling newly imported liquor.

But towards the end of Lloyd's life the sale of ships took a more important place in his turnover than claret and brandy. In 1711 fifteen vessels were put up for sale by candle in his rooms. These advertisements are not in themselves proof positive of a growing connection with shipping. They may have increased in number because the habit of press advertising had become more general; but they do point the same way as our other evidence, and they suggest that the dying Lloyd handed on to his successor a centre of shipping business well recognized and strongly established. But was it also a centre of marine underwriting? That question brings us to one of the most aggravating things in the early history of Lloyd's – our blank ignorance of when underwriting started there. We know near enough when its other activities began – its formal meetings, its auctions, its collection and distribution of news, its miscellaneous gatherings of City men who used it in the office of a club or market. But of the date when its permanent occupation, its predestined business of marine insurance, started we have no idea. And the reason for our ignorance lies in the organization of the London insurance market at the end of the seventeenth and the beginning of the eighteenth centuries – a matter that calls at this point for some notice.

. . . . . .

The market then, as now, was made up of brokers and underwriters. The underwriters accepted risks and the brokers (as agents for merchants and shipowners) fixed the terms with both parties, presenting underwriters with the policy to sign and handing it (when signed) to their principals. Essentially the brokers' business was the same then as it is today, but for reasons of their own they preferred not to be known as brokers. Instead they used the rather clumsy name of office-keepers; and it may be that they fought shy of the older style (in spite of its ancient and honourable connections) because it had come to be used by certain disreputable traders as a cover for shady practices, so that there hung about the word an aura of dishonesty. As far back as the beginning of James I's reign it had begun to smell, and in the year 1603 an Act had been passed which recorded the misuse of the name and set up penalties for the misbehaviour of people who called themselves brokers, but were in fact receivers of stolen goods. These men said the Act, calling themselves brokers, abused:

> . . . the true and honeste name and trade and many citizens being men of manuall occupation in the Citie and suburbes dailie doe leave and give over their handie and manuall occupations and dailie doe set up a trade of buying and selling and taking to pawne all kinde of worne apparell finding therebie the same is a more idle and easier kinde of trade of livinge than by their former manuall labours. The said kinde of counterfeit brokers being friperers and no brokers and there are not any garments apparell or households stuff being either stolen or robbed but these kinde of upstart brokers to uphold all kindes of lewd and bad persons to robbe and steale and presentlie utter, vent, sell and pawne the same for ready money.

A hundred years later the name broker lay under the same shadow, and tucked away at the British Museum in a collection of papers dated about 1720 there is a queer document described as 'a humble proposal to prevent the beginnings of thefte viz. the picking pockets of hankerchiefs.' The humble proposal is really a treatise on juvenile delinquency, and it attributes the evil entirely to brokers. 'Our thieves and robbers,' it said, 'arise and are trained up in the picking of pockets as the general school and first education in the art of thieving; and their way of getting money for their hankerchiefs by selling them to brokers of old goods whereby children are drawn young into crime.' If the word broker raised the picture of a fripperer, a corrupter of youth, a receiver, a spiv, then respectable insurance men would naturally dislike it and seek an alternative title for their own calling. And the alternative they chose was 'office-keeper'.

In course of time the word office-keeper, too, seems to have lost caste. By the middle of the century it described sometimes the humblest person in a Government department, and in *The Vicar of Wakefield* Goldsmith makes a rascally office-keeper try to kidnap young Primrose for the plantations. But in 1700 the word was specially appropriate to marine insurance brokers because they did keep offices for the business and nobody else did. They were the fixed point in a floating market. They were whole-time men; they made of insurance their full daily work; they depended on it for their livelihood; they had regular connections at home and abroad; and they must have offices where business could be discussed with clients, and letters could be written and received. Under-writers, on the other hand, did their business in such a way as to call for no separate offices. A few there may have been in the City who gave all their time to insurance, but for most of them it was a side line carried on at odd moments in the normal day of a merchant's life – or even, indeed, in the day of a journalist and a Civil Servant.

Daniel Defoe, first of the great English journalists, ruined himself by dabbling in marine underwriting; and Pepys, the Admiralty clerk, at least once kicked himself for not writing a line as he could have done on a ship which was thought to be at sea but was actually (as Pepys knew) safe in port. Instead of using his inside information he 'went like an asse to Alderman Bakewell and told him of it. Now what an opportunity had I to have concealed this and seemed to have made an insurance and got £100 with the least trouble and danger in the world. This troubles me to think that I should be so oversoon.'

But Pepys, nevertheless, did well enough at times out of insurance, usually with the help of a city merchant, his friend Warren, who went in for occasional underwriting. On 11th December, Pepys talked to Warren about insuring some Admiralty shipments 'whereby something may be saved to him and got to me'. Several little dinners followed the talk and on 26th January 'W. Hewer came to me with £320 from Sir William Warren whereof £220 is clearly got by a late business of insurance for which I ought and do bless God'. When Pepys turns pious and thanks the Almighty the bribe has usually reached the pocket. But he really is an infuriating person. If he is willing to blacken his own character in the diary, why be so shy of details? Why not record the whole transaction from A to Z and tell us how and where the risk was placed, who the broker was, what percentage he got for himself, how many underwriters wrote a line, whether there was a claim and (if there was) how it was settled? If only he had done that we might have today a straight picture of the marine market in action before our Coffee-House broke into the business.

As Pepys did not give the full tale to the twentieth century, the twentieth century must do the best it can to reconstruct the market without his help. And the central fact seems to be the difference in technique between broker and underwriter. Some underwriters attended at the Exchange, but the market was not concentrated there, and a broker with a risk to place had to run round the City seeking out merchants, bankers, and shipowners who were known to have the habit of playing a hand in the game. It would be too much perhaps to say that these men were professionals in their own trade and amateurs in underwriting; but for most of them insurance was a secondary interest to which they gave such time as they could spare from the management of their own business. When they underwrote (and this is a very important point), they usually were not acting as partners in a firm, but risking their private fortunes in such a way that there was no partnership control, no common liability, no check on what was written or who wrote it. It was a free-for-all trade and, so long as the office-keeper was willing to accept a man's security, there was no bar to the most unsuitable person committing himself to any extent on any risk. The one binding controlling element must have been the office-keeper's judgment; and his duty to his client was not only to get a risk completed at the best rate, but to make sure that it was placed with reliable men whose means would satisfy the claims when they arose. If his integrity and good sense failed, then the assured must suffer and the good name of the London market suffer with him.

By modern standards the whole arrangement is casual enough, especially when we remember how much of the business was done for foreign merchants. The mercantile connection of London and the Low Countries was close and continuous, and although there were critics in the eighteenth century who declared that Holland was shy of the security of a London policy, there is a good deal of evidence the other way, showing that orders came freely from Amsterdam to English offices, and that a substantial business was done here on Dutch account. It was the office-keepers who held this rather ramshackle scattered market together till its place could be taken by something more compact and more highly organized; and it is broadly true that the history of Lloyd's is the record of how a fluid, form-less, shapeless market grew into the controlled and safeguarded institution of the twentieth century.

To appreciate the dangers inherent in that market of two hundred and fifty years ago, you have only to picture an office-keeper with a difficult risk to place struggling with it for a week, hawking it round the City at the Royal Exchange, in Cornhill, in Lombard Street, in Crooked Lane, and in every other street, lane, or alley, from which an underwriter might with luck be flushed. At the end of the week he has almost got the risk finished, but there is still another £200 to do; and he has no idea where to look for an underwriter to accept it.

That is a situation in which every broker finds himself at one time or another in his career, and it is a very tantalizing one even today. But for the old office-keeper it had special temptations, which must sometimes have been very difficult to resist. He has exhausted his sound market and shown his risk to every available man of good credit. But somewhere in the City there are other men who might be willing to write it, though (as he suspects) they have no funds. They are men of straw. If he puts one of them on to the policy, the client in Amsterdam or Bristol will make no complaint, for the names mean nothing to the client and unless there is a claim he will never know that a goat is lurking among the sheep. If there should be a claim there might be trouble, but is it not better to run that risk rather than refuse the order? The tempted man yields. There is no claim. All is well. But next time the tempter goes a step further. What, after all, is the difference between a man of straw and a man who does not exist? Why pay a premium to John Smith, who (as you well know) could not pay a claim, when you could complete the policy with the purely fictitious name of Henry Robinson? It will make no difference to the client and you can keep the premium on £200 for yourself.

And that is just what happened at least once in the early 1700's. An insurance was going round on a vessel called the *Vansittart,* and the man who was placing it (being short of £200) inserted one or more false names. The forgeries were not detected at the time and never would have been detected if the vessel had not been a loss. But she was a loss. The claim was sent to London and the fraud discovered.

In the hurly-burly of dispute and argument that broke out round the London market in 1717, the *Vansittart* policy was not forgotten. Whole-sale charges were made against the office-keepers and proved very embarrassing to them. They found their own honour assailed on the strength of somebody else's crime, and eleven of them (being 'the persons who now keep offices for insurance near the Royal Exchange') published a dignified reply to what they called a scandalous reflection. Their mani-festo has survived and, after the passage of two hundred years and more, it wins our sympathy still.

We (they said) in justice to ourselves and that although our livelihood should be taken from us we may still be untainted in our reputation which we value more do in answer to such foul false and malicious a charge declare that we detest all such vile actions and do challenge all the merchants in England to produce one instance of any policy made in either of our offices underwrote with a fictitious name; which if they cannot do we humbly hope the honour and candour of those societies will be judged by this specimen since those who in order to get away our business have falsely laid forgery to our charge cannot be supposed to stick at anything that may be likely to accomplish their design. The policy hinted at on the *Vansittart* was made by a person since dead who

*1703*

*Octr 5*     Cpt Bowrie is debt.

      a protection for a mate & 

      Boatswaine for Cpt Wyborg —— 00 – 10 – 00

*11*     for a Letter of Marte —————— 11 – 00 – 00

      a protection for all his men   03 – 04 – 06

                          14   14   06

Recd Novbr: 10th 1703 .

fourteen pounds teen shill

in full ⅌ Edd Lloyd

A bill made out and receipted by Edward Lloyd in 1703. The protections (from the press gang) and Letter of Marque were to cover an East India voyage made by the *Riseing Sun*, in which Thomas Bowrey, the well-known master mariner and merchant, had a principal interest. Bowrey's account book, containing the 'cost and outset' of the voyage, is extant, and entries corresponding to the bill here reproduced confirm that the creditor was 'Mr Ed: Lloyd Coffeman'.

was not an office-keeper but one who acted as a broker for discounting notes and did sometimes make policies.[1]

There you have the honest office-keeper contrasted with the rascally broker – and there is no reason to believe that the office-keepers' claim was unsound. If these men had even occasionally been so fraudulent as to forge their documents, then the marine insurance market must have collapsed long before the dawn of the eighteenth century. But the weakness in their case was that they had no monopoly in placing risks, and they had to admit that anyone (whatever his style and character) could effect insurances for trusting folk at home and abroad with any Dick, Tom, or Harry, solvent or insolvent, living or dead, genuine or fictitious. The *Vansittart* scandal was a nasty hurdle for the office-keepers to take, and they came to it at a very inconvenient moment; for their market was soon to sustain the most dangerous attack ever made on it and they might well believe that their whole livelihood was threatened.

. . . . . .

The campaign against the insurance market was launched in 1717, and it took the form of a demand for chartered insurance companies to supplant, or to compete with, the individual underwriters. The underwriters and the office-keepers declared, and doubtless believed, that their enemies aimed at a monopoly; but their enemies denied it. All they wanted, they declared, was to introduce some healthy competition by starting two or perhaps three chartered companies, which (in their view) would do the work more efficiently, give better security, and draw more foreign business to London. If the old system was as good as it claimed to be, no harm would come to it; but if it wilted and collapsed under competition, that would only prove that it was a sickly plant which had properly been replaced by a healthier growth – a change clearly to the country's benefit. The advocates of insurance companies asked nothing more than a chance to show what they could do. Give them that and let the devil take the hindmost.

The campaign that these innovators started in 1717 lasted for about three years, taking a tortuous and not always a creditable course. To disentangle all the threads in the skein – the clean, the dirty, and the neutral – is practically impossible; and among the men who forwarded the scheme, it is usually not fair to say of this one, that he was a genuine believer in reform, or of the other, that he was a greedy speculator anxious only to

[1] British Museum 357 B 3/73.

c

make a quick fortune by corruption and share rigging. That there were merchants genuinely dissatisfied with the insurance market, critical of its slow movement and suspicious of its security, there can be no doubt; and in the battle of manifestos, petitions, and memoranda that was waged in these three years, the most impressive is a letter of which a copy still rests in the British Museum written by an anonymous merchant to an anonymous M.P.

> Put yourself (said the writer of the letter) in my position as a merchant and think what my situation is when I insure under the present system. I must go to the office where an office-keeper only attends who can't certainly inform me who shall subscribe my policy but I must leave directions with him to procure me one for such a sum. If it be a large one perhaps it may be some time before I can have it completed and when my policy is completed I find persons' names to it I have no acquaintance with or knowledge of. It is impossible I can be thought to have what satisfaction is necessary in an affair upon which my whole fortune depends.[1]

There is a ring of sincerity in that criticism and the author put his finger on the real problem – a problem that was insoluble so long as the market remained unorganized, and could be settled only after the underwriters had been brought under one roof. It was a problem that Lloyd's as Coffee-House, as Society, and as Corporation had to deal with, and slowly to solve in the next two hundred years.

But the author of the letter was not typical of the men who opposed the system of individual underwriting, for to tell the truth, most of them were a sorry crowd. They were corrupt; they were untruthful on their oath; they were professional speculators; and a fervour for the cause of sound insurance cloaked in most of them a desire for more shares and more money to go gambling with on 'change. For this was the time of the South Sea Bubble and men's minds were not attuned to the building up of solid business. They were concerned with something much more exciting, with new projects to tickle the public, with inflated capitals and clamorous coffee-houses, with the rigging of meaningless prices in the street at Jonathan's and at Garraway's, and possibly at Lloyd's. The wild boom was followed in due course by the suicidal depression; and the boom and depression together shaped the course of English insurance through the eighteenth century. Both had a direct vital influence on the development

[1] British Museum 357 B 3/62.

of Lloyd's, and although the story of the Bubble has been told so often, it has to be mentioned afresh whenever the history of Lloyd's is in question.

In 1711 the Chancellor of the Exchequer was wrestling with a national debt that had been mismanaged into a state of chaos, and he decided that unless some kind of order were introduced public credit would collapse. He thought of various devices and very nearly started an insurance company which was to make a profit of £1,000,000 a year and take a great part of the debt's burden off the taxpayer's back. If he had followed that plan the company, whatever else it did, would certainly not have given him his annual profit of £1,000,000. But it might have stifled private underwriting and would probably have killed the Lloyd's market before it was properly born. But he gave the notion up and fixed instead on a great commercial company that would enjoy a monopoly, trade under a charter, and at once develop the nation's trade and take over a large part of its debt.

The trading under a charter and the monopoly are clear enough. But how was the national debt to be taken over? The answer was that the holders of Government securities would exchange them for ordinary shares in the new company, and the company would thereby become the Government's chief creditor. It would be content with a reduced rate of interest from the Treasury, but it would make fine profits from its trading monopoly, and the shareholders would receive splendid dividends. Everybody would be better off – the Government because it had converted its debt, the Company because of its flourishing business, and the fund-holders because they had got rid of a bond with a dull fixed rate of interest, for an equity with exciting prospects and hopes of a glorious capital appreciation. The eighteenth-century investor would restore British finance by a switch from gilts to equities.

And what trade was this that was to make everybody's fortune? It was threefold: first, certain rather vague fishing rights; second, the right to deal in unwrought iron with the subjects of Spain; and third, the monopoly of trading with large parts of South America. There were no other assets, and if vast profits were to be made they must obviously be made out of trading with the Spanish possessions. But there had not been in the past any direct trade worth the name between South America and England. There was little or none at that moment. There was not much reason to expect any in the future. But the non-existent business was to support a company with a capital of £11,000,000 and make its ordinary stock a more desirable investment than the annuities of the British Government. If, in 1943, a company had been floated in London to develop British trade with Japan, to buy and sell base metals with Germany, and to run a fleet of trawlers to Iceland; and if the public had been pressed to exchange their savings certificates and defence bonds for the new company's ordinary shares, then the scheme would have been comparable with the South Sea project of 1711.

But the South Sea Company set out with banners and trumpets. It had an Act of Parliament and a charter of its own. Its capital grew quickly and £1,250,000 of it was spent on bribes. It had thirty-one directors and His Majesty King George I as its governor. It proposed to amalgamate with the Bank of England and the East India Company, and when the merger broke down it competed successfully with the Bank for taking over another £31,000,000 of the national debt. Above all, it worked up the price of its own £100 stock from £71 to £100, from £100 to £300, to £400, to £600 and, finally, to £1,000. To keep the public in the right mood, it was essential that the stock should be constantly rising and every known device was used to keep the market on the move. The company speculated in its own stock, lent generously on the security of its stock, and fostered the public's craze for gambling in its stock. The directors, it is true, expected the gambling mania to be confined to the South Sea capital. They did not mean the mixture they were boiling up in their own cauldron to run over into other people's. But when you set light to number 1 in a terrace of houses you are apt, before long, to find the fire reaching numbers 2, 3, 4 and 5, which you particularly wanted to leave undamaged. In the same way, the blaze of the South Sea Company's speculation spread far beyond the Company's own walls, growing so fierce that when the directors turned a hose on to their neighbour's property the water overflowed on to their own and extinguished the lot. By August 1720 the fire had burnt itself out. The boom was over.

That is the story of British finance from 1711 to 1720 and from the wreckage that was left at the end, when most of the wild-cat schemes and over-capitalized fraudulent companies had gone, three permanent things were salved – Guy's Hospital, the Royal Exchange Assurance Corporation, and the London Assurance. Guy's was founded on the profits made by Thomas Guy, a seller of bibles in the City, from the purchase of £45,000 of South Sea Stock,[1] while the Royal Exchange and the London Assurance survived on the strength of charters granted to them a few

[1] D.N.B.

months before the end of the boom. These two companies were not the first to handle insurance in London but they were the first to get charters – the first to do marine business and the first to challenge the individual underwriters who had hitherto had the marine market to themselves.

The older companies which were content with fire and life had comported themselves modestly, working with small capitals under deeds of settlements, and most of them in their simple way doing well enough. There seems, indeed, to have been no legitimate reason why the new marine companies should not have done the same, starting their underwriting without a charter and without an Act of Parliament. The private underwriters had no legal monopoly, and any group of men, so long as they did not claim to be a corporation, could club together and issue policies on ships and cargo. But in 1717 the projectors scorned small ventures and little partnerships. Everything must be on the grand scale, with big prospects, big promises, and big capital; and (above all) the capital must be transferable in stock that could change hands, have a quoted price, and be a good counter for playing the markets. And that was exactly what these Corporations provided. In the short time that passed between the first dealing in the Royal Exchange Company's shares and the bursting of the bubble the price of its shares (according to Maitland's *History of London*) actually rose from five guineas to £250. Results of that kind were not to be had from a deed of settlement and a capital of £15,000. That was the reason why the projectors set their hearts on a charter and a big capital.

The marine insurance projects were three, of which two survived; and as the career of both survivors followed the same course, it will be convenient to treat only of the one that seems to have taken the lead and been the more energetically pushed. It was known as the Mercers' Hall Subscription, and it was first opened at the Royal Exchange in August 1717. It was to have a capital of not less than £1,000,000 and not more than £2,000,000, and when the necessary subscriptions had been made, a charter was applied for, the petition being backed by three hundred signatures and opposed by counter-petitions carrying nearly four hundred names from London and from Bristol.

The dispute between petitions and counter-petitions was referred to the Attorney-General, Sir Edward Northey, and the Solicitor-General, Sir William Thompson; and in February 1718 the two lawyers sat together to weigh the evidence and report to His Majesty. But before the hearing started the petitioners had much to do in private. Evidence must be

collected and arguments prepared. About the theoretical arguments the
petitioners had no doubt; but the practical arguments were long and
anxiously canvassed and they all centred round one point – bribery. How
much hard cash would be needed to convince the law officers of the merits
of the scheme; how large a fee should be tendered for their professional
services; and what other inducements should be offered to help them in
their decision. Both officers were entitled to fees and the amount was not
fixed by law. It was a matter for negotiation, on the one hand between the
petitioners and the Attorney-General's clerk, and on the other between
their opponents and the same functionary. It was therefore of importance
to both sides to know what fees were being paid by the other, and the
barristers' clerks would say to each of them 'in a cursory way' that they
had better give handsomely as they were giving handsomely on the
other side.

It was a delicate situation. The two parties might have put their heads
together and reached a gentleman's agreement, but somehow that solution
did not occur to them and they continued fumbling in the dark to reach
the appropriate figure by guess-work. The petitioners decided to give
directions to their solicitors 'to do what was necessary', and the firm wrote
accordingly to the Attorney-General thanking him for the excellent
advice he had already given them, and for helping to foil the tricks of their
opponents. They went on:

> We are obliged to assure you that though we are wholly at our own
> charge and risque till we have a charter and cannot be so handsome in
> our fees as when we come to have money from the subscribers yet
> they have given us discretionary commission (and enquire not into
> particulars) and therefore the moment we have our charter the fee to you
> shall be 1,000 guineas which we will never directly or indirectly
> mention to any soul living. . . . We are satisfyd that your justice will
> make their unreasonable opposition signify little; we stand well with
> the Board of Trade and with Sir William Thompson.

That Sir William did not feel the insult keenly is certain for he frankly
told the petitioners that he was on their side. But something went wrong
and the two law officers reported against the scheme, which for the
moment fell through.

But the projectors had not shot their bolt. Disappointed of a new charter,
the Mercers' Hall men bought old charters granted by Elizabeth to the
Mines Royal and the Battery Works, two firms that had never had a

connection with insurance and, anyhow, were by this time defunct. But there the charters were and the right to dig minerals out of the ground might (so the argument ran) serve equally well to issue marine policies. So the scheme was launched under cover of the obsolete charters, and the Mines Royal began to issue policies in competition with the private underwriters.

Ten years earlier the trick might have worked, but in 1720 there were too many public subscriptions about – subscriptions for other insurance charters, for raising Thames water (£1,000,000), for suppressing thieves and robbers (£2,000,000), for furnishing funerals (£1,200,000), for fishing and whaling (£8,700,000); and as the rival gambling schemes crowded the City streets and coffee-houses, the South Sea Company became jealous and Parliament apprehensive. Prompted by the Company and, perhaps, by Walpole, the House of Commons turned its searchlight on the City and caught in its beams not only the patently fraudulent projects but the comparatively respectable marine insurance ventures. The House took note of a complaint that there were on foot 'several public and private subscriptions for several unjustifiable projects with undertakings whereby great mischiefs may accrue to the Publick'; and it appointed a committee to enquire into the several subscriptions for fisheries, insurances, annuities for lives, in and about the Cities of London and Westminster, and to enquire too (this must have made the Mercers' Hall men uncomfortable) into all undertakings for purchasing obsolete charters. On 18th March, 1720, the Committee met.

It opened with an almost incredible incident. When the first petition had been referred to the law officers, Northey had been Attorney-General and Thompson, Solicitor-General. In 1720 Thompson still held his office, but Northey had been followed as Attorney-General by Nicholas Lechmere, so that Thompson and Lechmere were members of the same Government and colleagues at the Head of the English Bar. But before the Committee began its real business, Thompson levelled at Lechmere, his own leader, an open and violent charge of corruption. He declared that Lechmere had taken large sums of money from the insurance interests; that his chambers had been crowded with their agents; that there had been open bidding for charters; and that the professional business of the Right Honourable the Attorney-General had been conducted like an auction sale. It must surely be the only case in English history of one law officer publicly accusing the other of taking bribes. The accusation, however, collapsed, and the Committee reported that Lechmere had discharged his trust with honour and integrity. He was soon afterwards raised to the peerage, and Thompson at once dismissed from his post. But the fall was softened for Thompson by his retaining the Recordership of London, and his appointment a few years later to a seat on the bench – to which he must have brought both an incorruptible mind and a high judicial impartiality.

That dispute being finished, the theoretical arguments on both sides were considered by the Parliamentary Committee. The petitioners maintained that underwriters constantly defaulted; that the market was too small; that foreigners refused to insure in London, and Londoners preferred to insure abroad. If the charters were granted, the companies would neither aim at nor achieve a monopoly, for that was the last thing they desired. The underwriters and the office-keepers *per contra* declared that failures were no more common in marine insurance than in any other trade; that the market could handle all the orders that came to it; that the foreigners liked the London market very much and Londoners detested the Dutch market; and that the aim of the petitioners was to establish a monopoly of marine insurance which would not only kill the business of the private underwriters and deprive them of their livelihood but do infinite harm to the trade of the country.

From the reports in the *House of Commons Journal* it does not appear that the members of the Committee paid very much attention to these arguments, or that they were primarily concerned with the well-being of the insurance market. What they were bothered about was the gambling fever and how to stop it. They reported in general terms to the House of Commons, which passed a short comprehensive resolution condemning the 'several large subscriptions made by great numbers of persons in the City of London', and the action of the subscribers as though they were 'corporate bodies without any legal authority for their so doing'. The House declared that several unwary persons had been drawn into 'unwarrantable undertakings' and that 'the said practices manifestly tended to the prejudice of the Publick Trade of the Kingdom'. At the same time it gave leave for a bill to be brought in restraining the extravagant and unwarrantable practice of raising money by voluntary subscriptions.

If matters had been left there the life of the two insurance companies would have been over. But the petitioners took quick and dramatic action. Over the heads of the Committee they appealed to Caesar. Or rather (to be more accurate) they offered Caesar a bribe and Caesar accepted it. It came to King George's knowledge that if the charters were granted his civil list would receive a gift of £300,000 from each of the companies – making £600,000 in all – a convincing argument which swung the issue in the right direction. Two days after the Commons' adverse resolution, a message reached the House from His Majesty giving it as his opinion that the two marine companies 'exclusive only of all other Corporations and Societies' might be of great advantage to the trade and commerce of the Kingdom and hoping that the House would give its 'ready concurrence' in granting such corporations. The obedient House gave its ready concurrence and the great Bubble Act[1] followed, at once condemning most of the things that the Mercers' Hall group had done in the past and giving it unique privileges to do what it wanted in the future. Thus propelled by the weight of King George, the Royal Exchange Assurance Corporation and the London Assurance were launched on their great careers.

The Act, in spite of the speed with which it was produced, was carefully drafted and it achieved successfully all the objects Parliament had in mind. The main purpose was to stop the companies which had no charter from behaving as though they had one; and it did it by declaring that all offenders against the Act should be deemed 'publick nuisances', liable to such fines, penalties, and punishment 'whereunto persons convicted for common and publick nuisances are subject'. And 'moreover they shall incur and sustain any further pains, penalties and forfeitures as were ordained by the Statute of Praemunire made in the reign of King Richard the Second'. That drastic step – for praemunire was not a pleasant weapon – disposed of the gambling counters and killed outright the crop of mushroom companies that the Bubble had produced. But it did not touch the problem of marine insurance, or the difficult relations between private underwriters and the two new corporations. That problem dealt with in other parts of the Act was solved on three principles:

1. Any private underwriter or particular person might still underwrite any policies or lend money on bottomry 'as if this Act had never been made'.

2. No private or particular persons might write policies or lend money on bottomry, either in partnerships or societies, or at the risque of a corporation or persons acting in a society or partnership.

3. No corporation, society or partnership, other than the Royal Exchange and the London, could assure ships or merchandise at sea or lend money on bottomry.

[1] 6 Geo. 1 c. 18.

In other words, marine policies were to be issued only by the Royal
Exchange Assurance, the London Assurance, and private underwriters
trading for their own account at their own risk. It has sometimes been
said that the Bubble Act gave Lloyd's and the two companies between
them the monopoly of marine underwriting, but in fact it did nothing of
the kind. The private or particular person whom the Act allowed to
underwrite need not be a frequenter of Lloyd's or any other place. He
might be anyone anywhere. The Archbishop of Canterbury, the Archbishop's scullion, a Cambridge undergraduate, a drunken sailor on leave
from his ship, had legally as full a right to sign the policy as the most
regular attendant at any coffee-house; and if an office-keeper were willing
to accept their names, a document could have been signed each for himself and not one for another by the Prelate, the Turnspit, the Student, and
the Drunken Seaman, and so signed could have been tendered to a merchant in satisfaction of his order to insure. The ban was on corporations,
societies, and partnerships only. Everything else got through the mesh.
So the law of marine underwriting by private individuals stood in 1721,
and so it stood for the next two hundred and twenty-five years till the
Assurance Companies Act of 1946 regulated the right of individuals to
sign and issue marine policies.

·     ·     ·     ·     ·     ·

The changes made by the Bubble Act were (so far as insurance was
concerned) much less violent than they were expected to be. In 1720, we
may safely picture the two companies with the charters on their plate,
gloating in triumph over a fallen enemy, while the office-keepers and
whole-time underwriters anticipated – *vae victis* – only ruin and a pauper's
funeral. For three years they had watched the enemy making his prepara-
tions. They had thrown up what defences they could. They had beaten
back the invaders once, and when a second assault was made, the line still
held and all looked well, until suddenly the flank was turned by an act of
treachery in the highest quarter, and the foe came swarming into their
territory. That was the scene as the beaten men saw it. But the true
situation was very different. Their defences had broken indeed, but no
sooner did the invaders get through, than they turned and helped rebuild
the line, repair the trenches, and put up fresh fortifications against another
attack. From now on, attackers and attacked were allies, sheltered by an
Act of Parliament and leagued together to protect their common interests.
And how much stronger that made the position of the private underwriter.

Hitherto any company or syndicate working under some deed of association could break into the business, cut out the office-keepers and reduce premiums to a point that would ruin the private underwriters. That could have happened at any moment, but now it was impossible. Against anything except these two corporations private underwriters were made secure, and if they could reach some *modus vivendi*, tacit or expressed, with the corporations' managers, the ball was at their feet.

And that is what happened. The Royal Exchange and the London, whose interest in marine underwriting (even before incorporation) was diplomatic rather than intelligent, quickly became short of money, defaulted in their payments to the King, and were saved from extinction only by another Act of Parliament which was, in effect, a deed of composition with their chief creditor. At the same time they turned to fire insurance, which they now found more attractive, and did so little in marine that over ninety per cent of the marine premiums still went into private pockets. The clouds that the fearful underwriters had so much dreaded turned out to be big with mercy and broke in blessings on their head.

# 3

## THE EIGHTEENTH-CENTURY LLOYD'S

*Growing importance of Lloyd's – National Prosperity – Heavy War losses –
The great disruption – Move to Royal Exchange – Lloyd's in 1810*

FORTIFIED BY THE MONOPOLY that they had so vigorously opposed, the
private underwriters set out in 1720 on the next stage of their career – a
stage that was to last for 104 years and carry Lloyd's Coffee-House to a
high level of wealth and importance.

How far at the beginning of the stage Lloyd's was a market for insurance
and a gathering place for underwriters is a matter of doubt. Was it already
recognized as the home of marine underwriting, or was it just one of half
a dozen city coffee-houses, of which all had a good connection among
merchants and shipowners, and none outdid the rest in standing and
dignity? In the controversies of 1718–20 over the future of marine insurance, the name of Lloyd's never cropped up. In the bitter disputes of
those years Sheppard, then owner of Lloyd's, never intervened. The
petitions and memorials were never signed by him, and it has been inferred
from his silence that Lloyd's was not in 1720 a place of special interest to
the office-keepers. The inference may be correct; but it must be remembered that even if Lloyd's had by that time completely beaten the competition of its rivals – and it certainly had not – there would still have been
no reason why its owner (being neither merchant nor underwriter)
should be asked to subscribe his name on a list of protesting underwriters
and merchants.

Nor was there any reason for the parties in the dispute to mention the
name of the coffee-house in which they were accustomed to meet. It was
their profession that was under assault, not their location; and however
much they valued Sheppard's services, he would not (if he was a man of
reasonable modesty) expect to be called in as an expert witness on the
basic needs of marine insurance. To take a modern analogy, there is today
in the City of London a restaurant that must get a large part of its trade
from members of the Stock Exchange; but, if the existence of the Stock

Exchange were ever challenged by a Labour Government, would
J. Lyons & Co., just because they are owners of the adjacent Throgmorton
Café, be likely to publish a memorandum on the economic advantages of
a free market for stocks and shares?

But that is all speculation. What is certain is that Lloyd's was a less
important place in 1720 than it was in 1740; that the habit of marine
insurance between those two dates increased considerably; that the private
underwriter got a bigger share of the business than the two companies;
that Lloyd's Coffee-House grew in strength and in repute, and that its
shipping news was fuller and more authoritative than it had ever been in
the time of Lloyd himself. In journalism, where Lloyd had suffered his
one major setback, Baker who came to the proprietorship in 1738 made
good. He managed to maintain a paper that was more successful and more
closely concerned with shipping than the original *Lloyd's News*. And the
paper that he (or it may have been Jemson) started has survived as *Lloyd's
List* until the present day. It is clear that a far greater volume of shipping
intelligence was, by this time, coming to the Coffee-House, and it is
probable that the demand for news among the customers had also grown.
Lloyd's had now more ties with overseas trade and marine underwriting
than it had had in 1700 or 1720.

The best proof of the reputation it had won came in 1740, when the
war of Jenkins' Ear was less than a year old, and the country enjoyed in
Admiral Vernon's capture of Portobello the first and almost the only
episode of glory in that drab and unsatisfactory war. Normally the earliest
reports of victory would have been brought to England by a fast sailing
frigate; but this time for some reason a merchant captain was first with the
news and when he landed he took it to the master at Lloyd's. The master
took it in turn direct to Walpole, 'first and most successful of our Peace
Ministers';[1] and the Prime Minister (as the custom then was) tipped him
for the good tidings that he brought. In 1697 Lloyd's reports from abroad
had been received in Whitehall with a condescending scepticism. In 1740
they were authoritative.

This improvement in the standing of Lloyd's is attributed by Wright
and Fayle in their *History of Lloyd's* to the disputes which preceded the
Act of 1720. The weakness of a scattered market had – they argue – been
emphasized with such damaging effect that underwriters and brokers
saw the importance of concentrating in one market and picked on Lloyd's
as the most convenient spot. That, no doubt, would be the natural path of

[1] J. R. Green.

evolution. But there were underlying causes for the success of the new market which went deeper than the Parliamentary squabbles of Northey and Thompson and all the rest of the self-seeking lawyers.

The nineteen years from 1720 to 1739 were a time of great prosperity for England; and the architect of that prosperity was Robert Walpole, the Norfolk squire, with a gift of common-sense that touched the heights of genius. His early career in politics had been discouraging, for he spent a year imprisoned in the Tower and was dismissed from office by the King. But in the turmoil of 1720 he was recalled because his ability was indispensable and, in spite of bitter hatred and opposition, he remained in power till 1742 – the longest uninterrupted period of office in the history of the Premiership. It was a comic situation. The King he served could talk no English. Walpole could talk no German. But the two of them got along splendidly in dog Latin.[1] Things, in fact, went so smoothly that in one year of Walpole's ministry the House of Commons despatched all the business it had to perform with only one division – a remarkable proof of harmony between the House of Commons and the Throne.[2]

Walpole saw that the rift between the Jacobites and the rest of the country must be healed and that the surest way to heal it was a policy of peace abroad and freer trade between England, her Colonies, and the continent of Europe. In one session he abolished export duty on one hundred and six articles, and import duty on thirty-eight raw materials.[3] He gave to the English in America greater commercial freedom than they had ever before enjoyed, and in twenty-three years he helped to raise the value of British exports to Pennsylvania alone from £15,000 to £500,000 per annum. In his unostentatious way he was the forerunner of Chatham, of Burke, and of Adam Smith. He was as much alive to the evils of war before war was declared, as other people were after nine years of schooling in casualty lists, semi-starvation, and bread riots; and if he were remembered for nothing else, two immortal sentences of his would survive. 'There are fifty thousand men slain this year in Europe and not one Englishman', and the other, 'They are ringing the bells now; soon they will be wringing their hands.'

This enlightened policy of Walpole's created exactly the atmosphere that suited the adolescent Lloyd's and stimulated its growth. The population of England increased; exports without the help of inflation doubled themselves in fifty years; the value of land rose; and the maritime interest

[1] In his book on Walpole Mr Plumb says this is a myth. What a pity.
[2] J. R. Green.       [3] Morley: *Walpole.*

gained an importance which it had scarcely enjoyed even in the days of
Elizabeth. The port of Bristol, then the second largest in the land, rose to a
very high level of wealth, and Liverpool shot up almost suddenly from a
little country town into our third largest port. To satisfy the growing
Colonial demand for British goods, Birmingham and Manchester, already
manufacturing towns, doubled in size within thirty years and London,
always pre-eminent, shared fully in the new prosperity of the Provinces.

Amongst other things that London supplied for the rest of the country
was insurance cover, without which our foreign trade would have been
impossible; and, even after the foundation of the two companies, marine
insurance in London was to the extent of at least ninety per cent in the
hands of the private underwriters.

The increase in our foreign trade itself would have been enough to
stimulate the demand for insurance cover and so swell the numbers of the
London underwriters; but there seems, also, to have been another and a
stranger reason. In 1741 the Admiralty recorded a minute on the number
of ships in convoy that insisted on breaking away from their companions.
The captains had the habit of racing ahead and running unnecessary risks
to get their cargo on to the market before the arrival of their competitors –
obviously a disturbing and worrying trick for the officers in command of
a war-time convoy. And the mischief had developed – so the sailors
believed – because the habit of insurance had grown since the war of
1718. Ship captains (knowing that ship and cargo were covered against
seizure) calculated that at somebody else's risk it was worth while to
endanger them both for a better price in the Bristol or London market.
If that official belief was correct; if the skippers were in fact more ready to
play reckless tricks in 1741 than they had been in 1718; and if the new
recklessness sprang from a larger proportion of them being insured, then
the only possible inference is that hitherto many merchants and owners
had as a matter of policy run their risks uncovered even in time of war. It
is not easy to accept that theory, and to believe that ships of two hundred
tons were sent to sea uninsured across an ocean dotted with privateers and
subject at any moment to the inroads of a hostile fleet. But it still may be a
fact that marine insurance had not become a general custom among
merchants and shipowners until nearly halfway through the eighteenth
century.

That crucial period then in the history both of Britain and of Lloyd's
was marked by three changes – a strong impetus given by Walpole to our
foreign trade; an increase (probably more than a proportionate increase)

in the volume of marine insurance; and a great improvement in the standing and importance of Lloyd's Coffee-House. Throughout the period marine underwriters were increasing in number and becoming more professional in character. And new men, as they started in the business, would naturally be attracted to a place which gave them the great advantage that only the masters of Lloyd's Coffee-House could provide. At other coffee-houses in the City they could no doubt get business accommodation free of rent. They need only frequent the places and spend a little money on food and drink to have a roof over their heads, pen ink and paper, a table to sit at and a fire to keep them warm. But at Lloyd's they got, as well, the best available news service about the world's shipping, messages from the Admiralty and from every British port, gossip brought by homeward-bound skippers from every part of the world in which they might be interested, and reports of casualties at the moment when they first reached London.

It was a wonderful arrangement for a budding underwriter, and with every year its advantages increased. For every year the Coffee-House became more of a market, with the brokers turning to it as their first place of call, and bringing to its underwriters the first show of the day's business. With all these attractions to offer – negligible working expenses, the first cut at the news and the first show of the brokers' risks – it is not surprising that Lloyd's drew the underwriters like a magnet, and proved far too much for the cumbrous heavily capitalized chartered companies. The attractions were all considerable, but the greatest of the three was the news service. It was on that rock that Lloyd's was built.

.    .    .    .    .    .    .

But the easy-going days of Walpole's government could not last for ever. He had many enemies at home. The second George, though he could talk the language most appropriate to the tongue of a British King, was on much worse terms with his Prime Minister than his German-speaking father had been. Spain and France were drawing together again; our efforts to develop trade with South America (from which so much had been expected) were being hampered; and our own people, perhaps, were growing tired of the prosperous, humdrum, unexciting existence that Walpole provided for them. The result was that in 1739 the country suffered a sharp attack of war fever, kindled fantastically by the appearance before a House of Commons Committee of Captain Robert Jenkins. He brought with him a piece of an ear – presumably in pickle – which had,

John Julius Angerstein, Chairman of Lloyd's, 1795; from the painting by Sir Thomas Lawrence in the Library at Lloyd's.

he declared, been sliced from his head seven years before by a Spanish coastguard off Havana. From 1731 to 1738 the incident (though known) had been almost unnoticed. But the war party in 1738 suddenly remembered it, discovered in their hearts a belated indignation, and arranged for the victim's appearance at Westminster. There he displayed a rather surprising turn for epigram, declaring to the House that when captured by the Spaniards he had commended his soul to God and his cause to his Country. The effect on public opinion was tremendous. The nation's temperature rose wildly; Walpole was forced to abandon his peace policy; and Lloyd's had to face its first experience of war since it had become the predominant market for marine insurance.

The war that started from half a pickled ear broadened out into the long struggle of the Austrian Succession, with France and Spain fighting against us side by side – France hoping to cripple her neighbours and win the hegemony of Europe, Spain itching to recapture Gibraltar and break the challenge of Britain in the West Indies and South America. For England it was (like all the wars of the eighteenth century) predominantly a sea war, fought by tedious blockades, by privateers against merchant ships, and by occasional dramatic actions between ships of the line. It was the first of four wars and out of the next seventy-six years Britain (if we neglect such interludes as the peace of Amiens) was to spend forty-five battling for her sea power, sometimes strengthening it, sometimes just holding it, sometimes losing it and struggling desperately to regain it.

In the 1739 war we had some bad patches when Spanish privateers made their way to the heart of the English Channel and captured our ships almost within sight of our own coast. At times our trade with the West Indies and the American Colonies was all but paralysed. City merchants complained furiously to the Admiralty of the Navy's inefficiency, and the Admiralty retorted with complaints about the behaviour of merchant captains in convoy. Wherever the blame lay the loss of our merchant tonnage was alarming. In 1741 the merchants themselves claimed that 300 ships had been captured in one year, while the Admiralty admitted to a hundred – and that figure is roughly confirmed by the surviving files of *Lloyd's List* which give the number as a hundred and seven. In the later stages of the war the losses became a good deal heavier for (according to *Lloyd's List*) two hundred and ninety-seven ships were captured in 1748, three hundred and seven in 1744, and in 1747 no less than four hundred and fifty-seven. And by far the greater part of the financial loss was carried by Lloyd's underwriters.

D

The burden that rested on the British Navy from 1739 to 1815 can be judged from the career of one man – the great Lord Howe. Born in 1726, Howe went into battle first in 1742, and in 1794, after fighting in four wars, crowned his career at the age of sixty-eight on the glorious First of June. He spent more than fifty years in the Navy and for thirty-one years he was on active service. And active service in the Navy of the eighteenth century was no picnic. A clerk[1] on holiday at the seaside, or a tragedian playing the lead for a week at the local theatre, would be seized by the press gang, and within a few days find himself beating about on blockade, packed with six hundred other men (some of them jailbirds with the jail fever still on them) in a ship a hundred and seventy or a hundred and eighty feet long. He was fed with maggoty food and foul water, and weakened in due course by scurvy and fever. He might go for incredible periods without setting foot ashore; and Nelson in one of his letters actually claimed to have been afloat continuously for two whole years.

There was always (it is true) the glittering chance of a good fat prize, and to the highest rank of officer the rewards of a fine capture might be sensational. But even then, however great the aggregate prize money might be, the junior officer, the petty officer, and the seaman came off badly. When Havana was captured in 1762 by a mixed naval and land force the total amount to be divided in prize money was £736,000, and it went like this to the various ranks:

| | | | |
|---|---|---|---|
| Admiral | £122,697 | 10 | 6 |
| General | £122,697 | 10 | 6 |
| Captain, R.N. | £1,600 | 10 | 10 |
| Petty Officer | £17 | 5 | 3 |
| Seaman | £3 | 14 | 9¼ |
| Marine | £3 | 14 | 9¼ |

'It was felt', said the historian of that action, 'and perhaps with reason, that the administration permitted the Commanding Officers to appropriate far too large a share of the spoils to themselves.'[2]

To Lloyd's underwriters, the state of the British Navy was clearly of overwhelming importance. Almost every policy they wrote covered the risk of capture, seizure and detention, and if our sea defences failed they were ruined. The angle from which most of us were taught our English history makes it difficult for us to think of the Navy as having been at any time anything but admirable; but there were periods in the eighteenth

[1] Sir George Trevelyan: *George III and Charles Fox*.
[2] Clowes: *History of the Royal Navy*.

century when (usually through the folly of Whitehall) it was a very insecure shield. In 1740, as we have seen, the outcry against it among City merchants was bitter; but the lowest point in its efficiency came in the American war, when Lord Sandwich (with his mistress and his large family of illegitimate children) was living at the Admiralty, controlling the Navy and ruling the service with a combination of party faction, cowardice, reckless mis-statement and congenital incompetence. He assured the nation – and incidentally the underwriters – that thirty-five ships of the line were ready to sail at a moment's notice, that twenty more could be placed in commission within a fortnight, and that ninety would be at sea within a year. When the year had gone by, Keppel, taking command in home waters, found only six ships ready; and 'viewing them with a seaman's eye I was not by any means pleased with their condition.'[1] Upkeep and repairs were so bad that the tragedy of the *Royal George* was caused by her rotten bottom falling out of her as she lay at Spithead.

Political feeling ran high among the officers, and when our fleet engaged the French fleet off Ushant in July 1778, with Admiral Keppel (who was a Whig M.P.) in command, and Vice-Admiral Palliser (a Tory M.P.) commanding the rear, Palliser refused to obey Keppel's repeated orders to come into the line, and by his disobedience robbed the fleet and the Admiral of a decisive victory. A tremendous row followed and the Vice-Admiral's conduct was attributed to the natural, and understandable, hatred that an M.P. on the Government benches would feel towards a member of the Opposition. The lower decks, too, were often in poor shape, physically and morally. Sickness accounted for far more deaths than fighting, and desertions were more frequent still. It has been estimated that in the Seven Years War, 184,893 men were serving at one time or another in the Navy, and more than 133,000 of them either died of sickness or were lost by desertion. In four years of the American War an official return issued in 1780 gave these figures:[2]

| | |
|---|---|
| Total raised | 175,990 |
| Killed | 1,243 |
| Died of disease | 18,541 |
| Deserted | 42,069 |

It was on a Navy so manned, and on such an administration in Whitehall,

[1] Sir George Trevelyan: *George III and Charles Fox*. See also Robson: *The American Revolution*: 'Among the reasons for the British defeat in the American War, not the least important, was the weakness of the Royal Navy' (Chapter 5).

[2] Clowes: *History of the Royal Navy*.

that the solvency of Lloyd's underwriters depended. And for all its faults the Navy by hook or by crook never completely failed them.

.     .     .     .     .     .

The war risks that the underwriters ran were three-fold – capture by privateers, capture in convoy, and seizure in port. The commonest of the dangers was the privateer which was always at work and – if the eighteenth century is taken as a whole – it accounted for most of the underwriting losses. The policy of using privateers – which Nelson on moral grounds detested – must have spread considerably as the wars went on, and sometimes neutral shipowners were willing enough to take a hand in the game and use their ships in a war to which their own government was not a party. In the early days of the American war, for example, the Americans sent to France bundles of Letters of Marque signed in blank by a competent American authority. On reaching Paris they were filled in with the name of a French ship, and taken as good justification for the Frenchmen to ply the profitable trade of interfering with British commerce. It was co-belligerency carried to an extreme, and it served its purpose until France openly joined the Americans by declaring war on England in 1778.

From then on our losses rose steadily and in 1779 the number of British ships captured amounted – on the figures in *Lloyd's List* –to six hundred and fifty-six. The right answer to the privateer was the convoy, but under Sandwich's administration convoying ships were so scarce that merchantmen (to their owners' great loss) spent long periods waiting for protection. At one time two hundred of them were in Portsmouth harbour for three months, while the West Indies were starving for want of the supplies with which the ships were loaded. Morale, too, was often bad on the merchant ships, and it was said at Lloyd's that when a skipper, with ship and cargo adequately insured, caught sight of an enemy privateer ahead of him he would clap on sail to make certain of being captured.[1] That statement may have been a falsehood and a libel, but that it could be made at all is evidence of a very bad state of affairs.

The capture of a convoy was a much rarer event than the capture of a single ship, but when it came it was infinitely more disastrous. And it was always a sword hanging over the underwriters' heads. One of the strangest incidents in the Seven Years War brought them within a hairsbreadth of a terrible calamity.[2] It came when we were at the very height of our Naval

[1] Weskett.          [2] Clowes.

strength; when the West and East Indies were ours; when the British Navy was lord of the seas from New York to India, and from India to the Philippines; when great portions of the Spanish Empire were capitulating almost before they knew they were at war; when a British Naval captain could call in disguise on the Governor of St Lucia one day and formally accept his surrender the next. We were like a triumphant football fifteen that has scored thirty points before half time, and spends the second half experimenting with new movements that up till then had been considered too dangerous to attempt.

In that scene of triumph, when the Coffee-House in Lombard Street must have been bursting with confidence, a French squadron slipped out of the Channel, and made its way across the Atlantic under orders to relieve Newfoundland. By sheer luck off the American coast it fell in with three British convoys combined. They were very rich convoys, inadequately protected, and the French Admiral had them practically at his mercy. Placed in that situation, surely nine hundred and ninety-nine men out of a thousand would have decided without a thought to attack the convoys and let Newfoundland go for another day or two unrelieved; and in taking that obvious decision they might well have given Lloyd's its death blow. But by an extraordinary piece of good fortune the French Admiral was the thousandth man. As he had been ordered to Newfoundland, his duty, as he saw it, was to go there with all speed letting nothing – not even a rich fat treble convoy – delay his movements. So he left the merchantmen uncaptured, temporarily recovered Newfoundland, and spared the underwriters at Lloyd's a loss worse than any of them had ever known.

The uncovenanted mercy of that escape from disaster came in the year 1762. Disaster itself came eighteen years later in August 1780. Then two convoys, one bound for the West Indies and the other for the East, had sailed together and as far as Finisterre had had adequate protection. But from Finisterre onwards their escort was reduced to one vessel of the line with two or three frigates and (so protected) the ships – three hundred miles off Cape St Vincent – met the combined fleets of France and Spain. The escort ran for safety. Out of the sixty-three merchantmen only eight escaped, and in addition to the ordinary cargo, vast quantities of military stores were captured by the enemy. It was, said Clowes in his naval history, one of the greater operations of the war and commercially it was undoubtedly the most destructive. It was described as the heaviest single blow that British commerce had received in living memory, the downfall of many respectable firms and the direct cause of half the underwriters in

Lloyd's Coffee-House failing to meet their obligations. That last statement
is no doubt an exaggeration. It comes from the mouth of one of the
Lloyd's defaulters, John Walter, who afterwards founded *The Times*
newspaper, and he may have stretched the number of the insolvencies to
put himself into good company and cover his own lack of underwriting
judgment.

But the failures at Lloyd's were certainly serious enough to be remembered against it for many years. Thirty years afterwards, when Lloyd's
was under fire in the Parliamentary Committee of 1810, the episode was
brought up against Angerstein as he gave his evidence; and in his cautious
answer he confessed to a 'belief' that it produced some considerable
failures. He had been at Lloyd's for twenty-four years when the disaster
happened. He must have known the facts and as he was a very canny
witness at the Committee, his guarded statement undoubtedly concealed
a most painful memory. Lloyd's had been hit very hard indeed. In fact
the only place in London where the incident was seen in a more cheerful
light was, strangely enough, the Admiralty itself. The officials there
noticed, and pointed out to the public, how fortunate it was that the
convoy had been given only a weak escort. If (they said) it had been
accompanied by a stronger squadron 'the Commodore might have been
tempted to fight in defence of the traders and would have lost some of his
own ships'. The public may, perhaps, have wondered in the light of this
authoritative comment why convoys were used at all, or valuable ships of
war were ever subjected to the undeniable hazards of a naval battle.

The third type of war loss that underwriters had to fear was the capture
of merchandise lying in a port; and the chief examples of it are the capture
of St Eustacius in 1781, the seizure of Dutch ships and cargo in 1794, and
the seizure of British ships and cargo by Russia during the Napoleonic war.

The first two of these disasters were caused by our own navy and our
own government, and both of them came from an outbreak of war with
Holland. St Eustacius is a tiny island, a blob of rock in the Western
Atlantic, that belonged to the Dutch and would never have been heard of
but for its importance as the centre of an illicit *entrepôt* trade with the
French. As neutral territory, it was a place of sanctuary for the blockade
runners in the American war, and goods said to be worth three million
pounds were piled up there, waiting to be distributed to the enemies of
Britain. The existence of this bolthole was a perpetual irritation to Rodney,
then in command in the West Indies, who disliked it in 1780 much in the
way that General MacArthur disliked Hong Kong in 1950. As soon as

Holland abandoned neutrality and declared war on Britain, Rodney appeared with his fleet before the island, received its submission, and took over the contents of its warehouses. Much of the merchandise was insured in London, and the capture was another very stiff blow to Lloyd's. And the blow was not softened by the disposal of the booty (which was handed over by the King to Vaughan and Rodney), or by Rodney's behaviour which 'gave rise to much scandal'. Finally, on its way back to England most of it was recaptured by the French and taken into Brest. Altogether it was not a happy incident.

The seizure of Dutch ships and cargoes by our own government, and of British merchandise by the Czar of Russia, were both severe knocks to Lloyd's, though the wound was assuaged in the Russian case by a fairly quick salvage. It is on record that the claims of one underwriter, in the two years 1794 and 1795, amounted to £190,000 and a very large part of that sum came from the loss of the Dutch ships. The Russian seizure was described by Angerstein as 'a complete loss for the time' and, although the position was soon improved by the assassination of the Czar, many underwriters took a poor view of their chances of recovery and were glad to sell their rights of subrogation to Angerstein for fifty or sixty per cent of their face value. Two years afterwards the losses were repaid to underwriters and Angerstein's speculation proved profitable – the first recorded case of an underwriter speculating on the prospects of salvage after payment of a total loss.

In the light of these great and – as one might think – terrifying risks inherent in underwriting during the second part of the eighteenth century, it is necessary to recall again the constitution of the market which faced and survived them. We must never forget that practically every policy signed at Lloyd's in those days covered the risk of war; that until 1769 Lloyd's was nothing but a coffee-house to which all the world had access; and that even after 1769 anyone in the place (without regard to his means) could write any risk on any voyage for any amount. After 1769, it is true, a rather more elaborate organization began to take shape, and in course of time it influenced and enhanced the sense of responsibility among underwriters. But the gravest risks were run by Lloyd's, and the worst disasters fell upon it before the security of a Lloyd's policy had been in any way improved.

. . . . . . .

The ownership of the Coffee-House had passed in 1754 to Samuel Saunders, a man of some wealth, who married one of the Baker girls and so got possession of the business. He held it for nine years and then, in 1763, obedient to the unwritten law which determined that the property should always pass laterally, he died and left it to his sister and her husband – Thomas Lawrence. And Thomas Lawrence was not a success. He was the first and only proprietor of Lloyd's who did not look after the management himself, preferring to leave the routine work to his head waiter. And the head waiter, too, was not a success. The management was no doubt slack and control, even over the manners of the customers, difficult. Handsome underwriting profits, made in the Seven Years War, must have attracted new customers to the place, all eager to make quick fortunes and disappointed on the return of peace by the collapse of the war time rates and the restoration of humdrum conditions of business. And the effect of all this was to produce under the guise of underwriting an outbreak of gambling that had nothing to do with legitimate insurance.

It became a regular habit for the death of prominent people to be covered without their knowledge by speculative folk who had no insurable interest in their lives, but betted on them as they would bet on a horse at Newmarket. As soon as the name of some prominent man appeared in the list of distinguished invalids, a market on the prospect of his survival would be established at Jonathan's, or at Lloyd's, sometimes at very high rates; and it was said that the effect on a sick man's condition when he read in the morning paper that Lloyd's brokers had been paying 90 per cent on him often proved disastrous. One can well believe it. It was a bad business, and the more serious-minded customers at Lloyd's disliked it so much that they decided, in 1769, to cut adrift from the old Coffee-House and set up in Pope's Head Alley a rival Lloyd's of their own.

In this way the new Lloyd's Coffee-House was founded. It was the great disruption. It was the death of the old Lloyd's and it may be regarded as the birth of the Society which has survived until today.

Although the gambling scandal was the immediate cause of the split, and although the scandal was probably serious enough to justify the seceders' behaviour, it is fairly clear that other forces were pulling in the same direction. One of Lawrence's waiters, who went off with the emigrants and became the master of the new house, got considerable benefit from the move; and his personal ambition perhaps helped to set the movement going. There was certainly some rather evil-smelling intrigue with Lawrence's manager who retired just at the moment when his retirement would do most harm to his chief. But probably the most

significant motive was a feeling in the minds of Lawrence's customers that
the old system of management had had its day and should be killed and
buried as quickly as possible. Anyone who could see beyond the toes of
his own shoes might notice that the arrangement by which underwriters
were nothing but unenfranchised customers of a coffee-house would not
work for ever. They and their predecessors had made Lloyd's. Without
their underwriting the place would still have been an ordinary shop, with
no connections more valuable than those of a dozen other restaurants and
with no claim to distinction except what it might get from serving the
best coffee. The work of the proprietors in collecting trustworthy
shipping news had been valuable – very valuable indeed. But the underwriters were breaking in even on the intelligence service, and without
help from the proprietor they had got together in 1763 their own register
of ships which was now essential to intelligent underwriting. They were
clearly capable of running their own establishment and it was time they
began to set it up.

And this decision brought Lloyd's for the first time into collision with a
problem that in the twentieth century has haunted its Committee almost
without interruption – the problem of premises. It was easy enough to
cut away from the old moorings, but not at all easy to find new ones.
You could tell Lawrence that his coffee-house was unsatisfactory, but
where could you find another? At first the seceders moved hurriedly to an
old house in Pope's Head Alley – a lane that is now little more than a
tunnel leading from Lombard Street to Cornhill, but in the eighteenth
century was one of the best addresses in the City. It was a sort of Bond
Street containing the best shops and the best hotels. It was there that Pepys
did his expensive shopping, to be troubled afterwards by the thought of
his own extravagance. It was there at the most famous hotel in the City
that wealthy merchants entertained him extensively and talked business
with him to his great advantage.

It was in Pope's Head Alley – at No. 5 – that the new Lloyd's started
its career. And very uncomfortable the place was. The house was old and
insanitary. The space was cramped; and in 1771, two years after the
underwriters had moved in, they decided that they must move out. And
this decision to move, important as it was in itself, led to another that was
infinitely more important – it led to the election of a committee and to the
payment of a subscription. The impetus that drove underwriters from
Pope's Head Alley gave the death blow to Lloyd's as a proprietary coffee-
house and assured its future as a self-governing body. There are half a

dozen vital dates in the history of Lloyd's, and the day when the first Committee was elected in 1771 is one of them.

For two years the Committee, still in Pope's Head Alley, struggled with the task of finding a new home for their subscribers. They tried houses in Freeman's Court and actually bought a lease there but never made use of it. They tried a place in Cornhill without success, and by the autumn of 1773 they were still floundering along with nothing to show for their efforts and no prospect of finding a new home. Anyone who has served on a modern building committee to decide on new premises, and remembers the endless discussions, the futile plans, and the everlasting postponement of a decision, can picture and sympathize with that eighteenth-century committee of Lloyd's underwriters. But on a modern committee it sometimes happens that, in the middle of the uncertainty and fruitless talk, one member of it will take charge and for good or ill will carry the others along on a flood of decision and action. Then for the first time results begin to show themselves.

Something of the same kind happened in 1773 at Lloyd's; but the man who took charge then and got things done was not a member of the Committee. He was an ordinary subscriber and a foreigner at that. He went over the Committee's head, approached the Mercers' Company (which managed the Royal Exchange), represented himself as the envoy of the 'Gentlemen who attend New Lloyd's Coffee-House'; demanded to be told whether there was any large room to be let over the Royal Exchange; was shown two rooms that might do; called on his own initiative a meeting of the subscribers; attended a meeting of the Committee to which he did not belong; and on the next day fixed the deal with the Mercers' Company at the very moderate rent of £160 per year. It has never been explained why the Committee of Lloyd's had fiddled about so long with premises that were much more expensive and much less convenient while two good cheap rooms were vacant at the Royal Exchange. Nor do we know whether they felt themselves humiliated at having their appointed task snatched out of their hands by John Julius Angerstein; but for the part he played then, Angerstein, the immigrant from the Baltic, became known to later generations as the Father of Lloyd's.

·        ·        ·        ·        ·

The secession of 1769 and the reforms that immediately followed it are all-important in the history of Lloyd's because they involved this revolutionary change: the underwriters were now the masters of the place, and the so-called masters had become their servants. Lloyd's, in fact, was now a society with a home of its own. It was a body of men recognizing to some extent their common interests, owning the authority of a committee which they themselves elected, and by implication at least gaining some control over the conduct of those who frequented their Coffee-House. The organization was still loose – so loose, indeed, that for years you could gatecrash into the Room and enjoy its amenities without the formality of paying a subscription. But it was definitely an organization. It was responsible, it was autonomous, and it had in it all the essential qualities which made possible the development of the next hundred and ninety years. The number of subscribers in 1771 was only seventy-nine, and even with the gatecrashers and the hangers-on the average daily attendance probably did not much exceed three or four hundred. But the young plant was well rooted and with a favouring Providence it might grow into a flourishing tree. And by good luck Providence, as things turned out, favoured Lloyd's.

.   .   .   .   .   .

Only two years after the move to the Royal Exchange the war of American Independence broke out, and underwriters had to face the greatest ordeal in the history of marine underwriting. But, mauled and battered though it was, Lloyd's emerged from the war in tolerable shape; and ten years later, when we went to war again with France, the under-writers were probably better fitted to insure British trade against men-of-war enemies, takings at sea, arrests, restraints and detainments, than they had been at the outbreak of any previous war that Lloyd's had known.

The British Navy, too, was in the Napoleonic wars a far more effective fighting force than it had been in 1775. Underwriters were not called on to pay enormous war losses like that of 1780, and could, after 1805, frame their policy on the calculable risks of privateers without taking into account the far more catastrophic loss of whole convoys. From 1801 to 1809, too, they had the great advantage of sharply rising commodity prices, so that the demand for marine insurance tended constantly to exceed the supply. They were trading comfortably on a sellers' market which generally enabled the eight hundred or nine hundred men (who then made up the body of Lloyd's underwriters) to get the rates they thought to be necessary and most of the merchants thought to be exces-sive. Altogether they were during the Napoleonic wars in a good bargaining position, and both their wealth and their standing in the City of London rose considerably. Seldom, if ever, has Lloyd's been more prosperous or more prominent than it was in the Napoleonic wars.

This period, too, is a turning point for the historian of Lloyd's. In one of his essays, Mr G. M. Young says that the historian's duty is to study his period until he can hear the people talking in the streets – an excellent maxim but a maxim that in the first hundred years of Lloyd's history is, for the amateur historian at any rate, too difficult to follow. With the best will in the world he cannot listen to the conversation of the old Coffee-House. But in 1781 his luck turns and he begins to tune in. In that year a peppery old underwriter called Weskett published a treatise on marine insurance and marine claims, and as you read it your ear catches a few familiar syllables. Indeed if your living memory of Lloyd's goes back to the beginning of the twentieth century you may even put a face that you seem to remember on to the choleric Weskett. Then you feel a certain nostalgic affection for that quarrelsome old claim settler of the eighteenth century. But it is about the year 1800, when war underwriting was in full spate, that for the first time you can begin to hold your own in the market gossip. And the reason is that then, for the first time, you have a description from Lloyd's men of how Lloyd's business was done. You have occasional books of account with figures of premiums and claims; you have Committee Minutes; and you have (what is perhaps the most educational of all the surviving matter) reports of grumbles and domestic squabbles. You begin, in fact, to feel at home.

Most of our information comes from the evidence given in 1810 to a Parliamentary Committee which sat to consider the monopoly and advise the government whether new companies should be allowed to start doing marine insurance. The question primarily concerned the Royal Exchange Assurance and the London Assurance, but most of the evidence given to this most important Committee was directed at Lloyd's. Most of the hostile witnesses devoted themselves to attacking Lloyd's; and most of the others spent their time in defending Lloyd's. The Parliamentary Committee of 1810, in fact, was a sort of Grand Assize, and Lloyd's was in the dock accused of inefficiency, inadequacy, and insolvency – three charges that it managed to refute with considerable success. The so-called monopoly (it is true) could not be defended. It was far too irrational; and in 1824 it was abolished by Act of Parliament. But in 1810 Lloyd's itself left the Court without a spot, or very nearly without a spot, on its character.

What sort of picture of marine insurance does the evidence at that 1810

Committee give? First it shows Great Britain as the most important country for marine insurance in the world. The Napoleonic wars were hampering its business on some voyages, and competitive companies had been started in India (which had now no regular mail service with Britain), while in America men were starting enterprises that cut into our trade with the West Indies. But for all that the insurance supremacy of Britain was not seriously challenged; and inside Britain London was easily first. Private underwriters were, it is true, established at some of the outposts – Bristol, Manchester, Liverpool, Hull, Glasgow and Greenock – and on the North East coast there were about twenty mutual clubs which were active (though with doubtful legality) in the insurance of coal-carrying hulls. But London was supreme, and in London Lloyd's under-writers had at least nine-tenths of the total business. The Royal Exchange and the London Assurance were too cautious and too fidgety to provide serious competition and were rather contemptuously (but quite incorrectly) described by one witness as almost obsolete. The two mutual clubs that worked in London had only eighty members each, and private under-writing outside Lloyd's (though it was still carried on in coffee-houses and merchants' offices) must have been a drop in the bucket compared with the volume of underwriting in the Room. It would, in fact, be only a minor exaggeration to say of Lloyd's in 1810 that it was the London marine insurance market.

.    .    .    .    .    .

And now let us try to get a view of that crowded bustling noisy place, that hybrid of coffee-house and market, in which millionaire under-writers, underwriters of doubtful solvency, brokers, penniless clerks, shipowners, attorneys touting for business, and merchants engaged in every sort of foreign trade jostled in the gangways, sat in their regular seats or stood like passengers in a tube railway carriage waiting for somebody else's seat to become vacant. We must see it as a few rooms of moderate size, equal perhaps to a dozen normal billiard rooms, filled to the point of acute discomfort with five hundred to a thousand men, of whom some four hundred are sitting down. It will probably be safe to assume that all the seated subscribers are engaged in underwriting. But it must not be assumed that underwriting is their only occupation; for between under-writer and broker and between broker and merchant the line of distinction is shadowy. Many, perhaps the majority, of the men who underwrite call themselves merchants and are in fact both underwriting merchants and broking underwriters. But they spend most of their time in the actual writing of risks. Some are irregular in their attendance and, when the autumn gales are due and winter voyages are being offered in the market, they have a habit of disappearing into the country – to the disgust of merchants with difficult risks to place. One of the underwriters actually admits that he spends only three months of the year in London and resides principally in Yorkshire, but he does not explain (as we should have liked him to explain) how on this timetable he contrives to hold his account together.

From such evidence as we have, and such calculations as we can make, it looks as though the total annual premium of Lloyd's underwriters in 1809 might have been about £5,000,000 gross. But this gross income was subject to many returns and deductions, and the net premium income from which all the claims had to be met was probably somewhere between three million pounds and four million pounds a year. It is of no use to ask in the early nineteenth century how many underwriters there are for nobody can tell you. The question was put more than once while the Parliamentary Committee was sitting, and even John Bennett, the secretary to the Committee of Lloyd's, could only say that the subscribers were between 1,400 and 1,500, that many of them never underwrote at all, and that his guess of the number who actually did underwrite would be about 1,000.

The reason for this curious uncertainty on such an elementary matter lies in the fact (which must never be forgotten) that there was no such thing as an underwriting member. Anyone who had access to the Room might write what he liked, and as much as he liked, without regard to his means or to his capital. The result was that, in point of strength and solvency, Lloyd's underwriters shaded down from spotless white to a questionable grey. The most respectable of them were men of large fortunes like Angerstein and Brook Watson, who was Member of Parliament for the City and Lord Mayor of London, and like Dicky Thornton who once (it is said) wrote £250,000 in his own name on one risk and offered to deposit exchequer bills for the whole sum as security. The less responsible were hangers-on, who wrote the worse risks at cheap rates; and the least responsible of all were dashing young clerks employed by merchants to place risks at Lloyd's, who swopped lines with each other as they went round the Room on their firm's business and had no money to pay for the losses that might ensue. But that unsatisfactory side of Lloyd's life was ignored (rather ostentatiously ignored) by the great men; and Angerstein, who showed his brokerage account to only two hundred out of the one thousand underwriters, dismissed the weakness with a careless shrug. 'I cannot speak to it', he said, 'I do not know their names.' So far as he was concerned these men without caste were just the untouchables beneath notice and best not spoken of in decent society.

A prosperous underwriter in time of war, at any rate, would have in his own name an annual premium income of over £40,000 gross. But for the outer fringe of underwriters life must have been difficult. Most of the risks that came to the Room were of comparatively low value and could be completed easily enough with less than four hundred men. Nine-tenths of the insurances were for less than £50,000 each and as an under-writer would take (on normally good business) a line of £200 to £500 on one risk, there cannot have been many crumbs left for the smaller men by the time the leaders had had their fill. Of the occasional big risks, the largest ever done was treasure on the *Diana* frigate from Vera Cruz to Britain. The voyage took place in 1807 and the placing of that insurance was the chief glory of Angerstein's career as a broker. The full value was £656,800. One of the companies took £25,000 and private under-writers £631,800; but not all these private men were at Lloyd's, for Angerstein as he showed the risk gave lines to people that 'had not taken a policy for years before'. He probably sent his policy round two or three other coffee-houses besides Lloyd's, and into a number of merchants' private counting houses as well. It was a *tour de force* not to be performed twice in the life of one broker.

Brokers until the outbreak of the Napoleonic wars handled practically all the business that came to Lloyd's. But the high wartime rates, and the corresponding increase in brokerage, tempted merchants to show their business themselves without employing a broker; and by the year 1810 underwriters were writing about as many risks to merchants direct as they were to the wholetime brokers. Indeed, according to the brokers' evidence, which was probably reliable, many of the complaints about the instability of Lloyd's were caused by the amateur broking of the merchants' clerks. How many firms of genuine brokers there were we do not know, but there were enough to make competition keen, and nothing hurt a broker's feelings more than the suggestion that he was overpaid for his services. He got a brokerage of 5 per cent; was given by underwriters anything from a year to three years credit; and when, at the end of the credit period, the time came for payment he was allowed to keep 12 per cent of this net balance as extra remuneration.

One elderly broker who had been Angerstein's partner for fourteen years declared that on these terms no one ever made a fortune out of broking, and only a minority made a competence. The luckier brokers he said had income enough to keep two maids and a manservant. The less lucky employed two maids, and many, of whom he himself (despite his partnership with Angerstein) was one, could afford only one maid-of-all-work. Another broker, challenged to justify his remuneration, burst into a positive threnody before the Parliamentary Committee. 'The labour,' he cried, 'the agitation of mind, the perpetual vexation, is not to be described. I would rather begin the world again and pursue any other line. It is painful to a degree; we can hardly ever satisfy our principal. If men got their twenty or thirty thousand a year the trouble is not too great for the compensation they receive.'

There seems to be no doubt that the insurance broker in the eighteenth century was not a feather-bedded person. His duties were many and exacting. He had to do all that his twentieth-century successors have to do in obtaining the best terms for his client; but he had another duty of which a modern Lloyd's broker is happily free – he had to guess correctly the means of the different underwriters, distinguish between the strong men and the weaklings, and see to it that, if possible, no policy sent out by him was signed by a man of doubtful standing. It must have been a difficult matter but somehow the brokers tackled it. They knew their men; they watched their methods; they detected the first sign of recklessness in an underwriter; and when one of the brokers was asked by the Parliamentary Committee whether he could form a correct judgment of the prudence with which individual underwriters carried on their business, he was able to answer proudly 'If I had not the means of judging it would be quite impossible I could have recovered about £280,000 in six years with less than £300 in bad debts.'

In the routine work of his business, too, the broker of 1800 had a harder time than his successor. Although he may have had an office staff it looks as though the principal had to do almost everything for himself. He had to show the risks, write out the policies, obtain the underwriters' signatures and adjust the claims. He had none of the modern apparatus of standardized clauses and wordings, and so far as can be judged from the evidence of 1810, the exact wording of each policy was thrashed out with underwriters at the moment the risk was being placed. If the broker did a risk with one of the companies, he was expected to sit beside the Company underwriter while the underwriter wrote out and signed the policy. If he placed a risk at Lloyd's he would sometimes use a slip in the modern

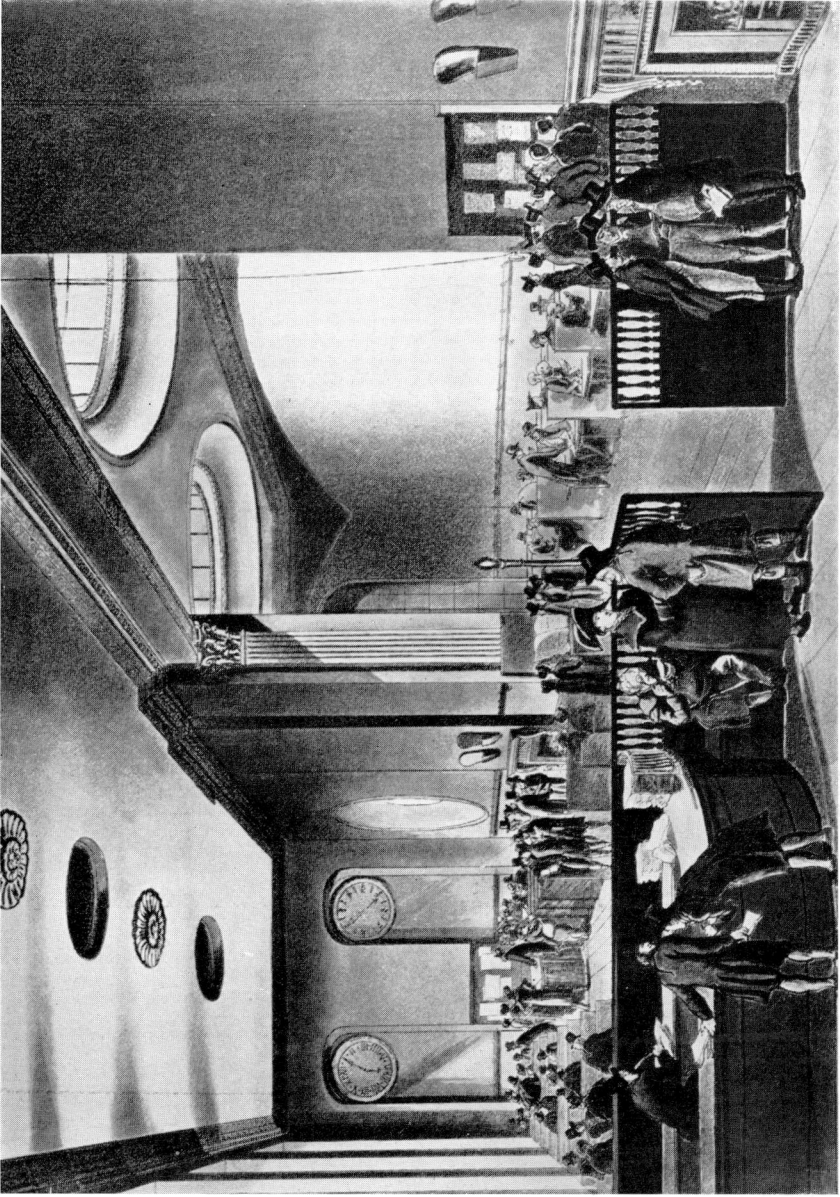

Lloyd's Subscription Rooms in the Second Royal Exchange; from a print by Pugin and Rowlandson published in 1809.

fashion, but more commonly he would prepare the policy before he went to Lloyd's and get it signed while he was actually doing the risk.

It sounds impossible, but it is on record that, using this system, a broker could take an order for £40,000 at lunch time and hand the policy written, signed, and in order, to his client at three of the afternoon. The broker's slip, which is today the keystone of his business system, came into fashion at some date not ascertained and was at one time regarded as a disreputable dodge to avoid the marine stamp duty. It was denounced by the government; more than one merchant was prosecuted for evading taxation by the use of it; and notices were put up in the Coffee-House warning underwriters never to write their names and lines on brokers' slips. The order was in general complied with, but the slip was too convenient to be banned altogether. People got round the difficulty by preparing slips in the same way that a modern broker prepares his; but instead of leaving the underwriter to put his line down for himself, the broker wrote down in his own writing the names and lines of all the underwriters who accepted part of the risk. The slip in fact became the broker's *aide-mémoire* until the next morning when the policy would be presented at Lloyd's for the underwriters' signatures. It was a curious arrangement but years went by before custom and common-sense together made an honest document of the underwriter-initialled slip.

. . . . . .

This short survey of the Coffee-House market and its functions in 1810 brings us face to face with the most interesting of all the questions connected with it. Why did not more underwriters fail? Here we have a casual group of unorganized, uncontrolled men, accepting separately enormous liabilities every year without any inquiry being made into their means, with no deposits or guarantees, without (in some cases) enjoying the respect or confidence even of the people with whom they rubbed shoulders in the daily work. They were supposed to pay only an entrance fee of £15 and a subscription of £2 2s. 0d. or £4 4s. 0d. per year – not in itself a severe test of solvency – and some men sneaked into the Room without making even that payment. Subscribers joining after 1800 had (it is true) to be spoken for by six other subscribers; but it was not an exacting formality and from 1773 to 1800 the Committee – or rather the masters – apparently made no sort of inquiry before giving a new man the right of entry.

E

Altogether it must have been a much easier thing to become a subscriber to Lloyd's than to join a moderately exclusive club. The greatest insurance market in the world, a market which offered its customers nothing but promises to pay, took no steps to see that the promises would ever be implemented. An organization that lived entirely by the good name and credit of its members allowed a young clerk as free a hand to trade on its good name as it allowed to Angerstein and Dicky Thornton. On paper the thing was impossible. It could not work. But in practice it worked astonishingly well, and the one conclusion that came out of the evidence given to the Parliamentary Committee of 1810 was that failures were rare occurrences. The convoy disaster of 1780 and the insolvencies that followed it still rankled in the minds of some of the witnesses. But the fact that men who were avowed enemies of Lloyd's, anxious to throw at Lloyd's all the mud they could collect, had to go back thirty years to fetch their ammunition, is proof in itself that their case against Lloyd's in the matter of security was a bad case. The security of a Lloyd's policy was good. By the standards of the early nineteenth century it was very good.

But how did such an unlikely tree bear such sound fruit? The answer most commonly given to that question is that Lloyd's was saved by the principle of individual liability, because an underwriter might be able to meet his underwriting debts even after the merchant firm in which he was a partner had gone bankrupt. The strength of a Lloyd's policy on this theory lay in the cardinal words, 'each for his own part', which put the liability squarely on to the shoulders of the individual.

Whatever force there may be in that explanation it is not wholly satisfactory, and we must look elsewhere for another reason. One attractive theory would give all the credit to the brokers – responsible men anxious not to have weak names on their policies, always vigilant to detect and avoid the unsafe underwriters. If every broker was a man of prudence and integrity, and gifted with an infallible judgment of his fellow men, that explanation might be sufficient. But there was no official check on brokers any more than there was on underwriters, and it is just impossible to believe that while underwriters could sometimes be rash and imprudent the brokers were always wise and cool. For the true answer to our question we must look a little further. The real reason for the security of a Lloyd's policy in the eighteenth century lay in the long credit that underwriters gave to brokers. They seem never to have allowed less than twelve months credit and sometimes as much as three years, and although they probably settled most of their claims by book-keeping entries, they had to be ready at any time to find cash for total losses. Unless a man's under-writing was very unprofitable he was always owed a considerable sum by the brokers, and the brokers' balances were a floating reserve which must have proved valuable if ever the underwriter were driven into insolvency by some staggering total loss.

That accounting system, which had grown up at Lloyd's no doubt for the convenience of brokers and their clients, was at the same time a safe-guard to any merchant who found he had a defaulting underwriter on his policy. It mitigated the mischief after the mischief was known. But it did a good deal more than that. It meant that a man when he started under-writing as a business knew that he must have a working capital equal to at least one year's losses. If he aimed at a premium income of £6,000 a year he knew that if he was going to be reasonably safe, let alone comfortable, he must have at least £6,000 of free capital to tide him over the early stages of his career. And no prudent man would launch out unless he had that sum behind him. The credit system, in fact, worked as a sort of means test and so far as serious underwriting went it kept the weaklings out. There were a certain number of irresponsible reckless men who hung about the Room and gambled without the means to pay when they lost; but Angerstein dismissed them as unimportant – and unimportant they may have been. There were others, no doubt (not meant by Nature to be underwriters), who by their bad judgment made losses year by year until their working capital was eaten up. Then they failed and the premium that the brokers owed them came in to the relief of the creditors.

But altogether the bad debts that merchants made on Lloyd's policies in 1800 and in the subsequent years were trifling – probably less than one quarter per cent of the total collected. That was not perfect security. But for an unorganized coffee-house it was almost miraculous, and in 1810 it was probably far better than the average credit in any other trade.

# 4

## THE BIRTH OF A CONSTITUTION

*The first Committee and the Masters – 'Mills' frigate – Lloyd's self-confidence
and authority – Connections with the Navy – Problem of subscribers – Underwriters' profits – Criticism of Committee – Trust Deed of 1811*

---

THE PARLIAMENTARY COMMITTEE of 1810, mentioned in the previous
chapter, reported to the House of Commons against the monopoly and in
favour of throwing marine insurance open to any corporations or companies that wished to engage in it. The old arrangement was, in truth,
indefensible, and no advice could be offered other than to destroy what the
Committee called 'this exclusive privilege'. But for fourteen years the
Committee's advice was neglected. Then in 1824, under the impulse of
the Alliance Assurance Company and the Quakers who were connected
with it, the attack on the monopoly was launched again. A Bill was passed
into law repealing those parts of the Act of 1720 that referred to marine
insurance, and thenceforward the Royal Exchange, the London, the
Underwriters at Lloyd's, and the few comparatively rare persons who
were still writing policies 'in the several coffee-houses round the Royal
Exchange' were to be exposed to the harsh wind of competition. A
closed meeting had been turned into the open championship.

At this point we must go back nearly fifty years and trace from
another aspect the development of Lloyd's in the second half of the
eighteenth century and the early years of the nineteenth. Our last chapter
was concerned mainly with the daily work of brokers and underwriters
during that period. This will deal with the events and reforms which in
the same period re-shaped a proprietary coffee-house into a compact,
autonomous and partially disciplined society. The change took place
mainly between 1771 and 1811 and of the various administrative steps
that helped to bring it about almost every one was taken, not as a move
in a plan of campaign, but as an expedient to meet some temporary and
immediate problem. The underwriters broke away from Lombard Street

in 1769 ostensibly, at least, because the management had deteriorated and an epidemic of gambling had broken out from which they desired to escape. Then from the rank and file of the frequenters they elected a committee, not because they particularly wanted to be managed by a committee, but because somebody had to find new premises, and a small committee seemed the most likely means of finding them.

In its immediate task that first committee certainly was not a success; but for all that it was the direct ancestor of the Lloyd's Committee of today and the vote that elected it was one of the cardinal events in the history of Lloyd's. The committee-men in due course assumed the owner-ship of the Coffee-House, but only because the new master was not a man of means and somebody had to supply the capital. They restricted, or tried to restrict, the use of the rooms to subscribers, not because they thought it right to control the quality of the brokers and underwriters who traded there, but because they needed money to keep the place going. Later on they took the shipping intelligence out of the master's hands into their own, and they did so only because a squabble – a not very important squabble – with one of the masters blew up during the Napoleonic wars. They got along comfortably enough without a paid secretary until (in 1804) the First Lord of the Admiralty refused to receive letters from 'a waiter', and then to relieve the nobleman's social queasiness (and for no other reason) they created the post of secretary to the Committee – which was to last for more than a century. They gave the title to one of the waiters who, from then on, corresponded with His Lordship to His Lordship's complete satisfaction. They signed a Trust Deed in 1811 because of a squabble between the subscribers and the Committee. The subscribers, because of that squabble, bound themselves for the first time to obey a code of rules and regulations, submitted themselves to a central discipline, and fixed the constitution of the society for another sixty years. The result of that step was the creation of an organized body, but the occasion was a trivial quarrel. At every point the temporary emergency produced the permanent reform.

In the early days at the Royal Exchange the constitution was partly a diarchy and partly a democracy. The power was divided between the Committee and the masters, and in the day by day control of the Room the masters were at first the more important. When the split came between the old Lloyd's and the new Lloyd's the management, and presumably the ownership, of the Coffee-House in Pope's Head Alley had gone to Thomas Fielding, one of the old waiters. And he probably carried on the business, much as Edward Lloyd had carried it on eighty years before and Newton, Sheppard, Jemson, and the others had managed it in their day. The place was still a private shop and the goodwill (we may assume) vested legally in the master. But four years later, in 1774, when Lloyd's moved into the Royal Exchange the balance of power shifted, and with that unexpected tilt the legal position was changed radically once and for all. The lease of the Room was granted by the Mercers' Company not to the masters but to certain members of the new Committee; and the new masters sank into the position of being tenants-at-will to the subscribers, who might 'turn them out and replace them and make such alterations as they shall think the merits of the party may require'.

When they accepted that position of tenants-at-will, the masters signed away their independence in perpetuity. It was, indeed, a curious and most unusual arrangement. The masters were partners in a flourishing business, running it for profit and sharing the profits between themselves in fixed stated proportions. But the proportions were not arrived at, as they generally are in partnerships, by voluntary agreement between the partners. They were imposed on them by the Committee. If there was ever a partnership deed between them or an understanding on the period of the partnership it was little better than a piece of camouflage, for any of them or all of them together could be dismissed and the partnership terminated or reconstituted by the Committee without notice or warning. But for all that they still behaved as though they were masters in fact as well as in name. They put their signatures as a firm to the letters that went out from Lloyd's, and there was nothing in their style to show that they were not the independent owners of the business.

In 1798 the Admiral commanding at Spithead – a very important person who had written an almost deferential letter to Lloyd's – received back a courteous complimentary acknowledgement, not from Lloyd's itself but from a firm that most members of Lloyd's today have never heard of – the firm of Bennett, Trebilcock and White. That style rather suggests an old-established very respectable firm of solicitors in Lincoln's Inn, but the names were actually those of three ex-waiters, each elevated to the state of master and living on the goodwill of a body of underwriters, liable to instant dismissal on the word of the Committee, and under open notice that if he took bribes from outsiders he would be discharged from his post.

It was a queer and, as one would think today, a humiliating situation; but the partnership was prosperous and the partners (though the sword was always over their heads) still had some power and authority. They received, or were entitled to receive, from each frequenter of the Coffee-House, an annual payment that varied from one guinea to three guineas. The size of their income obviously depended on the numbers of those who subscribed, and there was little they could do either to increase or diminish those numbers. But luck was with them. The roll of subscribers rose from 79 in the year 1769 to 179 in the year 1775, and to more than 2,000 in the year 1801; so that their revenue from subscriptions alone was steadily and rapidly advancing. The catering was in their hands, and as Lloyd's was still a Coffee-House, in fact as well as in name, that side of the business may have produced a substantial gross income. The news service was, to begin with, wholly under their control; and the profits of *Lloyd's List* went into the partnership's pocket. So long, too, as they remained on good terms with the Committee the work was interesting as well as profitable, for they probably knew more about the shipping of the country and the wars at sea than anyone else in the country. They acted as Secretaries and no doubt as advisors to the Committee and to its Chairman, and their power over the affairs of the society (though legally it might hang by a thread) must, in practice, have been considerable.

After twenty-one years of being master, Thomas Tayler told the Committee in 1795 that the management of the house 'under the Committee's direction' had ever been the pride of his heart, and the friendship of the subscribers in general would 'ever remain a grateful remembrance on his mind'. Language of that kind, coming from a man at his retirement, is proof enough of happy relations with his employers, and when Tayler died a year later, leaving a substantial estate, his will showed that he had meant what he said – that his heart had indeed been fully engaged in his life's work. To be a master of Lloyd's Coffee-House in 1795 was to have a profitable and interesting occupation.

So much for the masters. What of the other half of the diarchy – the Committee? It had nine members; it was elected for the first time when the move from Pope's Head Alley had become necessary; and it was given a very closely defined authority. The function of the Committee members was 'to provide and contract for a proper place whereon to carry the said scheme (i.e., the removal from Pope's Head Alley) into execution, and they may be at liberty to apply all or any part of the money to be paid into their hands in the purchase of such places as they shall provide and contract for'.

The money to be paid into their hands came from a guarantee given by seventy-nine frequenters of Lloyd's, each of whom bound himself to contribute up to £100. A call of £20 a head was made to provide a working capital, but after the subscribers had settled in at the Royal Exchange the Committee found that they had a surplus of cash, and returned £5 to each of the subscribers, so making his net contribution £15. That figure of £15 was purely fortuitous. It happened to be the cost per man of moving into the new premises and furnishing them. The cost might equally well have been £12, or £18, or £25, but the figure of £15 became standardized and from 1773 onwards everyone who applied to become a subscriber was charged £15 as his 'foundation subscription', or as we should call it now, his entrance fee. It was reasonable enough to make a new entrant pay his footing before he started business, but it seems a little strange to fix his fee at £15 and leave it for nearly half a century at £15 because of the original cost of fitting up the rooms. It was illogical. But it was strangely characteristic.

To speak disrespectfully of one's predecessors is a disagreeable experience, but it is sometimes necessary; and there is no blinking the fact that in its earliest days that Committee of nine Lloyd's subscribers was not at all an efficient body. Again and again it met, it debated, it separated, and it did nothing. And the first entry in its Minute Book must surely record the exasperation of someone who had sat through its several meetings.

> There have been (the minute runs) several meetings of the Committee but as nothing was determined at any of them no notice was taken of them.

An admirable minute. The Committee toyed with this idea and that. It tried premises in Freeman's Court and in Cornhill and it failed in both. It negotiated with Magdalen College, Oxford, for two houses that the College owned in the City and the negotiations collapsed after Lloyd's had accused the College of double dealing. The Committee was undoubtedly in a mess, and it was only the intervention of Angerstein that saved them. But they continued to function, and on the 24th November, 1773, at half past seven o'clock, they reported to a general meeting of subscribers that after many fruitless attempts to obtain a coffee-house in Freeman's Court and other places, they had succeeded with the Mercer's Company for a very roomy and convenient place on the north west side of the Royal Exchange. Nothing (so far as the records show) was said about Angerstein and the masterful lead he had given, but the Committee had a good meeting. Their proposal was well received; the Royal Exchange plan was adopted, apparently with only one dissentient, and in March 1774 Lloyd's moved house.

Now that underwriters were installed in their new home, it might have been expected that the Committee (its task discharged) would go into voluntary liquidation. It is difficult, indeed, to find legal justification for its continued life or basis for any of its subsequent actions. No general meeting of the subscribers had asked the members of the Committee to take charge; the Committee's original authority was confined strictly to the acquisition of premises, and said nothing about managing the affairs of the society after the acquisition was accomplished. But no one seems to have objected to the Committee going on or to have asked its members by what authority they claimed to act as managers; and it may be that by the general acquiescence of the subscribers some kind of power – what lawyers might call a constructive authority – was conferred upon them.

It was not a very onerous duty that the Committee had to discharge; nor was their work generally of epoch-making importance. But the Committee took it seriously. On the night of 24th November, 1773, when the general meeting which ratified the move to the Royal Exchange had broken up, a meeting of the Committee was convened (it must by this time have been well after nine o'clock) to discuss with a Mr Penton the provision of a wind dial and a clock in the subscribers' room, and to instruct him to go and look at wind dials at the Royal and at Sam's Coffee-House. At another meeting, in November 1773, even more important business had been debated – business which called for the personal attention of a strong sub-committee of two or three members to act as a deputation to the East India Company.

> It was resolved (say the minutes) that two or three of the Committee wait on the Committee of Warehouses of the East India Company and endeavour to obtain leave to carry a pipe for a necessary in their cess pool.

But with all its oddities, its fussiness, its failure to find the right premises, its doubtful legal standing and its apparent absorption in trivialities, the Committee did great service to the growing Lloyd's. Like the House of Lords at about the same period in English history, the Committee of Lloyd's for the most part did nothing in particular and did it very well. Until 1769 the Coffee-House had always been privately owned and managed by the proprietors and, if the Committee by a sudden gesture had wrenched the power out of Fielding's hands and assumed it themselves, the routine of the place might have been disturbed and the subscribers' comfort impaired. The prudent policy of the Committee was to interfere with the masters as little as possible, leave them to look after the room, let them collect and disseminate the news, let them manage the newspaper, let them take the subscriptions and carry on the correspondence; but at the same time to make it clear that the subscribers owned the Coffee-House and could get rid of the masters whenever they pleased. That position was always maintained and at no time, from 1774 onwards, was there any doubt about the ultimate balance of power in the diarchy, or any suggestion that the masters had proprietary or contractual rights. Nominally they were tenants. Actually they were servants with a wide range of free action.

But for the existence of an elected representative Committee it would have been difficult to prevent the full power and authority from slipping back into the hands of the masters. And this Committee of 1774 was undoubtedly representative. It was in close and constant touch with the body of subscribers. It frequently called general meetings to take the opinions of the rank and file; and the right of subscribers to summon a general meeting for the discussion of some particular matter was exercised far more often than it is in our own day. The young society was very much of a democracy and the Committee was its mouthpiece.

A very good example of the working of Lloyd's as a democracy (with the Committee speaking for it) comes from the famous case of the *Mills* frigate, a boat that in 1764 was insured by Lloyd's underwriters, became a total loss in the West Indies, and helped (in an action at the Guildhall) to build up the body of English Insurance Law.

But before we consider the circumstances of the *Mills* case something should be said (even at the risk of deviation) about the general attitude of eighteenth-century underwriters towards their claims. At the Parliamentary Committee of 1810 various opinions were expressed on this point, some witnesses declaring that underwriters were very obstructive, while others maintained that they were most generous. It is quite possible that both views were right; that underwriters sometimes paid claims for which they were not liable and sometimes resisted claims which they ought to have settled. But unhappily for the reputation of the early Lloyd's the claims that underwriters settle quietly are forgotten, and the cases they fight are recorded and remembered. And in some of those cases they appear at this distance to have been a good deal more obstinate than reasonable, while their competitors of the Royal Exchange Company sometimes laid themselves open to the same criticism. A boat, for instance, that had been insured with the Royal Exchange was damaged by heavy weather and put into port for repairs. The repairs necessitated the removal of rigging from ship to shore, and while the gear was on land, part or all of it was destroyed by fire – surely a straightforward claim on a marine policy. But the Royal Exchange refused to pay because the rigging was covered as part of the vessel, and (so the Company argued) the owners had put it outside the protection of the policy when they unshipped it.

Another case fought, this time by private underwriters, turned on a vessel that had been blown off her course and forced to run for safety to St Eustacius. Later on in the voyage she became a total loss and underwriters refused to pay the claim because the vessel had deviated and voided her insurance. Another vessel insured from Jamaica was warranted to sail before 2nd August – no doubt because of the approaching hurricane season. She left Saint Anne's Bay in good time and went round to Blue Fields on the south coast of the island to join her convoy. There she was detained by the naval authorities and did not leave Jamaican waters till after the warranty date. If she had left Blue Fields by herself she would have run unnecessary risks of capture and probably would have broken the law. By not sailing alone she broke (if underwriters were right) her sailing warranty. Was ever a ship more clearly between the devil and the deep sea? But on the way home she was lost or damaged and underwriters refused to pay because of the broken sailing warranty. They were taken to court by the owners, and there the owners very rightly won their case and got their money.

By modern standards these old underwriters and companies were behaving like obstructionists and deserved any criticism that may have been directed at them. But if they were still in a position to answer for themselves they might even today put up a fairly persuasive argument to justify their conduct. They could remind us that in a country which is governed by case law nobody knows what the law is until either he or somebody else has – at his own expense – fought an action to get the law determined. If any point has not been fought out in court then there is a vacuum; and in the early days of a legal system the vacuum must be wide and deep. It is all very well for underwriters and brokers of the twentieth century to take a high line and speak harshly of their predecessors for being too ready to litigate, but they have a mass of judgments to guide them and learned textbooks in which these judgments are collected and analysed. They have their Arnolds, their Gows, their Templemans, and their

Greenacres to elucidate separately every sentence in the marine policy; and when a dispute between assured and underwriter turns on a point of law, not on a point of fact, the odds are 90 to 1 that it can be cleared up without anybody having to trouble a Judge for his decision. That is a pleasant and comfortable situation to be in, and it is the old underwriters who are to be thanked for it. If the underwriters of the eighteenth and early nineteenth century had not been litigious; if instead of going to court they had agreed with their adversary while they were in the way with him; if, in fact, they had not blazed the legal trail for us; then the law of marine insurance would be as uncertain today as it was in 1750, before a Jacobite from Scotland, sitting as a judge in an English court of law, taught Hanoverian Englishmen what their law was. And but for the litigious marine underwriter the great Lord Mansfield would never have had the opportunity to teach us. The reeling English drunkard is supposed to have made the rolling English road – a very doubtful historical statement. But it is undeniably true that it was the quarrelsome English Litigant who made the English Case Law.

From that deviation on the claim-settling principles of the eighteenth century, we return to the case of the *Mills* frigate, one of the most famous of Lord Mansfield's law suits and for our immediate purpose the most important. The *Mills* was a trading frigate well owned and well thought of by underwriters, which became a total loss in the West Indies in the year 1764; was twice the subject of a trial in an English Court; and after the judgment in the second trial raised such a disturbance and such a wordy battle in the City of London as few legal disputes before or since have ever produced.

The facts were that in the early months of the year the *Mills* sailed from England on a voyage to Madeira, met with terrible weather, was blown off her course and finished up at Nevis in the West Indies. There her captain had her repaired, obtained a certificate of seaworthiness and sailed with a cargo of sugar on her return voyage to England. But before sailing he sent to his owners in London a detailed account of the damages their ship had received. The owners, when they insured the ship for her return voyage, showed the captain's letter to the leading underwriter who quoted a rate of £2 7s. 6d. per cent knowing as much about the condition of the vessel as the captain or the owners themselves. There could not have been a fuller disclosure. But there was in fact serious undiscovered damage in the ship and the *Mills* soon after sailing sprang a leak, made water rapidly, limped into a port of refuge and was there condemned. Her owners claimed on the underwriters and the underwriters decided to fight the case on the question of seaworthiness, declaring that a marine policy contained an implicit but absolute warranty that the ship is in a fit condition for the voyage.

The underwriters appear to have had a good defence on other grounds than seaworthiness, but it was on the point of seaworthiness that they won the case at the Guildhall before Lord Mansfield. And by that victory in court they established as a rule of law that in a voyage policy there is an absolute warranty of seaworthiness – that if a vessel, for any reason, is not fit for the voyage, then whether the owners knew of the weakness or not, whether the loss of the vessel was or was not caused by her unfitness, the insurance both on herself and her cargo is void and worthless.

In its simple absolute form that is a harsh doctrine, and since the days of the *Mills* frigate it has been so much softened both by law and by practice that it has ceased to be of very much general importance. But in 1764 Lord Mansfield's judgment hit the City of London like a thunderbolt. Merchants asked themselves, with a good deal of reason, what was the good of a contract expressed in a Lloyd's policy if it could be upset by some latent defect – a defect that nobody could know of or even suspect at the time the insurance was taken out. If that was the law, then the most careful, the most honourable ship owner, could never say 'I am insured'. The farthest he could go was to say 'I hope I am insured but only God knows whether I am or not'. Feeling ran high and a pamphleteering controversy of an almost theological bitterness broke out between merchants and underwriters.

The merchants accused the underwriters of being grasping and unfair, anticipating the charges that were to be brought against Lloyd's forty years afterwards at the Parliamentary Committee. The merchants in truth were very angry with the judgment itself. They were still more indignant when they heard that George Hayley, who was the leading underwriter on the policy and a member of the Committee of Lloyd's, the man who had laid so much stress at the trial on the vital importance of seaworthiness, was now actually writing policies with a clause admitting the seaworthiness of the insured ships and was charging no additional premium for doing it. Nor were they content with general expressions of indignation. For the use of merchants and for the discomfort of underwriters they drafted a ready-made clause declaring that 'Any insufficiency of the ship' unknown to the assured or his agents should not prejudice the insurance; and they recommended everyone who did business with Lloyd's to insist on the new clause going into the policy. They had in mind only the insurance of ships for a voyage, since time insurance then was very little practised. But it says much for the common-sense of these merchants that years later, when time insurance had become fashionable and the law of seaworthiness had to be restated in relation to time policies, the judges adopted, in effect, the same solution that the merchants had drafted for voyage insurance in 1755.

For a few years, too, the underwriters themselves seemed to have agreed to the merchants' clause, but the feeling at Lloyd's hardened against it, and in 1779 a meeting of subscribers was called presided over by the then Chairman of the Committee – the same George Hayley – and a drastic resolution was taken by a majority, or perhaps by a unanimous, vote. The vote not only banned the new merchants' clause, but actually outlawed any change in the printed wording of the marine policy and forbad any kind of addition to it. 'No policy', it said, 'shall be subscribed from this time knowingly that may be different from a form now produced' and 'we will not underwrite to any person or persons who may hereafter tender any policy otherwise printed.' It was surely a very high-handed line for men to take who claimed to be serving the interests of the community and supplying commerce with the sort of protection that commerce needed.

From our point of view the case of the *Mills* frigate is a curious and convincing proof (*a*) of the position that the Committee of Lloyd's now occupied in the affairs of the Coffee-House and (*b*) of the grip that the Coffee-House itself had secured on the country's marine insurance business. The meeting held at Lloyd's on the 12th January, 1779, 'to consider on the innovations' of the printed wording was an official general meeting, summoned by the Committee and presided over by its Chairman. Its resolutions were recorded in the Minute Book of the Committee and it dealt with a matter that had not the remotest connection with the purpose for which the Committee had been constituted eight years before. It had nothing to do with premises, or the provision of space, or with the collection of subscriptions. It was concerned with an underwriting matter and with nothing else, a point (as one would think) to be decided between individual underwriters and individual merchants in their normal daily bargaining over the terms of their insurances. But it was to the Committee that the subscribers turned to help them solve their underwriting problems, and it was under the shelter of the Committee that they enforced their demands against their clients.

It is clear that in the few years that had passed since 1774 both the Committee and the Coffee-House itself had undergone an almost violent change. The Committee had become the guardian of underwriters' general interests, their defender against attack and their mouthpiece when they wanted to speak as a body to the outside world. That it should be appealed to when common action had to be taken was accepted as the natural procedure. And through the changes and vicissitudes of nearly two hundred years we see the Committee of Lloyd's, in the eighth year of its life, discharging some of the same functions that it discharges now when it is more than a hundred and eighty years old. Its scope today is wider. Its reach is longer. Its regulations are more elaborate. But the core of its duties was the same a hundred and eighty years ago as it is now.

The *Mills* case, too, shows the Lloyd's subscribers in a most surprising light – powerful, self-confident, and astonishingly sure of themselves. The line they took towards their clients was a very strong one – stronger than the members of Lloyd's acting by themselves would think it wise to attempt at the present time. The merchants who were their clients had been antagonized by Lord Mansfield's judgment and by the advantage which, as they believed, it had given to the underwriters on every policy of marine insurance. The merchants had reacted in an obvious and natural way by insisting on an alteration in the printed wording of the policy. They had been largely successful in their attempt, and the fashion of admitting seaworthiness under certain conditions was probably by 1779 fairly well established at Lloyd's. Then suddenly the underwriters revolt, and at their general meeting they bind themselves never in any circumstances to vary the printed wording of the policy form or 'underwrite to any person who may hereafter tender any policy otherwise printed'. It was an affirmation of the literal inspiration of the policy. It sounds rather like the finish of the Book of Revelation which also deprecates any addition to its wording, and declares that if any man shall ever add anything to its contents, 'God shall add unto him the plagues that are written in this book'. The author of Revelation was definite, final, and uncompromising, and so were Lloyd's underwriters. Nothing must be added. And the decision was taken without apparently consulting anybody outside Lloyd's. There is nothing to show that the two companies were asked for their opinion, and it is quite certain that there were no trade organizations such as a Chamber of Commerce whose views could be taken. The subscribers were acting on their own responsibility, and at their own risk, and it speaks volumes for the position which the Coffee-House had attained that in the midst of the trials, problems, and perplexities of the American war, the subscribers felt themselves strong enough to challenge the merchants and declare boldly 'these are our terms and you may take them or leave them exactly as you think fit'.

.    .    .    .    .    .

The American war began in 1775 and ended in 1783, and although Lloyd's was suffering then the greatest disasters in its history, there is in the minutes of those eight years not one direct reference to the war or to the failures of subscribing underwriters. The corporate spirit was undoubtedly beginning to work, but it was working very patchily, and it had not yet reached the stage of producing either sympathy for the fallen or jealousy for the good name of the society. And ten years later, when we come to the outbreak of the war with revolutionary France and with Napoleon's empire, there is still not much evidence of a highly developed *esprit de corps* among the subscribers. When an underwriter or broker was unlucky enough to fall by the way that was his own affair. It made no difference either to Lloyd's or to the other subscribers whether he succeeded or failed; and as he dropped out his fellow travellers were content to march on leaving the body to rot at the side of the road. In 1801 it is true, someone at a general meeting did propose that help should be given from the society's funds to 'subscribers to this House who are now or shall be hereafter reduced to poverty and whose age shall not be less than 50 years', but the Committee would have none of it and the suggestion was dropped.

On the other hand, although the members of the Committee were indifferent to these personal failures after they had occurred, they did at least do their best to save underwriters from such disasters as had happened in 1780, and they were extremely active in their efforts to keep down the number of captures at sea. They gave a large part of their time to watching the convoy system, to checking mismanagement in the Navy, and to prosecuting merchant captains who broke the convoy laws or deliberately threw away their ships. That was not their only activity, for they regularly concerned themselves in those years with several other problems – with the lifeboat service which they helped to start all round the coast, with a Patriotic Fund and with the extension of their premises in the Royal Exchange. But their two most important tasks were: (1) to act as watchdog over shipping; and (2) to grapple with the problem of keeping

Sir Brook Watson, Chairman of Lloyd's, 1796–1806; from a painting by J. S. Copley
in the Herron Art Museum of the Art Association of Indianapolis.

subscribers in some sort of order and keeping gate-crashers out of the Room.

In the matter of shipping, Lloyd's in the Napoleonic wars held a position that no one had ever reached before and no one has ever had since. The news service that it had built up in the last forty years must have been far more efficient than anything that the Government possessed when war broke out, and underwriters' knowledge of what the merchant fleets required in the way of protection was unique. The result was that Lloyd's Committee could speak with authority to Admirals and Admiralty alike. It commended and it criticized with equal freedom, and neither praise, nor censure, nor advice was treated with disrespect so long as it came from the Coffee-House. The Committee told the Admiralty of French ships having been sighted off Cromer and received their Lordships' thanks for the information. In 1794 they reported to the Admiralty the capture of the British ship *Hopewell* off Lowestoft by a French privateer which it named; and when the Admiralty in reply asked Lloyd's in which convoy the *Hopewell* had sailed, the Committee answered back that there had been no convoy for the *Hopewell* to sail in. It knew the name of the Frenchman that had done the mischief, gave the exact date on which the enemy ship had sailed from Dunkirk and stated the number of prizes that it had taken.

It called the attention of the Navy to its unsatisfactory convoy arrangements at Falmouth, which made it easy for the enemy to pick up our westbound British ships while they hung about outside the port waiting for the Falmouth contingent to come and join them. It received from serving Admirals confidential details of the plans made for the assembly and despatch of convoys, and passed the Admirals' memoranda on to the Admiralty with a word of praise and a suggestion that the same plans should be adopted at other ports. It pointed out to the Admiralty that convoys were being sent off with only one ship of war to protect them, and the Admiralty respectfully attended to the complaint.

It was a kind of clearing-house, too, for complaints about the misbehaviour of the skippers of merchant ships; and naval captains at the end of a voyage would send to Lloyd's a note of the ships that had broken away or disobeyed orders, so that the Committee could weigh the evidence and send their judgment on to the Admiralty. If a case of dishonesty in a captain or an owner was mentioned to Lloyd's, the Committee would back a prosecution and charge the legal costs either to the society's funds or to the underwriters directly concerned. Sometimes – so great was its

F

prestige – the Committee was forced to remind naval captains that it had no special powers to punish the guilty men, since its members were ordinary citizens and enjoyed no punitive powers beyond those common to all His Majesty's subjects.

Occasionally the magic of the name Lloyd's failed of its purpose and then the Committee was snubbed. The Chancellor of the Exchequer, for example, would do nothing for it when it demanded a reduction in the marine stamp duty; and in 1795 Pitt did not trouble himself to answer a letter in which the Chairman asked for a personal interview to discuss the capture of Dutch shipping by the British Navy. Four months later the Chairman reminded Pitt that the first letter had not been answered and Pitt treated this second letter exactly as he had treated the first. The East India Company, too, which ran a separate convoy system for its own shipping, refused in the correspondence over the famous loss of the *Althea* to recognize any right in Lloyd's or in anybody else to dictate to it the management of its own affairs. But these cases were exceptional. In general, the arm of Lloyd's Committee stretched a long way, and in commercial matters its strength was probably greater than that of any other body or organization in Great Britain. To say of the Napoleonic wars that they were Lloyd's finest hour would be an exaggeration. But they were certainly its most glamorous.

The Committee's other main task – the supervision of subscribers and gate-crashers – was more difficult than its negotiations with the Admiralty, and for a period of some twenty-six years the Committee toiled and struggled with it unsuccessfully. And that was not surprising, for the Committee approached the problem with both hands tied behind its back. The original mandate to the Committee elected in 1772 had (as we have seen) restricted them to finding new premises – and that instruction had never formally been changed. And though the members of the Committee had in many directions been ready to assume powers of action that had never been granted to them, they were strangely coy when they came to the question of subscribers, and they refused to handle it firmly. The result was that hundreds of people used the subscribers' room as though it belonged to them, but never paid their subscription; and the Committee beyond threatening the intruders, stimulating the masters to action and issuing lists of those subscribers whose subscriptions had or had not been paid, did nothing to check the nuisance. Indeed they laid it down as a principle – and it is the only general principle recorded in those early minutes – that they had no authority to decide who should, and who should not, become a subscriber and unless a general meeting gave them a specific right to do so they would not undertake the work of selection. It was an odd line to take, for the members of the Committee were undoubtedly distressed by the misuse of the Rooms, and they must have seen that the only remedy was a form of election with a close scrutiny of those who applied for the right of entry. But for twenty-six years, while they alternately menaced the offenders and pleaded with them, they refused to bring in this obvious reform.

In 1775, for example, they instructed Fielding, the then master, to apply to Mr Alexander Aberdeen for his subscription and Fielding reported that Mr Aberdeen had 'peremptorily refused'. In 1779 they put a notice over the door declaring the rooms to be the property of subscribers and no others were to be admitted. In 1781 they had an alphabetical list made of subscribers 'together with the names of those who ought to pay'. In 1784 they resolved that a list of defaulters should be put up in the Coffee-House, and in 1785 they wrote letters to those who had not paid telling them that they would be refused admission. And so on, year by year. It was all terribly ineffective. The Committee were put into a most humiliating position and the Rooms became more and more crowded with these intruding underwriters.

It was, in fact, the overcrowding that at last brought matters to a head and led up to one of the cardinal reforms in the constitution of Lloyd's. In the year 1800 several subscribers (including Angerstein) told the Committee that they would move a resolution at a general meeting restricting the right of being a subscriber to merchants, underwriters, and brokers 'on being recommended by two or more members'. They asked the Committee not to wait for the resolution to be passed but to take action in the interim; but the Committee, while agreeing to the meeting, refused to take immediate steps for lack of authority. The date of the subscribers' letter was the 26th March, 1800, and on the 2nd April, 1800, the general meeting adopted the resolution with only one material change – the addition of bankers to the permitted occupations. So the Committee then were authorized, and instructed, to take upon themselves the task at which they had hitherto shied.

We should pause a moment at this point to lay a white stone on that date, 2nd April of the year 1800, for in the calendar of Lloyd's it is a day to be gratefully remembered and celebrated. It may indeed be regarded as the day on which the old Lloyd's died and the modern Lloyd's was born, the day on which the society finally outstripped the Coffee-House, the day on which the elected Committee received the power to choose the subscribers that it liked, and refuse those to whom it objected. From that simple reform of April 1800 stems everything that has since been done for the security of a Lloyd's policy, and it is to be noted that in their letter which prompted the reform Angerstein and his friends – perhaps by a slip of the pen but if so by a most happy one – used for the first time the word 'members' in place of the word 'subscribers'. It almost seems that they might have been looking forward forty-three years to the day when another meeting of Lloyd's subscribers, under the leadership of another Committee, would create the underwriting member and give to him, and to him alone, the right of accepting liability on a Lloyd's policy.

The subscribers and the Committeemen, it is true, had no such grandiloquent notions in their minds when they decided on these reforms. The only thing that worried them was the crowded discomfort in which they worked, aggravated by the throngs of gate-crashers swarming daily into the Room. If the Committee's new powers could set that trouble right they would be content. And although the powers were for ten years or so not exercised in full, they produced immediately a startling change of mind in the gate-crashers.

At last the resistance of these recusant men broke down and they came forward in their hundreds to pay their subscriptions – hardened sinners crowding the penitent form week by week and returning from it as honest subscription-paying underwriters. The Committee, indeed, soon found itself overburdened with the work of dealing with their penitents, and in May 1800 one of the Committee meetings had so much to do that it was adjourned with a large part of its agenda untouched – the first time that is known to have happened in the history of the Committee of Lloyd's. At the first meeting after the 2nd April, 1800, forty-five new names were recommended as subscribers; at the next, twenty-nine; then forty-nine; then eighty; then thirty-eight – a total of two hundred and forty-one elected at five Committee meetings. It is fair to assume that all, or almost all, of these recruits were people who had used the Room up till then without paying a subscription; and if that be so the non-payers must hitherto have made up a very substantial proportion of the whole Lloyd's market, acting no doubt as brokers and almost certainly as underwriters.

Once again the twentieth-century observer can only marvel that a market composed so largely of this type of person could, both in war and in peace, supply not only England but a great part of the world overseas with its marine insurance cover. The routine of dealing with the applications grew so heavy that the full Committee decided to delegate the work, and it was resolved that any two members of the Committee might deal with the candidates and admit them on their own judgment, referring to the main Committee only those cases in which they felt some hesitation. Here we have the germ of the Rota Committee which today sifts the candidates for membership, interviews them, and reports on them at the next Committee meeting; and those who have served on the Rota between 1945 and 1956 will know how to sympathize with their overworked predecessors in 1800.

. . . . . .

In general, the first ten or fifteen years of the new century were, so far as we can judge at this distance of time, a period of great prosperity for Lloyd's. Politically comparable to the years 1939 to 1945, they covered the disasters of Ulm, Austerlitz and Jena, the imminent danger of invasion from Boulogne, the isolation of Britain (which not for the first time or the last stood against a hostile continent alone) and the short, but ugly war with the United States. But it also included Trafalgar, the Peninsular War, the triumph of the Russians, and the crowning mercy of Waterloo. Marine underwriters had their black days, some of them due to the chops and changes of international politics and more of them to the privateers – those submarines of the Napoleonic wars which were always levying their toll on ships and cargoes insured at Lloyd's. But there is very little doubt that most of the subscribers ended their war underwriting a good deal richer than they started it. In the Library at Lloyd's there is a risk book of 1807, kept by an underwriter who was partner in a firm that has survived until today, and the figures of his accounts show that he, at any rate (and there is no reason to suppose that he was exceptionally prosperous), was piling up a fortune at a great pace. In one year, writing for himself and no others, he took in premiums £54,452 and paid out in losses £22,804, leaving a difference of £31,648. From that balance he had to find, presumably, a substantial amount for returns of premium, but the net profit when the final balance was struck must have been very considerable and – at a time when direct taxation was negligible – the additions to his fortune from the business of those twelve months was undoubtedly handsome. There were, of course, underwriters whose judgment or capital was inadequate to the risks they were running. Some of these less fortunate men failed and were reduced to hanging about the staircase at the Royal Exchange begging from their old associates. But they were few in number and Lloyd's itself was then beyond question a place of great wealth and large fortunes.

But for all the prosperity of the place there was an undercurrent of discontent. Perhaps the strain of writing incalculable war risks year after year had stretched the nerves of the underwriters and made them ready, on comparatively small provocation, to flare out into open revolt; for in the year 1811 they did what the subscribers and members have never done at any time in the history of Lloyd's. They passed a formal direct vote of censure on their Committee.

The incident, which is very fully described by Wright and Fayle in their *History of Lloyd's*, sprang from what underwriters considered to be a negligent use of the news service by the Committee's secretary, John Bennett. There had been heavy losses in the Baltic due to Napoleon's pressure on Sweden, Denmark and Prussia, and while the claims were being settled, the underwriters discovered that Bennett had had private information from the British Fleet in the Baltic which (so they claimed) would have warned them against writing freely in that area. The Committee had been told by Bennett of his confidential letters, but had not published them in the Room, and it is probably true that any other Committee of that period in the same circumstances would have taken the same line. But underwriters, being human, usually like to find an alternative explanation to excuse a fault in their own underwriting judgment, and the suppression of this correspondence was just the excuse they wanted. They turned on the members of the Committee and rent them, carrying at a general meeting a motion that 'the Committee for managing the affairs of this house . . . has in this instance neglected the interests of this house'. It was a stab in the back and the members of the Committee very properly resigned.

Though the vote of censure was, in effect, cancelled at a subsequent meeting the general body of subscribers did not come well out of the incident, and it is not one of the passages in Lloyd's history that one would choose to look back on with pride. But the results that flowed from it were excellent, for it produced the famous Trust Deed of 1811, under which the society was governed for sixty years. It established the authority of the Committee, changing it from an *ad hoc* body doubtful of its permanent rights and powers; and it led to the birth of that very important person – the Lloyd's Agent.

The path to these reforms lay through a special committee of twenty-one members, formed to consider the vital question of what reforms were necessary for the future control of business. It must have been an admirable Committee, for it presented a firm, practical and intelligent report, and although some of its recommendations were not adopted and others have long since lost their relevance or importance, the framework that it proposed is the framework of the modern Lloyd's. And whenever a new Committee of Lloyd's is elected in the twentieth century, whenever a member of the Committee having served for four continuous years retires and becomes for twelve months a private member, whenever the name of a candidate is brought forward for election as a subscriber or underwriting member, whenever a firm of merchants is appointed and authorized to act as Lloyd's agent in some distant port, then the machinery proposed by the Committee of twenty-one members is still in use and working smoothly. It is often said that small committees are much better than large ones, and that generalization may usually be true. But every rule has its exception and, if there is indeed a general rule that large committees are unwieldy, the shining exception to it is provided by that remarkable special Committee of 1811.

The recommendations of the Committees were accepted almost *en bloc* by the subscribers in July 1811, and in August another meeting agreed to the trust deed which (drafted though it was in general terms) vested in Lloyd's Committee legal powers to manage the affairs of the subscribers. In one very important sentence it bound the rank and file to:

...duly observe perform fulfil and keep all and singular the rules and regulations for the time being which have been heretofore passed and confirmed and also all such further rules as shall or may at any time hereafter be duly passed and confirmed by a majority of the subscribers for the time being present at two general meetings to be convened for that purpose.

That document gave Lloyd's a constitution; and henceforward the Committee, which for forty years had acted on an assumed authority, was a legal body working under the protection of an enforceable deed and exercising powers specifically granted to it by the subscribers. The deed itself was destroyed by fire in 1838 but a copy survived in the Minute Books which, by a special providence, escaped the flames and by that chance we know exactly how and when Lloyd's became a legal entity.

Not only were these reforms of 1811 excellent in themselves but they were carried out at a remarkable speed, and by the end of the year the new system was in working order. At that time there were still four years of war in front of Britain, and thirteen years of the monopoly before marine underwriters. To judge from the state of the country and the collapse of wholesale prices, the period of 1815–24 cannot have been an easy time either for Lloyd's or for the merchants and bankers who stood within the circle from which subscribers might be enlisted. And it was fortunate that the changes in the constitution were made when they were, that the house was rebuilt and strengthened before the rains descended, the floods came, and the winds blew and beat upon it. When the Act of 1824 destroying the monopoly was passed, Lloyd's had had fifty years of democratic government under an elected committee, which had no purpose other than to serve the interests of the subscribers. It had played gadfly to the Admiralty, watched the convoys, prosecuted fraudulent captains and shipowners, improved the news service, stabilized the printed wording of the policy, and at long last set up effective machinery to keep undesirables out of the market. Even when it had made mistakes it had been single minded in its efforts to fortify Lloyd's.

But in the catalogue of these efforts there is one gap – and to the modern eye that gap is perhaps the most surprising thing in the history of that half-century. From first to last there was never a step taken, or a hand moved, to improve the security of the Lloyd's policy; never a suggestion made that the Committee had some responsibility for seeing that the men of Lloyd's, when they accepted liability as underwriters had the means to fulfil their undertakings. In every other direction the corporate sense was growing, but in this matter of communal credit it had not been born. The credit of Lloyd's was still a blind spot. And the blindness was universal. Even the far-sighted Angerstein, when he was challenged with a record of failures among underwriters, was content to wash his hands of the whole business and say that he personally did no business with men of that type. The conception of Lloyd's as a society in which every member must be a Caesar's wife, as a place to which the public could go in complete confidence that its claims would be met; the conception of Lloyd's Committee as a body morally responsible for the underwriters' security and the protection of the assured – these conceptions which were to become axioms in the twentieth century were, in 1824, still a long way below the horizon.

# 5

## THE DOLDRUMS

*Many new companies – Numbers of Lloyd's subscribers declining – Fire Insurance at Lloyd's – Its disappearance and re-appearance – Low morale – Payment of committeemen – Growth of Lloyd's Agents – Coveted by insurance companies – Lloyd's burnt out*

THROUGHOUT ITS LIFE of 104 years the Bubble Act of 1720 had been fatal to all but two marine insurance companies and had dealt very gently with fire and life. Between 1720 and 1824 a few small mutual marine clubs had, it is true, been formed in spite of the Act, but not one marine company proper had slipped through the meshes. Non-marine companies, on the other hand, had wriggled through the net in considerable numbers. On the strict wording of the Act the legality of what the promoters of non-marine companies did was surely doubtful. But by one device and another; by entering into deeds of settlement; by straining the word partnership almost to bursting point; by making named individuals instead of the company itself liable for claims; and by gaining in time the sympathy of the Government, they managed to get the business going, and to lay a broader foundation for British company insurance than an exact interpretation of the law might have justified. In his very valuable book published in 1948, Mr Raynes tables thirty-two companies that were giving fire insurance cover in 1806 – eighteen years before the ban on companies was lifted; and his table makes it clear that the City of London which had always been the centre of marine insurance was also from the first the chief home of fire and life. The City had got away with a good start. Companies and quasi-companies had been founded there before the founding of a company was a legitimate operation, and they had already secured for London the lion's share of the fire business. On the other hand the individual underwriter whose right to transact fire insurance was indisputable, had for the most part stood back and allowed this great new industry to pass into other hands.

The passing of the Act of 1824 was followed at once by a flood of new promotions, and such was the public appetite for new shares that in one month (January 1825) the nominal capital offered for subscription in the City was over one hundred and sixty million pounds. The money was wanted for many and various purposes, insurance, mines, railways, political loans, canals, waterworks and pawnbroking. But of all the ventures, insurance (if we judge by nominal capital) was the most important; for out of the total of a hundred and sixty millions no less than thirty-two millions was wanted for insurance companies. In one year, ninety-two insurance companies were registered, and in nine years no fewer than three hundred and eleven. And here we meet a rather odd phenomenon. As the old embargo on companies had applied much more tightly to marine than to fire insurance; as the would-be marine companies had been effectively and persistently strangled at birth while the non-marine had been allowed both to be born and (if they could) to survive, one might anticipate in the flotations of 1825 a considerable majority of marine ventures. When a dam breaks you expect the biggest flow to come at the point where the heaviest weight of water has been banked up. But that is not what happened. The companies that took advantage of the public's new enthusiasm for buying shares were the fire and life companies, which had always had a certain amount of liberty, not the marine which had been in chains for more than a century. There is, in fact, this curious contrast between the boom of 1718 and the boom of 1824. In 1718 the promoters were hawking insurance shares which were mostly marine. In 1824 they were hawking insurance shares again but this time their companies were almost all to be engaged in fire and life.

But if we are to recapture the atmosphere of 1824, we must discard our twentieth-century conception of an insurance company as something powerful, wealthy and elaborately organized. Most of these boom concerns in their early days were neither powerful, nor wealthy, nor organized. Some (better managed than the rest) survived and flourished. Others never expected to survive. Some were flagrant long-firm swindles. In the four years from 1837 to 1841 fifteen or sixteen companies collapsed and others were regarded as certain to go. The most notorious of the swindles was the West Middlesex and General Annuity Association, which offered very favourable annuities to 'tradesmen, servants, male and female clerks, shopmen, and others' and, before its inevitable collapse, extracted from the public in payment of its worthless annuities about two hundred and forty thousand pounds. Its board included a gentleman from Dover, described as a Journeyman Shopkeeper and Smuggler, another gentleman from Hythe who was a footman and owner of a little oil shop, a bankrupt physician, and a porter journeyman locksmith or bell-hanger, who was paid a director's salary of five shillings a week and seems to have signed most of the policies. He was ready, he said, to sign policies or anything else that might be put before him. Among the victims of these men were elderly people living on tiny incomes, and one naval captain sank five hundred and fifty pounds in buying an annuity for his invalid brother then living in an asylum.

It is a little surprising that these scandals and semi-scandals did not kill the public's faith in insurance companies stone dead. It would have been easy for people who knew nothing of finance and were incapable of distinguishing a good concern from a bad, to lump them all together and decide that all insurance companies were cooked in the same saucepan. But that did not happen. The sound concerns started in the eighteenth century, and the more recent companies like the Alliance, saved the reputation of the industry. Within a few years their success had persuaded many level-headed people that the future of insurance lay with the companies, not with individuals; that Lloyd's, in spite of its useful work in the past, had no prospects; and that the private underwriter might conveniently be relegated to a museum of historical curiosities.

In 1841 a select committee was appointed to inquire into company law and it dealt, incidentally, with the position of insurance companies, *vis-à-vis* Lloyd's. One of the witnesses was a solicitor named Duncan who was legal adviser to a marine insurance company and clearly a person of some standing in the City. He told the Committee that while it was 'impossible to say that marine insurance must be essentially carried on by a joint stock company' yet 'from the extent and character of the business and the enormous amount of the risks undertaken being to the extent in some cases of a million per annum, I should think it useful to commerce if gradually private underwriting were extinguished and marine insurance confined to responsible joint stock companies'. That sweeping statement, mistaken as it was, probably represented well enough informed opinion about Lloyd's sixteen years after the markets had been thrown open to free competition.

What had happened to Lloyd's that within so short a period it should have fallen from the high pinnacle of Angerstein and Marryat to this low level at which its death was almost taken for granted? Why should men be getting ready to speak of it as a glory of the past like the Venetian Republic:

> *Men are we and must grieve when even the shade*
> *Of that which once was great has passed away.*

Were there signs of internal decay in Lloyd's itself to account for the decline in its reputation and standing? To answer that question we should naturally, if it were possible, watch the premium income of Lloyd's over the period, and see what it had to tell us about the state of its subscribers. But if there is one thing about Lloyd's that the most patient researcher will never discover, it is its exact premium income in the nineteenth century. No one has ever known it and no one ever will know it. So we are forced on to another line of approach. We must look round for some other test that may be available to us. And the only yardstick ready to hand is the annual list of subscribers in which their numbers are recorded year by year from 1771 onwards.

Those figures will not necessarily move in arithmetical rhythm with the amount of business transacted; but when we find over a range of years a steady increase in numbers, then we may safely infer prosperity. And *per contra* when the subscribers are becoming fewer every year it is obvious that the place must be going down hill, offering to young men starting out in life an ever poorer hope of a successful career. Let us see how the figures run. In the seventy-two years from 1771 to 1843 we find both movements – a steady uninterrupted climb until 1814, and then a steady uninterrupted drop until 1843. In 1771 there were only 79 subscribers. In 1811 there were about 1,500; in 1814 there were 2,150; in 1843 there were only 953. Here are the figures at various dates in tabular form:

SUBSCRIBERS TO LLOYD'S

| Year | | Number |
|------|---|--------|
| 1771 | — | 79 |
| 1814 | — | 2,150 |
| 1822 | — | 1,595 |
| 1832 | — | 1,320 |
| 1842 | — | 1,008 |
| 1843 | — | 953 |

The figures between 1771 and 1814 are affected by the influx of subscribers when the old Lloyd's collapsed, by the tightening up of the rules at the new Lloyd's, and by the suppression of the gate-crashers, all of which naturally increased the numbers of subscribers. But when allowance has been made for these disturbing factors, the jump in membership from 79 to 2,150 is an astonishing performance, and it could not have been achieved without the very great access of prosperity and importance that came to Lloyd's during the Napoleonic wars.

But in 1814 Lloyd's stood at a water shed. The track that had been running almost precipitously uphill had reached its peak, and for the next thirty years it was to move downwards, not quite so quickly as it had risen, but quickly enough to disturb any intelligent observer who cared about the future of Lloyd's. It was no light thing for the place to lose sixty per cent of its subscribers in twenty-nine years.

As this decline in the prosperity of Lloyd's started about the time when the old monopoly was destroyed, it would be easy to attribute it entirely to the growth of competition; and no doubt the rivalry of the new companies did have a great deal to do with the falling off in business. The weight of money behind the Alliance (started in 1824), the valuable connections of its board, and the profits made by it uninterruptedly over a long period, are enough in themselves to account for a drain on underwriters' premium incomes. The Indemnity Mutual Marine Insurance Co., too (started about the same time as the Alliance and mutual more in name than in fact), had a large board composed almost entirely of Lloyd's subscribers, who were either hedging their bets or leaving what they took to be a sinking ship. There were actually twenty-one of those renegade Lloyd's men on the Board and once they had gone over to the Company it is practically certain that they showed in the Room only such business as the Indemnity did not want. Abroad, too, companies were on the increase, and aided by the crushing stamp duty charged on British policies, Hamburg was becoming a serious competitor to London. But in England itself, apart from the Alliance, the Indemnity and a few not very important concerns in the north of England, there was in the years immediately following the repeal not much fresh marine competition to be faced and overcome by Lloyd's, and we shall probably be correct if we trace the decline of its underwriting largely to other causes. For more than twenty years Lloyd's underwriters had been living on war rates, rates that were not always adequate but had over a long period afforded a very handsome margin of profit. With the return of peace these high rates disappeared, and on voyages which had hitherto carried a rate of five to eight per cent underwriters had to be content with one or one and a half. Fed by the fat war premiums the market for twenty years had grown in numbers at breakneck speed; and when the war premiums disappeared there was not enough business to fill all the mouths that were still gaping for food. Too many birds were chasing too few worms.

There was, too, another and a more general reason for Lloyd's setback. Marine underwriting, like many other trades, does not thrive easily in a time of falling prices; and even before the battle of Waterloo, Lloyd's business had for several years been affected by a sharp decline in the commodity price curve. The index number of wholesale prices had risen sharply and persistently until 1808 and then as sharply it had fallen. It was a rather critical time and two years later, in 1810, Angerstein, giving his evidence on the state of Lloyd's to the Select Committee, declared:

> I have never written so little as for the last two or three years. I think premiums are too low. If I had thought the premiums adequate I would have written them.

That was the opinion of the world's leading marine underwriter two years after commodity prices had begun to fall; and it cannot be fanciful, or over-theoretical, to connect those 'too low premiums' of Angerstein's with the precipitous decline in the graph of wholesale prices.

Immediately after Waterloo prices, it is true, went up again, but from 1818 onwards there was an almost continuous drop till the middle of the century, the index number falling by about 10 per cent in every ten years. To the men of that generation it was a new and unexplained phenomenon. But in the 1820's and 1830's Lloyd's underwriters, though they cannot have appreciated what was happening, were in fact grappling with the same problems that their successors of the next century, in common with most British industries, had to meet and deal with as best they might between 1923 and 1935. Deflation is always a painful process and the adjustment of an inflated market to deflated values is in all circumstances uncomfortable. At Lloyd's in the nineteenth century we can see its effects in those dwindling figures of subscribers, in the rather sordid squabbles between underwriters that went on continuously for nearly fifteen years, in the tragedy of broken-down subscribers lurking about on the staircase and begging for alms, and in the true story of two subscribers' sons who were given jobs as waiters to fetch and carry for their fathers' friends and acquaintances in the Room where their fathers had been waited on as subscribers and underwriters. It was not a jolly time at Lloyd's.

· · · · · ·

To return for a moment to the companies. In the torrent of new promotions that hit the City of London intermittently between 1824 and

1850, there is one curious fact that must be noted here, for it is closely relevant to the development of Lloyd's itself. Many of the young companies proposed to transact fire insurance only; many were confined to life; and a certain number to marine. But so far as can be ascertained today not one of them was to be concerned both with fire and with marine. That is surely a curious thing, for the two Bubble companies had had from their early days both fire and marine departments and had driven the two horses abreast safely and prosperously for more than a century. The Alliance company, too, had originally meant to include marine with its fire and life, and divided the business into two separate companies only because there had been a slip in the prospectus, and a troublesome Lloyd's man (who had probably become a shareholder with malice prepense) stopped the parent concern from having a marine department. In these three successful companies, the London, the Royal Exchange and the Alliance, there would (one might think) have been precedent enough for the younger concerns, as they broke into the insurance business, to go in for a composite account and develop, during that formative and important period up to 1860, a mixture of fire, marine, and other types of insurance. But the precedent, if it was ever recognized, was ignored; and every one seems to have taken for granted that for the future there must be a high wall topped with broken glass to isolate marine from every other type of insurance. It was an unspoken but generally accepted dogma and no one had the imagination to challenge it. What the reason for this strange caution was we can but guess. It may have been an obtuse conservatism in the marine underwriters. It may have been that the men in control of the non-marine companies looked on marine underwriting as a mystery and were chary of risking the profits, which they expected to make out of fire, in the dark waters of an unfamiliar sea. Or it may have been simply lack of enterprise.

But what was the attitude of Lloyd's underwriters to this business of fire insurance? To anyone who has known Lloyd's in the first half of the twentieth century, and watched its annual fire and accident premiums rise from almost nothing to some hundred million pounds, the answer to that must be of great interest. And, fortunately, although the evidence about what happened between 1771 and 1841 is scanty, it is reasonably conclusive. Let us start with the year 1782.

In that year an Act was passed imposing a heavy tax on fire insurance premiums and making the fire companies responsible for collecting it from their policy holders. To make sure that the collection was properly done it was decreed that anyone who kept an insurance office should first obtain a licence and supply the government with a bond, being liable to forfeit fifty pounds a day if he dared to do business without having first secured the licence. For reasons doubtless connected with their old charters, the London and the Royal Exchange were allowed to continue without a licence, but everyone else whether 'corporate or consisting of a great number of partners' must be licensed before giving fire cover. And all the companies, including the London and the Royal Exchange, had to act as collectors of the taxes. The proceeds of the tax, even at the original rate of 1/6 per cent, were surprisingly large and one company (The Sun) in a single year brought into the Exchequer nearly £100,000.

Lloyd's underwriters on the other hand, so far as can be ascertained today, neither took out licences nor gave a bond, nor collected the tax. Whatever fire insurance policies they issued were tax free, so they were very favourably placed in relation to the companies. They were in the position in which a British manufacturer would have been in 1951 if he had been privileged to sell his output without having paid purchase tax on it. But did they issue fire policies at all? Almost certainly they did. Why did they not collect the tax? We do not know. How did they dodge the law's demand for a licence? Again we do not know. They may have found some flaw in the Act that exempted them, or they may have snapped their fingers at the Government and ignored the law; but what seems to be certain is that in 1791 – nine years after the Act was passed – they were doing fire insurance business and covering sometimes very considerable values.

We know this because of a big fire which on the 3rd March, 1791, destroyed the recently-built Albion Flour Mill on the south bank of the Thames opposite Blackfriars, and gave to the fire insurance market one of the biggest claims in its early history. In Ackermann's *Microcosm of London*, which was half guide book, half history, there is a description of that fire:

> This fire (Ackermann wrote) raged with such unabating fury that in about half an hour the whole of the extensive edifice together with a quantity of flour and grain was reduced to ashes. It was low water at the time the fire was first discovered and before the engines were collected there assistance was ineffectual. In the lane adjoining the mills one house was burnt to the ground and others considerably damaged.

Ackermann goes on to give a list of insurance companies that were on the

Richard Thornton (1776–1865); from a painting by an unknown artist in the Hall of the Leathersellers' Company. Thornton was one of the best known underwriters of his day.

risk including the Hand-in-Hand for £6,000 and the Phoenix for £5,000 and ends up with this remarkable statement:

The largest insurance was at Lloyd's to the amount of £20,000.[1]

If that is correct we must believe that by 1790 Lloyd's underwriters had broken into the fire market and were ready to play a considerable part in its operations. The non-marine market was undoubtedly in existence before the end of the eighteenth century.

But not for long. At some time between 1790 and 1810 the Government must have intervened and stopped the business so completely that property owners, who had come to rely on the Lloyd's market for fire cover, lost their market and complained to the Government about their plight. They were mostly merchants in the West Indian trade, and as the companies seem then to have been cautious about writing risks abroad, the business men of Trinidad and Jamaica brought their larger values to be insured at Lloyd's. And when the Government put Lloyd's out of bounds for fire insurance, the merchants had to remain uninsured on a good deal of property that in prudence they would have liked to cover. The Government in sympathy with their complaints decided to alter the regulations and make it possible for private underwriters to accept these foreign risks without a licence. A convenient opportunity for the reform came in 1810 when the necessity for pulling in more revenue drove the Government to raise the fire insurance tax by 1/- per cent. In the Act imposing that higher duty the Board of Trade, killing two birds with one stone, set up new and separate machinery for the individual fire underwriter – machinery which it was hoped might allow Lloyd's to remain in the business. The preamble to the Act recited the history of the duty and went on to deal with private underwriters without mentioning the name of Lloyd's:

And whereas (the Act said) many persons having property in Trinidad and in other of His Majesty's islands and possessions in the West Indies and elsewhere beyond the seas cannot procure the same to be insured against loss by fire to the amount desired by the public corporations or companies by whom insurances against fire are most commonly made and they cannot procure insurance to be made upon such property because of the regulations which are inconvenient as applied to them ...

Having thus stated the circumstances, the Act relieved the individual underwriters from the duty of getting a licence. In place of the tax that the companies had to collect it imposed a stamp duty rather more

[1] Ackermann: *Microcosm of London*, Vol. 2, p. 36.

onerous than the companies' tax. These provisions need not concern us here. What does concern us is that towards the end of the eighteenth century there was a substantial fire market among the individual underwriters of the City, that the majority of these underwriters were Lloyd's subscribers, and that the market was strangled by taxation imposed by politicians who were intent on milking a trade which they had never attempted to understand.

If the Government, when it produced this Act of 1810, genuinely meant to revive and preserve fire underwriting at Lloyd's it must have been disappointed. From 1810 onwards we find no evidence of a fire market there. On the contrary we have positive evidence in 1841 that no such market existed. The non-marine market by that time had long been dead and was, to all appearances, far beyond the hope of a resurrection. The same Mr Duncan who gave his opinion about the future of Lloyd's to the Select Committee of 1841, was also asked by that Committee for his views about the possibility of fire and life insurance being carried on by individual underwriters, and his opinion on that point was definite and final. 'No private individual', he said, 'has attempted or could attempt with success the business of fire and life insurance companies. I never knew an instance of an individual or a small private partnership attempting to take the risks of fire insurance and I only know of two cases of attempting life insurance by private individuals.'

The reasons Duncan gave for his emphatic statement that Lloyd's could not handle fire business are both familiar and illogical. A private person, he argued, subject to all the risks of mortality, might safely cover cargo for a voyage, but as he might die at any moment he was entirely unsuited for accepting liability which would last for a full twelve months. The notion was on the face of it absurd and would never be entertained by any sensible person. In his forecast of the future this dogmatic solicitor was magnificently wrong, but in his description of the state of affairs in the 1830's he was probably right. If there had been a regular fire market or anything like a regular fire market at Lloyd's he would, as solicitor to the Marine Company, have been almost certain to know about it; and, while we dismiss this legal gentleman of 1841 as a prophet of the future, we can safely accept him as a witness to contemporary fact. When he said there was no market he was correct. Lloyd's had long ago turned its back on non-marine business.

What reasoning, apart from the taxation difficulty, lay behind the deliberate or unconscious decision of underwriters to renounce fire insurance we cannot tell. They may have felt that they were ill-organized for this kind of underwriting; that they had no surveyors to warn them when a building was likely to burn and – what was even more important – no fire brigade to put a fire out when once it had started. The companies had both surveyors and fire brigades and – in addition – another type of employee who was known as the Inspector of Salvage. He performed a most useful service and sometimes acted for a good many offices.

At Liverpool there was one of these Inspectors of Salvage who looked after the interests of eleven different companies. His duty was to mark the position of fire plugs and look after salvage; and he was particularly instructed to 'ascertain whether the property on fire, or in danger, or adjoining to the fire, be insured at any of the offices upon whose behalf you are employed, and in no way to interfere unless such shall appear to be the case'. If the Inspector had ever discovered that property 'on fire or in danger or adjoining' was insured at Lloyd's, he would (we may be sure) have followed his brief and in no way interfered to check the spread of the fire. There was to be no nonsense about helping to reduce other people's loss ratios. The underwriters, in fact, might have been left to bat all the time on a damaged wicket, and perhaps they were prudent in their resolve to keep out of the game. Perhaps, too, their abstention from fire was not absolute; for there is in one of the volumes of the Chartered Insurance Institute a suggestion that in the latter part of the nineteenth century, before the modern non-marine market had been formed, Lloyd's under-writers did on occasion cut in with considerable courage and with drastic results. They are said, for example, to have written or offered to write petroleum stocks – which were not as good a risk then as they are now – at half the rate set out in the Companies tariff, and although considerable opposition was offered in the councils of the Tariff Office to any competitive reduction of rates, 'it was finally agreed to considerably modify them'.

But such efforts as that were, at the most, flashes in the pan, and it is broadly true that underwriters kept steadily out of the business until the century was more than half over. In the great growing era of British fire insurance they stood aside and let the risks and the profits go to the companies. It is tempting – though perhaps sterile – to speculate on what would have happened if in 1824 they had taken another course. What shape would the British insurance industry have assumed if in those sixty years 1824 to 1884 Lloyd's had competed with energy enough to secure a substantial share of the new fire insurance at home and abroad? How would the growth of the tariff system have been affected if a large body of fire underwriters had stood aloof from the tariffs while they were still a novelty, and before the public had learnt to regard them as a normal element in the commercial life of the country? Or would it have been possible for Lloyd's underwriters to adhere to the tariffs and become themselves an integral part of the system? And would they have been able to push out side by side with the companies, taking a part in the work of building up Britain's foreign fire connection which grew so rapidly between 1850 and 1880? To all these hypothetical questions any man's answer is as good as his neighbour's, and we must be content to record the fact that the underwriters postponed their entry until very late in the day – until long after the form and structure of British non-marine insurance had (as it seemed) been settled for good and all.

. . . . . . .

Fifty years later, when Lloyd's underwriters took the plunge and began seriously to do fire and accident insurance, the effect on the whole Lloyd's market was undoubtedly stimulating; and company managers would probably agree that the companies too, as they converted themselves from single purpose concerns into composite offices, drew great and unexpected benefits from the change. An insurance undertaking is apt to do best when it advances on a broad front. And it is possible – though here again we are indulging in sterile speculation – that Lloyd's would have done itself a vast amount of good if the underwriters had been encouraged in 1824 to come out boldly in competition with the new fire offices. A piece of enterprise of that sort might have acted as a pick-me-up.

At that moment a good strong pick-me-up was what the place sadly needed, for Lloyd's was in a poor way. The decline in the number of sub-scribers was already serious. In ten years the total had shrunk by a quarter. In the next five years it fell by another 13 per cent. And, what was even worse, the decline in quantity was matched by decline in quality. Through-out the Napoleonic wars the leaders of the market – Angerstein, Marryat, Brook Watson, Vaux, and the rest – walked the stage as great figures, men capable of rising to the level of events even in the heroic period of English history that covered Trafalgar and Waterloo. But their immediate successors in the work of leadership seem to have been men of a different kidney, and the rank and file, probably because they had not enough to do in their own business, seem for the most part to flit across the stage as quarrelsome, spiteful and short-sighted creatures with few gifts even for handling their own affairs. They disliked the new companies in such full measure that their bitterness overflowed and soured their relations with each other inside their own four walls. It must have been a painful and unpleasant time. At the general meetings they fought and squabbled over trivialities. In the intervals between general meetings they barked at the heels of the Committee. When a motion was proposed at one of the meetings deploring the quality of the men who were elected to seats on the Committee the motion was carried. And in the majority that carried it there was a member of the Committee itself. What morale! A member of Lloyd's Committee openly supporting a resolution that deplored the character of his colleagues. Is it to be wondered at if well-informed people were saying that the death and burial of Lloyd's would be a healthy clearance of bad rubbish?

Another incident recorded in the minutes of the Committee helps us (trivial as it is) to realize what a queer place Lloyd's could be during this unsatisfactory period of its history. In 1828 the Committee learned that the second waiter, a man named Bye, had been absent from duty for a whole week-end and they found on enquiry that he had been arrested for debt and clapped into gaol. Somehow or other he got his release and, returning to work, he was called before the Committee for an explanation of his conduct. He told the Committee that he had been speculating in stocks, and that mixed up in the deal had been one of Lloyd's subscribers, a Mr Stuart. The flutter had been a failure and he had found himself owing Mr Stuart money which he could not repay. Mr Stuart had then put the law on him and got him arrested for debt, no doubt by the same process that Mrs Bardell a few years later used to send Mr Pickwick to prison for his breach-of-promise damages. Whether the Committee was shocked by this revelation we do not know; but they were gentle with the waiter and retained him in the service of Lloyd's. At the same time they passed a resolution that any waiter speculating in stocks should be instantly dismissed. But they took no recorded steps to punish or censure Mr Stuart for his share in the scandal. In its small way it was really a dreadful affair. Whatever may have been the relations between the two men, the fact that a subscriber, without even consulting the Committee or asking its advice, could procure the arrest and imprisonment of one of the Committee's waiters, was an unforgivable thing; and the disgrace must surely be reflected both on the Society in which such behaviour was possible, and on the Committee which passed it over without rebuke or criticism.

The matter that at this time most deeply engaged the interest of

subscribers and raised their passions to the highest point was payment of
members of the Committee. The bye-laws then in force arranged for
meetings of the full Committee for general business to be held not more
often than once a week and not less often than once a fortnight, and in
addition the Committee-men had to take their turn at looking after the
correspondence. For every attendance, whether at the full Committee or
at the daily supervision of the letters, a member was to receive one guinea;
and it was that guinea that stuck painfully in the throats of the subscribers. They denounced it. They agitated against it. They canvassed
against it. They wrote letters to the papers against it. They moved resolutions and made impassioned speeches against it. They carried motions
against it in open meeting and they submitted it to the ordeal of a ballot.
It was all rather like a long-drawn-out Eatanswill election and the final
result of the subscribers' ballot was a tie, so that the proposal to abolish the
fee failed by one vote to carry the day, and the principle of payment of
members survived by the skin of its teeth. But as one reads the minutes of
that period it is difficult to know which to admire more – the fury of the
attempt to get the bone out of the dog's mouth, or the determination of
the dog not to let it go. You may in fact search the annals of Lloyd's with
a small-tooth comb and find nothing that, for lack of dignity, will compare
with this episode of the Committee's fees in 1830.

.     .     .     .     .

In this bleak and depressing era there stands out one most valuable piece
of work for which the various Committees, whatever their failings may
have been, deserve the thanks of succeeding generations and a niche
perhaps in Lloyd's Pantheon. They developed and supported the system of
Lloyd's agents throughout the world.

Before the year 1811, individual underwriters often had their own agents
at overseas ports, using them for the survey of damaged goods and ships
in which they were personally interested. How general the custom was and
exactly how an underwriter, sitting at a box in a coffee-house, could
establish and maintain a connection with firms overseas is not known; but
the connections undoubtedly existed, and the local man would be given
power of attorney by the underwriter in London to act on his behalf. In
the case of the *Mills* frigate one of the points made in argument was that
Hayley, the leading underwriter, happened not to have an agent at the
port into which the vessel put for refuge; and in 1811 the special Committee recommended that this habit of underwriters privately giving
power of attorney to local men should be discontinued.

In place of it, they proposed that the Committee of Lloyd's should have power to appoint Agents who would act for the benefit, not of one particular underwriter, but of all Lloyd's underwriters in any ports or places the Committee should think proper. That suggestion was adopted, and in August 1811 the Committee energetically set about the task of appointing these Agents. By the end of the year they were in touch with about a hundred and fifty firms. By 1819 they had two hundred and seventeen Agents. By 1829 they had over three hundred and fifty. In 1951, Agents and Sub-Agents together amounted to one thousand, three hundred and seventy-nine.

The immediate success of the Agency Scheme and its rapid growth were both remarkable. It went well at home and, although half the world was still at war, it went well abroad. Within four months, Agents had been appointed at many English and Scottish ports, at ports in Spain, Madeira, South America, the West Indies, Morocco, Algiers, Newfoundland, and even in the United States which were at that moment hovering on the edge of war with Great Britain. By the end of the year the Committee was well on the way to achieving the object they had in mind, which was explained in the first letter they sent out to the prospective agents:

> The intention of subscribers in leaving these appointments to their Committee was to make them subservient to the important object of establishing such a universal and regular system both of intelligence and superintendence as would diminish the temptation to attempt frauds upon underwriters by increasing the obstacles to their success.

The art of writing that sort of letter perished (except in Government departments) many years ago. But if the Committee of 1811 was pompous in its literary style it was also sensible in its actions. It told the firms exactly what they would have to do – send prompt news of arrivals, sailings, casualties, and movements of enemy privateers, deal with salvage claims, check the plundering of stranded goods, and furnish such precise information as would ensure that only damage properly attaching to the policy was paid for by underwriters.

The Committee made no promises of big rewards to the Agents. On the contrary, they told the Agents that they would have to recover their fees and disbursements from the owners of the vessels or the goods, and the Committee would not be responsible for any charges 'on business that you may be introduced to in consequence of your appointment'. The only attractions that the Committee held out were indirect and rather remote

They were led (so they told the Agents) 'to believe that the appointments are considered as highly desirable and honourable' and they 'have reason to think that they will eventually be productive of emolument'. That does not sound a very alluring prospectus, but the Committee's judgment was right. The position was attractive, and for a hundred and forty years the post of Lloyd's Agent has in truth been considered, both by merchant firms and by shipping companies, as highly desirable and honourable.

Having established the Agency System in 1811, the Committee carefully, patiently, and for a long period nursed it through its teething troubles, and devoted (so far as can be judged from the minutes) about seventy-five per cent of its time to correspondence with the Agents, advising them, encouraging them, reprimanding them and occasionally, when they got themselves into scrapes, dismissing them. From Kinsale, in 1824, there came a letter written by a Lloyd's Agent from a temporary address in the local gaol. He had, he explained, offered assistance to an American vessel in distress, which turned out to have a cargo of tobacco and was laid under seizure pending an action by the Crown. In faithful discharge of his duties the Agent joined the master in a bond. The master absconded. The cargo was condemned. He, Lloyd's Agent in person, was arrested and thrown into prison. What did the Committee advise? The Committee sent him a charming letter of sympathy and advised him to resign. He replied that that was unnecessary as he expected shortly to be released and would then resume his duties. But the heartless Committee sacked him without waiting for his discharge. Wales, too, was a difficult area, and in the 1830's two Lloyd's Agents at Aberystwyth resigned one after the other because their lives were endangered by 'lawless crews' who resented attempts to preserve shipwrecked property. Falmouth, on the other hand, so close to the centre of the Cornish wrecking industry, seems rather unexpectedly to have had a less troublesome history. It was one of the very early ports to have a Lloyd's Agent and the appointment remained with the same firm from 1811 to 1947.

This network of Agents, by whomsoever it was first suggested, was the life work of John Bennett, Junior. He was an able man and an excellent organizer. He was appointed secretary to the Committee in 1804. He became a master in 1811 and he died in 1834. And if he did nothing else for the advantage of Lloyd's, his careful nursing of the Agencies fairly won for him the position of honour that his portrait now occupies in Lloyd's Building. His Agents from the first performed a double service. They looked after the underwriters' interests in the districts to which they were appointed, and they fed Lloyd's with an unbroken supply of news about ships' movements – a supply that was unique in 1811 and is still unique in 1956. The Agents, in fact, were the linchpin of the intelligence service, and for some forty years the collection of the news was performed by them alone.

Later on the Committee began another source of supply by founding signal stations to report the movements of ships *en route* from port to port. Some of these stations were maintained and controlled by Lloyd's itself, and the men who managed them were Lloyd's employees, not its Agents. The first of them was planted at Deal in 1852, and by 1883 their number had grown to thirteen. The system was expanded fairly rapidly and at the beginning of this century the Committee was managing and maintaining in this country fifteen first-class stations and twenty-one second class; the stations achieved a fame and prestige of their own, and so did the intelligence service that Lloyd's, with the help of its Agencies and its stations, administered and maintained. The immediate benefit to the underwriters is obvious, but the indirect benefit was perhaps more valuable still. To be recognized as the clearing house of the world's shipping intelligence made Lloyd's in the nineteenth century what it had been for other reasons in the eighteenth – a national institution. It gave to the society a halo, and separated it in the public estimation from all its insurance rivals. The marine insurance companies were just companies, useful no doubt and honourably managed; but for them there was no halo. They were not Lloyd's. They lacked Lloyd's standing and prestige and the aura of mystery that hung about it. They were just trading for profit, while Lloyd's was performing a national service. This distinction in the public mind, unreasonable as it may have been, was of incalculable benefit to Lloyd's; and it may well be argued that in the lean periods which the place had at times to pass through between 1815 and 1909 it was the intelligence service that saved it.

Two examples, one taken from the Committee's minutes, and the other from a bitter attack made on Lloyd's by one of its open enemies, will show how much the agencies meant to it. For many years the Coffee-House had had favourable arrangements with the Post Office for the handling of its inward correspondence, and it had become the habit of the Committee to send, once a year, to the secretary of the General Post Office a whole turtle, which he would accept and courteously acknowledge. In 1838 the arrangement with the Post Office was either extended or confirmed, and the Committee of Lloyd's sent a circular to all its Agents in the United

Kingdom telling them that they need not stamp their letters to Lloyd's
so long as they contained only shipping intelligence. They might send
them unstamped direct to the Postmaster General with the word 'Lloyd's'
in the corner of the envelope, and the Postmaster General would forward
them to Lloyd's. And why should the Postmaster General do this for
Lloyd's? The Committee's letter tells us. He did it 'with a view to the
public benefit'. For the sake of the Agencies and the shipping news they
sent to London, and for the advantage their news letters brought to the
British Nation, Lloyd's underwriters had been, and were still to be,
treated as a privileged body.

The second tribute to Lloyd's system of Agencies and signal stations
comes from a monograph published in the year 1872, fifty-one years after
the first Agent had been appointed. It was reprinted with additions from the
*Shipping Gazette*. It was called 'About Lloyd's' and it was written by a
Mr J. T. Danson who was closely connected with marine insurance. He
was a Liverpudlian, a pompous foolish Liverpudlian, but he makes a
useful witness today because he blurted out things that the more sensible
enemies of Lloyd's probably thought, but were not silly enough to
express. His approach to the underwriters was this:

> You are living on your past, you are effete, your premium income
> compared with the companies is almost trivial, but you still behave as
> though the monopoly of 1720 had never been abolished. You are
> sheltering under your prestige, you are hucksters, you are running after
> plunder, you are walking in shackles and mistaking your awkwardness
> for dignity. You must immediately throw Lloyd's membership open to
> the companies and hand over to the companies the right to elect one-
> third or more of the members of Lloyd's Committee. That reform is
> essential if Lloyd's is to be allowed to continue. If you refuse you will be
> crushed and your news service taken from you.

Altogether the pamphlet was an ultimatum, a haughty confident ultimatum, and the author must have been disappointed when Lloyd's
neither accepted his terms nor collapsed according to his prediction.
Historically the interest in his work lies here – that he and the companies
whom he championed wanted at all costs to get hold of Lloyd's Agencies
and Lloyd's intelligence service. All the bombast and the rhetoric in
Danson's twenty-eight pages boil down to a simple statement that Lloyd's
had this one enormously valuable asset, which gave it high prestige both
in England and abroad; that the companies envied it and wanted it, and

were even prepared (for a time at any rate) to share the ownership and control of it with Lloyd's. The news service which that generation of Lloyd's men had inherited from John Bennett was a Naboth's vineyard. It will be remembered that according to the First Book of Kings, Ahab spake unto Naboth saying 'Give me thy vineyard that I may have it for a garden of herbs'. And Naboth said to Ahab 'The Lord forbid it me that I should give the inheritance of my fathers unto thee'. Naboth's vineyard is always a desirable property.

To hark back now from Danson's monograph and the year 1872 to the 1830's, the state of Lloyd's at the beginning of the year 1838 was this. Its numbers were declining and its business was indifferent. It was under heavy pressure from the competition of companies, and was destined to endure still fiercer competition in the future. But it had outstripped all its competitors at home and abroad in its almost world-wide organization of shipping news. It was still a national institution and still the hub of the wheel for the world's marine insurance. Then on the 10th January, 1838, at eleven o'clock p.m., the Royal Exchange was gutted by fire and next morning Lloyd's was homeless.

# 6

## THE EVOLUTION OF MEMBERSHIP

*Effects of the fire – London Tavern – South Sea House – Committee of twenty-one – Reorganization of Lloyd's – Membership – Merchants' Room – Return to Royal Exchange – Non-underwriting members – Numbers of underwriters – Changing character of Lloyd's – The index – Foreign names at Lloyd's – Discipline – Summary of dates*

---

THE FIRE OF 10TH JANUARY, 1838, visible at Windsor in the west and at Theydon in the east, was probably the worst conflagration London had had for a hundred and seventy years. It was generally regarded as a national disaster and was spoken of openly as a terrible omen for the reign of the young Queen Victoria. 'It affords', said the *Morning Herald*, 'but a melancholy subject for reflection that the commencement of the new reign has been distinguished by a rebellion in Canada and the burning down of the Royal Exchange in London. Persons whose minds are at all tinctured with superstition will look upon these calamities of fire and blood as omens of evil augury.' It did, indeed, look as though Fate, when it planned the fire, had used every trick in its repertory to make the destruction of the building certain. There was a delay in gaining entrance after the alarm was sounded. The thermometer had fallen to a point very seldom touched in Southern England, and the engines when they reached the spot had to be thawed before they could be worked. There was a scarcity of water, and when the water came it froze so quickly that the firemen were covered with ice, and every thoroughfare in the vicinity became a skating rink.

The building, too, admirable doubtless from an aesthetic standpoint, was a deplorably bad fire risk and burned so quickly that a few hours after the discovery of the fire, when 'the Lord Mayor, some of the Aldermen and many of the most respectable citizens were able to enter the Court, it was only to look upon the progress of the ruin which they were unable to arrest.' 'The persons employed', said the *Morning Chronicle* and the *Shipping*

*Gazette* (both of whom within a very few hours of the event published a highly-coloured 3,000 word report in identical language from start to finish), 'worked to the utmost, many of them up to their knees in water and ice, and they were encouraged in their efforts by the Lord Mayor and the Aldermen present, but unfortunately no one thought of providing any refreshment for the poor fellows.'

The walls in the interior of the Royal Exchange (said the *Morning Herald*) fell with a tremendous crash, carrying with them the statues of the kings and queens who have reigned in England from the time of William the Conqueror. A place that was the resort of merchants of all nations, derived a magnificent and picturesque effect from the sceptred effigies in characteristic costumes of the long line of England's monarchs, arranged in niches and presiding, in its favourite haunt, over the interests of that commerce to which this small island has been indebted for its proud position in the civilized world. The commercial inconvenience, if not embarrassment, which this destruction with the loss of an immense quantity of important documents will cause, we need not dwell upon.

Enormous crowds gathered to watch the fire and were complimented in the Press on their admirable behaviour, which 'did nothing to embarrass those who were engaged in very arduous duties', while the firemen, according to the same report, 'by a judicious but not very legitimate use of the engine hose kept the populace at a prudent distance.'

If the Press and the Public were overwhelmed by the calamity, Lloyd's subscribers, who were most closely concerned, took it with remarkable calm. In the papers of Thursday, 11th January, which gave them news of the fire, they found an advertisement offering Lloyd's immediate accommodation at the Jerusalem Coffee-House. And there they assembled early in the morning to carry on their business. There was no gap in the routine and, although the space was inadequate, the work of Lloyd's went on with no material interruption. The Committee, by a friendly gesture, were invited to meet at the offices of the London Assurance and in the company's boardroom they sat continuously from nine till five. They saw that the Jerusalem Coffee-House was too small to take the whole of Lloyd's; but the London Tavern in Bishopsgate provided more ample house-room and to that Inn, after one or two days, the body of the subscribers moved. It was there that the Chairman of Lloyd's addressed his subscribers on the Saturday morning and gave them an account of what was being done to secure the future.

The situation, as the Chairman explained it, was this. The hurriedly arranged tenancy of the London Tavern, in which the subscribers were met, would come to an end within a day or two, and some place must be found in which Lloyd's might carry on its business until a new permanent home could be arranged. The Committee had tried all round the City and considered nearly a dozen possibilities – The Commercial Sale Room, the Corn Market, Cross Keys in Wood Street, the Jamaica Coffee-House, Paty's premises in Aldermanbury, the private house of the Secretary of the East India Company in Leadenhall Street, and the City Club House in Broad Street – a place still very familiar to many members of Lloyd's. Of these sites none was satisfactory, and the Committee had by this Saturday morning narrowed their choice to a short list of two places – Draper's Hall, and the South Sea House which stood at the corner of Bishopsgate and Threadneedle Street – the spot where the British Linen Bank now has its City office. Of these two the South Sea House was the more suitable and was finally chosen. The South Sea Company's offer was 'accepted by the Committee with thankfulness'. The rent was fixed at £600 a year. A seating plan was arranged. Tables and benches were hired. And on 17th January, exactly one week after the fiery exodus from the Royal Exchange, the subscribers met at 9.30 a.m. in a room that was to be their home for more than six years.

The Committee had acted with speed, courage and determination, and the subscribers responded to their leadership with a cheerfulness and resolution that promised well for the future. Perhaps after the first gloom of the newspapers they were relieved to find the facts very much better than the reports. The *Shipping Gazette*'s reference to the immense loss of valuable documents turned out to be nonsense, for the Chairman of Lloyd's declared that no document of importance had been burnt. Financial embarrassment had been foretold; but the Chairman assured the meeting that there would be no great pecuniary loss to subscribers. The premises had been covered with the Royal Exchange Assurance for £6,000 and the fixtures with the Imperial Company for £3,000, and so far as money was concerned there was no reason to feel gloomy or disheartened about the future.

The Chairman told the subscribers nothing about the Committee's Minute Books which were in the building at the time of the fire; but in fact they had been saved by some devoted hero. Today they sleep their long sleep in a strong-room at Lloyd's building, with the edges of their pages brown and brittle where the heat singed them in their escape.

Here and there the writing cannot be read, but for the most part the fire was kind to the books. Their value as a record is unimpaired, and even today there is a strange thrill in the study of these scorched pages, so narrowly saved, to tell us almost everything we know of the Society in its rise to greatness. Whoever it was that rescued them on that freezing January night should be gratefully remembered by anyone who can find enjoyment either in writing or in reading the history of Lloyd's. The trust deed of 1811, that Magna Charta of Lloyd's, was not so lucky as the Minute Books for it was burnt without trace. Happily, however, a copy of it survived; and on legal advice the Committee had a new deed prepared which every then subscriber was called upon to sign, and every future member had to sign on election – until thirty-three years later Lloyd's received a fresh constitution from its own Act of Parliament. The document of 1838 had attached to it a copy of the old deed of 1811, and by that simple device the subscribers continued to be bound after the fire by exactly the same ties that had controlled them before.

To advertise the fact that there was no lack of confidence at Lloyd's and no depression the Chairman, before the end of the month, arranged a great banquet at the London Tavern. The dinner included 350 Lloyd's subscribers and a number of distinguished guests. The proceedings were adequately reported in *The Times* of 1st February, and the toast list (which the paper reproduced) is proof in itself that the evening was satisfactorily spent. The revellers drank to the young Queen and to the Queen Dowager; they drank to the Army and Navy; to the Lord Mayor and Corporation; to the Duke of Wellington, and the elder brethren of Trinity House; to the Chairman and Directors of the East India Company; to the Chairman of Lloyd's; to the Governor and Directors of the Bank of England; to the Governor and Directors of the South Sea Company; to the Commissioners of Exchequer Bills and West India Claims; to four gentlemen members of the legislature; to Mr Crawford and the merchants of the City of London. And then, said *The Times*, several other toasts having been drunk the company separated.

There is something very admirable in the courage of the Chairman and the subscribers at this moment of apparent disaster, following fourteen years of declining fortune and divided counsels; and it is hard to believe that the Lloyd's which in 1838 cheerfully cocked a snook at its evil star was the same Lloyd's that had grumbled so bitterly about the payment of fees to the Committee in 1828. Morale must surely have been rising, and from the moment that the Chairman made his fighting speech three days after the fire everything was activity and enterprise. The name of the then Chairman was George Richard Robinson, at various times M.P. for the City of Worcester and for Poole, a man whose memory (it may be thought) has not been honoured at Lloyd's in proportion to his deserts. For every ten Lloyd's men who are familiar today with the names and achievements of Angerstein and Marryat it is doubtful if there is one capable of telling you who G. R. Robinson was and what he did. In fact he led Lloyd's at a critical moment along the right path, in the right direction, with cool and almost faultless judgment.

The first step taken was the election of twelve subscribers to join the nine members of the Committee of Lloyd's and form with them a special committee of twenty-one. This collection of twenty-one men was not concerned with the ordinary government of the Coffee-House and its affairs. That was left to the Committee of nine. The twenty-one were to meet separately and their duty would be 'to make such arrangements as they think proper for the temporary accommodation of the subscribers'.

There is a curious parallel here between what happened in 1771 and what happened in 1838. In 1771, it will be remembered, the men of the new Lloyd's authorized a specially elected committee to deal with the problem of finding a new home. But the Committee stayed in office after the new home had been found and slid, by imperceptible degrees, into the body that has governed Lloyd's ever since. The special committee of 1838 did not, it is true, perpetuate itself in this way or try to supersede the old committee, for it claimed only the right to make whatever arrangements the immediate circumstances of the time required; but it interpreted its mandate very broadly and in the period of exile it played a big part, not only in restoring the prosperity of Lloyd's, but in settling its future constitution. Essentially the history of 1771 after the great disruption repeated itself between 1838 and 1845 after the great fire.

In 1841 the special committee of twenty-one members opened negotiations with the Gresham Committee – negotiations which three years later led to the return of Lloyd's to a new building on the old site. Having got that project under way, the same Committee started out on a not less important task. It began to consider and to settle plans for reforming the whole system of underwriting at Lloyd's, for altering the bye-laws, and for bringing people of importance into closer touch with the Rooms. They saw that Lloyd's badly needed modernizing, that new methods were necessary to meet the competition of the companies, and that the destruction of its former premises was in truth not a disaster but a precious

John Bennett, Jnr., Secretary of Lloyd's, 1804-34, first holder of the office; from a painting believed to be by the portrait painter Andrew Morton, in the Deputy-Chairman's room at Lloyd's.

opportunity. If Lloyd's showed courage to lay hold on this occasion; if it went about its business with faith and confidence; if it obtained adequate space in the Royal Exchange; if the subscribers were ready to spend more money and pay a higher rent; if they were willing to attract more men of various occupations to the Rooms and encourage everyone in the City who was at any point interested in shipping to make Lloyd's his second home; then business would again flow freely to Lloyd's and the competition that had started after the Act of 1824 would be successfully met and overcome. Their purpose, in their own words, was 'to maintain the pre-eminence of Lloyd's and to enlarge the sphere of Lloyd's influence and utility by opening its doors more widely and bringing Lloyd's into more immediate connection with the mercantile community by allowing annual subscribers access to the whole of the establishment for all purposes except underwriting'. In that statement of policy you have the genesis of the underwriting member. And underwriting membership is the seed from which the strength of the modern Lloyd's policy has grown.

· · · · · ·

Until the year 1843 every subscriber to Lloyd's had the full run of the place. Everyone who used it must pay an entrance fee of £25 and an annual subscription of 4 guineas. Unless he disbursed this money a man had no rights in the Room. If he disbursed it he had the right to use the Rooms for any purpose, underwriting, broking, or just an occasional sight of the shipping intelligence. It was all or nothing and there was no half-way house. Under this system the number of subscribers had gone down almost every year for nearly thirty years, falling from the peak figure of two thousand, one hundred and fifty in the year 1814 to nine hundred and fifty-three in the year 1843; and at that time the decline showed no sign of coming to an end. Of these nine hundred and fifty-three subscribers, only one hundred and ninety or so were professional underwriters, and of the other seven hundred and sixty (while a large number were doubtless brokers) many used the Rooms only for the sake of the shipping news or for some other purpose not connected with insurance. But the cost to all was the same.

As the fortunes of Lloyd's declined, the business of the companies, stimulated and supported by their valuable connections, had been increasing rapidly. What premium income had been built up by the Alliance Marine is not known, for its figures are not available. But its twin brother the Indemnity Mutual Marine had in 1838 an income of £384,000, and

H

in 1839 of £408,000, the bulk of which must have been taken from Lloyd's old connections. If the underwriter of the Indemnity, William Ellis, had been an ordinary man some part of the lost premiums would no doubt have drifted back to Lloyd's by way of re-insurance. But Ellis, who was very far from being an ordinary man, never re-insured a risk, and whatever business Lloyd's lost to him was lost completely. The Indemnity's competition must have been very serious and if we add to its £400,000 premium income another £X for the Alliance Marine, we reach for the two companies a very substantial deduction from what Lloyd's (but for the abolition of the monopoly) would have received from the commercial public. It is unlikely that the aggregate of Lloyd's premiums for a long time after the end of the Napoleonic wars ever exceeded £2,000,000 in one year, and at its lowest point it must have been considerably less. So by the time of the Royal Exchange fire the loss of some half a million a year to the two new companies must have proved an unpleasant drain on the means of the dwindling band of underwriters at Lloyd's. The place was in a decline, and a reasonable prognosis might have been death from inanition induced by creeping paralysis.

The task of the special committee then was to revive the public interest in Lloyd's by making it worth while for business men to use the Rooms more freely; and the first step to be taken must be towards a fairer disposition of the cost – between those whose main livelihood lay in the Underwriting Room and those to whom the right of entry was useful but not vital. The flat charge of £25 entrance fee and 4 guineas annual subscription would have to be given up, and some more elaborate arrangement substituted for it. The solution that the special committee decided upon was to start what it called a Merchants' Room, separate from the Underwriting Room, and open to a new class of subscriber who would have no right to enter the main Room where the business of underwriting was conducted. Altogether it proposed that there should be four sorts of subscriber:

Members
Annual Subscribers
Merchants' Room Subscribers
Captains' Room Subscribers

Of these four types the Members were to be what are now called Underwriting Members. They would have the run of the whole premises, and could write risks, sign policies, act as brokers if they so desired, vote at meetings, stand for the Committee, and use the Merchants' Room and the Captains' Room at their own pleasure. They were the full enfranchised owners of Lloyd's. But the most important thing about them was that they alone might sign a Lloyd's policy. It is probable that nobody at the time realized the full significance of this change, but in fact it meant that the old system of free-for-all underwriting with which the Coffee-House started – a system that had been slowly modified and imperfectly restricted over a period of 150 years – was finished once and for all in 1843. The creation of membership drove the last few nails into its coffin.

The second class proposed by the special Committee was the annual subscriber, who would be allowed to use all the Rooms with the same freedom as the member, but could not attend general meetings, vote or stand for the Committee, or sign a policy. He could, however, do his insurance business in the Underwriting Room and trade with any member who cared to write his risks for him. He was, in fact, to be the broker, and ever since the day when the special Committee gave him his own niche in the bye-laws of 1843, the words 'Annual Subscriber' have been associated primarily with the broker who takes orders from the insuring public and places them with the underwriting member.

The third class proposed by the special Committee was the Subscriber to the Merchants' Room, and though he was not a permanent addition to the personnel of Lloyd's, he was, in some ways, the most interesting of the three suggested types of subscriber.

It is usually dangerous to describe in detail the mental processes of men who lived and died a hundred years ago, but the reasoning in the minds of the special Committee seems, even at this distance of time, so clear that an attempt at reporting them verbatim may be forgivable. In effect they said to themselves, these twenty-one Committee-men, something like this:

Our underwriting at Lloyd's has been drifting into a backwater because we are out of direct touch with the commercial world and the merchants who ought to be coming to us are going to the companies instead. The brokers who ought to be bringing in new business are either failing to get it or are being forced into the companies' Underwriting Rooms. One reason for this unhappy drift of business is that our charges have been too heavy and the entrance fee of £25 plus the subscription of 4 guineas is deterring the right people from coming to Lloyd's. We can remedy that by relieving brokers from the entrance fee, but that in itself is not enough. Lloyd's was intended, expressly intended, for merchants, bankers and traders, as well as for whole-time brokers and underwriters; and we need to bring these merchants, bankers and traders, back into our circle. How can we do it? Well, we have one powerful attraction – our shipping news. Let us use that to recall the erring flock back into the fold. We don't want to clutter up the underwriting room with a lot of outsiders, but if we can get from the Gresham Committee an extra room in the new Royal Exchange, let us, even at the cost of doubling our rent, take a lease of it and for a small annual subscription give merchants, bankers and traders the right to use it. Let them come here to find out for themselves what is happening to the ships in which they are interested. Let them get into the habit of using this new room as their business club. Let them meet our brokers here. Let them (though the horrible phrase was not then invented) become Lloyd's-minded by being given a place of their own on Lloyd's premises.

So the special Committee developed the idea of the Merchants' Room, and laid it before their fellow subscribers as part of their prescription for the recovery of Lloyd's.

The fourth proposal was a special subscription giving outsiders the right to use the Captains' Room. This room, which was originally a meeting place for sea-faring men and a spot for selling ships and goods by auction, had undoubtedly been very useful to Lloyd's in its early days. Now under the scheme of 1843 it was to become a kind of separate club. Members, annual subscribers, and Merchants' Room subscribers, were to have the enjoyment of it without paying any additional subscription; but outsiders, who had no right of entry either to the Underwriting or to the Merchants' Room, could for an annual subscription be made free of the Captains' Room; and the auctions still held in it could be attended by the general public without charge. The room was open from 9 in the morning till 9 at night, and if the food and drink were satisfactory it might be expected to attract a considerable number of customers.

The fees for the various types of members and subscribers that the special Committee proposed, and the General Meeting accepted, were as follows:

| | | |
|---|---|---|
| Members entitled to underwrite | £25 Entrance Fee | 4 guineas subscription |
| Annual subscribers – not entitled to underwrite | No Entrance Fee | 4 guineas subscription |

| Merchants' Room subscribers | No Entrance Fee | 2 guineas subscription |
| Captains' Room subscribers | No Entrance Fee | 1 guinea subscription |

All these matters – the division of Lloyd's men into new classifications, the scheme to bring more merchants and ship owners into daily touch with Lloyd's, and the new scale of subscriptions – were arranged during the period of exile. The special Committee had the great advantage of designing simultaneously the premises Lloyd's was to rent, and the grouping of the people who were to occupy them. The floor space was increased from 7,500 square feet to 11,000 square feet, and the rent went up from £600 to £1,200 a year. There is no record of any opposition to the new arrangement, and the spirit of goodwill and enthusiasm displayed after the fire seems to have survived the five years of banishment and comparative discomfort of South Sea House. On the 22nd November 1843 the bye-laws embodying the new classes of members and subscribers were passed in general meeting, and thirteen months later, on 26th December 1844, the new Rooms at the Royal Exchange were occupied for the first time. The years of exile were ended. Lloyd's was home again, returned unto Zion and dwelling in the midst of Jerusalem.

When in 1843 the general meeting created or recognized for the first time the title of Member of Lloyd's, it had to decide what status should be given to the existing subscribers – and the right course to take was obvious. In future the initial difference between members and subscribers was to be the payment of an entrance fee. The candidate who wanted the right to sign policies must pay £25 down for the privilege. The candidate who was satisfied to act as a broker was to pay no entrance fee at all. That was the new scheme. But hitherto every candidate (underwriter and broker alike) had been charged the £25 on election, and – apart from substitutes – everyone using the place in November 1843 had at some time paid his entrance fee. Obviously then he must from now on be regarded as a member and must retain the right to sign policies.

So the change-over was simple. All the men who were subscribers in 1843 changed their title overnight. They went to bed subscribers. They rose next morning Members. Many of them never had exercised, and never would exercise, the power to underwrite, and among these men one might have expected to find grumblers bemoaning the waste of the £25 they had paid on election; but in the Minutes there is no trace of complaint and everybody, for the moment, appears to have been satisfied with the new situation. The nearest thing to a grumble came eight years later, and strangely enough from a gentleman in Quebec. In 1851 he wrote to the Committee from Canada saying that in the year 1814 he had become a subscriber and paid an entrance fee. Some time after his election he left England for Canada. He was now resident in Quebec and would thank the Committee of Lloyd's to send him back the £25 that he had paid them thirty-seven years ago.

Judged by the Minutes of the Committee, which are presumably both accurate and complete, the immediate success of the new scheme lay in the Merchants' Room; and whoever it was that suggested the institution of a Merchants' Room undoubtedly did Lloyd's a valuable service. Although the Room had only a short life it was extraordinarily popular while it lived, and apart from the benefit that it brought to Lloyd's in the way of fresh insurance business, it was soon paying for itself in subscriptions. At meeting after meeting of the Committee new candidates for the Merchants' Room were proposed and elected, and by 1850 the number of these subscribers had risen to 541, producing at 2 guineas a head an income of over £1,100 a year which almost covered the rent of the whole premises. The candidates for the most part described themselves as merchants, but some were more specifically designated Wharfingers; and it is practically certain that all of them were drawn to Lloyd's by their business interest in the movement of ships. The attracting magnet was still the same – a reliable supply of shipping intelligence provided by Lloyd's agents from every port of the world. What the Merchants' Room did for Lloyd's was to widen the area of attraction, pulling more people of means and standing into personal contact with the room.

The life of the Merchants' Room, however, in spite of the good work that it did for Lloyd's, was only ten years, for the pressure of space in the new premises grew very quickly after the return to the Royal Exchange, and it became embarrassing to the brokers and underwriters to have nearly 550 people using precious floor room for their own purposes. The scheme had been too successful. The Committee discovered, too, that at least one subscriber was doing without an office of his own, and seeing all his customers either in the Merchants' Room or at the Coal Exchange. So in October 1853 it was decided that the Room should be abolished and that its subscribers, if they wanted to continue, must be elected in the ordinary way as full annual subscribers, paying the full 4 guineas a year. Many of them must have accepted the offer, for in four years annual subscribers rose in number from 835 to 1,056. The experiment of the Merchants' Room had produced good results which continued even after its abandonment.

The scheme for the Captains' Room, on the other hand, was a failure. The catering rights were leased out under contract and there were all sorts of minor troubles springing from the arrangement. One morning, about five months after the new scheme started, members coming to work found the Sheriff's Officer in possession of the bar and were told that the liquor had been impounded for a private debt of the lessee's. The man's contract was cancelled and the business was then leased to a Mr Mabey, who managed to make about £200 a year out of it on a turnover of over £3,000. He was a person of some energy, and in his first enthusiasm he persuaded the Committee to allow him to furnish, at his own expense, what he called a Soup Room. To make way for this room it would be necessary to remove the central water closet in the Upper Room; and against that removal twenty-four members lodged a protest. It was a delicate problem for the Committee to solve but, a compromise of some sort having been reached between the two schools of thought, the Soup Room was furnished and started business without completely superseding the closet. For some reason, however, there was a prejudice against the place. Nobody used it and in due course Mabey asked and was given permission to shut it up.

In the main Captains' Room, on the other hand, he was suffering from too large a custom because the gate-crashing habit, which was stamped out before the fire, had started again; and outsiders, with no right of entry, were treating the Captains' Room as an ordinary restaurant. Mabey did not like this. Nor did the members. But the waiters encouraged the outsiders for the sake of their generous tips and gave them preferential treatment over the members. One member, a Mr William Gray, appeared in person full of indignation before the Committee, protesting that he could get no attention at meal times because the waiters were all fawning on the gate-crashers. The Committee promised him that the complaint would not escape their attention, but the nuisance still continued.

In 1843, when the subscribers *en masse* were converted into members, all of them were granted or retained the privilege of underwriting, and all appeared in the annual records of Lloyd's as men of equal rights and standing. But in 1846 came another important change. From that year onwards the members were divided into classes – those who had the privilege of underwriting, and those who had not – a distinction that had never previously been made but has existed ever since. The new bye-law produced, in fact if not in name, the non-underwriting member.

This alteration in the structure of Lloyd's was not made on principle, but was due entirely to want of money. Almost for the first time in its history the Society of Lloyd's was financially embarrassed. Moving house is an expensive process, and Lloyd's, which had moved twice within a period of seven years, had not only suffered the ordinary removal charges but had deliberately and very prudently adopted a progressive policy, doubling its rent, spending freely on decoration and drawing on its not very adequate capital. The income, despite the Merchants' Room sub-scriptions, was only just adequate to the outgoings. Expenses had been and still were going up. The more responsible subscribers and members had grown a little anxious about the immediate future, and their concern had been shown in a remarkable and significant way. One hundred and twelve members wrote to the Committee in 1846 offering to contribute personally to the removal expenses a sum of ten guineas each and, furthermore, to increase their annual subscriptions from four guineas to ten guineas until such time as a reserve fund of £10,000 had been built up.

That was a splendid gesture and a sure proof of a rise in morale. And the generosity was not restricted to members of Lloyd's. The Register of Shipping, which had been helped twelve years before by a gift of £1,000 from Lloyd's, returned the present now that its old friend was worse off than itself – much as members of the British Commonwealth made free gifts to Great Britain in her post-war impoverishment. Still more remark-able perhaps was a gift of £100 made to Lloyd's in 1846 by the Indemnity Mutual Marine Co., as 'a contribution towards the expense of fitting up the present subscription room'. A few years later the Indemnity showed its goodwill a second time. When Lloyd's decided to raise the subscription that the London companies paid for the shipping intelligence from £200 to £400, the Committee advised the four companies accordingly. In reply the Alliance gave a conditional suspicious consent. The London asked for a sight of Lloyd's accounts. The Royal Exchange agreed with a proviso that it did not bind itself for the future. But the Indemnity treated the demand as though it were a welcome invitation to a feast, declaring that it had much pleasure in complying with the suggestion for the augmentation of the company's subscription. In view of the relationship in which the Insurance companies stood to Lloyd's those were generous acts, and it is a pleasure to record them after more than one hundred years.

But charity is not enough, and the finances of Lloyd's obviously could not rest on goodwill contributions, either from inside or from outside the rooms. So the Committee in 1846 set to work on a re-arrangement of the subscription. The subscription of members at that time was four guineas a year, and for that sum a man was entitled to use the Underwriting Room for any business purpose. He could do as much underwriting as he liked and as much broking, engaging in both occupations or in either of them; but whether he launched out on a large underwriting account or did none at all his subscription was the same. In fact the underwriters were a comparatively small body, and of those who paid the four guineas in 1845 only one-fifth were underwriters, while four-fifths were simply brokers. It was thought, and no doubt with justice, that the brokers could not be asked for a much increased subscription, and the Merchants' Room subscribers were considered then too valuable as business producers to be asked for a larger subscription. But the underwriters were in a different position, and it was only right that they should bear a more than proportionate part of the new financial burden. At a meeting, therefore, in April 1846, the Committee proposed that Members of Lloyd's should henceforth be divided formally into two classes – underwriting and non-underwriting; that both classes should in future pay on election an entrance fee of £25, but that the first class – the underwriting class – should instead of four guineas as an annual subscription pay ten guineas. Clearly the members who had voluntarily contributed to the Society's funds could not oppose the Committee's suggestion, but there were others who objected to it with some vigour, and at the general meeting they resisted the official motion by moving an amendment.

The proposal of the Committee was nevertheless carried, and from 1846 onwards there have always been these two classes of member – the underwriting and the non-underwriting. For some years the non-underwriting class continued to outnumber the underwriting by three or four to one, but by 1860 the two were about equal and from then on the non-underwriting class has tended to become smaller almost every year. In 1956 there were more than four thousand underwriting members and only sixteen non-underwriting. Nevertheless, rare bird as he is today, the non-underwriting member has played his part in Lloyd's history and holds an honoured place in its constitution. It will be a great pity if ever he becomes extinct and passes over to join the mastodon and the megalosaurus in their retirement from active life.

The important alteration of 1846 had one interesting result. It disclosed for the first time how many men connected with Lloyd's did in fact write risks either with their own hands or through the agency of some other person. Angerstein (it will be remembered) said in 1810 that as a broker he showed his risks to about 200 underwriters; and John Bennett at the same time, guessed that about 900 to 1,000 subscribers were underwriters. John Bennett may possibly have been right in his guess but, if he was, the decline in Lloyd's underwriting between 1810 and 1849 – the first year when accurate knowledge is to be had – was very considerable indeed. In 1849 the ten-guinea-a-year men – the men whose names appeared on Lloyd's policies – were, all told, only one hundred and eighty-nine. It was this small body that constituted the underwriting community of the world's greatest marine insurance market.

The classification of subscribers and members seems, at this distance of time, to have been clear enough but misunderstandings did occur and some of them gave the Committee a certain amount of trouble. In 1849, six years after the terms of membership had been fixed, a Mr Thomas Stephens was denounced to the Committee for underwriting without paying a subscription and a Mr Ross was charged with the same offence, both men admitting that they had broken the rules but pleading that they had not understood them. On the other hand about the same time Mr Ironmonger, a new candidate, asked a member to put his name forward as an annual subscriber, and either through the obscurity with which he explained his wishes or through an extraordinary thick-headedness in the sponsor himself, the Committee were told that the candidate wanted to become a member. There was no objection to him. He was balloted for as a member and was elected. He was presented with a bill for his £25 entrance fee and given the trust deed to sign. Not knowing any better he paid the bill and signed the deed, but discovered some time afterwards that he had got into the wrong compartment and paid the first-class fare for a seat in a third-class carriage. On his lodging a complaint with the Committee his entrance fee was repaid, his name was deleted from the trust deed, and he took his rightful place as an annual subscriber – probably the only case in history of a man being elected a Member of Lloyd's against his will and by a misunderstanding of his intention.

.    .    .    .    .    .

The income that the Committee of Lloyd's had to dispose of in 1848 was about £9,000 a year, of which nearly £5,600 came from subscriptions, £400 from entrance fees, and over £1,400 from supplying shipping news to the companies and the newspapers. It was a much larger income than they had enjoyed before the fire, and the increase probably coincided with a rise in the premium income and the general prosperity of the Room. The number of men gainfully occupied as members or subscribers – apart from the Merchants' Room – rose from 940 in the year 1844 to 1,667 in the year 1854; and between 1849 and 1854 underwriting members went up in number from 189 to 280, a fairly reliable indication that business was good and underwriting profits on the upgrade. But how did Lloyd's as an institution stand in the public esteem? Was it still, in spite of the competition of the companies, recognized as the centre of marine insurance, the natural home of shipping? The answer seems to be 'Yes.' It was still the place to which ordinary people turned first when they wanted to make contact with a shipping authority, and the Admiralty used the Committee as its insurance experts in much the same way that the Treasury used the Bank of England for its dealings with the money market. The time had gone by when a naval officer would ask Lloyd's to help him, by its influence, to obtain promotion in the service, but if there was trouble at sea both the Admiralty and the public thought of Lloyd's at once, and very often Lloyd's could be useful to them.

An Act of Parliament in 1845 obliged receivers of wrecks to send reports and sworn statements to Lloyd's, and the Committee noted that 'the recognition of this establishment as a channel of communication to the mercantile body generally compensates for any trouble that may arise in consequence'. In 1840 the Admiralty wrote to Lloyd's about a schooner lying in the Downs which had been boarded by a naval lieutenant on rumours of trouble. The crew, it turned out, were at loggerheads with the master and they all volunteered on the spot to join the Navy. Following an old eighteenth-century custom the naval lieutenant then and there enrolled one of the schooner's crew as a member of his own. The schooner's captain (who was drunk) went ashore with his men, discharged them when he landed and took himself off to a public house where 'he lay at the time of writing in a state of insensibility'. It was clearly a matter for Lloyd's to handle.

In the same way in 1847 the Superintendent of Lowestoft harbour wrote to Lloyd's to say that he had been threatened with death by Lowestoft boatmen when the harbour tugs went out to salve a vessel in distress. Would Lloyd's help him?

A local insurance company at Kincardine in 1840 had insured a local boat. The skipper who was half-owner had scuttled her. His mother, who owned the other half, had claimed for a total loss by barratry and she had won her case against the insurers in a Scotch court. Would Lloyd's contribute to share the expense of an appeal? Lloyd's appreciated the compliment but would not contribute.

The Foreign Office were trying to collect nine guineas which the British Consul at Havre had spent in affording relief to the Master of a British schooner. Would the Committee favour Lord Palmerston with information as to the best means of recovering the amount? Where the Foreign Office had failed Lloyd's succeeded and Lord Palmerston wrote a grateful letter to the Committee for the help it had given.

The Governor of Malta was anxious to find a market in England for cotton sails which the Maltese were very skilful in making. Would Lloyd's advise him on the prospects of selling them to London ship owners? Lloyd's satisfied the Governor that there was no future for the sails.

The Royal Society were much interested in a strange bottle picked up near the River Ob in Siberia. Could Lloyd's tell them what it was? Yes, Lloyd's could. It was a bottle used by Norwegian fishermen to keep their nets afloat.

The Committee of Lloyd's to which these enquiries came was extremely busy too on its own affairs, and very soon had to ask the members to increase the number of Committee-men from nine to twelve, so heavily did the business of Lloyd's weigh upon them. They were perhaps not as good as they might have been in arranging their working day, and it may be thought remarkable that when a vacancy for a junior messenger had to be filled, the Committee summoned three boys before them, cross-examined each of them separately and then solemnly voted by ballot on which was to be considered the most worthy of the appointment. They had obviously not learnt the art of delegating work. But that lesson was certain to be mastered in time and, whatever other failings the Committee may have had, they were not hide-bound and they could adapt their ways quickly enough to the shifting needs of the Society that elected them.

Indeed, the Minutes of the Committee during the twenty years that followed the re-opening of the Royal Exchange reflect year by year the changing character and the development of the Society. The Committee itself, first a gathering of underwriters interested only in underwriting problems, grows by degrees into an administrative body controlling a large premises and a difficult staff, but still watching closely the technical interests of underwriters. Then very slowly under a new compelling sense of common interest, the Committee takes on the additional task of disciplining the members and protecting the good name of the whole body. Almost as you read the Minutes you can watch the sense of a corporate responsibility taking shape in the Committee men's minds, and if one had to select from the whole course of Lloyd's history the period in which the atmosphere of the place altered most noticeably, the choice would probably lie between the first twenty years of the twentieth century and the twenty-two years from 1844 to 1866. In 1844 Lloyd's refused to be concerned with the credit or the solvency of individuals, and a member who was insolvent or bankrupt did not necessarily give up his membership. In 1866 expulsion automatically followed known insolvency, and new candidates were depositing £5,000 a piece as security before they began to underwrite.

The Committee continued, too, to watch most carefully over their Agents at home and abroad and the service of shipping news that Lloyd's supplied to the public and to its own members. In 1840 the Chairman of Lloyd's himself paid a five months' visit to America, calling on Lloyd's Agents everywhere, and travelling up and down the East Coast of the United States, Canada and New Brunswick. If he had no private purpose in making this journey, his trip is a strong proof of the value of the Agency System and of Lloyd's connection with the United States, even when Lloyd's business was restricted to marine insurance. It was the first trip ever made to America by a Chairman of Lloyd's during his term of office, and it was the only one until Sir Eustace Pulbrook, a century later, flew to America and back on vital business connected with Lloyd's in the Second World War.

It is indeed remarkable to see how the Agents could be kept up to the mark by supervision and discipline exercised from the Committee Room. The right to be called Lloyd's Agents must have given a firm remarkable advantages, for in most cases the direct reward in money was not considerable, and even as late as the middle of the nineteenth century the duties of the Agents were sometimes uncomfortable or dangerous. In the smaller English ports tradition died hard, and in many of them a good fat wreck was still regarded as an Act of God from which the Almighty meant the resident longshoremen – and the resident longshoremen only – to benefit. So when some intrusive busybody in the name of a remote impersonal society in London claimed to interfere with this arrangement, it was clearly a pious duty to make his life as unpleasant as possible and employ whatever force was necessary if he was so unreasonable as to show fight. A letter from an Irish port came to the Secretary at Lloyd's warning him that the local Lloyd's Agent had been interfering with wrecks and would probably be shot if he left his house after dark. And threats were sometimes followed by action. In Lowestoft – often a turbulent spot – when a pitched battle took place on the beach between the local boatmen and the crew of a tug about to go to a vessel in distress, Lloyd's Agent at Lowestoft was afraid to report it to Lloyd's; but the Committee hearing about it asked for an explanation and instead of giving the true reason the Agent tried to belittle the whole affair. The Committee were very round with him, and when he came to London willing to suffer any humiliation if he could avoid dismissal, he was solemnly dismissed and returned home in disgrace. As between Agents and Committee there was no doubt who held the whip-hand.

·    ·    ·    ·    ·    ·

The administration of the Society's domestic affairs was often a troublesome, if not a burdensome, business and the staff that managed it seems generally to have been too small for efficiency. The Committee indeed would probably have been wiser if they had done less of the routine work themselves and employed more clerks to help them. Captain Halsted, R.N., who was elected Secretary in 1848, grappled with his difficulties for four years and then told the Committee that he could not manage. At one time the staff, apart from the Secretary, the masters, and the waiters, had amounted only to two in all, and even after the fire the whole work of management was performed by nine men of whom one, at a salary of one hundred pounds a year, was responsible both for changes that were being made in *Lloyd's List*, and for keeping the whole shipping index.

That famous index, which was started a few months before the fire, is the most complete record in the world of ships' movements. It has been from its beginning a most valuable aid to underwriters and a great asset to Lloyd's. But its preparation has always involved much clerical work, and originally it was accepted by the Committee as a temporary expedient and with some reluctance. At that time Lloyd's could get men, capable of taking responsibility and knowing two foreign languages, for a salary of £150 a year – which seems low. In considering the men's salaries the Committee's attitude towards pensions must be borne in mind, and pensions were thought so important by the Committee as to be given a bye-law to themselves. In the Rules of 1843, Section No. 73 declared:

No annuity in future be granted on the death or retirement of any person on the establishment, each party having the means to make provision for himself and his family by the exercise of judicious care and frugality in his mode of living.

That bye-law was obviously a precaution taken by the members of the Committee to prevent themselves from being swept suddenly away by an unexpected flood of generosity. If there had been a pension waiting for him some employee on £150 a year might have thrown judicious care and frugality to the winds and burst out with his family into riotous living.

After the middle of the nineteenth century the management of the Society's affairs was becoming a good deal more complex. Old problems were still unsolved and new ones were constantly coming to birth. Among the old ones, the provision of space for underwriting and the campaign against excessive policy duties were the most persistent. Soon after the return to the Royal Exchange in 1844 Lloyd's had found itself uncomfortably cramped, and the Committee explored various schemes for relieving the pressure. They had a chance to build a house of their own on land then occupied by the Customs and Excise, and they might have had South Sea House; but they rejected both sites and made do at the Royal Exchange, living there always apparently on the verge of discomfort. In the matter of policy duties, a running-fight was carried on for years between the Committee and the Treasury. The duties which amounted at times to 50 per cent of the premium were indefensible, either in equity, or by economic reasoning, and it was as plain as a pikestaff that because of them Britain was losing valuable business to the Continent. But the Treasury was obstinate as only the Treasury can be obstinate, and it was not till 1844 that reasonable concessions were made to the Committee of Lloyd's and the rest of the insurance industry.

After the fire there is recorded one incident, trivial in itself but in the light of subsequent events too apposite to be overlooked. When, in the 1890's, Lloyd's underwriters broke into the fire insurance market, they showed so little respect for tradition as to offer to the public policies of various sorts that the established companies had long refused to grant. One such document was a valued policy on the contents of premises, i.e. a policy which agreed beforehand the separate value of the articles and freed the assured from the necessity of proving after a fire what they were in fact worth. To the companies sixty years ago that was sheer heresy, and the thought of it roused in company fire managers the same sort of horror that a whiff of Arianism produced in the mind of an early Christian Father. It was taboo. Indeed, much of the resentment felt and expressed against

Lloyd's at the beginning of the twentieth century sprang from the success it achieved with these valued policies. But in truth they were no innovation. In the year 1838 the Committee decided to insure its fixtures for £1,000 at 2/- per cent with the Imperial Fire Insurance Company, and asked for a valued policy. The Imperial, after deliberation, refused to issue it because 'making the policy a valued policy was contrary to its present rules'. The stubborn Lloyd's men insisted. The company still declined. So Lloyd's offered the risk to the Royal Exchange Assurance which agreed to give a valued policy if the rate were raised from 2/- to 2/6 per cent. The bargain was struck and a valued policy issued. The Company had been seduced into grave heresy by an extra 6d. on the rate.

    .    .    .    .    .    .

By this time Lloyd's had been in existence for a hundred and sixty-two years or so, and the process of its evolution from Coffee-House to the Corporation, as we know it now, had gone about half-way. It had shed most of the outward signs of a Coffee-House and acquired in an elementary form many of the features that now distinguish it. The development must have been encouraged by the improvement of business. Owing partly to the revival of trade which followed the repeal of the Corn Laws and partly to the Crimean War, this was a time of rising commodity prices; and just as Lloyd's had suffered from the collapse of prices in 1818, so it benefited from the upward movement in the early 1850's. A mild inflation combined with the writing of War Risks gave a fillip to underwriting; and the number of men entitled under the arrangement of 1846 to underwrite and sign policies rose in a decade from 189 to 306 – an increase of fifty-one per cent, which could not have been possible if the premium income of the Room had not been moving sharply upwards.

In the lengthening lists of members and subscribers published at this period, a curious feature is the number of foreign names contained in them. In 1852 two members of the Ralli family had applied for membership, but they had never been naturalized and the Committee were doubtful whether they were eligible. The Committee asked Lloyd's solicitor for an opinion on the rights and wrongs of electing a foreigner, and he advised them that there was nothing in law or in the constitution of Lloyd's to exclude a foreigner from election. So the two gentlemen became members. That precedent was followed for years, and many of the candidates – many, too, of the men who afterwards failed – in this period had

The Underwriting Room in the Third Royal Exchange c. 1875; from an illustration in *Picture Post* Library.

obviously come from the Mediterranean or from Germany. It has sometimes been said that of all commercial institutions Lloyd's is the most English. But if a compulsory roll call of its members and subscribers had been held in 1854 then Mr Brachi, Mr Bernouilli, Mr Englehart, Mr Focca, Mr Greverus, Mr Hava, Mr De Sa, two Mr Ionides, Mr Lozano, Mr Murieta, Mr Mussabini, Mr Peynado, Mr Schilizzi, Mr Schlemmer, Mr Segelke, Mr Sichel, Mr Schunk, Mr Spartali, Mr Steinmetz, Mr Thielcke, Mr Zulueta, and Mr Zygomalas, would all have joined in the responses. None of their names had been recorded in the printed list of underwriters at the beginning of the century, and all of them had disappeared before its end. But in the middle years they made up, with numerous other foreign names, a substantial proportion of the whole Lloyd's market. Lloyd's must have had some attraction for foreigners in 1850 that had not existed in 1800 and had evaporated by 1899.

Another notable thing in the membership of this period is the fact that several of the members had been underwriters elsewhere before they applied for the right to underwrite at Lloyd's. When S. I. da Costa, who was later on a leader in the market, applied for membership in 1858 he described his profession as underwriting. About the same time a Quaker, John Gurney Fry, and a Mr Hambro both described themselves in the same way when they were recommended for membership; and Edward Bagehot, who from his address must have been brother to Walter Bagehot, is described in the minutes as shipowner and underwriter. There was, too, a Charles Walton with an address at Holborn – a queer spot for a marine underwriter to have his office – who called himself simply 'underwriter'. It is certain that in 1850, and for long afterwards, Lloyd's had not achieved a complete monopoly of individual marine underwriting in London. Somewhere – probably at the Jerusalem Coffee-House or in the partners' rooms of banks and merchants – a few men were still following the procedure of the seventeenth century, dabbling in underwriting privately or even making it their main occupation. As the competition of Lloyd's and the companies increased these men would find that they got nothing but crumbs fallen from the high table, and rather than give the business up altogether they might decide to hire a seat at the table for themselves. It is quite possible, too, that some of them wanted the *entrée* to Lloyd's to place the reinsurances of their own underwriting, and if that was their motive then the appearance of these gentlemen would indicate the growth at Lloyd's of a market for reinsurance which, since then, has become an important part in underwriters' economy.

As the membership of the Society increased a certain amount of discipline had to be exercised on the subscribers; and cases of misbehaviour or dishonesty had to be appropriately dealt with. But in the original bye-laws no scrap of power had been given to the Committee to expel underwriters or to take action against them however gross might be their offence. Non-payment of the annual subscription was the only crime officially recognized in Lloyd's code, and the word defaulter signified not a man who had failed to pay his claims but a man whose subscription was overdue. For a long time Lloyd's got along without giving to the Committee any greater authority than that.

It is difficult to see how a place run on such a loose organization could have gone for fifty years without a scandal grave enough to justify expulsion. But in fact there is no record of anyone being expelled until the year 1828 – fifty-four years after the move to the Royal Exchange. Then it was discovered that a firm of brokers had collected a return of premium from underwriters by giving false information and without passing the money on to their clients. Taking a line that at that time was almost certainly *ultra vires* the Committee, with one dissentient, resolved that the names of Hoskin & Russell be erased from the list of subscribers, and that the men should never again be eligible for election. Fifteen years later, in 1843, the bye-laws were altered and from then onwards the Committee had power to decline a renewal of subscription from any person not being a member if they thought it desirable to do so. That gave them the right to expel annual subscribers, but Members (subject to the payment of their subscription) were still freeholders and however rank their offence they could never (if the law were strictly followed) be evicted. Even subscribers had to be guilty of something pretty startling before they were refused, but in 1853 two men named Bell were proved to have issued a false policy by forging the names of genuine underwriters; and not merely were their subscriptions refused but the door-keepers were instructed to deny them admission to the Room. The Committee had no right to exclude them summarily in this way but its usurped power was effective. Two years later a broker, accused by underwriters of a fraudulent concealment of material fact, was allowed to continue in business but warned that he had better behave himself and remember that the Committee could deal with him in a summary way.

On the whole the standard of behaviour at Lloyd's was high, but the vital question of the solvency of underwriting members and the credit of Lloyd's was a more pressing matter. From the year 1850 onwards it was engaging the attention of members, and for the last 100 years the preservation of a high standard has been recognized as the main preoccupation of the Committee.

To round off this somewhat discursive chapter it may be useful to summarise a few dates which mark steps in the development of Lloyd's at this period. Here they are:

1828 – First recorded expulsion of a subscriber.

1838 – The great fire.

1843 – Creation of membership.

1843 – Committee given power to exclude subscribers by refusal of subscription.

1844 – Return to Royal Exchange.

1846 – Separation of underwriting from non-underwriting members.

1851 – Resolution that insolvent members shall lose their membership.

It remains to deal with the problem of the credit of Lloyd's which must be handled in the next chapter.

# 7

## CHANGES AND INCORPORATION

*Modern Insurance Companies – First Legislation – Laissez-Faire – Reformers at Lloyd's – Helplessness of Committee to deal with insolvency – Bye-law of 1851 – Guarantees for members – The first deposit 1857 – Lloyd's a pioneer in security – Insolvencies – Misgivings of reformers – Increase of membership – Deposits oust Guarantees – Need for more discipline – Minor scandals – The 'Venezuelan' quarrel – Committee's blunders – A crashing judgment against Lloyd's – Act of 1871 – Its effects – Lloyd's policy – The anchor*

---

NOTHING IN THE HISTORY of Lloyd's is more remarkable to modern eyes than the slowness – one might almost say the reluctance – with which members came to recognize their common interest in the security of a Lloyd's policy. To us, indeed, as we watch the apparently tardy steps taken first to exclude insolvent underwriters and afterwards to prevent the weaker underwriters from slipping unnoticed into insolvency, the complacence of the Committee and the leaders of the market may seem not remarkable only but reprehensible. But the members of the Committee were children of the age in which they lived, and they can be judged fairly only by the standards of their day. For this reason, the story of what went on at Lloyd's should be preceded by a description of what was expected by the Public in the nineteenth century and ordained by Parliament in its treatment of the insurance companies.

The modern insurance office may be said to date from the year 1844, when Gladstone steered the first Company Act through the House of Commons and incidentally fixed the pattern of the new type of insurance office. Until that Act was passed it was common for the liability on companies' policies to fall legally, not on the companies themselves, but on two or three selected men – trustees or directors – who actually signed the policies, entered into the contract with the assured, and were personally suable if a claim were put forward and disputed. That was a curious arrangement, and while it lasted the activity of insurance companies must have been a good deal restricted by the unwillingness of private persons to act as potential whipping boys for their fellow shareholders. It is not surprising that the Act of 1844 (which made this legal device unnecessary) was followed by a rush of new insurance flotation.[1] In one year ninety-two new companies were registered, in another fifty-two, and in nine years three hundred and eleven. It must have been obvious that there was not enough business for them all and that many of them would be certain to fail. And fail they certainly did. By 1853 only ninety-six of them were still in business and the finance of many surviving companies was wasteful almost to the point of fraud. But Parliament did nothing. It believed in the principle of *caveat emptor*, and saw no reason to interfere between the weak insurer and the misguided assured.

In 1867, twenty-three years after the Company Act had been passed, the legislature did, it is true, take one short step towards enforcing security. It put through a complicated Act which stipulated that certain bonding companies must make a deposit with the Board of Trade before they guaranteed the fidelity of civil servants. Any other type of insurance contract – any other fidelity guarantee – might be entered into by a company without any kind of security. But the honesty of a civil servant could be guaranteed only by an office that had made a deposit. It was the first introduction of deposits into British insurance law, and it is most significant that the Government insisted on this security for its own protection, not for the general public's. It was anxious to safeguard the Treasury, which could well stand a loss, and content to leave the uninstructed citizen who might be ruined by the failure of his insuring company with no security at all. And that attitude of mind no doubt represented well enough the public opinion of the mid-Victorian era.

Three years later the Government was forced by the number of defaulting life offices slightly to change its attitude, and it brought in the Life Insurance Companies' Act of 1870. For the protection of Policy Holders the Act demanded a £20,000 deposit, the separation of life funds from those of other departments, and the return of accounts to the Government in a statutory form. From the point of view of protection there were several weak spots in the scheme, but the Act was revolutionary, in the sense that it recognized for the first time that the Government had a responsibility for looking after the interests of the insuring public. It was, however, unique. Throughout the nineteenth century this Life Assurance Act and one amending Act of 1872 were – apart from the queer legislation

[1] Raynes: *A History of British Insurance.*

of 1867 – the only statutes in the book bearing on the security of an insurance company.

It was not until 1909 that a British Government attempted any control over fire and accident insurance; not until 1946 that it laid hands on marine. In Britain (we must remember) the 1840's and 1850's were the high summer of those maligned people the *laissez-faire* economists; and it was in that school, so careful of the type, so careless of the single life, that most of our British insurance companies were reared. Today the *laissez-faire* economists are dead. Their school is closed, and none so poor to do it reverence. But there are two sides to its portrait. The failure of inefficient concerns undoubtedly caused suffering to individuals; but the efficient companies were given freedom, opportunity, and elbow room, and without those conditions the Victorian age would not have produced (as it did produce in Britain) the finest system of company insurance in the world.

The Victorian insurance companies in fact were rather like the large Victorian family. The duty of Victorian parents was to produce anything up to a dozen children, and if seventy per cent of them reached manhood that was considered a satisfactory result. It was bad luck no doubt for the children who died; but the survivors were of necessity tough and enterprising, and if when they grew up they found it too difficult to make their way in Britain they moved off to the Colonies. When food was short at home they went foraging overseas and there they built up the British Empire. Very much the same thing was happening with the insurance companies. The weaklings were going to the wall and the survivors were not only supplying this country with the insurance it needed, but were ranging far afield to feed the home office with premiums from the East, the United States, from Canada, and from Australia. If they had been tied all the time to Whitehall; if they had been born in accordance with standard instructions from the Board of Trade and watched, guided, and controlled throughout their lives by official superintendents acting under statutory rules, then those early failures might have been avoided, but it is most unlikely that our insurance industry would have become a world power. On the long view British insurance was fortunate in not being smothered by cotton wool in its boyhood.

While the *laissez-faire* attitude of mind prevailed throughout the country and coloured the Government's treatment of the insurance companies, it is not surprising that the Members of Lloyd's were affected by it when they considered their own constitution. They could argue, if ever they put their working philosophy into words, that sauce for the goose was sauce for the gander; that if companies started and failed without any steps being taken to prevent them from going under, surely it was reasonable that Lloyd's underwriters should be left to look after themselves without guidance, supervision, or interference. For a member of the public it was no worse to lose money through the insolvency of a member of Lloyd's than to lose it through the collapse of a company; and if the facts were known it would almost certainly appear that less money had been wasted by failures in the Lloyd's than in the company market. In any case, Lloyd's was not a trading entity but a collection of individuals making up a market, just as the companies were separate concerns making up their market. The merchant who made a bad choice among the companies when he arranged his insurance had his own poor judgment to blame for the result, and the merchant who had bad underwriters on his Lloyd's policy must do the same. If he had gone to a competent broker, who looked after his interests properly, there would have been no doubtful names on the document and he could have recovered his claims to the utmost farthing. That had been the attitude of the great Angerstein, who knew his business and dealt only with sound underwriters; and what was good enough for Angerstein in 1810 should be good enough for his successors in 1850.

We can see now that, Angerstein or no Angerstein, the reasoning was imperfect. The public receiving a single Lloyd's policy bearing a hundred names would regard them as one concern; and as the general standard of security among banks and insurance companies rose it would be useless to say to a disgruntled policy holder 'if you had picked your broker more cleverly all this trouble would have been spared you'. To take that line was to represent the policy as a kind of lucky dip, and that sort of cover would not for ever satisfy the merchants and shipowners who wanted not a gamble but security. But in the middle years of the nineteenth century public opinion had not advanced to the point of demanding complete security, and in the 1840's (despite the great advances made by Lloyd's in that period) the Angerstein point of view seems to have been practically universal. It is only at the turn of the half century that we begin to find signs of misgiving among the members and subscribers.

In 1850 we are still twenty years away from the first serious attempt of the British Government to enforce security among insurance companies, but already there is something stirring at Lloyd's. The more foresighted men there were beginning to think that the Committee's powers ought to be increased, first in the direction of getting rid of insolvent members, and afterwards in protecting the public against future insolvencies. On the first point – the exclusion of insolvent members – the reformers' case was overwhelming. An underwriting member at that time could fail to pay his liabilities, could make a composition with his creditors, could even pass through the bankruptcy court, and still use the room for broking and underwriting without any interference from the Committee. The Committee had no power to act, and its only course in dealing with a broken-down underwriter was to tell the doorkeepers not to let the man pass the barrier. That was a simple method. It was direct. To some extent it was effective. But it was not legal. And if any insolvent underwriter had had the physical strength to barge through the barricade or the moral determination to take action at law against the Committee, nothing apparently could have prevented him from continuing to subscribe any policy that was offered to him. Membership of Lloyd's was then a sacred freehold and it remained so until December 1851.

At a general meeting in that month an alteration was proposed in bye-law No. 12, a bye-law which in the course of sixty years was tinkered with and re-tinkered with, as the Committee claimed more and more power over the Underwriting Members. Until 1851 this bye-law had given the Committee the right to refuse the subscription of any person not being a member, but left all the members (so long as they paid their subscriptions) completely outside the Committee's control. The only crime that involved the banishment of a member was a failure to meet his annual subscription. Let him pay that and he was safe. But at the 1851 meeting it was decided that:

> If any member or annual subscriber become bankrupt or take the benefit of any Act of Parliament for the relief of insolvent debtors or compound with his creditors he shall cease to be a member or annual subscriber.

Four years later the bye-law was again altered, not in the sense of changing its intention, but to stop a few holes by a more complete definition of insolvency; and from that time onwards the doorkeepers were relieved of the prime responsibility for keeping the Room free of bankrupt underwriters. The Committee (whether or not with complete legality) had acquired, and was ready to exercise, a right of expulsion. Henceforward, no man who was admittedly insolvent could do business at Lloyd's. But by a curious latitude the bankrupt could, if he so desired, apply for re-election and the Committee, if it thought fit, could restore him to membership. The bye-law continued:

... such person shall be again admissible on a new recommendation of six members or Subscribers.

It seems strange that men who had once let the side down should so readily be allowed a second chance. But for all that, Lloyd's was feeling its way towards an efficient control over its members.

The bye-law of 1851, though it effectively prevented members known to be insolvent from trading, did nothing to ensure the solvency of those who were still allowed to trade; and in this matter the Committee was slower to take action. It may be remembered that in the days of Angerstein a suggestion had been made that 'the more trustworthy Underwriters should invest a certain sum in Government Securities' as an indication of strength and a protection for the Assured. But the scheme had never been adopted. Angerstein himself said that it would not answer and openly threw cold water on it. It was not mooted again for forty-five years, but in 1855 a member named Carruthers wrote to the Committee and suggested that provision should be made by the laws 'for taking security for a time from members who commenced underwriting in their own names'. What kind of security Carruthers had in mind is not known. He may have been asking only for guarantees, but it is quite likely that he was thinking of a deposit such as Angerstein had pooh-poohed in 1810. Whatever it was, the Committee seem to have been nervous about it, for they proposed no immediate change in the laws; and Carruthers having made his bow as one of Lloyd's reformers dropped out of the discussions.

But things were on the move. Though candidates were still being accepted without security of any kind, the Committee were beginning to call (in some cases) for guarantees, and insisting on the safeguard being provided before a man started underwriting. There had been such a case as early as 1852, and in five years four men at least with names that have ever since been familiar at Lloyd's were elected underwriting members on the strength of these guarantees. One of these elections was particularly interesting and deserves to be saved from oblivion.

On the 16th April 1856, a young man applied for underwriting membership and was supported by his father-in-law or brother-in-law who offered to stand security for his underwriting liabilities. His name was Henry John Philip Dumas and his relative was John Fairie, a sugar merchant of Church Lane, Whitechapel, who offered to guarantee him for £5,000. The Committee elected Dumas. He made a great success of his business and his son (who many years later was deputy chairman of Lloyd's) used to tell a curious story of the Committee's subsequent attitude to his father.

In the days of his growing prosperity Dumas was still underwriting on the strength of Fairie's guarantee, but thinking that he ought to come into line with other later elected members he voluntarily offered to the Committee a deposit in its place. The Committee refused the offer and Dumas continued, perforce, to write under the old guarantee.

That attitude of the Committee seems strange. Why should they refuse a deposit voluntarily offered? Why disdain anything which strengthened the security of the policy? Why force a guarantor to continue a guarantee that could have been replaced by a deposit with advantage to everyone of the three parties concerned? The answer is that the Committee would have liked to accept Dumas' offer but were advised by lawyers that a voluntary settlement made after election without consideration would not be valid in case of insolvency. Consequently, if they had exchanged the guarantee for a deposit after Dumas had become a member, they would be sacrificing security instead of improving it. So Dumas and many other underwriting members continued to trade on the strength of a friend's promise to pay, trading sometimes till the promise was fifty years old – a troublesome indigestible item in some deceased estate.

A year after Dumas' election we come to another landmark – the first deposit against insolvency ever made by a Lloyd's underwriter – and, extraordinary as it may seem, the making of this first deposit was not demanded by the Committee as a duty but conceded by it as a privilege. In March 1857, a Mr Sharp wanted to make his son an underwriting member and wrote to the Committee asking that the young man's name might be put forward. He himself (he wrote) would never let his son want for any monetary help that might be needed, but he had a strong personal repugnance against guarantees and he would be grateful if in place of a guarantee the Committee would consent to his son's election on the strength of a deposit of £5,000, which would at once be handed over to the young man's sponsor. Sharp wrote as one asking a favour and it was as men granting a favour that the Committee answered him. As Sharp had this prejudice against guarantees they would fall in with his wishes and accept £5,000 cash down. The young man was elected and the sum of £5,000 that his father had suggested became in time the standard figure for Lloyd's marine deposit. It was for many years the sum taken from every candidate and for nearly a century after young Sharp was elected it remained Lloyd's basic minimum deposit. In an earlier chapter we saw how the original Lloyd's entrance fee was fixed at £15 by the chance cost of moving from Pope's Head Alley to the Royal Exchange. Here we see how eighty years later the deposit was fixed at £5,000 by the chance offer of a wealthy indulgent parent anxious to advance his son's career.

There is another point in connection with this period in the history of Lloyd's that must be mentioned and remembered to its credit. In this matter of deposits Lloyd's was acting as a pioneer and setting an example that the British Government followed consistently when it became concerned to prevent loss by the failures of insurance companies. In the seventeenth century, it is true, there had been some talk of young companies setting sums aside for the protection of policy holders, but at no time in the eighteenth century, or the first sixty years of the nineteenth, did anybody except Lloyd's underwriters put money into the hands of trustees to stay there and to be available for debts in the event of insolvency. When the Board of Trade, first in 1867 and afterwards in 1870 and 1909, stipulated that certain insurance companies should make deposits it was treading in the footsteps of the Committee of Lloyd's. It is not, of course, suggested that the well-managed insurance offices, either then or now, offered to the public a less satisfactory security than Lloyd's underwriters; but the particular type of precaution that the Government adopted was copied from Lloyd's. To the deposit system unsupported by other precautions there are (as is now realised) serious drawbacks, and those drawbacks Lloyd's underwriters were the first to recognize; but for a number of years the deposit was the only known safeguard that could be imposed on an insurer from outside and that safeguard originated in the Underwriting and Committee Rooms of Lloyd's.

The Committee at this time had cause enough to worry about the standing of Lloyd's underwriters. The rules which enforced the expulsion of insolvent members and subscribers had uncovered a great deal of trouble and were followed at the Committee's weekly meetings by constant reports of failures and bankruptcies. On the 25th April 1855, just a fortnight after one of the bye-laws had been carried, twenty-five members and subscribers were struck off the list and for a few years after that the task of dealing with known insolvencies was a constantly recurring duty. It is true that not all the insolvencies touched the credit of a Lloyd's policy. Most of the defaulters were subscribers who had never underwritten a risk, and it is likely that a large number of the failed subscribers were not even wholetime brokers but merchants and bankers who had run into difficulties not connected with Lloyd's. Such failures as these did not react on the reputation of the Room and perhaps they mattered little to Lloyd's. But for all that, there were insolvencies enough among members to set the

Lloyd's of London

more serious-minded people thinking. Again and again the Committee directed that 'the usual letter should be written' to defaulters and the usual directions given to the doorkeepers. And as they gave the orders the members of the Committee must surely have felt in their hearts an uncomfortable qualm and misgiving – some stirring of that corporate sense which has transfigured Lloyd's since their day.

Occasionally as you read the minutes of the time you catch the first undertones of that new conscience. In April 1855, an underwriter named Gibson was declared a bankrupt and struck off the list of members. Two months later the Committee had a letter from a firm in Liverpool, complaining that it could not get a claim settled on a policy that had been effected by Gibson's brokerage firm and doubtless underwritten by Gibson himself as member. Would the Committee intervene and see that the claim was paid. The Committee replied, rather peremptorily, that Gibson was no longer a member of Lloyd's, that they had no power to interfere, and they refused to 'enter on the subject'. Perhaps that answer in the Committee's view should have ended the business for good and all, but the firm in Liverpool persisted and the Committee had to re-state its position. This time they sent a more explanatory letter:

It is not (they said) within the province of this Committee to enter upon the subject, they not being in connection with the proceedings of individual underwriters but simply a Committee for managing the affairs of the establishment of Lloyd's.

It looks as though the members of the Committee were not happy in their minds. Whatever the legal position was, they knew that in truth they were concerned with the proceedings of underwriters, and that the management of the establishment did involve some control over individuals. We know that they had already exacted guarantees before election. We know that they had bound Scottish members to appear in an English court when sued. We know that they had practically forced recusant underwriters to sign policies in accordance with the slip. We know that they had reprimanded and successfully threatened brokers whom they believed to be guilty of foul dealings. We know that they were prepared (if asked) to advise and issue instructions on the affairs of a defaulting member.

Perhaps we can detect in that second letter a suspicion in the minds of the Committee that their answer was inadequate, since they had already assumed the very responsibility that they were disclaiming. They felt that they could not go on as they were and, however much they disliked the thought of having to safeguard a Lloyd's policy, they would soon have to move much farther along the path of control. Like the prophet Jonah they had heard the word of the Lord directing them to set about a most unwelcome duty, and like Jonah they would have preferred to flee unto Tarshish. But like Jonah they found the pressure of surrounding circumstance too strong for them, and a few months after the Gibson correspondence they called for young Mr Dumas' guarantee. In the next year they accepted Mr Sharp's deposit and the field was set for the developments of the next one hundred years.

But although the Committee had started along the path of duty and ultimately persevered in it, there was a certain hesitation in their early steps. They did not demand either a guarantee or a deposit from every candidate but picked and chose, letting some through without any kind of safeguard, taking a guarantee from others and a deposit from the remainder. There were three kinds of treatment available and we do not know how or why they applied them to the different candidates. In December 1857, H. de Rougemont was elected to membership without any mention of deposit or guarantee, and in 1858 so was S. I. da Costa. But the Committee's action was having a good effect. In 1849 the underwriting members had numbered one hundred and eighty-nine. In 1855 they had risen to two hundred and eighty-two; in 1860 to three hundred and twenty-five; and in 1870 to four hundred and two. There was, therefore, an increase of a hundred and twelve per cent in a period of twenty-one years, and that fact is enough to show that although Lloyd's men were beginning to be disturbed by the run of failures in the Room, the credit of Lloyd's with the public had not been shaken. If the insuring public had been nervous of accepting a Lloyd's policy the premium income must have fallen. And if the income were falling the movement of underwriters would have been away from Lloyd's, not towards it.

It shows, too, that the Committee's new demands on candidates were not deterring members. We may assume that in the ten years from 1860 to 1870 the Committee found that it could, with advantage and without repelling desirable candidates, enforce either a guarantee or a deposit. We see that the deposit system gradually ousted the guarantees, that within ten years deposits became the general form, but that until the year 1882 neither deposits nor guarantees were universal. For some thirty years the Committee gave itself power to differentiate between the candidates and exercised the power according to some formula which was doubtless reasonable. But it died with the members of the Committee and is not now open to criticism or inspection.

It would be interesting to know with certainty how many of the candidates coming forward at this time got through on a guarantee, how many on a deposit, and how many without either. It looks as though the turning point came in the year 1860, and that after that date not many men were elected without provision of one kind or another being made for their possible insolvency. By 1866 the deposit system, though not universally applied, was well established. But the machinery was defective and in January 1866 the Committee consulted a solicitor about introducing a uniform trust deed. The solicitor produced a draft, and at a special meeting it was resolved that 'in such cases of admission of underwriters in which the Committee require a money deposit the deed of trust approved by Mr Walton be adopted'.

It was still possible to enter the circle of membership with a guarantee only, or with nothing at all. But the tide was flowing strongly both against these unsecured candidates and against the guarantees.

Deposits were what the members wanted from the newcomers, and four years later a number of Lloyd's men sent into the Committee a requisition asking that a deposit of not less than £5,000 in approved securities be exacted from all candidates. A general meeting was called and a new bye-law was carried by a show of hands making it compulsory for every candidate for underwriting membership to deposit at least £3,000. But it was never effective. A poll was demanded. The motion was defeated and the word deposit has never appeared in any bye-law. And a very good thing too. Deposits fixed by statute or bye-law are inelastic and unsatisfactory – as the Acts of Parliament dealing with companies' deposits proves. Lloyd's method has been to give the Committee full discretion to fix deposits; and that is certainly the best plan. Whatever may have been the motive of the men who kept deposits out of the bye-laws, they did a good thing for Lloyd's when they voted as they did in January 1871.

In 1870, too, the Committee had other things than deposits to bother them, for they were plunging head over heels into problems of discipline and a wholesale reform of the constitution. Into this boiling controversy we must now follow them.

     .     .     .     .     .

It is greatly to the credit of Lloyd's members that in a society so loosely organized serious scandals were extremely rare and that the Committee were seldom called on to exercise such powers of punishment as they possessed. And it was lucky that the occasions were rare, for the right to discipline either a member or a subscriber was vague and doubtful in the extreme. Whatever power the Committee had sprang from the old Trust Deed of 1811 by which members, but not subscribers, bound themselves to 'observe, perform, fulfil, and keep' all the rules and regulations ordained by a majority in general meeting. That so far as it went was good enough. But if a member failed in his obligations to observe, perform, fulfil, and keep, what happened then? What could the Committee do to penalize him? Could they fine him? No. Could they expel him? Not legally. What then, could they do? They could bluff him by pretending to powers that they did not possess, and they could cause him acute embarrassment by orders given to the doorkeepers. It would be a disrespectful thing to say of the Committee of Lloyd's that their power over members depended on the muscular strength of the chucker-out, but it would not be very far from the truth. And it is a tribute to the moral leadership of the Committee that their authority was able for so many years to keep the place free from major trouble without actually resorting to the technique of the pot house.

The misdeeds whose memory has been preserved for our instruction were of various kinds, some serious, some trivial, some farcical. There was the affair (already recorded) of the forged policy in 1853. There was the case of a member who was found guilty in a police court of cruelty to his wife, but satisfied the Committee that the report was inaccurate and retained his membership. There was a subscriber whose cheques were returned 'R/D' but were subsequently met. There was an extraordinary case of a cheque for premiums sent to an underwriter from a broker's office that was mysteriously cashed in the Captains' Room – an episode that one would like to know more about, but it is too scantily treated in the minutes for anyone to get to the bottom of it now. There were fairly frequent rows about underwriters refusing to sign policies in accordance with the slip which usually ended in the policy being signed under pressure from the Committee.

There was a very queer case in 1861 of an Aberdonian who – putting up for election as an underwriting member – was blackmailed by one of Lloyd's subscribers. Between him and the subscriber there had been in the past some squabble about premiums owing; and when the Aberdonian's name went up on the board as a candidate for membership the subscriber saw his opportunity to settle the dispute in his own favour. He wrote to the candidate in Aberdeen and told him that, unless the money for the disputed premiums came back by return of post, arrangements would be made to have him blackballed at the election. The Aberdonian sent the letter to the Committee and the subscriber was severely censured.

Another strange incident arose out of an election for the Committee. In 1852 there were two brothers at Lloyd's named Natusch, one an under-writer and the other a clerk on the staff of the Committee. The under-writer put up for election to the Committee and the clerk in an excess of brotherly affection carried on an active canvas on his behalf. There was no rule against canvassing by clerks but an edict was at once issued that such behaviour would in future mean a forced resignation from the staff.

Strangest of all, perhaps, were the quarrels about seats in the Room. For many years now underwriters have rented seats from the Committee and so obtained a legal right to them, but until the year 1871 there was no right to a seat except squatters' right and the fiercest conflicts arose between competing claimants. More than one squabble was referred to solicitors of high standing and one was sent to an eminent Chancery counsel. The opinion counsel gave was that the point was one of no little difficulty. But after carefully reviewing the authorities he advised the Committee that their right course was to have a member of their staff always at hand ready to fill the disputed seat in the morning before either of the claimants arrived; ready to give it up to the claimant favoured by the Committee as soon as he appeared; ready to slip into it again at lunch time; and ready to give it up again to the right claimant when he returned in the afternoon. Expensive though it was in manpower the solution was admirable – one of the devices by which the old Trust Deed was made to fit the changing Lloyd's.

For Lloyd's was changing fast, and in these diverse cases of wrongdoing which came to the Committee the changes are clearly reflected. Originally the Committee were concerned to stop gambling policies which had been in 1771 the avowed cause of the great disruption. Then for years their thunderbolts were kept for the gate-crashers who would not pay their subscriptions. But after 1850, when a stronger sense of responsibility for the behaviour of members had forced its way into the Committee Room, the serious charges that were brought there arose usually out of an alleged breach of commercial morality – complaints to which thirty years before the Committee would have turned a deaf ear. In an earlier chapter the story was told of a member who advised one of the waiters to speculate on the stock markets. Then, it will be remembered, the waiter took the punishment and the member was not even censured. In 1869 a rather similar incident occurred over the writing of three overdues, but now the attitude of the Committee was very different and their indignation against the erring subscriber was intense.

His name was Farrar and his offence arose out of orders he had received to reinsure lines on three overdue vessels. They must have been very bad risks, for instead of placing them in the regular market he persuaded a clerk named Morris (who was somebody's substitute) to write all three. None of the three ships arrived and Morris, who had no money, could not pay the claims. The Committee heard of the scandal and were furious. They sent for Farrar and accused him of breaking the bye-laws by doing business with a man who was not an underwriting member, a thing (they declared) that was expressly forbidden by Rule No. 20 in the bye-laws as they then stood. 'Nothing of the kind' said Farrar. 'These bye-laws are concerned with what goes on in the Room itself and cannot touch anything I do or leave undone once I get into the open air. I offered the risk to Morris outside Lloyd's. Morris wrote it to me outside Lloyd's. Both the broking and the underwriting therefore were beyond the jurisdiction of your bye-laws and you cannot touch me.' That was a facer for the Committee who referred the problem to their solicitor and got back from him a most discouraging reply. 'The only bye-law', said the solicitor, 'under which you could hope to punish Farrar is so loosely worded as to be unintelligible.' 'I cannot advise you', he said, 'to take action against Farrar on the strength of it and the best thing you can do is to leave Farrar alone for the time being and get all the bye-laws revised and made intelligible.' So Farrar for the moment escaped. Morris, under the old chucker-out technique, was at once refused access to the Room and the Committee began to think about getting the constitution of Lloyd's overhauled and repaired.

.　　.　　.　　.　　.　　.

The episode of Farrar and the overdues that were losses occurred in 1869, and it was followed a year later by the much more serious affair of Forwood and the overdue that arrived – an incident which clinched the determination of the Committee to have a thorough-going reform. Forwood lived in Liverpool. He was a shipowner of some wealth, and managing director of the West India and Pacific Steamship Company. He was also an underwriting member of Lloyd's. In March 1870, one of his ships, the *Venezuelan*, sailed from Barbados for this country and six days out had an accident that carried away her rudder and stern post and

K

filled an after compartment with water. In this plight she was sighted by a ship on passage to New York which took off the *Venezuelan*'s mail, her passengers, and her purser. Arrived in America, the purser sent a telegram to Forwood who passed it on to the Liverpool Underwriters' Association with an encouraging comment that he knew the after compartment to be small. The Association telegraphed the news to Lloyd's where it was put on the Casualty Board and Ross, who was Forwood's London representative, told the Secretary of Lloyd's that he personally had no misgiving about the ship's safety.

So far everything was well, but as several days passed without further news underwriters began to be fidgety, and the rate on the *Venezuelan* was pushed up to the neighbourhood of fifty per cent. Ross, still believing that the boat was safe, telegraphed to Forwood suggesting that he should write a line at fifty guineas if he could get it. Then the trouble started.

The morning after Ross had told Forwood of the high rate in London the *Liverpool Courier* reprinted an article from the *New York Herald*, in which the story was sensationally written up and given a banner headline, 'Mid-ocean horror'. In those days American methods of journalism were not as familiar to English readers as they afterwards became, and what with the headline and the write-up, underwriters' nerves at Lloyd's were unnecessarily jangled. The price on the *Venezuelan* was firm at fifty guineas and the market was growing more apprehensive.

Arriving at his office in Liverpool that morning, Forwood found a letter from his Captain, forwarded by the purser from New York, giving roughly the same information that had appeared in the article, but giving it in sober language that left a very different impression. There was nothing in the letter about a mid-ocean horror, but there was a calm statement that the bulkhead was tight and the screw uninjured, and that a safe arrival could be expected if the weather kept fine. Having read the letter, Forwood telegraphed instructions to Ross to write £1,000 and later in the day sent a copy of the Captain's letter to the Underwriters' Association in Liverpool. The Association's secretary did not think it sufficiently important to be telegraphed to Lloyd's and instead forwarded it by post. Underwriters at Lloyd's next morning read the Captain's prognosis some twenty hours after the owner had made £500 by backing his ship to arrive. There was a fierce outcry against him and the men who had paid the £500 demanded their money back.

It is necessary to tell this story in some detail because it leads up to a chain of the silliest blunders that any Committee of Lloyd's ever made, and the blunders led up to the first Parliamentary Charter that Lloyd's ever received. In the hot clamour over the Captain's letter a sub-committee was appointed at Lloyd's to examine the facts and advise. Without even interviewing Forwood they found him guilty and recommended that he should be excluded from the Room unless, and until, he repaid the premium. The main committee adopted the sub-committee's report and decided that Forwood should be forbidden to enter Lloyd's.

That was all very impressive but somebody pointed out that the bye-laws gave no authority to the Committee or to any other body to throw a solvent member out against his will. The Committee, faced with this objection, decided with an almost incredible lack of judgment to propound a new bye-law and treat it as retrospective. For that purpose they proposed at the next meeting a resolution to this effect:

> Any member or annual subscriber who shall fail or refuse to comply with a resolution or a requisition expressed in a resolution passed by a general meeting shall cease to be a member or subscriber at the expiration of one week after the passing of such resolution.

Any man of sense must, one would think, have felt qualms about the validity of such a totalitarian device, but with one not very important change the resolution was carried, balloted on, and confirmed by the necessary majority. Lloyd's had declared open war on one of its members.

The date of that spirited gesture was 5th October 1870, and two months afterwards the Committee, with its tail between its legs, came to another general meeting to confess that their brave talk could not be followed by action. Forwood had applied for an injunction against the Chairman and Committee to restrain them from using the powers that they thought they had been given. Nothing for the moment could be done. The Committee had led Lloyd's into a ridiculous and most humiliating position. They had made it impossible for Forwood to submit to their authority (such as it was) without pleading guilty to grave dishonesty, and they had made it impossible for themselves to comply with the resolution of a general meeting which required that all general meeting resolutions should be complied with. They had blundered badly and they still continued to blunder. Forwood had been pressing them for a copy of the sub-committee's report and the evidence on which it was based, and it was only reasonable that he should have it. But the Committee refused it to him and when he applied to the courts for a discovery order they resisted his application and ignominiously failed in their resistance. Then they passed a resolution that his subscription at the end of the year should be refused, and having refused it they had not the courage to deny him entrance.

When the application for an injunction finally came before the Lord Chancellor, Lloyd's counsel put up no defence, admitted that the Committee had been in the wrong, protested that they had no longer any intention of excluding the plaintiff, but argued – of all things – that the plaintiff should not have pursued the action and ought not to be allowed his costs. The Committee had accused him openly of dishonesty and passed a bye-law to drum him out of the Society in disgrace. Now to avoid paying £815 14s. 7d. in costs they made a complaint of his bringing the charges into the open. Instead of wearing a white sheet with as good a grace as might be, they posed in court as injured men with a grievance against the man whom they had slandered.

If ever a defendant asked for a crashing judgment against himself, it was the Committee of Lloyd's in this case of Forwood *v.* Goschen. And a crashing judgment was exactly what they got. As a question of fact the Lord Chancellor found that the Captain's letter was not a material fact that ought to have been shown to underwriters and that Forwood had not behaved dishonourably when he decided not to disclose it. As a question of law he found that the Committee had unjustifiably assumed rights over its members which, if exercisable at all, could be exercised only by a court of law. At every point the Committee had been in the wrong. At one stage in the controversy (so close to hysteria were emotions running) an underwriting member actually approached the Committee and offered to launch a criminal prosecution against Forwood – an offer that even that Committee refused. But when another member with a cooler head had implored them to take counsel's opinion before they committed Lloyd's to open battle, the Committee had declined that suggestion too. Amazing as it must appear, they had gone ahead on their own judgment, dragging their doubtless reluctant solicitor with them, without obtaining the opinion of counsel. The incident happily is unique in the history of Lloyd's.

Before the issue was decided in this battle of the *Venezuelan*, Lloyd's – or the more intelligent of its members – had come to realise the weakness of the constitution under which they were trading. It had taken them a very long time to appreciate the fact that once a man was elected a member and had paid his entrance fee he was beyond the Committee's control, and that even a subscriber, whose position was much less secure, could only be disciplined at the year's end by the refusal of his subscription which was tantamount to killing his business. For a member there was no punishment. For a subscriber there was nothing but the death penalty.

· · · · · ·

The Forwood case had not provided the ideal atmosphere for thinking out a new constitution, but the need for reform was urgent, and in 1870 – three years before the Lord Chancellor gave his judgment – the leaders of Lloyd's set about the task of drafting a bill which would give Lloyd's its charter and turn a society into a corporation. And the Act of 1871, though it has been trimmed and altered by subsequent Acts, is still after more than eighty years the second most important document in Lloyd's history. It made the Society what it never had been before – a legal entity. It defined its objects, arranged for a proper system of bye-laws, and fixed the election, the authority, and the duties of the Committee. It said nothing about the election of subscribers and members or about the punishment of peccant subscribers. But it had a great deal to say about the punishment of members and here the shadow of the Forwood case is cast unmistakably over the Act.

Every reader of the Act should remember that it was promoted by a body whose recent behaviour was still *sub judice*, a body which was being accused of high-handed illegal conduct towards an unpopular member, a body which was believed to be capable (if it could not get its way by legitimate means) of stretching the law to breaking point and far beyond it. In consequence whole sections of the Act are devoted to circumscribing the power both of the members of Lloyd's and of the Committee – making sure that they cannot deal harshly or unreasonably with one of their colleagues. Bankruptcy and conviction for fraud or any infamous crime are to be good grounds for loss of membership; but if a member is accused of discreditable conduct in his business he can only be expelled after (*a*) two arbitrators or the Recorder of the City of London or a Q.C. sitting as umpire, and (*b*) a four-fifth majority at a general meeting have assented to his disgrace. It is an extraordinarily elaborate procedure and it has never once been set in motion. But the purpose of a good criminal code is not so much to punish people as to remain in the background and deter them; and judged by that standard the punitive clauses of the 1871 Act must be written down a success.

Apart from crime and from discreditable conduct in his business there are five other offences for which a member may be expelled. They are set out in a schedule to the Act called the 'fundamental rules of the Society'.

The rules, fortified though they are with the word 'fundamental', have no greater force or sanctity than the rest of the Act and why the draftsman gave them a schedule to themselves and gave them their unusual title is not clear. But there they are and there they will remain unless, and until, there is a fundamental change in the Act itself.

The five offences are:

    1.   The acceptance by a non-underwriting member of a risk at Lloyd's.

    2.   Conducting underwriting business at Lloyd's outside the Underwriting Rooms.

    3.   Underwriting in the name of a partnership or otherwise than in the name of one individual for each separate line subscribed.

    4.   Underwriting for the benefit of a company or association in any place other than its ordinary place of business.

    5.   The opening by a member of an insurance account in the name of any person who is not a member or subscriber.

For any one of these five fundamental sins, expulsion is the ordained punishment, and at one time or another since 1871 four at least of them have been committed, and some of them committed over and over again, but nobody has ever been expelled.

Within a few months of the Bill becoming law an underwriter was charged by some informer with a breach of fundamental Rule 4 (1) which runs as follows:

> An underwriting member shall not underwrite in the City of London a policy of insurance otherwise than in the name of one individual (being an underwriting member of the Society).

The accused member admitted that he had written in the name of an individual who was not an underwriting member of the Society, but declared in spite of all the emphasis and the publicity of the fundamental rule – that he was not aware of the law in question. So difficult is it to make men grasp an inconvenient truth and get them to surrender their old habits.

More remarkable still was the action of the members of the Committee itself when they were confronted with one very inconvenient result of the fundamental rules and were a good deal embarrassed by it. Indeed they were so much embarrassed that they took legal opinion on the best way of evading the rules which they themselves had just made. They had always known that certain very respectable merchant firms engaged in counting house underwriting outside Lloyd's, some of whom had partners who were themselves underwriting members of Lloyd's and were subject to the fundamental rules contained in the Act. It had never been the intention of the Committee to stop this counting-house underwriting but someone pointed out to them that it was forbidden by Rule No. 4 and there was no doubt that the charge was correct. These highly respected members were in breach of a fundamental rule. What were the Committee to do? They could not after stressing the rules so vigorously turn a blind eye to them. They must support them. On the other hand the last thing they wanted was to make a nuisance of themselves to firms of merchants who brought valuable business to Lloyd's market. In their own words 'they felt considerable difficulty about taking extreme measures' and they would obviously catch at any straw likely to get them out of their trouble. Happily an escape route was found. The counting-house underwriting was reconciled with the fundamental rule by a legal fiction and, for all that is known to the contrary, it may still be in operation today.

If an intelligent member of Lloyd's had been asked in 1871 what in his opinion was the most valuable service that the Act did for Lloyd's, he would probably have answered 'the power that it gives to the Committee over the members of the Society'. No one would want to depreciate the importance of that power today; but looking back over the years that have passed since the legislation of 1871 an intelligent member in 1956 might take a different view. He might reasonably say that the Act's supreme value lay not in the control that it made possible over the members of Lloyd's, but in the very effective control it established over people outside Lloyd's. It was not the fundamental rules that had been so beneficial but Section 31 – the section which made it a crime for an outsider to sign a Lloyd's policy. It is worth while to stop for a moment and dwell on the significance of that change.

Let us imagine, then, some far-seeing Lloyd's member in 1869 pondering on the reforms that he would insist on in the new Bill. How would his thoughts have run? First, he would have seen that within the last few years Lloyd's had become a new place. From a haphazard collection of individuals, in which the ties between one man and the next were no stronger than they would be in a second-rate social club, it was evolving into an institution with a credit of its own that could be injured by the weakness of any one of its members, and sustained only by the maintenance of a high standard at every underwriting box in the Room. He would have seen that the deposits were only the first link in a long chain of reforms that would have to be made within the next fifty years. The goal to be reached was the perfect security of a Lloyd's policy.

But what was a Lloyd's policy? Surely a policy which could contain no names but those of elected Lloyd's members, a policy which no outsider could sign. And at that time no such policy existed. There was nothing whatever to prevent an outsider from signing the same policy as Lloyd's members. He could sign in such a way that a policy-holder could not tell the difference between the man who had been elected to Lloyd's and the man who owed no allegiance to Lloyd's, had made no deposits and was completely outside the control of the Committee. There were still people in London writing marine risks for themselves or for their firms, and before 1871 there was nothing to prevent a merchant from placing fifty per cent of a risk through a Lloyd's broker with Lloyd's underwriters, and the other fifty with outsiders who would be indistinguishable from the Lloyd's names. All would appear together on one policy.

While this state of affairs continued, while the same policy could be part Lloyd's and part not Lloyd's, the old grievance against Lloyd's still had weight and there was still no answer to the complaint of the eigh- teenth-century merchant:

> When my policy is completed I find persons names to it I have no acquaintance with or knowledge of. It is impossible I can be thought to have what satisfaction is necessary.

So long as an outsider might add his signature to the same policy that Lloyd's underwriters had signed there could be no satisfactory reply to that criticism, and the pains that the Committee were taking to safeguard the credit of the Society must be ineffective. After a policy left Lloyd's with nothing on it but Lloyd's names it might have added to it a dozen others, all names of straw. The public would not know the difference and the failure of an outsider might do as much harm to Lloyd's as the failure of an authorized Lloyd's underwriter. In those circumstances the credit of a Lloyd's policy could not reach the standard of Caesar's wife, and it was to that standard that the Committee aspired.

It should be superfluous to labour so obvious a point as that; but every generation takes for granted the amenities of life that it has inherited from its predecessors and is apt to overlook the debt it owes to the men who first thought of them. Most Lloyd's men of this generation take for granted the existence of a Lloyd's policy. They do not realise that for a hundred and eighty years in the life of Lloyd's there was in the true sense of the word no such thing, and that but for the prudence of the men who framed the Act of 1871 there might not be one today. Without a document, confined by law to the signatures of underwriting members, the value of all the safeguards introduced in the last hundred years – deposits, audits, guarantees, central funds, would have been greatly impaired, and the credit of Lloyd's, by virtue of which Lloyd's men make their living today, would have the strength only of a half-baked brick.

The men who drafted the Act of 1871 understood the importance of making Lloyd's policy sacrosanct and they were determined to restrict the privilege of signing it to elected members of their Society. They saw, too, that for this purpose civil actions were all but useless. If the cuckoo was to be kept away from the nest it must be outlawed. It must be made a criminal offence for anyone not an underwriting member to sign his name to a Lloyd's policy, and so Section 31 of the Act laid it down that:

> If any person . . . imitates or copies any stamp mark or other thing for the time being used by the Society to distinguish forms of policies of marine insurance underwritten by members of the Society or offers or utters or uses any form of policy bearing any such stamp mark or other thing as aforesaid he shall for every such offence be liable on summary conviction before two justices to a penalty not exceeding £20.

To protect the policy under this Section it was obviously necessary to give it 'a stamp mark or other thing' and the seal chosen was the picture of an anchor. It is imprinted now on every Lloyd's policy, marine and non-marine, and it carries with it a warning that trespassers will be prosecuted:

> Any person not an underwriting member of Lloyd's subscribing this policy or any person uttering the same if so subscribed will be liable to be proceeded against under Lloyd's Act.

That is the story of Lloyd's anchor – a symbol or trade mark that is not yet a hundred years old.

The Act has been widened and amplified by later legislation but it is still Lloyd's Charter and its purpose should be understood by every student of Lloyd's history. Its main features may conveniently be set out in summary form.

1. Lloyd's was made by the Act into a legal entity.
2. The Act contemplated no kind of insurance except marine.

3. The Act confirmed the distinction between underwriting and non-underwriting members.

4. It forbad an underwriting member of Lloyd's to write a policy in the City of London in the name of a partnership or for the benefit of a company or association not subscribing to Lloyd's, but it allowed him to do as he liked outside the city.

5. It forbad a non-underwriting member to write a policy at Lloyd's but permitted him to write one anywhere else.

6. It legalised the bye-laws but forbad any attempt to exclude members by passing a new bye-law.

7. It settled the offences for which a member could be excluded from the Corporation and fixed the machinery for expelling him.

8. It specifically recognized as one of the three objects of Lloyd's the collection, publication and diffusion of shipping intelligence.

9. It made it a crime for any unauthorized person to use or utter any policy bearing a distinguishing mark of Lloyd's or to imitate or copy any such mark.

That, in brief, is the constitution of Lloyd's as it was fixed in 1871 and in 1956 it is but little changed. For eighty years it has worked well enough, and, with the help of three or four amending Acts, has adapted itself comfortably to a dozen minor revolutions in the conduct of business at Lloyd's. But two omissions in it may be noted. The original Act is rich in references to Lloyd's underwriters but neither in it, nor in any of its successors, is there a single mention of Lloyd's brokers. And nowhere in any of the Acts is there a direct reference to the position, rights, or duties of annual subscribers. Historically the subscriber has a much longer pedigree than the member. For more than seventy years before members were thought of he ran Lloyd's. For another thirty years he still outnumbered the underwriting members and it was not until 1888 (exactly two hundred years after the opening of the Coffee-House) that he was overtaken by them. There are still over three hundred of him – almost all active. But he has no vote and no legal rights beyond the end of the year for which his subscription has been paid. He can be excluded without fuss or bother in any December by a refusal of his subscription, and his security of tenure is no stronger than that. Yet generation after generation, with his living dependent on one thread, the annual subscriber carries on and contributes a great deal more than a mite to the general prosperity of the Society.

# 8

## A GREAT SECRETARY

*Outside Chairmen – Disadvantages of the system – Members-in-attendance – Powers of the Secretary – Bennett, Halsted and Stephenson – Salvage Association's proposals to Lloyd's – Lloyd's saved from great mistake – Extraordinary suggestion refused – Hozier – Ruled Lloyd's – His innovations – Signal Stations – His work – Clash with Boulton – Wireless – Marconi and Lloyd's – Law suit – Arrangements with Marconi and Post Office*

---

GEORGE ROBINSON, the Chairman who had seen Lloyd's through its troubles in 1839, died eleven years afterwards, and the Committee, for a reason which at the time may have been sound, came to a remarkable decision. Robinson, though M.P. for Poole (and previously for Worcester), had been – like all his predecessors in the Chair – a Lloyd's man. Underwriter and shipowner, his fortunes had been linked with those of his fellow underwriters. His mind was schooled in the day-to-day management of marine business and for years he had filled the Chair at Lloyd's with courage and success. But in 1850, despite Robinson's good record, the Committee in choosing his successor sought a man of different quality, someone of high social connections who need not take part in the day-to-day running of the Society, but could make a figure in the world, stand up for Lloyd's in a crisis and face the greatest Parliamentary personages on equal terms.

Their choice fell on Thomas Baring – grandson of the founder of Baring Brothers – who certainly had the qualifications that the Committee wanted. He was a member of Parliament – he had very nearly been elected for the City of London and was actually member for Huntingdon. He was nephew to one Chancellor of the Exchequer and brother to another, and he himself was twice offered and twice refused the post of Chancellor in a Tory government. He had been a member of Lloyd's, though not an active member, for twenty years, and when he was asked to become Chairman he agreed. He held the post continuously for eighteen

145

years and his second refusal of the Treasury came while he was in office at Lloyd's. He has, in fact, the distinction of being the only man in history to reject the Chancellor's robes for the unadorned dignity of Lloyd's Chairmanship. Perhaps his biographer had that fact in mind when he wrote 'If Thomas Baring had been ambitious he might have played a greater part in history'.

In 1868 Baring retired from the Chair and the Committee following the same principle as in 1850 looked round for a promising politician to take his place. This time they chose George Joachim Goschen who was not a member of Lloyd's – a Liberal who had been elected to Parliament unopposed and was to be one of the great figures in English political life for the next forty years. In the same year that he became Chairman, he entered Gladstone's first Cabinet as President of the Poor Law Board. In that office he partially reformed local government in this country and three years later he became First Lord of the Admiralty. He visited Egypt to set the Egyptian finances in order; was British Ambassador to Turkey; refused the Viceroyalty of India and the Speakership of the House of Commons; fought vigorously against the radical policy of Chamberlain and passionately against the Irish policy of Gladstone; became Salisbury's Chancellor of the Exchequer; and re-emerged from retirement in 1903 to campaign against the Tariff proposals of Chamberlain. For eighteen years this active party politician was Chairman of Lloyd's. He doubled the part with the Presidency of the Poor Law Board, with the First Lordship of the Admiralty, the Ambassadorship at Constantinople, the economic control of Egypt and the active participation, on one side or the other, in every party scrap that made up the civil history of this country from 1868 to 1886. In the intervals between his various occupations he performed his duties as Chairman; but they lay on his shoulders so lightly that the Dictionary of National Biography, while it records the fact that he was head boy at Rugby, says not a word of his being Chairman of Lloyd's.

The truth seems to be (at any rate after Goschen's election) that the system which apparently satisfied the members of Lloyd's for another thirty-three years was not very satisfactory. At the best it gave Lloyd's a non-playing captain, at the worst an absentee figurehead; and the fact that it survived so long is one of the minor puzzles in the history of Lloyd's. It was modified in 1880 and abolished in 1901, but it lasted altogether for half a century and produced four chairmen, two from the Baring and two from the Goschen family:

Thomas Baring                       1851–1868
George Joachim Goschen              1869–1886
Lord Revelstoke                     1887–1892
Charles Hermann Goschen            1893–1901

If we accept the principle of a non-playing captain, these four chairmen were no doubt as distinguished and appropriate as any that could have been chosen. But in 1893 somebody – either a member of the Committee or a private member flying a kite for the Committee – did a most extraordinary thing. He approached Lord Rothschild and asked him whether he would accept the position. Now Lord Rothschild, desirable as he was for every one of his personal qualities, was a member of the family which started the Alliance Marine Insurance Company for the express purpose of taking business away from Lloyd's. Outside his banking the Alliance was his main commercial interest. He was its chairman and actively engaged in advancing its prosperity. The parent Alliance Company was one of the leading British fire offices; and at the very moment when Lord Rothschild was approached by Lloyd's, Lloyd's underwriters were busy challenging the *de facto* monopoly of the companies in fire insurance, just as a former Rothschild seventy years earlier had challenged the *de jure* monopoly of individual underwriters in marine. It is difficult to think of any situation more embarrassing than to be simultaneously chairman of Lloyd's and chairman of the Alliance, and it passes the wit of man to discover the Committee's reason for thinking the arrangement possible.

Lord Rothschild, with the good sense that one would have expected from him, declined the informal invitation and the second Goschen became head of the Society. He retired in 1901 and the fashion of electing distinguished outsiders to the chairmanship of Lloyd's came to an end. And it was very lucky for Lloyd's that it did. At that moment in 1901 the Society was entering on the most critical phase of its history and the new system of electing chairmen from amongst the active members meant that one of Lloyd's own sons was to lead it through danger to security – a feat that might have been beyond the power of any outsider, however able and however distinguished.

With the Chairman sitting on Olympus and giving only an occasional glance to his subjects at the Royal Exchange, how was the place managed and how had the thousand and one matters that must have cropped up day by day been decided?

They were decided by the Member-in-Attendance. And who was this Member-in-Attendance? He was one of the Committee appointed to stand-by for a month at a time, and for that short period he acted as the absentee Chairman's Vice-Regent. Personal complaints, squabbles, and offences were referred to him, and he would give an immediate decision or postpone the difficulty to the next meeting of the Committee. He had general supervision over the correspondence and presumably any caller at Lloyd's who was not satisfied with an interview with the Secretary would be seen by him. In his period of office he was (nominally at any rate) the most important person in the Room; and every member of the Committee took his turn to fill the position, spatchcocking his official duties into the intervals of his underwriting, or it may be spatchcocking his underwriting into the intervals of his official duties.

It is obvious that under such a system as that, a system which shifted responsibility at monthly intervals from one member of the Committee to another, the real power would lie with the only man who was on duty the whole time – and that man was the Secretary to the Committee. One has only to picture an inexperienced or half-experienced Member-in-Attendance presented by the Secretary with some knotty point for determination, to see him humming and hawing, groping around for a precedent, silently cursing his own indecision and finally asking the Secretary what he thought of the business himself and accepting the Secretary's advice. As the fixed point in a floating scene the Secretary, if he were a man of ability and ambition, would have no difficulty in getting most of the strings into his own hands. If he lacked ability and ambition the danger was that the strings would hang loose, with nobody to take a grasp of them. Everything depended on the character of the Secretary and (on the whole) Lloyd's was fortunate in its appointments.

The first Secretary, John Bennett Junior (1804–34), was one of the greatest figures in Lloyd's history and his work in developing the news service and appointing agents was perhaps the most valuable contribution that any man ever made to Lloyd's. Captain Halsted, R.N., too (1848–68), was a good administrator, ready to stand up to his Committee, and to him must go the credit for insisting on a proper staff to manage the Society's affairs and for shaking the Members out of a pettyfogging policy of economy enforced at the sacrifice of efficient management. Stephenson, his successor (1868–74), had before his appointment to Lloyd's been a clerk at the Treasury and seems in his new position to have been a square peg in a round hole. His heart perhaps was not in his work. Or perhaps he was a weak man unable to force a consistent policy on the Members in attendance, or to guide the Committee as the Committee needed to be guided by the permanent officials. In the last chapter some space was devoted to the case of the *Venezuelan*. While the responsibility for all the bungling and mismanagement of that dispute must ultimately fall on Goschen, who was too busy to bother about it, and on the Committee men who ought to have known better how to handle Forwood, it is impossible not to connect the fiasco with the deficiencies of Stephenson and his failure to understand what was required of him. He left Lloyd's to take up another position in 1874, and is said to have written a light opera which provided Hayden Coffin (the romantic tenor) with a life's career assuring a lady friend that she was 'Queen of his heart tonight'. That is perhaps Lloyd's only point of contact with the professional stage.

· · · · · · ·

During Stephenson's Secretaryship there occurred an episode that might have ended disastrously for Lloyd's, but luckily came to nothing and left the future of the Society almost unaffected. It will be remembered that in 1872 J. T. Danson published an attack on Lloyd's and demanded of the Committee that they should hand over to another body the ownership and control of the agencies and the shipping intelligence. When he wrote his masterpiece Danson was not drawing a bow at a venture. The project he advocated was being actively discussed at the time, and his spluttering rhetoric was intended either to push the Committee in the direction he wanted them to take or to express his indignation at their refusal to do what he wanted.

The details of the incident are not all clear, but the broad facts are these: It was suggested that there should be an amalgamation between Lloyd's and the Salvage Association and that the control, both of Lloyd's Agencies all over the world and of the shipping intelligence, should be taken away from the Committee and handed over to a new body in which Lloyd's would have only a partial interest.

With whom the plan originated is not known, but in the early stages of the discussion the Committee not only agreed to the scheme in principle but were eager to see it brought to completion. The reason may have been that they were nervous about future competition from the Salvage Association. The Association had been formed in 1856. Its capital had been supplied by Lloyd's itself, by individual underwriters, by the five leading marine insurance companies and, to a trifling extent, by ship owners. It was a composite business in which the various marine interests were to co-operate. Charles Wright, who was at one time Chairman of the Salvage

Association, described it as a body concerned 'only in promoting the profit and welfare of all the interests committed to their charge'. On the Committee of the Association Lloyd's, though represented, had only a minority interest. Out of thirty-three members it supplied eleven, while the companies had thirteen and the other interests nine or ten. It was anything but a predominantly Lloyd's institution.

The Salvage Association was a success, and in December 1871 the Committee of Lloyd's delegated three of their members to discuss with it the possibility of fusion. Meetings took place, and a plan was conceived for forming a new organization which would take from Lloyd's the management of Lloyd's agencies and the whole of the intelligence. That would have been a drastic revolutionary change and the negotiations for its completion went a considerable distance until, early in 1872, Counsel's opinion was taken on the best way of forming the new organization. All this was happening, it must be remembered, within a few months of the passing of Lloyd's Act of 1871 and it is probably a very fortunate thing for Lloyd's that the Act had been passed before the plan was broached; for the Act killed the plan. When learned Counsel was asked how the transfer of functions should be arranged his answer was definite. It cannot (he told the Committee) be arranged without another Act of Parliament. You have (he said in effect) been given by Parliament the right and the duty to protect the interests of members of the Society in respect of shipping cargoes and freight, and also to collect, publish, and diffuse intelligence and information with regard to shipping. Both right and duty were conferred on Lloyd's, and Lloyd's cannot without fresh permission hand it over to any other body. It has a statutory responsibility and what was given by Statute, only Statute can take away. There can be no question of passing it over to a new institution either by resolution of the Committee or by vote of the members. So the plan for a separate organization was dead.

But negotiations still continued. If it was impossible to form a new body it might surely be in order to extend the Agency Committee of Lloyd's, and include in it representatives of the Salvage Association and the marine companies. Delegates of Lloyd's and the Salvage Association discussed the possibilities for nearly a year, and in November it was informally reported to Lloyd's Committee that the Salvage Association had a scheme ready for discussion.

The proposal that the Association had prepared was extraordinary and startling – nothing less than this: A new Committee was to be formed and

Colonel Sir Henry Hozier, Secretary of Lloyd's, 1874–1906.

styled 'The General Committee of Lloyd's' which among other functions would have complete control of Lloyd's Agents everywhere, collect the shipping intelligence from all over the world, arrange for its distribution and presumably have the management and ownership of *Lloyd's List*. The old Committee of Lloyd's was to divest itself of all interest in these matters and transfer it to this new Committee. And how was the Committee to be constituted? It was to be constituted in such a way that Lloyd's representatives on it would be for ever in a minority. It was to have altogether forty-nine members of whom sixteen would be chosen by the Insurance companies, sixteen by merchants or ship owners, and seventeen by Lloyd's; so that in a full meeting Lloyd's delegates would be outnumbered by thirty-two to seventeen, and even a partial combination of merchants and company men could force through any resolution however disastrous it might be for Lloyd's. The spirit of J. T. Danson breathed through the plan and for all that is known to the contrary he may have drafted it himself. If it had been accepted Lloyd's would have jeopardised or destroyed outright the brilliant future that lay before it. At a stroke it would have thrown away its most valuable possession, would have ceased to be the nerve-centre of the world's shipping, would have sacrificed its contacts with the Government, and at the end might have dropped back into the position of an undistinguished moribund gathering of marine underwriters. But happily the Committee, when the scheme was proposed to them, realised the issues that were at stake.

Whoever it was that had conceived the plan had overplayed his hand. The trap was too obvious. Too unmistakably Ahab was demanding from Naboth the vineyard, the whole vineyard, and nothing but the vineyard. But between the author of the scheme and Ahab there was an important difference. Ahab was a despot armed with all the power of the throne and dealing with a helpless subject, while the author of the Danson scheme had no weapon in his hands but bluff. And when you flourish the weapon of bluff too vigorously it is apt to break in your hands – as it certainly broke now.

The Committee of Lloyd's saw that the other side aimed at the virtual destruction of Lloyd's and they reacted vigorously. They accused the Salvage Association of double-dealing and going back on statements previously made, and on the 6th November 1872, they indignantly passed a resolution that 'the propositions are quite inadmissible'. They told the Salvage Association what they thought and the Association prudently decided to drop the scheme. In place of it, it was agreed that the

L

marine companies should be represented on a Sub-Committee of Lloyd's for looking after the agencies – but not apparently the intelligence – and that the Sub-Committee should see all resolutions of the Committee of Lloyd's dealing with Agents and all correspondence passing between the Agents and Lloyd's. But it was to be advisory, not executive. Neither the management of Lloyd's Agencies, nor the proprietary rights in the intelligence, nor the goodwill in either of them passed from the possession or control of Lloyd's. On those terms the representation of companies on the Agency Sub-Committee has continued to the present day.

About a year after this dangerous incident was ended Stephenson resigned his post to take up another and the following advertisement appeared in the London Press:

> The Committee of Lloyd's are prepared to receive applications from gentlemen of liberal education between thirty and forty-five who may be desirous of filling the post of Secretary of Lloyd's.

The appointment (at a salary of £1,000 a year) went to an Army captain named Hozier who held it for thirty-two years. At one time and another Lloyd's has produced many able men and many interesting men, but in the combination of intelligence and personality few of them have surpassed Henry Hozier. He was a born autocrat and he carried into a civilian life a belief in discipline natural to an Army officer of eighty years ago. Probably to the end of his career he divided mankind into two classes – officers and men; but he was an able man, an excellent mathematician and a good amateur scientist. He was one of the pioneer enthusiasts of wireless-telegraphy and at the end of his career he fought hard to secure for Lloyd's permanent wireless rights at the signal stations which were his own creation. He had a quick eye for a man and once, when he was interviewing a Christ's Hospital boy for a post on the Committee's staff, he first put the usual general questions and then said 'Where is Galle?' 'Ceylon', said the boy. 'Start on Monday', said Hozier. The boy started on Monday and some forty years later became Principal Clerk to the Committee, discharging with great ability almost the same duties that Hozier used to discharge when he was Secretary.

As soon as he was put into the driving seat Hozier grasped the reins tightly. He was appointed on 13th March; he started work on the 1st April; and on the 8th April he laid before the Committee suggestions for the better management of their Society. Not for nothing did destiny choose him to be the father-in-law of Sir Winston Churchill.

Before long Hozier was the ruler of Lloyd's. Most of a chairman's duties were performed by him and the occasions on which the Committee rejected his advice must have been very few. He had them in chains. But they were pleasant chains, and in 1882 the Committee thanked him for his extraordinary service and asked him to accept a gift of five hundred guineas as a mark of their appreciation, putting his salary a little later up to £2,000 a year. Even the minutes of the Committee change in tone after his appointment and give the impression that the Secretary was telling the Committee just as much as he thought it good for them to know, while behind the scenes a routine, firmly controlled and smoothly running, was efficiently doing their work for them. The minutes of the Hozier period are (it must be admitted) dull. They have scarcely any of those touches of entertainment that occasionally brighten them before Hozier's time. Almost the only amusing entry is a resolution to offer a reward of twenty pounds for information leading to the discovery and conviction of the 'person or persons who cut fifty-five pages from volume ten of the *Encyclopaedia Britannica*' in the Members' Library. There is no further mention of the outrage and we do not know whether there was an arrest or conviction, or who the villain was. We can only hope that he turned out to be a prominent underwriting member. There is, too, a curious record of a formal protest lodged by H. J. P. Dumas against Messrs Bradford, because Bradford's office had been used for a meeting of the Primrose League, which Dumas strongly resented. The Committee resolved that 'it could not interfere in the matter'.

One of Hozier's most useful gifts to Lloyd's was the system of paying cargo claims at foreign ports, which he organized and got adopted in 1886. It had always been a weakness of Lloyd's that the whole of its work had to be done in London. A merchant in some distant port, with a claim on a Lloyd's policy, must send the papers by sea mail to England and wait months for his money while the process of settlement was gone through at the Royal Exchange. The difficulty of Indian merchants in dealing with underwriters thousands of miles away was one of the points made against Lloyd's in the dispute about the monopoly in 1810, and (so far as claims were concerned) the objection had not been removed even by the coming of the telegraph. Underwriters were, in this matter, at a disadvantage compared with the companies, which had branches and correspondents in foreign ports, competent to settle claims on the spot for local merchants. Hozier thought that what the companies' correspondents did for the marine companies Lloyd's agents might do for underwriters; and in the face probably of serious difficulties he organized a claim-settling service, first in the Far East and Australia and afterwards in other parts of the world. He had to persuade conservative-minded underwriters to give authority to the agents and the agents to accept this extra duty on behalf of under-writers, and he succeeded at both ends. The scheme was adopted by the Committee and on the 27th May 1886 the following notice appeared in an insignificant advertisement in *Lloyd's List*:

> The Committee of Lloyd's desire to give notice that on and after the 1st June 1886 arrangements will come into force by which claims on policies underwritten at Lloyd's will be payable at the principal ports in India, China and Australia.

The payable abroad system had been started and three generations of underwriters since 1886 have had cause to thank Hozier for securing much cargo business that without his organizing foresight would have been lost to them.

Valuable as this innovation of Hozier's was, his name is most commonly associated with another department of Lloyd's work – the Signal Stations. He became interested in them soon after his appointment almost by chance; but from the moment that he first got into touch with a station his imagination was fired by its possibilities. He saw what a place on the coast equipped with a telegraph wire might do to improve and increase the service of Lloyd's shipping intelligence. Perched on a remote almost unreachable spot like Cape Ross or Malin Head it would watch the passing of ships and send the news of their position to London in a few seconds – send it while it was still news and still valuable to underwriters and owners.

The telegraph had come to England in the 1840's and in 1847 it was still enough of a novelty to be exhibited to curious sightseers at country fetes. In Tennyson's *Princess* the Squire, when he arranged a treat for his tenants, put up a line of posts in his park to instruct and amuse them with the new toy. Tennyson describes how:

> *Through twenty posts of telegraph*
> *They flashed a saucy message to and fro.*

The Committee of Lloyd's, who were not present at the Squire's party, were not as quick as they might have been to see what telegraphy could do for remote signal stations on the coast; and in 1870 when a Falmouth firm offered to co-operate with them in running a station at the Lizard,

Stephenson (then still Secretary) did not trouble to acknowledge the offer. The firm assumed from his silence that Lloyd's were not interested and went on with the telegraph-equipped signal station as a private venture of their own. A dispute arose between the firm and their rivals at Falmouth, who were Lloyd's Agents. The Post Office intervened, and if Stephenson had still been in office the Lizard station and others as well would certainly have gone to the Government in perpetuity. But Hozier, appealed to by both the Falmouth firms, took the long journey to Cornwall, saw the opportunity, rescued the Lizard station from the Post Office, co-operated in running it in Lloyd's interests, and finally bought it for the sole use of Lloyd's. Lloyd's flag was now planted on England's Atlantic outpost.

His successful visit to Cornwall convinced Hozier that a system of signal stations equipped with telegraphic apparatus or in immediate touch with a local telegraph office would be of the greatest value to shipowners and merchants. At various other points round the coast a certain number of private people were already working stations, and Hozier started out on a pilgrimage both to bring them over to Lloyd's and to buy land in suitable spots for the erection of fresh stations. He was, we must believe, trying to corner the market and in that he was justified. It was obviously better from every point of view that the collection of shipping news should be centralized, and no one was likely to do the work so well as the Corporation of Lloyd's.

So Hozier bought land here and land there, sometimes because he wanted to build a station himself and sometimes because he suspected that the men at the Admiralty were thinking of putting one on the spot and he thought it wise to forestall them. Occasionally when he found the owner of a private station reluctant to sell he would call ostentatiously on land owners and land agents in the district with enquiries for suitable places to build a new station, and in the result the station owner usually came along with an offer to sell. The ethics may have been doubtful but not the success; and in twenty years he had acquired for Lloyd's signal stations at all the best points in Great Britain and Ireland and a chain of stations abroad. His relations with the Admiralty were friendly and in course of time there grew up between the Navy and Lloyd's a working partnership which in 1901 was expressed in a fifty-years agreement for co-operation in peace and war. The Post Office, which had intervened at the Lizard to protect its monopoly, seems to have lost interest in the stations, and once its own position as a monopolist was secured it remained disinterested till the introduction of wireless gave it a new monopoly. Then the Post Office vigorously exercised its rights to the disadvantage of Lloyd's and to the great disappointment of Hozier.

How far the Victorian underwriters drew direct benefit from Hozier's signal stations is an open question, but their usefulness to shipowners and to merchants is beyond doubt. And the indirect advantage to Lloyd's in maintaining its reputation as the centre of the world's shipping news is certain. To appreciate the value of what Lloyd's did, one must remember the conditions of trade in the nineteenth century when the price mechanism worked without interference. It was then the merchant's task to see that his goods were carried to the market in which they could at a given moment fetch the best price – London, Liverpool, Antwerp or Hamburg. Prices moved quickly; ships moved slowly; and when a sailing ship left a South American or an Australian port for Europe no one could tell what the value of its cargo would be on reaching the English Channel or where it could be sold at the best price.

To get round the difficulty the buyer of the cargo would instruct the Captain, through the owner, to call for orders at a place on the English coast, and as the time of the ship's arrival approached he would decide which was the best market for his goods and send orders to the Captain to proceed accordingly. And what place could be more convenient for the despatch of those orders than the Lizard, or Barry Island, or the Old Head of Kinsale? Without going into port the ship could come close to land, report to a station and receive quickly the instructions which the owner had telegraphed to Lloyd's. It was an admirable system and it fitted perfectly into the scheme of international trade as international trade was then carried on.

Lloyd's signal stations had a very active part to play in this machinery. In those days (except in times of prolonged fog or gales) to be a Lloyd's signalman was to lead a busy life. It was a common sight to see ten or fifteen sailing ships beating about off the Cornish, Welsh or Irish headland waiting for their owners' orders to be signalled from Lloyd's; and Hozier claimed in 1884 that more than ninety per cent of ocean-going vessels bound for this country were spoken to before arrival in port by one or other of his stations. And the station was always Lloyd's. Even today, though the Lizard signal station is now controlled by the Ministry of Transport, the people of the Lizard, when they speak of Lloyd's, mean not the great building in Leadenhall Street but a little, squat, storm-beaten house on the cliff's edge which for half a century greeted English sailormen with their first welcome home.

Within ten years of his first visit to the Lizard, Hozier had secured for Lloyd's seventeen stations in Great Britain and Ireland and six abroad. At the height of the stations' activity there were about forty at work at home and messages were regularly received from more than a hundred stations in foreign territory – some owned and controlled by Lloyd's itself and some supplying information under agreement with foreign governments.

The motive power throughout was the energy of Hozier; but among his many good qualities he could not claim to have a passion for economy. He was, in fact, a great spender and personally a great lover of foreign travel; and in forty-five years the upbringing of this favourite child of his cost Lloyd's on a careful estimate over £140,000, of which £25,500 had been spent on his own globe-trotting. It is not for us to say whether the expense was justified, but for a good many years the Committee made no objection to it. Then in 1902 a new-comer was elected to the Committee, a dynamic personality named Sidney Boulton, who challenged Hozier's policy, questioned the accuracy of his figures and argued almost violently that the value of these stations to Lloyd's underwriters and Lloyd's prestige had been greatly exaggerated. The clash between the two men was something like an irresistible force meeting an immovable body and in the first round the immovable body won. But it was shaken. And years afterwards, when Sidney Boulton became Chairman of Lloyd's, he set on foot an enquiry that satisfied him at least that in the past there had been excessive expenditure. But on the broad question whether the stations were of service to Lloyd's there can be no doubt. They clinched Lloyd's grip on the world's shipping intelligence, continued in a new sphere the work that John Bennett had started so successfully at the beginning of the century and confirmed for the Corporation a prestige both with the Government and with shipowners that is still one of its greatest assets. The fifty-years agreement of 1901 between Lloyd's and the Admiralty is proof enough of that.

Towards the end of the century came the invention of wireless telegraphy and it would be superfluous to stress the effect of a widespread reliable wireless service on a signalling system of flags and lights. It was some years, however, before the use of wireless was either widespread or reliable. In 1892 Sir Oliver Lodge sent a message three miles, and four years later Marconi covered nine miles. From the first Hozier was intensely interested and despite his routine duties as Secretary of Lloyd's he took up the study of the new science with enthusiasm. In conjunction with

Neville Maskelyne, the conjuror (who fancied wireless as an aid to his tricks), he invented a certain amount of apparatus, and in one place, at least, where Marconi himself had failed he succeeded in sending reasonably clear messages. He became a director of one of Marconi's companies and secured for Lloyd's a government licence to receive and despatch, by virtue of which he got five of his signal stations in the United Kingdom working a regular wireless service to and from ships at sea.

Hozier's work, in fact, was important enough to induce Marconi in 1901 to enter into an agreement with Lloyd's for some of the signal stations to handle ship-to-shore messages of every kind on behalf of the Marconi company. Not only did Lloyd's take reports of ships' positions. They handled as well private messages, so that the Corporation was in a fair way to become a public telegraph company. It was a bold venture, but wireless (as we can see now) was too big to be managed as a sideshow to marine insurance, and after a few years Marconi's claimed these stations for their own. The agreement between them and Lloyd's had given them the right to step in if they could make a *bona fide* complaint that the service was insufficient. And in 1906 they brought an action against Lloyd's on the grounds that they had such a *bona fide* complaint. Marconi's won and Lloyd's lost. Out of six stations in dispute, Marconi's were willing to leave four with Lloyd's but insisted on having the two they wanted most – Crookhaven and Malin Head. For the second time in fifty years Lloyd's as a Corporation had fought and lost an action.

It was probably as a result of this dispute between Marconi and Lloyd's that Sydney Buxton – a descendant of Fowell Buxton who helped to break the monopoly in 1810 – when he was Postmaster General in the Liberal government of 1906, withdrew Lloyd's wireless licence and knocked the Corporation right out of the wireless business. To Hozier it was a bitter blow – probably the worst he had had at any point in his career; and in his bitterness he involved himself in a fantastic incident that has never been forgotten. When Buxton was explaining his policy to the House of Commons he had criticised the figures with which Hozier had supported his case against the Post Office, and whether the criticism was fair or not Hozier was terribly incensed. Parliamentary privilege protected Buxton from a legal action and Hozier could not start proceedings. So he challenged Buxton to a duel in a letter which was dictated to one of the Committee's clerks to be taken down in shorthand. That fact seems somehow to complete the queerness of the whole episode. To summon a man to ordeal by combat in the year 1906 is strange enough in itself. But to ring an electric bell for your stenographer, have your challenge taken down in Pitman's shorthand and sign it with the rest of your day's letters before they go off to the post – that is surely a most unknightly way of throwing down the gage.

It is probable that Hozier's indignation against Buxton arose more from the disappointment of all his hopes for the future of Lloyd's than from a sense of injured honour. He was too experienced, too much a man of affairs, to treat as a reflection on his integrity a debating point made by a party politician in the House of Commons. And, to speak truly, if a charge of inaccuracy in statistics was good cause for a duel, he would have been better justified in sending his challenge to Sidney Boulton than to Sydney Buxton. Boulton prepared and circulated his careful memoranda to the Committee to prove that the figures given by Hozier to the Committee were misleading; and from the investigation which Boulton inaugurated when he was Chairman, it looks as though Hozier did conceal from the Committee at least as much as he disclosed. But it was Buxton who was the object of his attack and Hozier is said to have sent to members of both Houses of Parliament a circular stating his case against the Postmaster General. He resigned from Lloyd's in 1906, was made an Honorary Member – a very high distinction – and a year later died at Panama on one of his foreign trips looking for new sites for signal stations. With all his faults, his tendency to extravagance and his perhaps excessive love of power, he was (on the evidence of all who can still recall him) a great Lloyd's man, and one can only regret that he did not live long enough to see how the organization he had created was able to survive what he doubtless took to be its death-blow. He would have liked to know that in spite of what Buxton did, in spite of all the intervening changes of forty-four years, his signal stations relayed more messages in 1950 than they did in 1906.

Hozier's forebodings about the future were shared by others than himself and the Clerk on whom he most relied at Lloyd's warned the Intelligence Department at the time that the signal stations were doomed. That pessimistic view was almost certainly general in the years that followed Hozier's death. But arrangements were made with Marconi's and the Post Office, both of which found Lloyd's a useful partner in the distributing side of their work, and the reports, visual and wireless, which were received and sent out by Lloyd's to owners and agents increased considerably in numbers after the wireless licence had been revoked.

Here are the figures of the reports despatched in various years since
1906:

| | |
|---|---|
| 1906 | 38,890 |
| 1910 | 49,532 |
| 1920 | 90,771 |
| 1930 | 73,313 |
| 1940 | 42,059 |
| 1950 | 57,897 |

When Britain is at war the signallers are on war service and of great use to
the Admiralty. Then the general distribution of shipping news is of course
severely controlled, but in 1940 forty-two thousand messages were sent
to owners and agents in Great Britain and in 1945 sixty-one thousand.
The value of Hozier's organization, altered out of recognition from what
it was in his day, is still of great importance in time of peace and vital in
time of war.

# 9

## THE GROWTH OF NON-MARINE BUSINESS

*Heath's work – Not the originator of fire insurance at Lloyd's – Fire risks placed before 1874 – Heath's first fire risk – His attitude of mind – New kinds of insurance including Burglary – Committee not hostile – Complications about deposits – Committee's dilemma – Two standards of security – Committee's advertisement – Anchorless policies – Non-Marine deposits at last permitted – Act of 1911 – Growth of large syndicates*

CUTHBERT EDEN HEATH, the son of an Admiral, was elected an under-writing member in 1880. By his experiments and achievements in fire and accident insurance he did more than any other man of the last hundred years to change the character of Lloyd's and fix the pattern of its future. There are today few Lloyd's underwriters and no Lloyd's brokers whose business has not been revolutionized by what he did; and to his imagination and foresight even the insurance companies owe much of their present prosperity. It would be no overstatement to say of him that he was the father of the modern Lloyd's and scarcely an overstatement to call him the foster-father of modern company insurance.

Round men of Heath's stature tradition grows quickly. Events are dramatized to sharpen their effect and unconsciously distorted to increase the interest of his story. It is a process common to most pioneering move-ments, and Heath, who was essentially a pioneer, has not been exempt from it. Some of the current beliefs about him will not stand examination. It is for example generally thought at Lloyd's that he was the first man ever to write a fire risk there; that until he began business everyone had taken for granted the inability of Lloyd's underwriters to write anything but marine risks; that the rest of the Lloyd's market looked on his experiments with alarm verging on horror; and that the Committee, hidebound, obstructive, conservative, threw in his path every obstacle that their ingenuity could discover and their cowardice would permit them to employ.

The true facts are different. Fire insurance in the last quarter of the

nineteenth century was not a new thing at Lloyd's. As far back as the
eighteenth century fire risks were placed at Lloyd's on property both at
home and abroad; and the business came to a temporary end only because
of high taxation on fire policies, collected by a method to which Lloyd's
underwriters could not adapt themselves. It was an unusually stupid form
of taxation but it lasted for many years, and after the Napoleonic wars it
was modified only by slow degrees. Various reductions in the tax were
made at different times, and then Gladstone in the Budget of 1865 brought
it down to 1*d.* stamp per policy per annum. By that change he re-created
fire insurance at Lloyd's and within a few years a regular fire market
had been established by Lloyd's brokers with Lloyd's underwriters.

To say that there grew up immediately a non-marine market in the
modern sense would be a great exaggeration and Lloyd's was still quite
properly regarded as essentially a place of marine business. But before or
soon after 1870 a small market was established and some brokers (probably
while Heath was still a schoolboy at Brighton College) had established a
fire connection on which they set considerable value. We know this
because of an entry in a book of legal opinions that the Committee started
about that time, which reveals the existence of a market, active and, in a
modest way, flourishing in the year 1874 – six years before Heath's
election.

There was at that time a firm called Stock, White & Co. whose partners
were worried about the legality of placing fire insurance at Lloyd's and for
some reason decided to take the opinion of the Inland Revenue. One can
well understand them writing to the Revenue authorities to find out what
the stamp duty on a particular type of policy should be; but why they
should have asked that particular office whether the transaction itself was
legal is not clear. But it was to the Inland Revenue that Stock, White &
Co. carried their misgivings and the letter they wrote is illuminating. It
contained the following sentence:

> We frequently have to effect fire as well as marine insurances at
> Lloyd's.

That was written in the year 1874, nine years after the stamp duty had been
reduced to 1*d.*, and the solicitor to the Inland Revenue rather surprisingly
was willing to give an official opinion in reply. He answered Stock, White
& Co.'s letter with a firm statement that he knew of no reason why the
business should not be done. His opinion was passed on to the Committee.
The Committee thought it important enough to be recorded in their

archives. And there it stands as a proof that before the days of Heath underwriters were writing frequent fire risks with the blessing of the Inland Revenue and without opposition from their own Committee. A non-marine market was already in existence with the expressed approval of the Government and with the tacit consent of the Committee of Lloyd's.

In those early days there was no specialization in fire insurance business at Lloyd's, no syndicates given over to it entirely, no underwriters who made it their life's work. Whatever was done, was done as a side-line by marine underwriters who supplemented the premiums they derived from ships and cargo by the subsidiary underwriting of buildings and equipment. Fire was incidental to marine and even today the phrase 'Incidental non-marine' is in common use at Lloyd's to describe the premium income of marine underwriters who flavour their normal business with a dash of fire and accident. The pre-Heath non-marine insurance at Lloyd's was all of it 'incidental', and Heath himself not only started life as a marine underwriter but wrote a regular marine account to the end of his business life. But in the course of his career marine and non-marine changed places. At first he was a marine man incidentally writing non-marine. Afterwards he was a non-marine man incidentally writing marine.

What is believed to be his first large venture in fire insurance came to him through his father who was a director of the Hand in Hand Fire Office. That was a non-tariff office, unable to place its reinsurances with tariff companies and hard put to it to get all the re-insurance cover it needed for the safe running of its account. Admiral Heath told his son about the difficulty and the son saw no reason why he should not help the company out with a re-insurance treaty. That phrase 'saw no reason why he should not' points to one of the reasons for Heath's success as a pioneer underwriter. Where other men, presented with a new or unusual enquiry, would see twenty reasons for not accepting it – all twenty stemming from the root fact that such an insurance had never been done before – Heath found the novelty an attraction, not a deterrent. If there was a reason to prevent him from writing the risk it must lie in the quality of the risk itself. If the risk was a bad one, then either the rate must be raised to an appropriate level or it must be turned down. But a risk that had nothing against it except its novelty was (as Heath saw) the best of all risks to write, for the underwriter who accepted it would be starting on the ground floor and establishing himself as a market before his competitors. If an enquiry of a new kind came to an underwriter it proved that people needed that kind of insurance. There was clearly a demand for it. So judge it on its merits and be not frightened by its novelty.

The truth is that Heath's mind was not only original but extraordinarily receptive, always ready to listen to new suggestions and to consider impartially any new form of enterprise. It was this quality, more than any other, that helped him to reinvigorate the non-marine market at Lloyd's, to create the conditions of prosperity for hundreds of other underwriters and brokers, and to widen the scope of almost every insurance company in the world. In 1885 he accepted the Hand in Hand re-insurance treaty on English business and a few years later, when he was approached by the American branch of another English company, he gave it too a treaty of re-insurance. And from that treaty sprang the long and fruitful connection between Lloyd's non-marine market and the United States – a connection that for at least fifty years has been useful both to British and Americans. The day on which Heath wrote that American risk is another of the days in Lloyd's history to be marked with a white stone.

But if Heath had confined himself to ordinary fire insurance the revolution he started would have been a comparatively mild thing. There are after all limits to the insurance of buildings and property against fire, and the ground was already so well covered by the companies that for Lloyd's to challenge them on that alone would have involved a long and difficult struggle before Heath could find for himself and his fellow-underwriters even a niche in the market. What Heath wanted, and what the non-marine market wanted, was new kinds of insurance in which Lloyd's underwriters would be the sitting tenants and the companies the new-comers; and Heath found them by listening to brokers' enquiries with an open mind – with an inclination to accept rather than a bias towards refusal.

Perhaps the best known example of this open-mindedness of Heath's is his first burglary policy. Eighty years ago nobody in this country, householder or merchant, ever insured his property against burglary. He did not insure because there was no one in England – company or underwriter – willing to accept the risk. But at some time in 1887 a Lloyd's broker, who was placing the fire insurance on his own furniture, asked 'more in fun than in earnest' whether Heath would care to cover him against burglary as well. Even a casual jest could set Heath's imagination working, and again he saw no reason why he should refuse to give the broker what the broker wanted. The first burglary policy was written; and two years later in 1889 the old *Pall Mall Gazette* (an evening paper beloved by

Victorian London) published as a rather sensational piece of news an interview with a Lloyd's broker headed:

## INSURANCE AGAINST BURGLARY
### The history of the latest insurance scheme

The broker explained in the interview how his lighthearted proposal was 'after a little calculation accepted in all seriousness and the policy made out'. The scheme got wind and several other brokers and their friends effected similar insurances. The firm who had placed the first risk issued a circular announcing that they were prepared to effect insurances at Lloyd's against theft and robbery with or without violence or against burglary, the rates varying from 2s. 6d. per cent to 5s. per cent according to circumstance. As proof of his bona fides the broker added 'several losses have already been made good, notably one quite recently at Harringay for £25' which seems to have been considered a remarkably big claim.

Out of burglary insurance there was born another type of policy which brought a large volume of business from both sides of the Atlantic. A relative of Heath's, who had insured with him her jewellery against burglary and theft, sent in a claim for a piece that had been lost but not apparently stolen. She was told that mere loss was not one of the insured perils and consequently underwriters were not liable. She was naturally disappointed and Heath again saw no reason why the risk of loss should not be covered. The premium would have to be higher than the rate for theft, but why not cover deprivation from any cause? A satisfactory rate he thought would be 10s. per cent instead of 2s. 6d. and he began to cover jewellery at the cost of 10s. for every £100. That was the origin of 'all risks' insurance which produces today hundreds of thousands of pounds in premium every year. For fifty years or so the rate that Heath quoted to his relative was the standard all-risks rate on jewellery in this country, and it is a remarkable example of his underwriting instinct that he hit at first attempt on a rate that for so long a time would satisfy the assured and leave the underwriters with a reasonable profit.

Another policy of Heath's invention, not unlike the all-risks policy on personal jewellery, came about in much the same way. A man who kept the books of a diamond merchant in Holborn was impressed by the great risks his employer ran on his stock as he carried it round the circle of his customers. He spoke about it to his employer and wondered whether it would be possible to get some kind of policy covering the goods when they were outside as well as inside the office. The merchant told the book-keeper to see what he could do and the book-keeper, through a broker, approached Heath. Heath quoted a premium to insure the stock wherever it might be; the merchant accepted it; and the first jeweller's block policy was signed. Who it was that christened it 'block' is not known, but the name is derived from the peculiar method of working out the premium and from the fact that the policy is not subject to average. Anyhow the book-keeper was so pleased with his success that he invited other diamond merchants to take out block policies too, and in time he was doing well enough to give up book-keeping and start as an insurance broker on his own account. His business was almost entirely made up of jewellers' policies, but he became a member of Lloyd's and for years was an under-writing name in Heath's syndicate. His career indeed is a pretty example of one man's enterprise making other men's fortunes. Other brokers took the business up and today most dealers in precious stones in Britain, America, Holland, Belgium, France and the British Dominions protect themselves by block policies usually placed at Lloyd's.

These are a few of the many new insurances invented by Heath and the school of underwriting that he founded, and it was in this inventiveness and enterprise that his great achievement lay. His name is honoured today not because he started non-marine underwriting at Lloyd's, but because he revolutionized, both at Lloyd's and elsewhere, the business of non-marine insurance and enormously widened the service it offered to the commercial world. Both he and Lloyd's were extraordinarily fortunate in their con-nection with each other – he because Lloyd's provided him with just the field he needed for his experiments, and Lloyd's underwriters because he put them into the van of the new movement. Where he sowed they have ever since been reaping. Today whenever a man says, as men often do say (though not with perfect accuracy), that Lloyd's will insure anything, he is paying a conscious tribute to Lloyd's, and another, probably unconscious, to the genius of Cuthbert Heath.

While insurance was taking on this new look at Lloyd's many company managers were shaking their heads over Heath's recklessness and expect-ing disaster. But so long as he confined himself to fancy risks in which they were not concerned they could watch him with detachment or a mild professional interest. Their attitude was very different when Heath started new forms of fire insurance; for fire was the company's own province and there the game must be played according to the command-ments. And the first and greatest of the commandments was this: A fire

Cuthbert Heath (1859–1939), from a painting by John Hay, R.P., in the Library at Lloyd's.

policy is a policy of indemnity and thou shalt not recover after a fire more than the amount of thy material loss. If a building burns the assured must get no more than the cost of repairing it at the time of the fire. If merchandise burns he must have no more than the value of the merchandise at the time of the fire. Give him a right to more than that, tell him that he is entitled to consequential loss over and above the material value, and you are inviting him to become a criminal, to commit arson, to make fraudulent claims, to fake his books, to jettison his honour, and all at the expense of his insurers. Moral hazard (that jewel beyond price) will be damaged; fire insurance will go to the dogs and anyone who offers to cover consequential loss will be laying a rod in pickle not only for his own back but for every legitimate fire office in the land.

Heath took a more charitable view of human nature and was not deterred by the prophecies of the companies. He saw that the loss of business following a fire might be as serious as the immediate material loss. He believed that the companies in their anxiety to give a policy-holder no more than a bare indemnity were in fact giving him a good deal less; that there was a gap in the British system of fire insurance which could safely be filled; and that he was justified in filling it. In the event he proved to be correct and today there is probably not one fire office in the country that refuses to give cover for loss of profits; not one that does not value a branch of its business which Heath's enterprise forced them to start so reluctantly at the end of the nineteenth century. They are rather like the man in O. Henry's story who found himself a millionaire against his better judgment.

Experiments in non-marine business followed each other quickly and most of them were successful. One or two went wrong; the insurance against war loss of property in South Africa before the Boer War left underwriters with a substantial loss; and the attempt to cover farmers in Southern Europe against hail damage was not profitable. But on the whole the new risks paid, and they certainly multiplied and spread. In 1886 Lloyd's agent in New York was writing to the Committee for advice on how to deal with Lloyd's share in a big fire on Broadway, and an enterprising firm in Chicago was enquiring for some reason about Lloyd's losses on fire claims. A firm of London solicitors was asking about the insurance of a mill at Kidderminster and the Metropolitan Water Board about fire insurance at Lloyd's on property in its London territory. The brokers were certainly getting around and bringing a show of non-marine business to the Room.

M

That fact in itself goes a long way to dispose of the commonly accepted view that the Committee of Lloyd's were hampering Heath and that everything he did was done in the teeth of official obstruction. If the Committee had in truth desired to strangle the infant market at birth there were many ways of doing it. But the minutes of the period contain no evidence that the Committee ever wanted to compass the death of the child or took counsel against it to kill it. The natural conservatism of human nature may to some extent have coloured the minds of the Committee; and some members in their hearts may have regarded these new forms of insurance as intruders into Lloyd's – much as old-fashioned surgeons regarded Lister's aseptic methods as intruders into the operating theatre. The adjective that the Committee applied to the new risks was 'extraneous', and when they used that adjective they were clearly thinking of the non-marine insurance as a side-show to the real work of the place. And who can blame them? Lloyd's always had been a place of marine insurance and marine was still king. The new non-marine premiums were a drop in the bucket compared to the marine premiums and the Committee could not possibly foresee the time when extraneous risks would overtake in size and importance their elder brother marine.

The greatest difficulty the Committee had in dealing with the new market came not from their own antipathy but from the question of deposits and their relation to non-marine security – a very prickly problem. For years one Committee after another wrestled with it and one Committee after another was thrown by it. And here we must pause to consider the tangled difficulties that the Committee in this matter of underwriting deposits had to unravel.

.    .    .    .    .    .    .

Heath's underwriting started about thirty years after the first deposit had been made and about fifteen years after Lloyd's Act had received the Royal Assent. And both deposit and Act had been shaped to fit a purely marine business. 'The objects of the Society', said the Act, 'shall be the carrying on of the business of marine insurance by members of the Society.' The claims for which the deposit shall be available (said the Deposit Trust Deed) shall be claims on marine policies. Whatever rights had been given to the Society, whatever security had been provided for the policy-holders, were given and provided on the assumption that Lloyd's under-writers did no insurance except on ships and cargo. And here were underwriters accepting (apparently as members of Lloyd's) risks that had nothing to do with the sea, underwriting them under the wording of a Deed that restricted itself to marine liabilities.

Thirty years before this time the Committee would probably have been indifferent to the new ventures so long as they did not come under the head of gambling. But in those distant days there had been no Lloyd's Act. The idea that Lloyd's had a duty to protect the credit of its members was at that time still struggling to its birth, and such things as deposits against the insolvency of underwriters were unknown. If someone in 1855 had begun to write burglary risks and jewellery risks and consequential loss risks the Committee might have thought him mad and expected his failure; but they would not have conceived it as their duty to warn him that he was endangering the credit of Lloyd's. They were still in the state of mind which prompted them to write the letter to an angry policy-holder in 1855.[1]

It is not within the province of this Committee to enter upon the subject [i.e. a member's failure], they not being in connection with the proceedings of individual underwriters.

But even in the earliest days of Heath's underwriting the Committee had moved a long way from that attitude of remoteness. They were now very much in connection with the proceedings of individual underwriters and they had established a system of deposits which provided, as they thought, an almost perfect security for the payment of underwriting liabilities even when the underwriter had drifted into insolvency. In the new security of Lloyd's the deposit was the cornerstone and it held chief place in all Lloyd's propaganda.

In their annual reports the Committee spoke almost boastfully of what had been done in the way of taking deposits. They referred to a general meeting at which members had insisted on a deposit of £5,000 from every new candidate; they advertised the fact that the total value of the deposits was £2,695,000 – more than twice as much as the old-fashioned guarantees – and that the average sum deposited or guaranteed per under-writing member was close on £6,500. They were proud of what had been done and wanted all the world to know of it. And now, just as everything was comfortably arranged, along comes this young man encouraging brokers to bring in a lot of new-fangled business, business that lay right outside the protection both of deposits and of guarantees. What were the Committee to do?

[1] See page 130.

The first thing they did was to make sure that their reading of the Trust Deeds, signed by members at their election, was correct and that non-marine risks did in truth lie outside the scope of the underwriter's deposit. They instructed Hozier to write to the Corporation's solicitor telling him that many underwriters at Lloyd's were writing fire risks and asking him whether the deposits could be used in case of need for claims on these policies. His reply was emphatic. For fire losses falling on a marine policy – e.g. losses through fire on cargo insured in transit as an adjunct to a sea voyage – the deposits would be available; but for losses arising out of a straightforward fire policy they were useless. That was clear and it settled the first of the Committee's queries. But they had a further sugges-tion to put to the solicitor. Could we not (they asked him) promote another Act of Parliament to widen the scope of Lloyd's underwriting and 'make our object the effecting of fire and other insurances as well as marine' and if that were done would not the deposit made under the existing Trust Deed automatically become liable for claims on fire policies?

Here again we must consider that letter of the Committee's in the light of accusations made against them that they were unfriendly to the new non-marine market. If their attitude towards the new underwriting was hostile surely it was a very strange thing for them to suggest the promotion of a new Act of Parliament to give it legal standing. But that was exactly what the Committee were trying to do, and they only dropped the idea because their solicitor discouraged them. To promote a new Act, he said, might be actively dangerous and the Committee would be wise to abandon any thought of legislation.

Foiled in their first approach to the problem, the Committee tried various other ways in the hope that one of them might lead to their goal. If they had in truth been unfriendly to the non-marine underwriting it would have been simple to declare at once that it could not be fitted into the Lloyd's scheme and must be given up. But they did not take that line. They persevered in one attempt after another to find a solution, and there can be no doubt that their minds were honestly set on the purpose they proclaimed. They tried to alter the old Trust Deeds to make them com-prehend non-marine business, but their solicitor was against it as strongly as he had been against the new Act of Parliament. They considered altering the old guarantees, but the solicitor (quite rightly) advised them that guarantors could not be expected to extend the liability which they had originally assumed. They thought of a system of voluntary deposits, but the solicitor told them that the deposits would not be valid against a member's outside creditors and would therefore be a most dangerous innovation. Whenever the Committee seemed to be getting near the goal the solicitor blew his whistle and told them they were off-side. It was all very frustrating, and in the light of what happened a few years afterwards it is difficult not to think that the very distinguished lawyer who was then solicitor to the Corporation of Lloyd's was being just a little bit fussy and over-cautious.

The only positive advice the solicitor gave was to insert in all new Trust Deeds a clause stating explicitly that claims on fire policies were not covered by the deposits. That was done and for three years all new Trust Deeds specifically excluded fire policies, making it clear that there was no security behind fire policies except the premiums and the private means of underwriters. So far so good. But if the Committee thought that they had settled the matter they were reckoning without their Heath. To them non-marine business still meant fire and nothing but fire. To Heath it meant burglary, theft, and any other sort of cover that the public wanted and he was willing to give. So in 1889 the Committee had to write to their solicitor again, telling him that theft and burglary were being covered at Lloyd's and should be excluded from the Trust Deeds as well as fire. Would he draft an appropriate clause to be added to the new Deeds? He did it. But in doing it he overshot the mark and raised an outcry among the marine underwriters. He had managed to exclude from the deposits not only ordinary theft and burglary policies but insurances on bonds and securities in transit, which from time immemorial had been regarded as marine business and were among the most attractive risks in under-writers' books. The marine men were not going to admit that their specie risks ranked with fire and burglary policies and they forced the solicitor to change the Deeds again.

It was almost a race between Heath and the lawyer – Heath inventing new policies and the solicitor catching up with new clauses to exclude them from the deposits. At last the lawyer hit on a comprehensive wording which shut out all insurances not contemplated by the Lloyd's Act as being within the scope of Lloyd's underwriting.

Then Lloyd's settled down to two different standards of security – the marine fortified by deposits and guarantees and the non-marine dependent only on current premiums and the underwriters' uncharged capital.

The objections to this dual system of security are manifest and the Committee cannot have been blind to them. But after the failure of all their attempts to solve the problems they seem to have taken up a fatalistic attitude and let things run their course. Heath and his innovations were given unofficially the run of the market and nothing was done either to suppress them or to give them a settled position in the scheme of Lloyd's. But it was considered necessary both to protect the marine underwriters against loss of credit in case of a non-marine failure and to safeguard the insuring public against misconceptions about the security of a fire policy. The first purpose was achieved by confining the use of the Lloyd's anchor to marine policies and denying it to non-marine, so that it could if necessary be pointed out to a disgruntled policy-holder that his policy (though signed by underwriting members of Lloyd's) was not officially a Lloyd's policy. That sounds like a weak compromise – Pilate washing his hands of responsibility. And if ever the difference between a Lloyd's policy *cum* anchor and a Lloyd's policy *sans* anchor had been brought to the public notice in the courts of law the damage done to Lloyd's credit might have been very considerable. Fortunately that never happened and it is doubtful whether any outsider ever noticed that the fire policy on his furniture differed from the marine policy on his cargo to the extent of one trademark.

The other step taken by the Committee was essential in the interests of the assured. The public, who had been told so often about the deposits of Lloyd's underwriting members and had learned to base their confidence in Lloyd's largely on those deposits, must know now that the deposits were not available for the payment of extraneous claims. So an advertisement was inserted in *The Times* and regularly printed in *Lloyd's List* pointing out that deposits and securities were applicable only to certain

> . . . subject matters of insurance, viz. vessels of any description, cargoes, freights and other interests which may be legally insured in, by or in relation to vessels cargo and freight.

It was almost certainly the publication of this advertisement that started the traditional belief in the Committee's hostility to non-marine business, and the advertisement undoubtedly did raise resentful feelings in the pioneers, who saw in fire and accident business a great new venture for Lloyd's underwriting.

Their resentment is easily understood. For more than twenty years Lloyd's had pointed to the deposits of its members as the source of their security; and the commercial world had grown accustomed to thinking of them in that light. Lloyd's security and Lloyd's deposits were closely linked together in the public mind, and Lloyd's brokers had very properly concentrated on the deposit and guarantee system when they were called on to defend the strength of the policy. And now after all these years of talk and propaganda the Committee not only refused to extend the deposits to cover the valuable new non-marine business, but blazoned a warning that people who insured at Lloyd's against extraneous risks would be fools to expect any advantage from this security. The whole force of the campaign in favour of deposits would now recoil to the detriment of one set of underwriters.

If a rather strained analogy may be allowed, it was as though a manufacturer has for twenty years been using in the make-up of his products a raw material that he genuinely believes to have unique virtues. He has based his advertising entirely on the merits of that one ingredient. It is his best selling point and he has greatly increased his turnover on the strength of it. Then one of his departments puts on to the market a new brand that does not contain the much-advertised substance and the manufacturer starts another advertising campaign – this time to tell the world that the magic raw material has no place in his new product. The two campaigns continue side by side and cancel each other out. That would be lunatic advertising and the manager of the new department would resign his post at the earliest possible moment. Lloyd's non-marine underwriters could not resign theirs. But like the departmental manager they were sore and restless, and at one time there was actually talk of non-marine members forming themselves into a company for undertaking fire insurance. The talk came to nothing but the idea lasted long enough for the Committee to consult their lawyers on its feasibility. And some time afterwards Heath (for other reasons) did start an insurance company which he managed in close connection with his Lloyd's underwriting and is still a prosperous flourishing concern with a large capital and premium income.

Looking back on those problems of seventy years ago one must sympathise with both parties. The non-marine underwriters were in an exasperating position, while the Committee, so long as non-marine deposits were impossible, could not honestly allow fire and accident policies to get into the hands of the public without a warning that they were not protected by the same arrangement as the old-fashioned better-known marine document.

The root of the whole trouble was that the transaction of anything but marine insurance, if it was done under the aegis of Lloyd's Committee, was *ultra vires*. On that point the Act of 1871 was clear. It limited the objects of the Society to marine insurance and the powers of the Committee were restricted to marine matters. There was not a word in it to allow a member of Lloyd's – so long as he was acting as a member – to dabble in fire, burglary or other extraneous risks. It seems indeed impossible to resist the conclusion that if Heath wrote these risks in his capacity as a member of Lloyd's he was well on the wrong side of the law. He was never challenged, and so far as is known never had to defend his actions. But if his legal position had been called in question what defence could he have put up?

He would have admitted that nothing but marine insurance and the handling of shipping news was contemplated by the Act of 1871 and that the powers given to the Committee were restricted to the advancement of those interests. He would have admitted, too, that the non-marine policies he signed could not strictly be described as Lloyd's policies. But he would have pointed out that the Act did not interfere with his rights as a private person and that, unless he hampered the business of marine underwriters, the Committee had no jurisdiction over what he did when he was not writing marine risks. If he made trouble in the Room and impaired the comfort of marine underwriters the Committee could step in and prevent him. But there were a thousand things he could do in the Room unconnected with marine insurance without being subject to the Committee's authority. He could read *The Times*, talk to his fellow-members, consult his solicitor or stock-broker, guarantee another man's liabilities – transact in fact any personal business of his own – and he would not be breaking the law or offending against the bye-laws. By the same reasoning he could write whatever extraneous risks he liked and sign any policies he liked; and if in writing them he did not (*a*) injure marine underwriters or (*b*) use the distinguishing trademark of an anchor he would be doing nothing wrong. The fact that the non-marine policies were signed in the Room did not make them in the legal sense Lloyd's policies. That by the terms of the Act could only be done by the imprint of the Lloyd's trademark. And so long as a man avoided the anchor he could do what he wanted, write what he chose, and be free of any restrictions of the Committee.

That line of reasoning was nowhere put into writing; but from the advice the Lloyd's solicitor offered from time to time to the Committee there can be little doubt that it was present in his mind. And it is the clue to all the answers he gave to Hozier's questions. He conceived of the Lloyd's underwriter as a dual personality – a member of Lloyd's when he initialled a marine slip and a private individual when he initialled a non-marine; and subtle as that distinction may sound it provided Lloyd's with just the opportunity it needed to develop its new enterprise. It would have been better probably to ask Parliament for a new Act which would establish non-marine on the same level as marine and enable the Committee to control both types of business, taking separate deposits for each of them. But the Committee for a long time fought shy of that solution and preferred to carry on with the legal fiction – if legal fiction is the right term – that a non-marine policy signed by a Lloyd's underwriter was not a Lloyd's policy. On that legal fiction the modern non-marine market existed and flourished throughout its early years.

. . . . . . .

As the years went by non-marine business grew at a surprising speed and at the beginning of the century only a small minority of members were confining themselves to orthodox marine underwriting. The rest were taking advantage of the legal fiction, signing some policies decorated with the picture of an anchor and some not so decorated – some backed by deposits, some unsecured. As the fashion developed the nervousness of the Committee returned, and in 1902 they made another attempt to establish non-marine deposits for new members as they were elected. And this time they went to Counsel and got from him an opinion different from any that their solicitor had given them. They pointed out to Counsel that in the general interests of the Society it was desirable to have separate and additional security 'to ensure the discharge of liabilities on these extraneous risks'; that if failures occurred on non-marine policies discredit would fall on the Society as a whole; that the scandal would impair the reputation of marine as well as non-marine policies. Did Counsel think that the Committee could legally take security either by way of deposit or a guarantee policy for the protection of non-marine policy-holders? They would like to do so if they could, but had they the power?

Counsel's opinion was exactly what the Committee wanted and in flat contradiction to what they had been told in the past.

I do not see (he said) that there was any obligation on the Society to permit Lloyd's to be used as a place for non-marine underwriting at all, but since they do in fact permit it I think that they are entitled to take such precautions as they think fit to ensure that this non-marine business shall be carried on in such a manner as not to discredit the legitimate marine business. There is no reason why the Society should not impose as a term of admission any conditions which it thinks necessary for the maintenance of its reputation.

On the strength of that opinion Lloyd's began to receive non-marine deposits, and Heath, who for years had been trying to get his deposits accepted, was allowed to put up £2,000. Guarantee policies were freely asked for and supplied, and the legal fiction was on its deathbed.

A few years later the fiction had grown so feeble that Lloyd's did what it would have been wise perhaps to do ten or twenty years before. It promoted in 1911 an Act of Parliament altering and extending the objects of the Society and substituting for the wording of 1871 a new and much fuller definition which would give underwriters all the elbow-room they needed without fear or apprehension of breaking the law. Here are the two definitions side by side:

| [1871] | [1911] |
|---|---|
| The carrying on of the business of marine insurance by members of the Society. | The carrying on of the business of insurance of every description including guarantee policies by members of the Society. |

The Bill in which the change was made was introduced first in the Lords and afterwards in the Lower House, and despite a certain amount of criticism (which even at this distance of time does not increase one's respect for the intelligence of our legislators) it got through with flying colours. It was the belated charter of the non-marine market. At the moment when it became law the legal fiction finally disappeared. The distinction between official policies and unofficial was abolished. And the anchor from henceforth would be stamped on non-marine documents. Hitherto the non-marine market had been the illegitimate scion of a noble house, living, it is true, at the family mansion and feeding at the family table, but never recognized officially as a member of the family. Now it was openly and unashamedly a son of the house enjoying the same rights and the same privileges as its elder and hitherto more respectable brother.

The long delay before the business was legitimized may be regarded as a blunder, for it threw the Society wide open to the accusation of having two standards of security, one for marine and the other for non-marine. If the weaker of the two securities had been the marine policy it would not have mattered so much; but unhappily it was the non-marine policy that carried no anchor, that was backed by no deposit, that had no guarantees. And it was the non-marine policy that the critics of Lloyd's most earnestly wanted to assail. Lloyd's had made the tactical mistake of neglecting its defences just where a break-through would pay the enemy best.

·　　·　　·　　·　　·　　·

Apart from its effect on the premium income of Lloyd's the non-marine market had a considerable indirect influence both on Lloyd's itself and on the rest of the insurance industry. Two examples of this influence may be mentioned. First it widened the interest of Lloyd's and helped to break down the rather close barriers within which the old-fashioned marine underwriters, both at Lloyd's and in the companies, did their work. It is no disparagement of those Victorian underwriters to say that their outlook tended to be narrow. It could be nothing else. Their minds were concentrated on the qualities of ships and cargoes and on the relative dangers of different voyages; and within that sphere the knowledge of a good underwriter was detailed and exact. On the other hand the new forms of non-marine business, touching life at many points, brought the underwriter into contact with all sorts of trades that had no interest for the marine market. If an underwriter was writing a general non-marine account it called for a knowledge less detailed indeed than the old marine underwriters' but covering a much wider area. A very able and successful marine underwriter, who had passed a distinguished life in the service of a great company, still remembers the surprise with which he once watched a non-marine underwriter handling a batch of risks that a broker had brought him for writing or quotation.[1] Accustomed to the stately ritual of a company underwriting room, he saw with astonishment, perhaps, thirty insurances dealt with in a few minutes and almost every one of them different from the others. Fire, burglary, third-party, loss of profits, all came up for judgment; and as he watched the non-marine underwriter switching his mind from one to the other, the marine man felt that in its variety and speed this technique was so different from underwriting (as he knew it) that it was scarcely to be recognized as part of the same industry. The impact of this change on the mentality of Lloyd's is something that cannot be measured, but those whose memories of Lloyd's go back fifty years will probably agree that it has been considerable.

The second example of the influence of the non-marine market is more technical. It is the growth of the big underwriting syndicate, a subject that for its importance might almost deserve a chapter to itself.

In the very early days of marine underwriting every man signed on the policy a line for himself and himself alone. But it soon became convenient for an underwriting member to authorize someone to write his line for him; and to that end he appointed what he called a substitute but we in

[1] Information of Mr Ernest Jacobs, formerly underwriter of the Alliance, whose recollections of the insurance market are most valuable.

our modern jargon call an underwriting agent. At some date not known
someone, whose name has not been preserved, finding that he could
profitably act as substitute for A decided to increase his income by writing
for B as well; and on the day he first put down two separate lines on the
same risk, one for A and another for B, the modern underwriting syndicate
was conceived. But the fashion grew very slowly and even a hundred
years ago it was still in its infancy. We have a pretty good idea of how
things stood then because a broker named Forbes kept a record, which is
still in existence, of the underwriters with whom he did business. He had
accounts with seventy-four Lloyd's underwriters, of whom fourteen
worked for themselves alone, twenty-eight were in groups of twos,
eighteen in groups of threes, eight in groups of fours and six in groups of
sixes. From these figures it is apparent that a group of six was in 1865
exceptionally large.

By 1890 things had moved and it was remarked as a modern phenomenon that some agents were writing for 'half a score of names', a
dangerously large number, which was thought by some to be the main
source of the troubles from which the market was then suffering. That
diagnosis was nonsense, but we do get from it the fact that when the non-
marine market was first finding its feet a syndicate of ten names was
considered to be perilously large. On the other hand, in 1952 one Lloyd's
underwriter was writing for over three hundred names and another for
over two hundred. Fourteen underwriters were writing for between one
hundred and two hundred each. No less than two thousand, two hundred
and thirty-five names were then crowded into sixteen syndicates.

The change marked by those figures is striking enough but what is the
connection between non-marine insurance and these large syndicates?
Why should one lead to the other? The answer lies in the composition of
the non-marine market for the first fifteen or twenty years of its life and
in its subsequent evolution. It was at first a market in which one man did
all the thinking and the rest did all the following. That statement is not
literally accurate; but it is as true as most generalizations, and it is not an
unfair description of the machinery existing between 1890 and 1905. In
those days a broker with a large fire insurance to place must first take it to
Heath, and with Heath's name on the slip he would expect to place anything up to £200,000 on a single risk. But he would not do what he
normally does today – show it to other underwriters specializing like
Heath in non-marine business. He would take it after Heath had written
it to a marine underwriter, a man with a great knowledge of ships who

could read and understand *Lloyd's Register* as easily as he could read the *Daily Mail* and could tell exactly the kind of damage to which any particular cargo was subject. On the other hand he knew nothing, and claimed to know nothing, about fire, burglary or accident. But he would write the non-marine risk and write it for one reason only – because Heath had written it first. In course of time he may have learned something through repeatedly following the master; but he can never have been anything more than an amateur and, so far as this department of his business went, he was almost as completely in the hands of Heath as the names themselves who made up Heath's syndicate.

It was of such underwriters as these that the non-marine market was mainly composed – marine specialists backing their faith in one man whose judgment in non-marine risks they trusted.

One odd feature of this amateur market was that several of the marine underwriters though they followed Heath blindly in some kinds of fire and accident insurance refused to follow him in others. One man would write any fire risk led by him on property in the United Kingdom but refused everything he had written on the Continent and in America. Another would have nothing to do with fire risks in any part of the world even though Heath had led them, but followed him (strange to say) on American bankers' policies – perhaps the most speculative risk of any that Heath wrote. These underwriters might almost be compared to a group of intelligent boys in the Mathematical Sixth, sitting under the master but picking and choosing what to believe and what to reject in the stuff he taught them. One would accept everything he had to say about Trigonometry but mistrusted his views on Higher Algebra, and another would follow him on the Differential Calculus but refuse his instruction in every other branch of Mathematics. It sounds queer and illogical but it worked, and the pupils were usually contented enough at the end of the scholastic year when the results of their education were worked out in pounds, shillings and pence.

If non-marine business was to grow that organization of the market clearly could not be permanent. The market would have to broaden out. More underwriters and syndicates would have to specialize in fire and accident, and marine underwriters if they remained in the market would have to take a much less important place in it. There must be more underwriters familiar with the new underwriting. Many names who had hitherto done nothing but marine business wanted to branch out; and underwriting agents who found it inconvenient to develop their own non-marine account themselves were looking for a suitable man to do it for them. But where was a suitable man to be found? The obvious place to begin the search was Heath's underwriting box at which young men were being trained under the master's eye and should after a year or two be capable of taking charge of a syndicate themselves. Young men, too, were learning the ropes of non-marine insurance in brokers' offices and they could apply to underwriting the lore they had gathered in broking. There was in fact a seller's market for anyone with non-marine experience, and as non-marine business took shape in the first ten years of this century, the underwriting was mainly done by youngsters graduating from the school of Heath or from the offices of brokers with a large non-marine connection. But the number of these graduates was comparatively small; the names who wanted their services were many; and if the new syndicates had been limited to the old-fashioned eight or ten men, demand would have far outrun supply. To accommodate everyone who wanted to come in, the size of the syndicates must be increased and underwriting agents must get into the way of acting for battalions rather than platoons. The enormous modern syndicate sprang out of the rapid growth of non-marine business and the scarcity of non-marine underwriters.

It may perhaps seem that the difference between large syndicates and small is unimportant and nothing more than a question of convenience. But that would be a mistaken view. It is a matter of great moment and although there are many things to be said in favour of the old fashion as against the new, it is on balance true that the big syndicate has brought great advantages to Lloyd's. It has enabled large transactions to be carried through for which the old machinery would have been inadequate. In fifty years the premium income of Lloyd's has grown from a figure of perhaps seven million to a figure of about two hundred million, and it is difficult to believe that that increase could have been accomplished by syndicates however numerous – of ten to fifteen names each.

# 10

## THE COMING OF THE AUDIT

*Turning point in Lloyd's history – Conditions in 1900 – Burnand scandal –*
*Non-Marine deposits – Premiums not in trust – Genesis of the audit – First steps –*
*'Times' article – Underwriters' meeting – The audit scheme – Opposition over-*
*come – Audit and trust fund adopted – New insurance Act*

IN 1897 BRITAIN CELEBRATED with gaiety and magnificence the Diamond
Jubilee of Queen Victoria. It was the nineteenth century's last fling and it
was very well done. The Fleet assembled in the Solent; foreign royalties
(not then in short supply) were to be seen everywhere; the highways of
London almost lost their identity in the bunting that swathed and the
lights that transfigured them; sightseers revelled in the streets; fireworks
and chains of bonfires lighted the countryside, and in the daytime Her
Majesty drove through noisy and adoring crowds to her thanksgiving
service in St Paul's Cathedral. Land and sea gave themselves up to jollity
and into that splendid merrymaking Lloyd's wholeheartedly threw itself.
The Committee 'with enthusiastic acclamation' resolved to present a
humble and dutiful Address to the Throne, and for the festivities in the
Room itself they made precise and careful arrangements. Happily a
printed copy of the programme was for the benefit of future generations
bound in with the Committee's Minutes of 1897, and it still gives us a
picture of the ritual at Lloyd's on that memorable day. It occupied two
pages, of which the first reproduced the Committee's loyal resolution and
the second was as follows:

[*Chorus:*]
*God Save our Gracious Queen,*
*Long live our Noble Queen,*
 *God Save the Queen.*
*Send Her victorious,*
*Happy and glorious,*
*Long to reign over us;*
 *God Save the Queen.*

[*Soli:*]
Thy choicest gifts in store
On Her be pleased to pour;
Long may She reign.

[*Chorus:*]
May She defend our laws,
And ever give us cause
To sing with heart and voice,
God Save the Queen.

After the singing of the National Anthem (said the programme) 'three cheers for the Queen will be given'. That concluded the jubilations at Lloyd's and as the echo of the third cheer died away in the Room the excited members went back to their normal avocations.

The Diamond Jubilee, the close of the century, and the death of Queen Victoria have always been regarded as marking a turning point in English history. And the century's end was certainly a turning point in the history of Lloyd's. In 1900, whether the members of Lloyd's knew it or not, they were in truth on the threshold of a new era – an era first of trouble and anxiety, then of recovery and improved security, and finally of almost incredible expansion. The early troubles were serious enough but they paved the way for the prosperity that followed them; and as we look back across the years even the worries and perplexities of 1900 to 1912 fit into the pattern of success which the Society has enjoyed in the past half-century. But to understand the history of those years it is necessary to take a short survey of Lloyd's as it was in 1900.

When the first underwriting deposit was recorded in 1857 the number of underwriting members was 272. In 1900, when the deposit system was well established and applied to all new candidates, the number was 548. And the great majority of the members were then backed by a deposit of not less than £5,000. Those figures indicate not a very rapid but a regular, satisfactory and substantial increase in underwriting membership and a very considerable growth in the security of a Lloyd's policy. The deposits indeed were valuable and well suited to the conditions of underwriting in the middle of the nineteenth century. Their general efficiency at that time cannot be doubted. In the records of the Committee between 1870 and 1891 there are only six members whose deposits had to be sold for payment of their underwriting debts, and it is probable that in every case the amount realised from the sale was large enough to satisfy all the creditors so that the loss to the insuring public (if there was any loss at all) was negligible. In the last ten years of the century there was a slight increase in defaults but here again it is unlikely that policy-holders went short of the full amount of their claims. The deposit-guarantee system was up to this point an almost complete success and on past results there was in 1900 no very obvious reason for disquiet or concern.

But things were not as good as they appeared. In the first few years of the new century they took a turn for the worse and the number of regrettable incidents was beginning to increase. For this sudden deterioration it is difficult to pick out any single cause; but the whole marine market – companies as well as Lloyd's – was passing through one of those unprofitable periods which are bound to occur in insurance and are specially apt to affect the marine underwriter. That fact helped no doubt to weaken underwriters. Then the growing fashion of writing in syndicates provided opportunities for some underwriters to misuse premiums belonging to their names – premiums not yet carried to a trust fund (as they are today) but free to be handled at will by an inexperienced or too-optimistic underwriting agent, who could be at the same time an efficient underwriter and a miserably bad investor. The third cause of the trouble lay, it must be admitted, in some of the extraneous risks which had been spreading round the market and were occasionally a snare and pitfall to men trying to emulate Heath but deficient in Heath's underwriting genius.

The first and worst of the regrettable incidents occurred in 1903. Springing from a combination of misused premiums, reckless writing, and flagrant dishonesty, it led to the collapse of a marine syndicate through the default of all the names in it (except one) and to a most unhappy lawsuit calculated to do Lloyd's credit a vast amount of harm. It was a terrible affair due to a marine underwriter abusing his powers as agent and writing extraneous risks at his names' expense to bolster up his own outside interests.

The underwriter was a man named Burnand who had been elected an underwriting member in 1885, had deposited his £5,000, and had built up what was believed to be a sound and profitable marine account. Unhappily both for himself and for Lloyd's he joined the board of a company called Gaze and Sons Ltd which owned and managed a travel agency, and he became deeply interested in its business. Whether he invested much of his own money in it is not known; but he had its survival so much at heart that he was willing to risk not only everything he possessed himself but everything that his names possessed, if only he could put Gaze and Sons on to a prosperous footing. According to a High Court judge, who knew the facts, the firm of Gaze and Sons was never solvent, and the contemporary belief was that it took its death-blow from the postponement of King Edward VII's Coronation in 1902. It had (so it is said) invested freely in seats for Coronation sightseers, and when the King fell ill and the Coronation was put off, the loss broke the Company's back. It tried to raise money by putting its bills on to the market but the accepting banks were shy of them and soon refused to take them unless they were backed by some other security.

That security Burnand provided by signing policies with his syndicate of five names (including himself), binding them to pay if the insured's bill was not met within thirty days of the due date – policies that were not against insolvency (which would have been bad enough) but against failure from any cause to meet the bill promptly.

The bills were renewed several times and then, even though a Lloyd's policy was behind them, the accepting banks became nervous again. They sought further security and got it from an insurance company which (difficult as it is to believe) actually guaranteed the guarantors – covering the solvency of Burnand and his names signed on anchorless unofficial Lloyd's policies. The result was that the banks now had a treble protection (1) the drawer, (2) the Lloyd's policy, (3) the Company's policy – a curious and interesting situation. One can well understand the insurance company being anxious to oblige the banks; but it is surely impossible to believe that it would have given a guarantee of this kind unless it was satisfied that in any circumstances a Lloyd's policy signed by Burnand's syndicate was sound. Its action at least shows the high credit of a Lloyd's policy at the beginning of the century.

The rate of premium charged for the Lloyd's cover was nominally one per cent of the maturing value of the bills, but in fact no premium was ever paid or any entry made in Burnand's books. He had – of all incongruous things – a gentleman's agreement with Gaze and Sons that the transaction should cost them nothing, and he saddled his names with a liability of over £100,000 without crediting them with a single penny of premium. To the names he said nothing. On the contrary he intercepted and destroyed letters that came addressed to them at Lloyd's. When one of the names heard a whisper that something was wrong and called at Gaze and Sons' office to ask point-blank whether he was backing their bills, Gaze and Sons gave him a written assurance that there was not a word of truth in the rumour. His name they told him had never been used on such a policy. Soon after this cheerful reassurance he found that he was defendant in an action on the bills and the policies, and that his personal liability was at least £20,000. The matter when it came to trial produced one of the most interesting, and to Lloyd's men one of the most painful, judgments ever delivered in a commercial court. The upshot was the failure of three names, the impoverishment of a fourth and the destitution of Burnand himself. It is difficult to say which is the more astonishing – Burnand's wickedness in ruining his names or his folly in ruining and disgracing himself.

The Burnand scandal was in truth a horrible thing and even at a distance of fifty years writing about it is a distasteful business. But it cannot be passed over in silence for it had a great influence on the development of Lloyd's and it might without exaggeration be described as the spring that set in motion all the reforms introduced between 1908 and 1926. It shook both the Committee and the general body of members. It destroyed once and for all the legal fiction that policies on extraneous risks were not Lloyd's documents. And it undermined the compromise by which the Committee allowed such policies to be signed but refused all responsibility for protecting the policy-holder.

So far were the Committee now from maintaining their old aloof attitude that they prepared and published a memorandum to blunt the many criticisms of Lloyd's current after the trial and they admitted by inference, if not expressly, that the credit of Lloyd's marine and non-marine underwriting was indivisible. No longer could it be said that a policy must be safeguarded if it carried a picture of an anchor but might be left to look after itself if the anchor was not there; for it was patent now that a failure on one type of policy reacted and always would react on the other, and that the good name of Lloyd's could not survive unless the distinction between official risks and unofficial risks was jettisoned. 'The United States', said Lincoln, 'cannot endure permanently half slave and half free.' And by the same reasoning all intelligent members of Lloyd's saw in 1903 that Lloyd's underwriting could not much longer continue half-insecure and half-protected.

It will be remembered that 1903 – the year of Burnand's action – was also the year in which the Committee obtained Counsel's opinion on taking deposits from new non-marine underwriters and began for the first time to accept them from existing members. In 1903 Heath, who had been pressing the Committee for years to take a non-marine deposit from

him and had grown indignant at their constant refusal, was allowed for the
first time to give security for his extraneous underwriting; and it is quite
likely that other established non-marine underwriters did the same thing.
Strangely enough, however, the first candidate for membership from
whom a non-marine deposit was actually demanded by the Committee
was elected only in 1918; but the battle of the non-marine deposits was
really won in 1903 and it was Burnand's catastrophe that made the
victory possible.

But deposits were not everything. Any intelligent person pondering the
facts of Burnand's downfall must see at once that even if he had had
behind him a deposit of £5,000 available for non-marine claims his
creditors would still not have been paid in full. The trouble had been
going on too long and the liabilities had been piling up too secretly for the
deposits (when the smash came) to be a complete safeguard. While the
syndicate's underwriting assets were being dissipated by Burnand neither
the names who had trusted him, nor the brokers who had shown him their
business, nor the underwriters who had guaranteed him, knew that anything was wrong; and by the time they found out what was happening the
losses had swelled to a disastrous figure. By the old nineteenth-century
traditions it was a broker's duty to distinguish between weak underwriters
and strong. But the tradition, if ever it was sound, could not survive a
disaster that had been blowing up undetected, and it was apparent that
something more than a broker's vigilance plus a deposit would be needed
if a Lloyd's policy was to be restored to its old high standing. That was the
train of thought stimulated by Burnand's failure. It led five years later to
the Lloyd's audit and to premiums in trust.

. . . . . .

Those two reforms – a solvency audit and a trust fund for premiums –
are the two main pillars on which Lloyd's security for some fifty years has
now rested. Theoretically the audit and the trust fund are distinct but in
practice they are inseparable; without the other either would lose much, if
not all, of its value. They are like the two blades of a pair of scissors, very
useful when joined and not nearly so good apart.

Before discussing these two vitally important reforms we must pay
some attention to the weaknesses they were designed to cure. For fifty
years Lloyd's had been thinking of security in terms of funds to be kept
ready for payment of an underwriter's claim after he had defaulted. That
was the purpose of the deposit and a very proper and reasonable purpose

it was. But the method had its limitations of which the most obvious was this: it took no cognisance of an underwriting account until it had gone wrong and it allowed a foolish or incompetent underwriter to scatter his funds, to pay out profits which had never been earned, to pile one year's losses on to another and even to increase his underwriting liabilities in the hope of getting more funds for the payment of previous years' claims. In course of time he might default and only then would the protection of the deposits begin to operate. The scheme in fact concentrated on trouble after it had flared up and did nothing to prevent it from starting. It stood by for an emergency operation when the patient had collapsed and neglected the treatment that might have prevented him from collapsing at all.

A most dangerous aspect of the old system was the underwriting agent's uncontrolled freedom to use premiums as they were paid to him for any purpose, wise or unwise, that might take his fancy. Premiums were not in trust as the deposits were; they were not (as the deposits were) protected against the underwriter's outside creditors and there was no check to prevent, or penalty to punish, their misuse. Perhaps the most remarkable illustration of what could happen is the story of an underwriter in the early days of deposits who put up the security demanded by the Committee and proceeded to conduct an apparently normal business. But he had in fact borrowed the money for the deposit from a friend, and without telling the Committee what he was doing he had agreed to pay the debt back to the lender as he received the brokers' quarterly cheques for premiums. By this means in eighteen months or so he had satisfactorily discharged his personal debt, but there was no money left in his account to pay his underwriting claims. Before the claims on last year's policies had been adjusted and presented, his last year's premiums had found their way back into his benefactor's pocket. So he defaulted. Not many men could be found foolish enough to do a thing like that and the Committee could scarcely be blamed for not anticipating such madness; but the incident (now long forgotten) pointed the danger of a system which relied entirely on deposits for the security of a man's underwriting liabilities. Lloyd's was ready for audit and trust funds.

When there are two alternative versions of the same event tradition usually chooses the more dramatic of them. That happened in the story of the audit. The view commonly held at Lloyd's is that the audit and the trust funds were originated, discussed and put into shape at the nineteenth hole of Littlestone Golf Club by two members of Lloyd's who in 1907 or 1908 were enjoying a weekend at that pleasant spot. That they did play golf at Littlestone is doubtless true. That they talked shop between the games may be taken for granted. But the idea that these reforms were first conceived in the Littlestone Club house is not correct. The reforms had actually been in the air for a long time, and as far back as the year 1890 they had been advocated by an anonymous writer who must have been a Lloyd's man. He may, of course, have been expounding his own unaided brainwave but it is much more probable that he was putting into print notions which even then were current among the more enlightened members and subscribers.

In 1890 the *Economist* newspaper had two contributed articles on the position of Lloyd's and the need for reform; and the second of the two dealt with the necessity of earmarking premiums for the payment of claims. The writer's argument was (1) that premiums paid to underwriters could be and in fact were being dissipated before the risks had run off and the profit ascertained, and (2) that it was the duty of Lloyd's Committee to prevent that happening.

'Is there any sufficient reason', the article ran, 'why the Committee should not see to it that premiums taken in the Room shall be first available for the payment of underwriting losses and the balance only of his legitimate profit be at the disposal of the underwriter? Your security then would cease to be a fixed fund regardless of the size of the account and would grow with the increase of liabilities. Let the deposit remain as at present but in front of it place all premiums received. Put premiums in joint names of themselves and an officer of Lloyd's. Profits would be payable as ascertained.' That was the gist of the article. Underwriting funds were to be held in a joint account and profits were to be certified before money was distributed to the names. It was the first open suggestion of premiums in trust and the first hint of an annual audit. The name of the writer is not known but he may possibly have been one of the pioneers who helped to put the changes through in 1908. At the time he wrote his articles he did not, to be quite frank, get much of a reception; and in a lively correspondence that followed the publication of the two articles his proposals went almost unnoticed.

But the ideas he had expressed were germinating and three years later there is a curious entry in the Committee Minutes which seems to indicate that a shoot from the seed had appeared above ground. In 1893 a young man named Hayman was a candidate for underwriting membership, his deposit being supplied by his father who also provided £500 as working capital. The arrangement is noted in the Minutes in these words:

F. Hayman writes that the securities provided for his son H. Hayman are a free gift and that the premiums received after the payment of £500 advanced for immediate use will be held in trust.

It may be that father Hayman gave this undertaking at the request of the Committee and if that is so the Committee must have been more influenced by the *Economist*'s article than they had admitted. Or it may be that Hayman came to his decision of his own free will because he thought it sensible and businesslike. If that is so we have here another case of a prudent outsider giving an epoch-making lead to the Committee. In 1857 it was Sharp who craved the Committee's permission to put up a deposit for his son and in doing that started the deposit system. In 1893 it may have been Hayman who insisted on a trust deed for his son and so initiated the system of putting premiums in trust.

Whatever the true explanation is, the idea of premiums in trust was not adopted officially for another fifteen years and the movement towards reform was slowed down, if not actually stopped, until the Burnand scandal gave it fresh life in the early years of the twentieth century.

. . . . . . .

The Committee at that time thought of reform in much the same way that the Prayer Book speaks of Marriage – a good thing in itself but 'not by any to be enterprised, unadvisedly, lightly, or wantonly'. In accordance with that outlook they made up their minds very slowly, and when at last they moved, their action was anything but dramatic. It had no immediate effect on anybody and did little more than show which way the wind was blowing.

The first step was taken in 1903, soon after the Burnand catastrophe, and it consisted of asking every new candidate before election whether he would agree (if called upon) to put all his premiums in trust so that they would be available only for his underwriting liabilities. Naturally everybody agreed and so far things were going well. The change was a move in the right direction, and whenever it became possible to call on the names to implement their promises it could be very effective. But when could the time come? Not for many years. Almost every new name was going into an existing group or syndicate and it would be impossible for an agent to treat the premiums of one name in a syndicate as in trust and the premiums of the rest as free. Consequently the Committee would not be able to make any one candidate's undertaking effective until all the old underwriters (who had given no undertaking) had either retired or died or voluntarily consented to the change. It was doubtless a sound move to exact the promise just as it is a sound move to lay the foundation stone of a building; but in this case the building could not be put up until a whole generation of Lloyd's underwriters had passed away. And reform could not be postponed for a generation.

Burnand had already done great harm to the credit of the Room and within the next five years other less-serious failures also touched the good name of Lloyd's. The challenge of the non-marine market to old-established insurance offices both in this country and aboard was raising a new kind of opposition, and the Press both in this country and in America was beginning to write critically about the value of a Lloyd's policy. As time passed the attacks increased in number and some American newspapers were almost violently sceptical about the future of Lloyd's. Lloyd's replied by taking advertising space in American papers and pointed out to the Americans that Lloyd's underwriters had proved their strength by paying all their losses in the San Francisco earthquake. But that did not silence the voice of criticism. The Press in England was restless. *The Daily Telegraph* had spoken out and motorists were advised in their technical papers not to insure their cars at Lloyd's. But it was the London *Times* that brought the criticisms to a head and clinched the victory for reform. It did that in a single article in its financial supplement, a semi-magazine publication that the paper used to produce once a week and has long ago dropped. The article on Lloyd's appeared in it on 17th July 1908.

The Editor of the supplement – and almost certainly the writer of the article on Lloyd's – was a journalist called Kitchin who specialised in insurance and considered himself to be among the three leading financial writers of his generation. He had started his career in the Life department of the Alliance Assurance Company and he was the author of a not very profound book on fire insurance. He had never worked at Lloyd's but he claimed to be the first man ever to discover the news value of Lloyd's underwriting.[1] He certainly had several useful contacts among underwriters and he boasted that instead of his going to Lloyd's for news Lloyd's men came and pressed the news on him. He was not an outstandingly modest person but this claim of his was probably correct. He did, in fact, become the mouthpiece of people in the Room when they wanted their views aired in public. And one of his close acquaintances at Lloyd's was Sidney Boulton, the fighting reformer, who believed passionately that

[1] Harcourt Kitchin: *Moberly Bell and His Times.*

Lloyd's must either reform itself or sink into obscurity. There can be little doubt the *The Times* article which had so great an influence on the development of Lloyd's, though written by Kitchin in Printing House Square, was a loudspeaker for Sidney Boulton sitting at his box in the Room. Kitchin was the medium. Boulton was the control.

The article began with a short description of Lloyd's underwriting and distinguished between the treatment of defaulters on the Stock Exchange and at Lloyd's. Lloyd's brokers, it said, rather than return a name, would make good his quota out of their own pockets – a proof of the extreme jealousy with which members of Lloyd's guarded the reputation of their colleagues. 'And that', said *The Times*, 'is in itself a great merit and one of the reasons why the Room has gained such a high reputation.' But it was obvious that if business was being conducted for any length of time on an unsound basis this generous method of bearing one another's burdens might be too great for even the strongest brokers to bear. The large syndicates of underwriters had premium incomes of half a million to a million pounds a year and no policy-holder had any knowledge of how the premiums were used or the funds invested. As compared with the large sums which should be readily available to meet liabilities the amount of official deposits was insignificant.

That was the hub of the argument. Lloyd's had outgrown its underwriting deposits. A new line of defence must be built up to supplement the old and that line must be an auditor's certificate.

We believe, the article continued, that the public would be satisfied if the underwriting syndicates had properly audited balance sheets prepared every year and submitted them privately to the Committee of Lloyd's. The mere fact that such a balance sheet had to be submitted would automatically compel underwriters to make sure that all their liabilities for unexpired risks were provided for and their funds properly invested . . . There is no doubt that the incidents of the last two or three weeks have done a great deal of harm to the general credit of Lloyd's . . . We believe that the credit of underwriting members would again become practically invulnerable if they took the necessary step to secure a semi-private audit.

.    .    .    .    .    .

A week after the appearance of that article in 1908 a meeting of underwriters was held which sanctioned the appointment of a special joint committee to hammer out the audit scheme. In a little over three months (although the summer holidays were in full swing) the special committee had done its work and was able to report to another meeting of active underwriters.

The task of the special committee was twofold, first to consider possible schemes for the audit and second to influence the opinion of members in preparation for another meeting to be held in the autumn. In the first part of their work – the preparation of the scheme – the Committee were lucky. They had a prototype provided by Heath who was already something of an expert in this matter. He had devised a standard form of certificate to test the standing and solvency of a Lloyd's underwriter and his action had come about in this way. He refused to guarantee any of his fellow-members unless their account had been audited and an auditor's certificate given. And that certificate of Heath's was the matrix of the audit certificate devised in 1908 – the certificate which *mutatis mutandis* has for nearly fifty years been the foundation of Lloyd's security.

But an underwriting account is a long-lived thing and it is only after many months of waiting that the underwriter knows with certainty whether he has been trading at a profit or at a loss. His harvest sometimes good, sometimes bad, is always long-delayed. Generally it takes three years for an account to run off and it will only be at the end of 1956 that an underwriter will allow himself to say either that he made a profit of £x or suffered a loss of £x in 1954. That delay is inherent in the business and (since that is so) how can he at any moment between January 1954 and December 1956 be satisfied that his assets are sufficient to meet his liabilities for the year? Still more how can an accountant, unless he has second sight, give a certificate that they are adequate?

Heath's system had solved the difficulty by making an underwriter's past years the yardstick for his present underwriting. The auditor was told to look back at a man's figures for the last three 'closed' years and find out from them what percentage of the year's premium income had been settled at the end of the first year of an account; what percentage at the end of the second; and what percentage at the end of the third. The percentages of these closed years must then be applied to the open years as they came under the audit.

For illustration let us take an imaginary account. An underwriter's accounts are being tested at the end of 1954. Two years, 1953 and 1954, are still open. One year 1952 is about to be closed. The last three closed years are 1949, 1950 and 1951, and his results in those years were:

SETTLEMENTS OF 1949 UNDERWRITING

At end of first year　　　26 per cent of the premiums
At end of second year　　68 per cent of the premiums
At end of third year　　　85 per cent of the premiums

SETTLEMENTS OF 1950 UNDERWRITING

At end of first year　　　29 per cent of the premiums
At end of second year　　70 per cent of the premiums
At end of third year　　　87 per cent of the premiums

SETTLEMENTS OF 1951 UNDERWRITING

At end of first year　　　28 per cent of the premiums
At end of second year　　69 per cent of the premiums
At end of third year　　　86 per cent of the premiums

Having got the percentages, the auditor took the average of the closed years and he would find that the underwriter on the average had settled 27·6 per cent of his premium income in the first twelve months of an account, 69 per cent at the end of twenty-four months and 86 per cent in the full thirty-six months. He applied those averages to the open years that he was auditing and so he reached an estimate of the sum needed to pay future claims on them.

That was the Heath scheme, and it was the scheme that the Special Committee adopted and put before the body of underwriters in 1908. Since that time there have been many changes in it. Underwriters in general are no longer judged by their own past percentages. The percentages to be used are now supplied by the Committee of Lloyd's who are the sole judges of what is an adequate test; and elaborate instructions are given to auditors for the treatment of different kinds of underwriting. The changes made since 1908 are important but they are not changes of principle. As Sir Winston Churchill said when he re-visited Niagara twenty-five years after his first visit: 'The principle doesn't seem to have changed.'

·　　·　　·　　·　　·　　·

The preparation of the audit and the certificate completed the first part of the Special Committee's task. They had spent the whole of October working on it. But it was not the whole of their task. At the beginning of November they would have to put their case to a meeting of Members. At that meeting they must, if their plans were to go through, get a very strong vote in their favour; and they had no weapon to rely on except personal persuasion. The gathering was not an official meeting that could make or alter bye-laws, but an unofficial off-the-record talk that could take no decision or force any corporate action. It was more like a temperance meeting called to induce erring souls individually to sign the pledge. Those present would be active underwriters listening to suggestions which each of them separately could accept or refuse. The whole thing was voluntary, even academic; but the meeting was the most important in the modern history of Lloyd's and more than one member of the Special Committee believed that the whole future of the Society was staked upon it.

The omens as read by the reformers were not all favourable. The chairman of Lloyd's himself told his colleagues that he was very nervous and uncertain of the result. Boulton's closest associate in business was bitterly opposed to the audit and profuse in arguments against a scheme that he described as: 'inquisitorial, oppressive, offensive, and disgustingly insulting beyond all expression.' He argued simultaneously (*a*) that Lloyd's was very strong and powerful and (*b*) that if underwriters' actual figures were published as a result of the audit they might bring the credit of Lloyd's to the ground. Another leading underwriter declared that the scheme was 'only pandering to the taste of the present time and to our Continental colleagues. We should be practically saying that we are not solvent and are now trying to strengthen our position'.

The members of the Special Committee themselves were so little sure of the result that they carefully avoided any reference to premiums in trust. They thought that if they put forward both halves of the scheme (trust funds as well as audit) they might be trying 'to carry more cargo than they could cross the bar with'. So they brought into the open only one blade of the scissors – the audit, and left the other blade in the cupboard against a more suitable occasion. As things turned out the second blade was forcibly dragged out by a Member in the body of the meeting and the two were then and there joined by an amendment that he proposed and carried.

In truth the reformers' misgivings were unnecessary and their prospects far brighter than they feared. The meeting was to be held on 3rd November and the effect of *The Times* article of July was still powerful. Important holders of Lloyd's policies were known to be contemplating a change in their insurance arrangements and all but the toughest diehards at Lloyd's were now fearful of a second thunderbolt from Printing House Square.

Another blow, too, had been struck for reform and this time is was a decisive blow – a blow that could not fail to send the opposition down for the full count. It was struck by Heath who drew up in his own hand-writing a manifesto to the Committee of Lloyd's as follows:

> We, the undersigned underwriting Members would agree to hand in to the Committee of Lloyd's annually a statement, signed by an approved accountant, that we were in possession of assets reasonably sufficient to wind up our underwriting accounts.

To this declaration he obtained the signatures of forty-two underwriting agents and among those forty-two were almost all the leading men of the market. It was scribbled casually on a cheap piece of foolscap paper and it bore no date. It was typical of the casualness with which Lloyd's brokers and underwriters used in those days at any rate to carry on their business. But by a happy chance it was kept and filed in the Minute Book and it remains there today to be revered as one of the most important documents in the Society's archives. For we can see now that once that manifesto had been signed, once its existence was known, the victory of reform at the November meeting was certain. If these leading underwriters were willing to submit themselves to an audit, no other underwriter would dare to hang back.

Perhaps the situation can best be described in Biblical language. At the meeting in November the sheep were going to be divided from the goats. Heath, when he collected the forty-two names, was taking a preliminary census of the sheep. The list was there for anybody to sign. Anyone who liked could add his name to it and by doing so secure for himself a place in the fold. But if he resisted, if he refused to sign, if he declared openly that he would not undergo an audit or provide a certificate, if in a word he took his place among the goats, what would be thought of him? His obstinacy would be taken for nervousness about his own solvency. Cautious brokers with good risks to place would fight shy of him. Prudent merchants and shipowners would tell their brokers to do their business only with audited names. Surely he and all the other unaudited underwriters would lose all the business that was worth having and finally be squeezed out of the market altogether. It was an unpleasant outlook and formidable enough to make the most recalcitrant member swallow his prejudices and the most timid brace himself for the ordeal.

The meeting was held and it is highly probable that few, if any, of the underwriters had consulted their Names before they attended. They were committing the Names to a vital change in the management of their underwriting, agreeing on their behalf that they would submit themselves to a test not contemplated in their underwriting agreements and putting them to the hazard of either surviving the auditors' scrutiny or abandoning their business as underwriters. It was a good deal to ask, and the Chairman was still so doubtful that he invited Boulton, the chief champion of reform inside the Committee, to sit next to him for his moral support. In his opening speech he spoke of adverse Press criticisms both in England and abroad and he described the object of the meeting as being only to receive a report of the proceedings of the Special Committee. He made no mention of any resolutions to be taken that day. The report was as follows:

> This Committee is of opinion that in view of the large increase in business the deposits or guarantee in cases where the premium income exceeds £7,500 should be supplemented by the production of a certificate approved by the Committee of Lloyd's and that a list of Members complying with these conditions be posted on the board on 31st March of each year.

The debate that followed the Chairman's speech was not impressive. The opposition was feeble, and Boulton seeing that the hour had come to strike whispered to the Chairman 'Take a vote at once'. Accordingly, the Chairman put an appropriate resolution to the meeting.

That brought to his feet a private Member, Mr F. A. White, who made an unanswerable speech in favour of including 'premiums in trust' with the audit. He referred to Burnand's mad dissipation of his premiums and the danger in which Lloyd's would always stand so long as an underwriting agent could use his underwriting money for outside purposes and an outside creditor could attach his premiums for debts that had nothing to do with the underwriting. Finally he moved that words be added linking a deed of trust approved by the Committee to the audit itself. There was no opposition and both amendment and resolution were carried by a unanimous vote.

· · · · · ·

That unofficial meeting fixed the future of Lloyd's. By 31st December all the arrangements for the audit were complete and before 31st March in the succeeding year all the accounts had been audited. To arrange the details and have the machinery ready for action between the beginning of November and the end of the year must have been a considerable feat of organization. But the staff performed it as it seems always to perform everything. Lloyd's Committees have for many years been extraordinarily fortunate in the staff that has served them and in the administrative ability on which they have been able to call. In the way of organization nothing seems to be beyond the capacity of the officials. The tasks given them in the last fifty years have included among many other things the billeting at a moment's notice of scores of evacuated clerks on the householders of Ruislip and Ickenham; the setting up almost at a moment's notice of a special trust fund to take all dollar premiums; the support of a Lloyd's chairman in his conferences with high-ranking American officers in New York; the implementing of decisions made at those conferences; the organizing and reorganizing of machinery for signing every Lloyd's policy; the supervision and construction of two large buildings; and the staging, without hitch or flaw, of the pageant and ceremonial for those Royal visits which, now and again, like rich and various gems inlay the otherwise unadorned routine of broking and underwriting. No emergency has been too much for them. Never have they failed in their task. And it would be an unworthy history of Lloyd's that did not at least once record the supreme value of their services. For one member at any rate it is a very great pleasure to be able to acknowledge the debt he owes to them.

.    .    .    .    .

To return to 1908. It was a wonderful piece of luck for Lloyd's that the audit came into being just at that moment, for in 1909, within a few months of its establishment, a new Insurance Bill was laid before Parliament and Lloyd's place in the insurance firmament had to be fixed by law. The guts of the Bill were that insurance companies doing life, fire, and accident or bond business would in future have to deposit with the Board of Trade a sum of £20,000 and make annual returns of their business in a prescribed form. It was rather a half-hearted Bill, very emphatic and exacting in its earlier sections but easing off most of its demands twelve pages further on. Every assurance company, said Section 2, must deposit a separate sum of £20,000 as respects each class of business that it transacts. That was clear and precise. But in Sections 31–34 it said:

> Such of the provisions of this Act as relate to deposits shall not apply if the company concerned has commenced to carry on the business in the United Kingdom before the passing of this Act.

A similar provision covered the Employers' Liability, the only difference between it and other kinds of insurance being the date on which exemption from deposits depended.

Existing companies in fact got off almost untouched and most of them, whether they were bursting with money or skirting the edge of insolvency, would be able to carry on their business after the Bill became law without a deposit. But for all that, Lloyd's underwriters, now that they were in the fire and accident market, had to be dealt with; for the companies would never submit even to a shadow of control if their chief competitors were left out of the Bill altogether. Something must be done about the non-marine underwriters and the burden put on them must be made to appear at least equal in weight to the burden laid on the companies. How was that to be done?

The Board of Trade began by demanding from every Lloyd's under-writer transacting fire and accident business a deposit of £2,000, which would have produced from the whole of Lloyd's about £1,500,000. As the fire and accident premium of the whole of Lloyd's was at that time probably less than that of one large office, and as the existing offices were not being asked to put up one penny of deposit for that type of business, the scheme was obviously unfair to Lloyd's and the Committee very properly resisted it. But it would not be enough to meet the Government with a blank refusal. Governments are made up of politicians, and politicians naturally try to avoid giving offence to an influential body of citizens, such as the staff and the shareholders of the large insurance companies whose votes might be valuable at the next Election. If the Committee wanted to save the non-marine market from putting up deposits with the Government, they must make some proposal that would save the Government's face and bring Lloyd's within the scope of the Bill.

And this is where the audit came in. Let us (argued the Committee) accept the £2,000 deposit as it stands. Let us leave it in the Bill but at the same time suggest an alternative which every non-marine underwriter will be at liberty to accept. We will not make a frontal attack but get round the flank and by-pass the position. So they proposed that the clause dealing with Lloyd's should not be amended or the deposit of £2,000 interfered with, but that the following alternative should be appended to it:

If an underwriter could show (a) that he had complied with the audit requirements and produce his certificate of solvency, and (b) that he had provided the Committee with a non-marine security either by deposit or by guarantee policy for an amount equal to one year's premium income, he should be forgiven the £2,000 deposit with the Board of Trade.

We the undersigned underwriting
members would agree to hand in
to the Committee of Lloyds annually
a statement signed by an approved
accountant that we were in possession
of assets reasonably sufficient to wind
up our underwriting accounts.
　　We suggest that a Committee should
be appointed to consider the best
method of carrying out the above proposal.

| Names | Suggestions |
|---|---|
| John V Dawson | |
| B H Ackerman | |
| Geo H. Faber | |
| F W Marten | |
| Albert N Read | Provided the suggestion be generally adopted. |
| Erro Richardson | — do — |
| C. E Heath | |
| A White | |
| Jas Forbes | do. |
| Charle Ht Rosevear | |
| B. R. Fleming. | |
| John Fleming | |
| J Mackintosh | |
| Raymond Beck | |
| Edward Kitts | That statement may be called for any time. |
| D Poole | |
| S Hubyn Greene | |
| H E Hoford | |
| Alfred Faber | |
| Geng A Sims | |
| A Charteris | |

The turning point in the campaign for compulsory audit: the 'manifesto' drawn up
by Heath in his own hand on a sheet of foolscap and signed by most of the leading underwriting agents. The signatures run on to a second page.

That proposal was accepted by the Government and the Bill, when it was published, did for Lloyd's almost exactly what it did for the existing companies. It enforced a deposit in one of its sections and cancelled it in another. First the cane was flourished and the victim put into the appropriate attitude. Then the cane was put back into the cupboard and the unscathed victim resumed his upright posture.

For the companies, who had been treated so gently, it was practically impossible to put up a serious resistance to the proposals for Lloyd's, and neither in the Lords nor in the Commons was there any serious opposition to the Lloyd's part of the Bill. Slight changes were made but the pith of the scheme was unaltered. So everybody was happy – the companies because they had got what they wanted for themselves and Lloyd's because the Bill which might have proved a nuisance had become an asset. Until it became law the Lloyd's audit was not obligatory either for marine or non-marine. It was a work of supererogation. At any time an underwriter could refuse to submit himself to it and might have got away with the refusal, still retaining his business as an underwriter. But henceforward the audit for non-marine business had legal backing and if ever a fire or accident underwriter showed signs of kicking over the traces, the Board of Trade was there to apply the necessary discipline. Most happily the Committee had made the best of both worlds and if ever men earned the gratitude of succeeding generations they were the leaders of Lloyd's for what they did between January 1908 and December 1909.

# 11

## ADAPTABILITY AND EXPANSION
## AMERICAN BUSINESS

*Immediate result of audit – Benefit to Names – A Name's position – Decline in number of candidates – Rise in underwriting profits – National prosperity – Total premium income – Growing need for insurance – Accident business – Its importance to Lloyd's – The adaptability of Lloyd's – American business – Abuse of Lloyd's name – Queer policies – Re-insurance – Excess policies – Catastrophe re-insurance*

---

THE FIRST AUDIT went off in the early months of 1909 with less difficulty than the pessimists had expected. But it did produce immediately some astonishing results – results so astonishing that one hesitates to accept the record of them at its face value. It exposed, too, some queer things that unbeknown to the general body of members had undoubtedly been going on for years. Some underwriters for example passed the audit on their open underwriting but were in heavy trouble on business that they had been conducting under the counter. Policies in those days were usually signed with rubber stamps containing a list of underwriters' names. Every syndicate had its own stamps which would be banged on to policy after policy as they were presented to the underwriters for signature. They ought obviously to have been kept and guarded with great care; but at least one underwriter left a spare stamp in his office, to which favoured brokers had access, using it to stamp policies at their pleasure without consulting the underwriter. The risk on those policies nominally borne by the underwriters named in the stamps was actually run by the brokers themselves, who were not underwriting members but (as a side-line) did an underwriting business under a borrowed name. They were wolves, so to speak, in sheep's clothing. They evaded the audit and helped to ruin the underwriter whose folly had given them their opportunity.

Another underwriting member had quite a large syndicate, of which all the members passed the 1909 audit. But he had another account – a specially privileged account – shared between himself and a friend. This subsidiary account was not submitted to the audit and it brought down both the names concerned in it – an unhappy incident, but of some historical interest because the brokers, who had given the little syndicate the bulk of its business, held a meeting and undertook to pay the underwriters' claims out of their own pockets.

Apart from a general improvement in the credit of Lloyd's policy the check that the audit imposed on this hugger-mugger type of underwriting was one of the great benefits it conferred on Lloyd's. And another notable result was the protection that it gave to the Names themselves. Before the audit it was often impossible for the Names to know what their true position was. Some received no annual account from their agents and many others, though they got statements, could not understand them. The audit changed all that and put them *vis-à-vis* their underwriting agents into a position of safety that they had never enjoyed before. It gave them a confidence which they may have felt in the old days but were not always justified in feeling and (when properly conducted) it guaranteed them early information of trouble, if trouble should unhappily be brewing. Designed as the policy-holder's charter, which it certainly is, the audit is the Names' charter too, and if it had never been adopted the number of underwriting members at Lloyd's would scarcely have risen to its present level.

To appreciate the importance of this change one need only consider the unique position of a Lloyd's Name. When a man becomes an underwriting member and a Name he accepts (as he always has accepted) unlimited liability and stakes everything he has – on what? On the prudence, honour and ability of the man who will be underwriting for him. He himself has no underwriting skill or experience and usually he has at best but a general notion of the kind of risks the agent is going to take on his behalf. He probably has by agreement a right to examine the underwriting books at such times as may suit the agent's convenience, but the right in practice is seldom (if ever) exercised, and if Names did start examining the books in numbers they would learn very little and the result would be chaotic. The annual accounts cannot disclose to an outsider anything more precise than an overall impression of how the business is running; and even an expert cannot read them aright unless the ascertained results are appallingly bad or he is provided with a good deal of information (which the accounts given to the Name do not usually disclose) about the nature of the business the agent is doing. To be properly understood almost every commercial balance sheet needs explanations from inside the business and to that general principle Lloyd's underwriting accounts are not an exception.

Before the institution of the audit a Lloyd's Name had no help at all towards understanding his financial position. He walked by faith, unaided by authority and sometimes as we have seen (though very seldom) the faith was misplaced. Without his knowledge losses might have been piling up. The ship might have been drifting closer and closer to the rocks, while he slept comfortably in his berth; and the first intimation of danger he received might be the crash as she stranded. That danger is removed by an honestly conducted audit, for the audit's first and most important duty is to act as a red light to detect underwriting losses not after but before they have occurred; to put its finger on any weak spot before the weakness spreads; and to check the effects of bad or unlucky underwriting before they develop into failures. The audit is no guarantee for the Name that he will have good results and handsome profits. That has never been claimed for it. But it is a guarantee that when things are going wrong he will know about them. It is an assurance that every year his account will be examined by an expert provided with a mass of information about his underwriting; and once that expert's certificate has been delivered he may be reasonably satisfied that all losses, actual and prospective, are covered by the assets already in his trust fund. If things are bad and the Name cannot get the certificate without drawing a cheque to bring his funds up to the audit level he will naturally be disappointed. But let him be grateful that the demand comes when it does and is not postponed till the required cheque has risen – as before the audit it could rise – to many times its present figure. Of all the expenses that an underwriting member of Lloyd's pays for the privilege of being an underwriter, not one from his own point of view gives better value for money than the auditor's fee.

In 1908 these considerations were not appreciated by the merchants, bankers and shipowners whose ranks supplied Lloyd's with most of its recruits for underwriting membership; and it is probable that many of them regarded the audit not as a pledge of future safety but as an indication of weakness and a warning to keep clear. The necessity for introducing such a safeguard was in itself taken as a red light not a green one; and of those who would normally have become members, many at this time must have changed their minds about the proposition and determined not to risk their fortunes at Lloyd's.

Of these men, who were deterred by their knowledge of what had been happening, there were probably about a hundred; and for about ten years their abstention made an appreciable difference in underwriting member-ship. For some reason not now clear, there had been between 1898 and 1907 a remarkable increase in the number of Lloyd's underwriting members. The total rises in that period from five hundred and thirty-three to seven hundred and ten – a jump of about thirty-three per cent in ten years. Those years had included a bad time for marine underwriting in which many companies, and not a few Lloyd's men, found it impossible to make a profit. They included also the appalling Burnand episode and the blasting judgment of Mr Justice Bigham. There had been much criticism of Lloyd's up and down the City and many misgivings at Lloyd's about its own future. And yet membership rose and went on rising until the audit came to the rescue. From that auspicious moment it began to fall and entrance fees paid by new members dropped by two-thirds.

Membership remained at a low level throughout the First War (in which war risks were generally profitable and produced for many syndicates large incomes) but as soon as the war was over, and the stern difficulties of peace lay ahead, it began to go up again so quickly that it very nearly doubled itself in ten years. The tendency often is for candidates to come forward on stories of underwriting profits made in a past period of prosperity and to be deterred by reports of bad times long after the bad times are over. In fine weather they carry umbrellas to protect themselves from last week's rain, and in bad they leave them at home as a tribute to last month's sunshine.

In fact the year 1909 (when men in the know made up their minds not to become underwriters) was about as good a time as there ever was for a new member to come in. The marine market reached the end of its bad patch in 1908, and from 1909 onwards it had a long series of good years with profits rising very rapidly. There were, of course, exceptions to the general prosperity, as exceptions there always will be, but neither the good underwriter nor the average underwriter had any reason to complain.

But how is it possible to make such a definite statement about a body of men who published no accounts, kept their results to themselves and jealously guarded, man by man, the secrets of their business? We can make the statement because a set of figures has been preserved in Lloyd's files which give us the aggregate premium incomes, the aggregate claims and the aggregate net profits of nineteen representative marine syndicates from the year 1907 to the year 1913. How the underwriting agents were persuaded to part with their most private statistics and why the records were preserved we do not know; but there it is – the only extant collection of underwriting results at Lloyd's to be had at any time between 1688 and 1947. The figures given below are net profits after deduction of all out-goings, including the agents' commission, and they are per syndicate, not per name.

NINETEEN SYNDICATES' AGGREGATE NET PROFIT

|  | Total £ | Average per Syndicate £ |
|---|---|---|
| 1907 | 99,259 | 5,251 |
| 1908 | 55,099 | 2,889 |
| 1909 | 122,903 | 6,468 |
| 1910 | 157,024 | 7,933 |
| 1911 | 212,868 | 11,203 |
| 1912 | 242,708 | 12,773 |
| 1913 | 427,853 | 22,308 |

The syndicates varied greatly, both in the number of their Names and in the size of their business. The lowest premium income recorded by any syndicate was £10,958 on which the profit was £294 and the highest (this from a big syndicate) £550,949 on which the profit was £45,222.

To a serious student of Lloyd's and to anyone contemplating member-ship in the future, those figures should be of interest. They show what an up-and-down affair marine underwriting can be and how difficult it is to forecast results over a long period, or even for a particular year until its account has been opened for twelve or eighteen months. In the doldrums of 1908 no one could possibly have foreseen five prosperous years smiling at him in the immediate future, and in June 1912 very few would have dared to prophesy that that particular year was going to be better than any previous year in his experience. For 1912 was the year of the *Titanic*, and the *Titanic* was one of the heaviest single marine losses ever suffered by the market. One member at least, whose memory goes back a deplorably long way, can recall an experienced underwriter's claim settler saying to him after the tragedy: 'Any hope of making a profit on this year's under-writing has disappeared'. But in fact that year's underwriting was to prove the best he had ever had. In marine underwriting the wise course is not to count a chicken till it is hatched or to start crying over milk till you are certain it has been spilt.

It would be pleasant to connect the remarkable advance in profits between 1909 and 1913 with the audit instituted exactly at the moment when the tide turned, and to attribute the improvement in underwriting figures to greater caution imposed by the thought of judgment day

waiting for a punter at the year's end. It is indeed a fact that several underwriters voluntarily retired in 1908 because they could not make a profit,
and the audit may have had something to do with their decision. But
probably the coincidence of the audit and the return of prosperity was
coincidence only – not cause and effect; and the reason why underwriters
at Lloyd's began to do better in 1909 was not something peculiar to the
place itself but the fact that business people were beginning to do better
all over the country.

In 1907 there had been a big financial crisis in New York – not as big
as the economic blizzard of 1929 but bad enough to cause suffering throughout America, to bring many banks there to ruin and to enforce a sharp
fall in the prices of commodities on both sides of the Atlantic. The United
States were already important enough to affect very closely the economic
climate of Europe and both the booms and the depressions that came to us
usually moved eastwards across the Atlantic. As a result of the trouble in
New York in 1907 our bank rate rose in the autumn from four per cent to
seven per cent; wholesale prices fell; and the *Economist* price index number
dropped from 2,600 to 2,190. Imports and exports both declined; unem-
ployment increased; a large guarantee insurance company failed, and
everybody was conscious that trade was bad and money tight. It is not
surprising that in 1908 the average profit of those nineteen syndicates at
Lloyd's was less than £3,000 and the average profit per name well below
£300.

In 1909 on the other hand the state of trade was improving. America
was getting over her troubles far more quickly than she did twenty-two
years later and confidence began to return. Prices in England rose again and
continued to rise, the index number going up from the 2,190 of 1908 to
over 2,300 in 1913. Our foreign trade was moving upwards and almost
the only trouble from which business at that moment suffered was (as the
business world realised) excessive taxation. A crushing weight of additional taxes was imposed by the famous Lloyd–George budget of 1909 – a
burden recognized by experts as reaching, if not passing, the limit of the
country's taxable capacity. Income tax rose from 1s. to 1s. 2d. in the £
and a new imposition (christened Super Tax) swallowed another sixpence
in the £ on part of all personal income of more than £5,000 a year. The
consequence was that a man with an unearned income of £20,000 a year
would pay in taxes nearly £1,800 per annum and be left after taxation
with only ninety per cent of his gross income for his own use. At that
time a rearmament campaign was in progress and a sense of patriotism

helped men to bear the all but intolerable burden; but it was recognized that such penal taxation could not continue permanently without draining the national resources and reducing Britain to the level of a second-class power. Despite it all, however, prosperity persisted and it was on the flood of that general prosperity that marine underwriters recovered theirs.

If the underwriting membership varied between six hundred and seven hundred during their times of alternating trouble and prosperity what was the amount of business to be divided between the underwriters? In 1908 it was estimated that the marine premium income was six million pounds which would supply an average premium per underwriter of about £8,400. By 1913, thanks to information provided by the audit, we know the exact premium income and have moved from guesswork to knowledge. The aggregate marine income in 1913 was £8,860,992 and as under-writing membership had declined to six hundred and twenty-one, the average premium income per underwriter was over £14,000 a year. Being an underwriter was now a bigger and better business than it had been five years before. The companies were going ahead too. In 1908 ten companies between them had an aggregate loss on their marine business of more than £14,000; but by 1910 they were making a profit, and their premium income like that of Lloyd's underwriters was moving upwards. The total of the companies' marine premium income was prob-ably about three and a quarter million pounds in 1908 and perhaps four million, two hundred thousand pounds in 1913. If those estimates are correct Lloyd's at that time was doing between a half and two-thirds of all the marine insurance effected by British underwriters – companies and Lloyd's – at home and abroad.

.    .    .    .    .    .

The non-marine market at Lloyd's was still much smaller than the marine and its income was probably not more than £2,500,000 a year. But its future was assured and its development certain. For conditions were all in its favour and if the non-marine underwriters had selected their own time for launching out in competition with the companies they could not have picked a happier moment. For this was the period in which accident insurance was born and started out on a career that was to produce a revolution in the insurance industry. In that revolution Lloyd's played a very active part. But for a moment let us forget Lloyd's and fix our attention on the companies.

At the beginning of this century most of the companies confined them-selves practically if not entirely to life and fire, and the few who specialized in accident business did nothing in either fire or life. But fresh legislation (notably the Workmen's Compensation Act) suddenly opened up the field of accident insurance; and the fire offices, spurred on perhaps by the impending Assurance Companies Act, discarded their old conservative tradition and threw an invading force into the new territory. Simultaneously by way of retaliation the accident companies attacked the citadel of the fire offices. An article on insurance published in a financial paper in the early months of 1909 remarked that in that year most of the fire companies' reports for the first time in their history contained an accident account; and several of the accident companies' reports for the first time contained a fire account. The amount of premium derived from accident business was not large. It was got mainly from Employers' Liability and Personal Injuries, and even in 1911 the total of the companies' accident premiums was only a little more than five million pounds. What premiums were contributed by motor insurance is not known but it cannot have been large, and the accident revenue of all the companies put together can scarcely have amounted in 1908 to five millions – less than a quarter of the fire premiums then reported by the tariff offices.

Now turn to 1951. In that year, although the statutory liability of employers had in this country been taken over by the Government and only the common law liability remained for the open market, the accident departments produced for the companies established in Great Britain a premium income of £96,000,000. Motor premiums (which are kept separate) amounted to £102,000,000 and the combined income of the companies' accident departments reached a figure of £199,000,000.

Thus in forty years the accident managers had added some one hundred and ninety millions to the companies' revenue and had outstripped the income of their colleagues of the fire department by about thirty-one millions. For some of this remarkable increase Acts of Parliament here and legislation abroad were responsible. Workmen's Compensation Acts had thrown on to employers a liability that few of them cared to carry themselves, and industrial companies turned in thousands to underwriters and companies who would bear the risks for them. The Road Traffic Acts, which made third-party insurance for motorists compulsory, had no very great immediate effect on the volume of premiums. But it made some difference and by advertising the importance of third-party cover probably helped to make the public more sensitive to the value of insurance in other departments than fire and life.

The impact of legislation on the business of accident insurance was clearly very powerful. But it may be suggested that more important even than the Workmen's Compensation and the Road Traffic Acts was a change of climate in the Law Courts themselves, a difference in the mental attitude of judges. The old doctrine that he who keeps a tiger is liable for the damage his tiger does was extended by quick degrees until the onus of proof seemed almost to have been shifted off the plaintiff's shoulders and on to the defendant's. Instead of the injured man having to prove negligence on the part of the tortfeasor it almost looked at times as though the defendant had to show proof that he had not been negligent. The best-known illustration of this shift in judicial bias – if the word bias may be used without contempt of court – was the doctrine of common employment.

Fifty years ago that doctrine almost completely protected an employer from claims for injury done by one man to another in same employ. And it was carried to extreme lengths. A mineworker was incapacitated in a train accident on his way home from work. The accident was admittedly due to the negligence of the train's driver; but there was held to be no liability on the railway because mine and railway were both owned by the same company. It was harsh treatment arising out of harsh law and the law was abolished in 1948. But years before it was abolished it had been growing less and less important. The judges by making subtle distinctions between the reported cases and the cases they were themselves trying, had gone far to whittle the doctrine away. In sympathy with the more generous treatment of workmen that had grown up since they themselves addressed the court as advocates, they reduced the defence of common employment to less than half its former strength.

As time passed that change of atmosphere affected the courts over the whole sphere of tort and negligence, and as business men appreciated the change their thoughts naturally veered to fresh kinds of insurance. That in turn affected the minds of juries who would assume in a case of tort that the nominal defendant was not the real defendant. They took for granted that damages, if awarded, would be paid by a wealthy insurance company or an anonymous Lloyd's underwriter, who could afford the loss better than the unfortunate plaintiff. So they allowed their sympathy with an injured man to colour their view of the accident, the tort, the liability and the consequences in human suffering.

The effect of this attitude has extended far beyond the bounds of commerce and touched even professional men. Amongst them the doctors are specially vulnerable, and it is said that one of the reasons for the very high cost of our National Health Service is the modern fashion of patients suing surgeons and physicians for negligence whenever they are disappointed with the result of their treatment. The chain of cause and effect is curious. Patients of this mentality – which seems to spread and become more common every year – will always hold their doctor liable for continued bad health; and many of them, either spontaneously or at the prompting of a solicitor, are quick to accuse him of carelessness in his diagnosis – the favourite plea being that no X-ray photo has been taken. The doctors now appreciate this danger and send case after case to the X-ray room, not because they hope for guidance from the photograph but to be able to say in court 'The man was sent to be X-rayed'. The result is that thousands of unnecessary photographs are taken every week of the year. Expensive X-ray departments are overworked, and Britain instead of exporting films as she did before the war, now uses all she can make herself and imports further supplies from Belgium. Such is the effect of a plaintiff's market in the administration of justice.

The doctors, who have their own Defence Union, do not usually bring their risks to the ordinary insurance market, but most business and professional men do. Factory owners, building contractors, petroleum companies, engineers, accountants, solicitors, bankers, stockbrokers, newspaper proprietors, hotels, restaurants, theatres, schools, colleges, and householders all come to Lloyd's or to companies for third-party cover. For most of them special types of policy have been drafted and a substantial part of the accident premium income is derived from this public liability in one form or another. At the beginning of the century the business scarcely existed and almost the whole structure has been built up in fifty years. The scope of insurance has been widened and changed out of recognition; new departments have been created and a vast new service provided on which the social revolution both here and abroad has in part depended. In less than the lifetime of one man, accident insurance has done what marine and fire took centuries to achieve.

How much of the new accident business is concerned directly with public liability it is impossible to say. Many policies cover both material damage and the third-party risk in one document and the main stream is fed by a number of tributaries springing from the most various and miscellaneous sources. For accident insurance is essentially a miscellaneous affair, the product of many different experiments in underwriting. Each experiment is made by some pioneer ready to back his judgment on a risk that has no history behind it. He quotes premiums with no statistics to justify them, guesses where he cannot reason, believes where he cannot see.

When the first motor-car risk was shown the rate quoted and paid can have been nothing more than a shot in the dark. When Heath offered to write private furniture against burglary at 2s. 6d. per cent he may have done some mental arithmetic first but it must have been pretty sketchy. When he began on Workmen's Compensation he is said to have known something about results in Germany, but they misled him and his rates proved too low for this country. When he quoted a rate for his first blanket policy for bankers, or his one-half per cent for private jewellery, he must have been trusting to his instinct and his instinct alone. Fanciful as the simile may seem the early underwriters can be compared to researchers at work in a laboratory, trying everything but never knowing whether a new line of enquiry will be a cul-de-sac or lead them to a treasure-trove.

It is important to emphasize this feature of business in the last fifty years because it has much to do with the recent success of Lloyd's. In an age of adventure there is no insurer so well placed as the individual underwriter. To realise that fact one needs only to contrast the position of an under-writer with that of his opposite number in charge of a company's depart-ment. The manager is set under authority; the assistant general managers are above him; a general manager is above them; and a board of directors is over all. Every man of them must account for his mistakes. If the departmental manager tries an experiment and it goes wrong he must explain to the higher powers why he ran the risk and be ready to meet their objections, answer their criticisms and perhaps endure their censure. In most cases he will find that the minds of the higher powers have a conservative tinge. They have to remember their next profit and loss account and their annual report to the shareholders; and it is no criticism of them to say that they may tend to be shy of innovations and cautious in trying fresh experiments. They are admirably placed for managing a going concern and developing it along recognized lines, but they are not in so good a position to chance their luck, to walk by faith and to encourage practical experiments at the risk of the company's shareholders. The work they have done in developing their world-wide connections has been of the greatest value to this country. That is surely too obvious to need saying. But it is also true that they are less happily constituted for the more adventurous side of insurance life.

The position of a Lloyd's underwriter is very different. He has not (as a company manager has) a world-wide efficient machinery behind him and his daily intake of premiums depends entirely on the brokers who come to his box. No brokers, no business. But on the other hand he is usually his own master. He has his Names to consider and if he is persistently unsuccessful he will be in danger of losing them. But they cannot command him in his daily work. They have given him freedom to write what he likes within very wide limits, and none of them will know what he is doing – how he selects his risks, what lines of business are profitable and what are unsatisfactory. Still less have they the right to dictate. In the 1930's a military gentleman, already a non-marine name, thought of joining a marine syndicate. But for some reason he had grave doubts about the seaworthiness of a certain famous liner. He approached one or two marine underwriters asking if they would write for him, but stipulating that he should not be given a line on that particular vessel. The answer from each underwriter was 'Either you trust me or you don't. If you join my syndicate you must give me complete freedom of judgment'. That is indeed the only condition on which a Lloyd's underwriting agent can accept Names. He must be untrammelled and he must accept full responsibility. There can be no back-seat driving and if things go wrong there must be no one but himself to take the blame. If the Names are not satisfied with his results they can go, but while the results are in the making they must leave the man at the wheel to steer his own course.

The relationship between Name and underwriter involves an act of faith that must be almost unique in the commercial world. But it is essential to the system of individual underwriting and it lies at the root of Lloyd's success. It is particularly useful in a period of growth and new enterprise, when the public are conscious of new risks and new kinds of insurance that they would like to take out. It provides a market of two or three hundred experts or quasi-experts all on the look-out for new business, all masters in their own houses, all able to make a quick decision and give an answer on the spot, all – if they are good underwriters – of receptive minds. And that brings us again to Cuthbert Heath. Of the many services that he did to Lloyd's perhaps the greatest is the tradition that he established and bequeathed to the non-marine market – the tradition of the open mind. Never turn a risk down for the sake of turning it down. Never say 'Is there any reason why I should write it?' but 'Is there any reason why I should not write it?' If there are good reasons against writing it, refuse it; but weigh them carefully and don't reckon as an objection the fact that you have never seen a risk of that kind before. Every serious new enquiry indicates an unsatisfied need and as underwriters we should try to meet it. It was exactly the state of mind needed in the insurance world between

1908 and 1930. Combine it with the freedom of action that a Lloyd's underwriter enjoys and you have the ideal equipment for the period.

Those early days of the modern non-marine market were indeed a great time. They were the Elizabethan age of Lloyd's underwriting, full of go and enterprise and adventure, with risks hitherto unthought of coming almost weekly to a market that was waiting for them. Brokers were scouring the world to find new business, raking it in from the Americas, from the Far East, from Australia, from South Africa and from Europe, backed by the prestige of Lloyd's as 'a market where you can insure anything'. Business was constantly on the increase and in eight years the non-marine premium income rose by nearly three hundred per cent. And most of the new income was acquired by new types of policy – some fire, some accident. The majority of them originated at Lloyd's, shaped at an underwriter's box in discussion between the underwriter and an importunate broker.

No one with a trace of imagination can follow in detail the expanding history of Lloyd's without feeling sometimes that a guardian angel of exceptional ability was assigned to it at its birth. In many of the troubles that Lloyd's from time to time got into and escaped from, one is conscious of the angel working at a distance. But now and again he hovers so close that one can hear the beating of his wings. And never did he come so close as in the years between 1908 and 1914. The combination of circumstance then was from the Lloyd's point of view almost perfect. The establishment of a vigorous non-marine market, the advent of new legislation and the passing of the Assurance Companies Act of 1909, the throng of new risks calling for the very service that Lloyd's was best qualified to give, and the foundation in the nick of time of Lloyd's audit conspired together to produce exactly the conditions that a benevolent omniscient far-seeing observer would have demanded for the Society.

And the crowning mercy was its audit. If there had been no audit in being at the start of 1909 Lloyd's would not have secured the treatment that it got in the Insurance Companies Act of that year. If the audit had not worked efficiently it could not have killed the suspicion of Lloyd's security that had been creeping over the commercial world after the scandals of 1903 and 1908.

If the audit had not been an exacting test it might not have kept in bounds the enthusiasm of the young non-marine market or enforced the caution that was necessary for the success of its experiments. The standard objections to Lloyd's non-marine underwriters, put forward by their rivals, all pivoted on this one argument that Lloyd's men were irresponsible amateurs dabbling in business they did not understand, without experience and without security to offer to the insuring public. And to all these arguments the audit was the answer. No security? The audit, combined with the premium trust deeds, the deposits and the guarantees, is the finest possible security. Irresponsible underwriters? The audit is the strongest check on irresponsible underwriting ever invented. So long as they submit themselves to a properly conducted audit every year Lloyd's under-writers can go on writing their new-fangled risks and giving the public the service that it wants.

.     .     .     .     .     .

Another piece of good fortune was the fact that America, just at the moment when these changes were taking place at Lloyd's, was ready to send business to the underwriters in considerable quantities, and under-writers were able to give America just the kind of cover that she needed. From 1900 till the crisis of 1907 the United States enjoyed a great burst of prosperity, opening new industries, reorganizing old ones, producing millionaires by the dozen and absorbing in one year alone more than a million and a quarter immigrants from Europe. The country's capital at that time must have been stretched near to breaking point. Her demand for insurance exceeded the capacity of her own companies and she had for some time been relying on foreign insurers to fill the gap.

Even in the 1890's (which were not an outstandingly prosperous period) America had turned to Lloyd's non-marine market with the crumbs that fell from her overloaded table. A Lloyd's broker, touring the United States in 1899, secured in a few months enough business to give him £1,000 a year in commission; and on the large department stores growing up in the American cities underwriters could get all the fire risk they wanted at rates of two and two and a half per cent per annum. Of necessity the business population of America was insurance-minded. The rewards of success in business were so great and the cost of failure so heavy that men looked round for insurance far more readily than their fellows in the more settled countries of the Old World. And if Lloyd's underwriters could provide policies of the kind that America wanted, America was ready to send her orders in profusion. It was just the place for the young non-marine market to sell its wares, and the new types of policy that had been thought out for British merchants began to be exported to the United States, while others which would have been unsaleable in Europe but were suited to America, were thought out for American consumption.

Orders came quickly and within a few years of Heath's first adventure in fire insurance the name of Lloyd's as a market for fire risks was so well known in America that an active bootlegging business sprang up there based on the reputation its policies had already gained. One American after another who had no connection with the real Lloyd's assumed the name as his trading sign and secured business from Americans who were probably misled into the idea that they were insuring with Lloyd's of London. The thing became a minor scandal, and in 1892 the State of New York passed a new law which would make it difficult for companies to practice this particular deception. On the day before the law came into force thirty different firms and companies in a single afternoon registered themselves in New York under the name of Lloyd's. It was a queer racket for many of the applicants had no intention of trading themselves but went straight out of the Registrar's office to hawk their so-called charters round the city, looking for the highest bidder to buy the right of trading under a deceptive alias.

It is a remarkable fact that Lloyd's had acquired so quickly a reputation strong enough to make this illicit trading worth while, and it is equally remarkable that with so many spurious Lloyd's in the market the real Lloyd's policies still remained in circulation. As bad money drives out good, so the bad policies carrying Lloyd's name might have been expected to drive out the genuine article. But they did not and the two trades, legitimate and illegitimate, went on side by side for years. In 1910 the New York Insurance Department said that there were still thirty-seven institutions trading under the name in the State of New York alone, and one fraudulent Anglo-American concern, which circulated imitation Lloyd's policies in America, directed its operations from an office in Queen Victoria Street, London. Its turnover must have been substantial for the Committee of Lloyd's actually advertised in *The Times* a disclaimer warning the public against its faked documents, and the advertisement was enforced by a leading article in *The Times Financial Supplement*. The episode at least emphasizes the good name of Lloyd's and the usefulness of the young non-marine market to the American public.

Jewellers and diamond merchants insured their stocks with Lloyd's policies; bankers covered their securities and their liabilities with blanket policies; millionaires insured against damage done to the pictures which Joseph Duveen was so busy selling to them; millionaires' wives covered their pearls and diamonds and it was once said maliciously that in New York there was not one lady of easy virtue whose sin-won jewellery was

At the Third Royal Exchange in 1924, four years before the move to Leadenhall Street; the Caller in the Rostrum, and the *Lutine* Bell.

not covered by some syndicate at Lloyd's. In course of time film producers insured against the illness of their stars which might bring the shooting of an expensive picture to a dead end; and the stars themselves insured against personal injury and the consequent fall in the screen value of a handsome face or an attractive pair of legs. But perhaps the queerest of these extraneous risks was the insurance of saloon keepers' liability which later on produced a substantial volume of premiums.

In some States of the Union laws were passed to protect the public against physical injury done by drunken men to innocent third parties; and as the drunks would usually be men of straw, unable to pay damages, the liability was thrown back on to the owner of the saloon in which the man had got drunk. If an American citizen drank himself into a condition of violence and assaulted a fellow-citizen on the sidewalk, the police or the injured party would trace his movements and find the saloon at which he had been drinking. If they found it and could prove the fact, then an action would lie against the saloon keeper who would be liable for the injury that his drunken customer had inflicted. Saloon keepers, faced with this new liability, sent the risks via American brokers to Lloyd's and there established a market in which it could be insured.

Heaven knows how the underwriters rated the first risk of this sort that came to them; but rate it they did and the business began to flow. But underwriters were too innocent and trustful, too little alive to the wickedness of human nature. Before long they discovered that they were standing free drinks plus a bonus to the wide boys of some American States. The system that had grown up was simple. Citizen A would offer Citizen B enough cash to drink himself into a state of semi-drunkenness on the understanding that Citizen B as he emerged from the saloon would assault Citizen A with just enough force to justify a claim on the saloon keeper, who was known to be insured. To the right type of mind the prospect of unlimited drink, with a profit commission thrown in, was naturally attractive. On the other hand a minor or simulated physical injury was a small price for the victim of the assault to pay for the certainty of substantial cash damages. But one would like to know the percentage split when the spoils were finally divided between the tortfeasor, the tort receiver and the saloon keeper. The story is a good example of how legislation conceived on prudent lines will stimulate business. But while the racket lasted the saloon keepers' liability policy was not the most profitable section of underwriters' accounts.

·   ·   ·   ·   ·   ·   ·

P

American fire business, beginning with lines placed at Lloyd's by owners of large buildings, moved on to reinsurance. And the greater part of the dollar fire premium income that now comes to Lloyd's from America is placed for the account of American insurance companies limiting their liability by laying off their risks in London. Reinsurance is an old department of fire insurance and goes back beyond the beginning of the modern non-marine market at Lloyd's. But underwriters with their exploring minds have been able to make great changes in the mechanics of reinsurance and have provided newer and less cumbersome types of policy than the old schemes which satisfied fire managers fifty years ago. As many of the American non-marine connections of Lloyd's underwriters have long been intimately connected with reinsurance, a brief reference to the history of this specialized trade may be appropriate at this point.

The original form of fire reinsurance was the facultative policy[1] which covered a particular risk that a company's fire manager wanted to be rid of either in whole or in part. Looking back on its early forms, one must admit that the managers of those days succeeded in making a very elaborate business of what was really a simple transaction. The documents that passed between a ceding company and its reinsurer before the deal was finished read less like an ordinary business correspondence than an exchange of diplomatic notes between two high-contracting parties preparing an international treaty. First, the ceding company would send out a slip to the accepting company for its consideration. The slip if accepted would be initialled by the reinsuring company and once that was done cover (it would seem) had been given. But the slip would be followed up by a formal written request from the ceding to the reinsuring company for a guarantee. The reinsuring company, though it had already initialled the slip, would send a formal reply with what was called a take-note signifying its acceptance of the proposal. The ceding company, having received the take-note and so satisfied itself (1) that the slip had not been initialled by mistake, and (2) that the ceding company had not changed its mind, would make out copies of the provisional policy or detailed specifications of the risk and send one to each of the reinsurance companies. Then, and not till then, the reinsurance policies were written and issued and the transaction was complete.

Altogether it was a strangely intricate procedure and in course of time it was largely superseded by what was known as the surplus treaty. This

[1] See C. E. Golding: *The Law and Practice of Reinsurance*. A short authoritative and admirable book.

method was more convenient than the facultative cover but it still involved a prodigious amount of clerical work. The basis of a surplus treaty was that the ceding company could retain whatever amount it thought fit on any risks that it had written and place the balance up to a certain limit in stated proportions between its reinsurers. The reinsurers would be bound to accept the lines given them in accordance with the treaty and as soon as the ceding company had decided on the amount of its retention on any particular business, and the retention had been noted in the appropriate register, all the reinsurers were automatically on risk. But they all wanted to know just what risk they had been given. So the ceding company at regular intervals sent an elaborate bordereau to every company on its treaty and the reinsuring companies were supposed to note and enter all the lines on the bordereaux in their own books.

The truth may be that the bordereaux were never conned over as they were supposed to be, that between two honourable parties the precaution never had been necessary and that the system was continued only because man is a conservative animal, who will go on doing a lot of superfluous things for no better reason than that they always have been done. And in this country it took a world-wide war to upset the tradition of the bordereau.

During the war with labour scarce and thousands of new urgent problems to be solved, office managers looked round for chances to economise in clerical work. Underwriters began to doubt the need for the elaborate statistical systems they had always maintained, which had in peacetime been the pride of their hearts. On the altar of economy many underwriting statistics were sacrificed for the duration of the war, and underwriters, finding that their business did just as well without them, realised that they might have been discarded without ill effects any time in the last twenty years. The company fire managers, giving up their elaborate reinsurance bordereaux, made the same discovery and came very close to abolishing them altogether. It used to be said by John Bright that the only good thing war did was to teach people geography. But we know now that modern war teaches us a good deal more. It teaches us what a lot of things we can do without and be all the better for the lack of them. Amongst these things are reinsurance bordereaux.

Under these conditions a new type of reinsurance cover (originated at Lloyd's before the war) was widely adopted. It may be remembered that when Cuthbert Heath was re-establishing the fire market at Lloyd's his early steps pointed westward to America. He wrote in the 1880's the first

Lloyd's reinsurance on American risks for an English company doing business in the States, and doubtless gained the reputation there for being helpful in reinsurance matters. Years later – soon after the San Francisco earthquake – he was approached by the Hartford Company of America, which was concerned to limit the consequences of another catastrophe in the future. It did not want from Heath the old-fashioned type of treaty. It wanted something simpler, something that would involve no great amount of clerical work, something that would need no bordereaux or elaborate monthly accounts, but would nevertheless protect it from the effects of a single great conflagration. Could Heath think of anything? He could. He devised an excess loss reinsurance – an insurance that would pay no regard to ordinary losses and operate only when the ceding company had to pay unusually heavy claims arising from a single fire. It would concern itself with big fires that cost a lot of money but, unlike the old bordereau reinsurance, it would not bother about small ones. The figure at which the reinsurers would begin to pay was fixed in the treaty and so was the maximum of their liability in respect of any one fire, but between these two points the ceding company was completely reinsured and the brunt of any disastrous fire would be borne by the Lloyd's underwriters.

The placing of that first surplus reinsurance, like the placing of the first burglary insurance and the first jewellers' block policy, is an illustration of Heath's readiness to meet people on their own ground and try to give them what they themselves wanted in the light of their own experience. The old-fashioned insurer had (to use his own language) 'granted' insurances – a word that suggests a benevolent despot deciding what his subjects ought to want and then doling it out to them. Heath worked the other way. He first found out what his clients thought they needed and then did his best to supply it. And it was by doing that that he set Lloyd's going as a big non-marine market. It was by doing that that he started a revolution in reinsurance.

Some years after that first successful policy for the Hartford Company, an American expert in the insurance of cotton, named Carpenter, thought of another new type of insurance that he fancied might suit his own business; and he brought the idea to Lloyd's as a place where experiments in insurance were carried out. His idea was that every year's fire premium should be based on the average of the last three years' results – on the actual cost of paying for the fire damage plus a loading for expenses and profit. The assured would enter into a seven-year or a five-year contract and in each of the years the premium would be adjusted to the burning cost of the last three. That is how the 'burning cost' system came into existence.

It may seem paradoxical that individual underwriters in London should cover the catastrophe risk for great American fire and accident offices; but it is a service that they are well fitted to give – a service that they understand thoroughly and they watch it with a care born of long experience. It has been of value both to the companies and to Lloyd's and it has been partly responsible for a curious link inside Lloyd's between the marine and the non-marine market. Every marine underwriter has the right to do a certain amount of non-marine business and it has been worth while for many of them to write reinsurances of the liability of their non-marine colleagues. As the non-marine men at Lloyd's write excess loss liability for companies, so the marine men in turn write excess loss policies for the non-marine underwriters; and if a very large fire or accident loss hits the Lloyd's market, part of it filters along the channel of these internal reinsurance treaties to the marine boxes. When hurricanes, escaping from their normal track in 1950 and 1954, swept the east coast of the United States and laid flat buildings and tens of thousands of television aerials the loss ran into many millions of dollars. Much of it fell on Lloyd's non-marine market via the companies' excess loss reinsurance treaties and much of the loss was passed on by the non-marine underwriters to the marine syndicates under their excess treaties. That is a good example of the advantage of having a market not too rigidly boxed into watertight compartments.

# 12

## LLOYD'S IN TWO WORLD WARS

*War risks traditionally covered by marine policies – Changed conditions disturb underwriters – War crises – Suggestion from insurance company declined – Lloyd's Underwriters adopt f.c. & s. clause – Government Committee – Restlessness among Underwriters – Disturbing situation – Another Government Committee – Government decides to provide cover in 1914 war – Weaknesses in Government's original scheme – Air damage insurance in 1914 – 1938 and 1939 – Government scheme – Partial monopoly – War risks on land – The Dixey agreement to exclude – Its wisdom and value – Government schemes – Dollar trust funds – A century's retrospect – Shipping news in wartime – Pulbrook's agreement with American authorities – Its working success*

---

THE TRADITIONAL FORM of marine policy names fifteen different perils and adventures that are borne and taken upon them by underwriters. And of these fifteen, eleven relate to war, piracy, and violence on the high seas. Those eleven disasters make an impressive and rather fascinating list, and the care with which they are enumerated in detail indicates the importance that eighteenth-century merchants and underwriters attached both in peace and war to the possibility of capture at sea. Of all the protection provided by the policies, the cover against violence was probably the most highly valued, and to give that cover was perhaps regarded as an underwriter's primary duty. For the most part underwriters did well enough out of the risk. Now and again, as in the disaster of 1780 and the Russian seizures of 1800, they took an unpleasant tumble; but on the whole, with all its hazards, war had not treated Lloyd's unkindly. The war risks of the Napoleonic Wars were largely responsible for the Society's pre-eminence at the beginning of the nineteenth century, but by the end of the century the Napoleonic Wars were eighty-five years away, and in the interval there had been no war in which Britain's naval supremacy had been challenged. Neither the strength of our national forces nor the capacity of underwriters had been tested by experience.

For almost the whole of the nineteenth century the traditions in favour of writing war risks remained at Lloyd's unbroken. It was still thought to be at once the duty and the advantage of a marine underwriter to cover war as willingly as he covered collision, fire, or stranding. But in the 1890's, when the Napoleonic wars had receded into schoolbook history, there were signs at Lloyd's and in the companies that the tradition was wearing a little thin – signs of some uneasiness about what the next war at sea would be like, and searching of hearts as to how far the ordinary machinery of insurance would stand the strain of a modern war. There were some obvious reasons for that apprehension. In 1893 the French Navy launched its first submarine and the idea of a hidden underwater ship, against which there was no known protection, hit the British imagination hard. Conan Doyle about that time wrote a successful short story in which he looked forward to the effect of a single enemy sub-marine stationed at the mouth of the Thames, picking off merchantmen one by one as they moved in and out the river; and it seemed then that his picture might be something more than the fantasy of a professional story-teller. The propelled torpedo, invented in 1862, had seldom been used in action but when it had been used its destructive powers were unmistakable, and naval theorists realized that this new weapon might do almost as much to change sea strategy as the steam engine itself. In the matter of war risks underwriters began to tell each other what Adam told Eve as they left the Garden of Eden, 'my dear we are living in an age of transition'.

And as the weapons of attack were growing in power so the objects at which they might be aimed were growing in value. In Napoleon's day it was exceptional for the value of a merchant ship and her cargo combined to exceed fifty thousand pounds, but in 1900 a liner and her cargo could easily be worth three-quarters of a million, and if part of the cargo was specie they could exceed that total by hundreds of thousands of pounds. The market was larger no doubt than it had been in Napoleon's day but was it large enough to absorb such amounts as these without imposing dangerous lines both on the syndicates at Lloyd's and on the marine companies?

While thoughts such as these were passing through the minds of under-writers, two incidents occurred that brought the market face to face with these problems in their immediate form. At that time the Royal Navy was the largest naval force in the world. Its two nearest rivals were the navies of France and the United States. In a period of ten years between 1890 and 1900 we were at different times on the edge of war with both these countries, and British people learnt afresh how easily some remote

unexpected trivial incident could drag us into a life-and-death struggle for
our foreign trade.

The trouble with America came in 1895 through a petty frontier
squabble between Venezuela and British Guiana – two places that most
Englishmen could not without some guidance have pointed out in an
atlas of the world. But the squabble touched British prestige and fired
American pride. And so near did we come to war with the United States
that President Cleveland actually sent a message to Congress which in
itself was almost an ultimatum to Great Britain. Three years later came
the crisis with France when a French expedition to Fashoda challenged
British claims to the Sudan. Until that happened not one Briton in a
hundred thousand had heard of Fashoda, and except to historians and to
the men and women who were boys and girls in 1898, the name can mean
very little today. But in 1898 in the name of Fashoda the two navies,
French and British, were ready to spring at each other's throats and for
some time it was a toss-up whether they would be unleashed or not. So
within three years the British Fleet was within a touch of fighting the two
foreign navies which twenty years later – when the great naval war did
break out – were to be their comrades-in-arms.

Of the nervousness that underwriters were beginning to feel about the
possibility of a modern sea war, we come across the first recorded evidence
(in an unexpected place) a few months after the danger of war with the
United States had disappeared. At the beginning of 1896 the London
Assurance wrote to the Committee of Lloyd's suggesting that the marine
insurance market's traditional attitude to war risks should be changed;
that a clause excluding them should be inserted in marine policies, companies' as well as at Lloyd's; and that the Committee of Lloyd's should
propose the reform to their members with the authority of the Committee
behind it. Whether that letter represented only the views of a single underwriter or was a kite flown on behalf of all the companies is not clear; but
whatever its origin it had a very cold reception from the Committee. In
those days the feeling of Lloyd's underwriters towards the marine companies was not one of brotherly love. Any letter coming from a company
was probably suspect even before its envelope was opened, and in this
case the Committee simply told the London Assurance that in such a
matter they could not bind the members of Lloyd's, nor would they consent to call a General Meeting for the consideration of the idea.

That looked final enough, but two and a half years later, when the
trouble with France was blowing up, the Committee made a *volte-face* and

did what they had refused to do when the London Assurance asked them. They called a meeting of members to ballot on a resolution that in future in all Lloyd's policies the risk of war should be excluded unless a special agreement had been reached that it should be covered. The meeting was far from being unanimous and there was considerable opposition. But the resolution was carried by a working majority and has never been rescinded. For the last fifty years all marine policies at Lloyd's have, despite the eleven types of violence mentioned in the body of the wording, been free of capture, seizure, and detention, unless the F.C. and S. clause has been specifically deleted. The resolution of 1898 was in effect a decree of divorce between war and marine. By special agreement, which must be made clear on the slip, the two risks may be and constantly are brought together temporarily on one policy, but the old lasting bond between them has been broken. The twain have not been one flesh since the General Meeting of Lloyd's on 15th June 1898.

The adequacy of the market which would have to insure our seaborne traffic in case of naval war was clearly a matter of national interest. And five years after the decision of 1898 the British Government, with one eye on a still hostile France and the other on the new German Fleet, appointed a Committee to consider whether merchants and shipowners had in the past found it difficult to cover against war and whether they were likely to do so in the future. That Committee – known as the Austen Chamberlain Committee – went into great detail and Hozier supplied it with a statement showing the exact position of all British ships on a given day in 1903. It is perhaps surprising, in view of the facts which must have been given them, that the members of the Committee reported as they did. They decided that private enterprise would be able to carry the burden of the next war without help from the Treasury or the Board of Trade. That is surprising both because of the international situation in 1903 and because of the restlessness of the marine underwriters, on whose willingness to write war risks the sufficiency of the market depended. If in 1904 Britain had slipped into war with a great naval power, it would have been (as we can see now) extremely doubtful whether Lloyd's underwriters and the companies between them could have supplied from the word 'go' an adequate market that would have lasted through thick and thin to the war's end.

In the first ten years of this century the outlook did not improve. Underwriters lost a good deal of money on war risks in the Russo-Japanese War and the success of the Japanese Fleet was due so much to the use of the torpedo that the importance of this weapon was put beyond dispute. The German Navy grew everyday more powerful and feeling between ourselves and Germany was growing bitter. The insurance of hulls against war risks had practically deserted the open market and gone over to mutual clubs, which supplied a temporary and very inadequate cover against the King's enemies for a short period after the outbreak of war. Some of the marine companies declared openly that they would not give war cover on cargoes except to their regular clients, and a number of underwriters at Lloyd's were threatening to refuse war business, saying that if there were no other reason against it they would be deterred by the difficulty of selling securities at a moment of crisis to supply themselves with cash for the payment of heavy war losses. In 1913 only about two-thirds of British tonnage was insured against war with the clubs; not more than ten per cent of the cargoes in British bottoms were covered against war; and if a sudden emergency arose it was likely that a large proportion of our shipping would be paralysed, while the sudden rush of cargo coming to be insured would choke the open market. No one could say with any confidence that either the shipowners or the merchants, when war broke out, would get the insurance they needed at rates that the nation could afford to pay. Then what would happen to our vital overseas trade either at the first impact of war or in the black patches of ill-fortune that would be certain to come before the war was over?

The prospect was so disturbing to the Government that in 1913 – they had left things pretty late – they appointed the Huth Jackson Committee to reconsider the problem on which its predecessor of 1903 had been so optimistically confident. And the Huth Jackson Committee came to a different conclusion. It was a small efficient body including Raymond Beck, then a member of the Committee of Lloyd's and destined to be its Chairman in two years of the First World War. On the evidence given to it, the Committee decided that the mutual clubs left to themselves could not be relied on to provide British hulls with war cover, and that immediately a war in which Britain was a belligerent broke out the Government should assume eighty per cent of the risk, even on ships which at that moment were in the middle of a voyage. Thereafter, voyage by voyage, by a simple reinsurance arrangement, the risks should be divided between the Treasury and the clubs in the proportion of eighty to twenty, and the fixing of rates and the settlement of claims should both be controlled by Government regulations. The business, in fact, would be managed by a partnership between the clubs and the Government. And the Government would be the senior partner.

The insurance of cargoes was a more complicated problem and it called for a more direct interference by the Government. The Huth Jackson Committee decided that immediately after the declaration of war the Government ought to open a State Insurance Office which would issue direct policies to merchants voyage by voyage. Only cargoes in British bottoms would be insured and the rates charged by the Government at any given moment should be the same for all voyages, whether more or less hazardous. The Government should claim no monopoly for war insurance and underwriters at Lloyd's and in the Companies should be at liberty to write what they liked at whatever rate they liked; to compete with the Government office if they chose to do so, or (if they preferred it) to pass the business and let the whole burden be carried by the Government. The scheme was adopted by the Government and came into force on 5th August 1914.

As the Government offered a uniform rate for all voyages, the advantages given by the scheme to Companies and Lloyd's underwriters are obvious. As there was to be only a single rate, some voyages must be rated by the Government much too high and some much too low. Even if the Mediterranean was full of enemy submarines, the Government would charge the same for a voyage from Bristol to Bordeaux as from Hull to Greece; and naturally all the cargo for Bordeaux would be insured at Lloyd's or the Companies, while everything sent to Greece would go to the Government and be borne by the British taxpayer. From the taxpayer's point of view it was a very bad arrangement and it seems at first sight astonishing that a scheme so inequitable should have been either proposed by the Huth Jackson Committee or accepted by His Majesty's Government. Why was it that both of them fell for it? The explanation is given in the Huth Jackson Report which recognized the anomaly and forestalled the criticisms. It was possible, the Report said, that:

> the State will get all the bad risks and the market all the good ones. This is quite true but we recognize that the main object of the State will be not to compete with the insurance market, but only to secure a continuance of voyages after the outbreak of war which might be arrested owing to inability to insure against King's enemies. It will not mind therefore if it does little business so long as these risks are being covered elsewhere.

To us, as we look back over two wars, that seems a strange statement but the truth probably is that Huth Jackson and his colleagues were anxious to keep their scheme simple, and that they were thinking in terms of a short war which would be decided by the events of the first few weeks.[1] They were not expecting either a struggle that would last for years or a long-drawn-out combat with submarines ordered to sink merchantmen at sight. They thought probably of one sharp decisive action, an up-to-date Trafalgar, to settle the issue between the belligerent navies and after that at the most some sporadic raids by German light cruisers and armed merchantmen which would offer no vital threat to our trade lines. Their miscalculations were not the fault of the Huth Jackson Committee, but as the war developed the scheme's inequity became intolerable and the Government altered it by introducing different rates for different voyages. By that time, however, the market had been allowed to make too large a profit; and both Lloyd's underwriters and the companies might have been better without the money which some of them undoubtedly accumulated.

Between 1914 and 1918 the Government lost on cargo insurance seven million five hundred thousand pounds. On hulls and in other branches of its war insurance it made a gross profit of thirty-two million pounds. That profit may be thought unnecessarily high, but so was the loss on cargo. And the loss might have been avoided if the Government underwriting had been more elastic, if the principle of one standard rate had never been adopted, or if it had been given up directly the pre-war misconceptions were dissipated by experience.

Of all the Government's ventures in the field of insurance during the 1914 war, the most successful financially was its cover against aircraft bombardment and in view of what happened in the Second World War the origin of this business is of considerable interest. Until 1914 no one had ever thought of the risk and even at the outbreak of war, when the Zeppelins were recognized as a great potential danger, it is probable that there were no bomb-damage policies in existence anywhere. But in the very early days of the war the owners of a building in the City of London enquired at Lloyd's for a rate to cover it against bomb-damage. The enquiry was taken to Sidney Boulton who had never seen such a risk before and he quoted 2s. per £100. The rate was accepted by the property owners and it then turned out that Boulton had not taken the enquiry seriously. His quotation had been a jest but he stood by it and wrote the risk – the first of its kind in world history. Lloyd's had invented another new insurance and again it was exactly what the public wanted. The tariff companies preferred to leave the business alone and for three years

[1] See A. J. P. Taylor: *The Struggle for Mastery in Europe* (p. 530).

Lloyd's, which was the main market for air-raid damage, was flooded with orders and the underwriters did very well out of them.

Except perhaps at the docks the conflagration risk arising from air bombing was not serious. The Zeppelins were a failure and the planes that succeeded them did comparatively little damage. For three years Lloyd's had almost a monopoly, one of the few companies that accepted the risks actually reinsuring the lot at Lloyd's. Then in the autumn of 1917 the Government launched its own scheme for insuring against bomb-damage and used the companies as its collecting agents. In fourteen months it took £13,610,000 in premiums and paid £2,970,000 in claims, finishing the war with a profit of seventy-one per cent of its premium income. And the Government rate at the end of the war was within a few pence of the rate that Sidney Boulton had quoted in 1914.

The story of war insurance in the Second World War differed widely from the First. The destructive power of the aeroplane, the comparative weakness of our Air Force, the range of the submarine, the certainty that the Germans would sink without warning from the first day of the war, combined to increase the hazards of underwriting and to preach the need for caution. The market, too, had had a sharp warning at the time of the Munich crisis and had realized then one vital difference between its position in 1914 and in 1938. In 1914 most cargo policies contained the F.C. and S. clause, which meant that most merchants were running the war risks on their shipments uninsured. It was usual for specie to be covered against war but not for ordinary merchandise; and in 1914, with very few war risks on their books, underwriters had had a free hand to take business at rates appropriate not to a war that might or might not break out but to a war actually raging at the moment.

On the other hand in September 1938, when war seemed inevitable, underwriters were already heavily committed. Between the two wars it had become the fashion to include war risks at nominal rates in almost all cargo covers and the only safeguard underwriters had was the right to cancel war risks from the covers on giving forty-eight hours' notice. So far as future shipments were concerned that was a great protection, but for cargo already shipped it was useless. Once cargo had been loaded the war risk had to be covered and underwriters' books at the outbreak of war would be full of cargo insured for a shilling or two per cent against war risks which called for a premium of at least four or five pounds per cent.

That was the unhappy situation of the marine market while the Chamberlain-Hitler negotiations were in progress in 1938. Rates for reinsurances and for new risks were at sixes and sevens. The market was chaotic and the underwriters who had passed through the worst week in their business lives were publicly accused of profiteering and holding the country up to ransom. It was a very unfair charge. The dilemma was not of the underwriters' making and in the circumstances it is difficult to see that they could have done anything but what they did.

For a year after Munich Britain lived in a limbo that was neither peace nor war, and it had never been so difficult as it was in those months to reconcile the interests of merchants and the safety of underwriters. The underwriter said quite rightly: 'War may break out at any moment and I dare not commit myself to fixed war rates that will hold good for weeks ahead or quote rates that would normally satisfy me in times of peace'. The merchant with equal justice said: 'War may break out at any moment and I must be insured against the risk. I cannot pay high rates before it has actually begun and if I am to place forward contracts with my customers, as I am bound to do, I must have a firm rate for insuring the cargoes when they are shipped'. It was very nearly a dead-lock of conflicting necessities.

At a moment when the nation was bent on rearmament a check to the stream of imports and exports might well prove a calamity and the Government was forced to intervene. While there was still a chance of preserving peace the Cabinet was reluctant to set up formally a war risk insurance office on the lines of the 1914 organization; but it put through Parliament an Act authorizing the Board of Trade to reinsure the 'King's enemy risk' on ships and cargoes by sea and air. On the strength of that Act, the Board of Trade arranged with the marine market that underwriters should accept the King's enemy risks offered to them exactly as they would accept them in normal times but should reinsure them all with His Majesty's Government. It was an ingenious plan and it worked admirably. Rates were kept down to a comparatively low level; the merchants were able to make their contracts; trade flowed and the raw materials for ships, guns, and planes were brought to Britain.

That reinsurance arrangement lasted only for a few months, for as soon as Hitler struck at Poland the war risk insurance office opened its doors to accept war risks direct. But the lesson of the last War had not been forgotten and the organization this time was different. The Government had made up its mind that the old plan which forced the War Risks Office to take all the bad risks, while the good went to Lloyd's and the companies, would not do. One way of achieving the Government's purpose would have been to give the Board of Trade a monopoly of all war risks at sea, forbidding underwriters to accept them. But that would have been a dangerous policy. It would have been easy to prevent Lloyd's underwriters from taking on war risks, but foreign underwriters were free; and since sea insurance is an international business, no power on earth could force foreign merchants to insure their war risks with His Britannic Majesty's Government. New York had a big marine underwriting market and would have stretched itself to swallow all the good risks in competition with the official organization here. The ordinary marine risk would tend to go with the war, and a valuable invisible export would have been lost to us perhaps for ever. There is only one way in which premiums can be brought to Britain and that is for British underwriters to quote the lowest rate.

Instead of creating a monopoly for itself the Government came to a gentleman's agreement with Lloyd's and the companies. It split war risks on cargo into two groups: (1) voyages to and from this country, and (2) voyages between two countries overseas. In the first group it was agreed that underwriters if they ever quoted a rate would quote one that was higher than the published rate of the Government. That arrangement secured the Government against competition by rate cutting and still made it possible for a foreigner who objected (as some did) to covering his risks with the British Government to insure at a higher rate in the British open market. In the second group – the cross-voyages between two overseas countries – underwriters were to have a free hand to quote what they liked and write what they liked without regard to the current official rate. So it is roughly true that the war risk on all cargo imported into Britain and exported from it would be a Government preserve, while all other cargo remained an open field. The agreement was perfectly observed and the bulk of the war premiums that came to Lloyd's between 1939 and 1945 was paid on cross-voyages which did not touch Great Britain.

It was a sensible arrangement which at once protected the British tax-payers, preserved an invisible export, and brought us during the war millions of pounds worth of foreign currency. It also guaranteed the survival of our marine insurance market after the war was over. But seven years after the war ended politicians were still complaining about the arrangement, protesting that the insurance of war risks had been rigged in favour of Lloyd's underwriters who got all the good business while the State got all the bad. It was not an effective criticism. Most underwriters, it is true, made a profit on the war risks at sea but so did the Government;

and it is certainly not true that Lloyd's got nothing but good business and the Government nothing but bad.

Perhaps the worst period of the whole war at sea was the first half of 1942, when German submarines were concentrating on the Western Atlantic before the American defences were complete, and doing enormous damage to ships and cargoes in and to the north of the Caribbean. The insurance in this area was shared between underwriters in America and underwriters in Britain. A great number of risks had been written while the United States were still neutral and the route from U.S.A. to West Indies comparatively safe. The losses between January and June 1942 were many and expensive; the rates had been inadequate; and those foreign underwriters who threw in their hands and abandoned war risks half-way through the year must have finished 1942 with uncommonly bad figures. Lloyd's underwriters, true to their tradition, adjusted their rates and went on writing war risks. A still greater volume of business in the Western Atlantic came to Lloyd's and thanks to their courage and perseverance underwriters closed the year without disastrous results. But such profits as they made, they made not because they were featherbedded. They made them because they had the right underwriting spirit and were not frightened by a succession of heavy losses.

· · · · · · ·

The story of insurance against war risks on land between the Wars and in the Second War is a good deal more complicated than the sea story. The very large sums paid during the 1914 War in premiums against bomb-damage and the big percentage of profit made out of them would naturally dispose underwriters favourably towards the risk. And after 1918 they continued to write not only the bombing risk but other war damage in various parts of the world. They wrote it in Ethiopia, in China, in Palestine, and in Spain – above all in Spain. And it was Spain that pulled them up short, for there they learnt how many claims a single raid on a comparatively small town could produce. The early reports of the destruction done by aircraft in the Spanish Civil War were exaggerated, but the figures when they reached London were bad enough to show that the experience of 1914–18 was no guide to what would happen in the next Anglo-German War. To Spain Hitler had sent only a few squadrons of bombers and they dropped their bombs on a poor country with few rich cities and little concentration of wealth in its crowded areas. He had sent them in an experimental mood, much as a theatrical manager sends a new

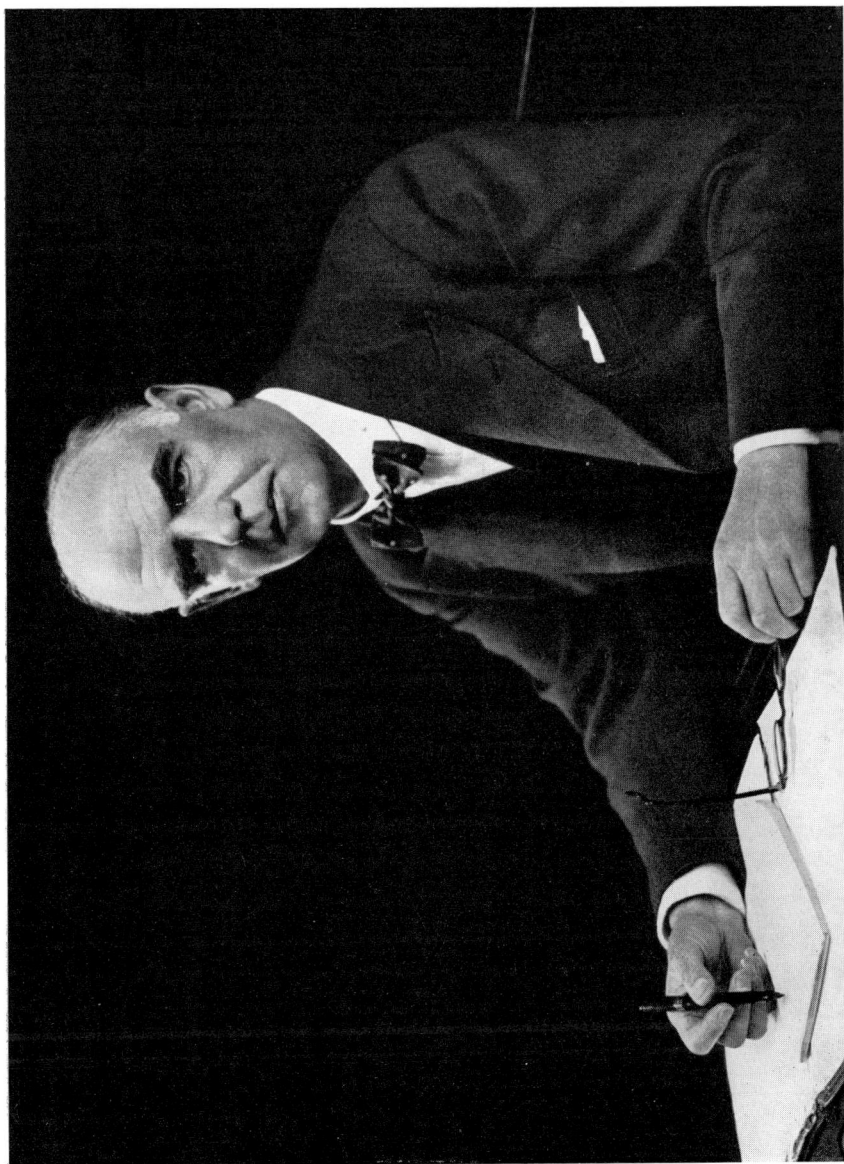

Neville Dixey, Chairman of Lloyd's, 1931, 1934 and 1936.

play to Brighton or Manchester to try it out and give the cast an opportunity to settle down before they open in London. It was a useful experience for the Luftwaffe and an equally useful lesson for Lloyd's underwriters. If damage done by three or four squadrons of bombers over a poor country amounts to say two millions, what will be the destruction when the whole bomber force of Germany is directed against London, the Midlands, and the North?

At the beginning of 1936 non-marine underwriters were writing bomb risks freely not only in Spain but in England. Large insurances were known to be running on many buildings in this country and on much merchandise in the London docks. The more cautious underwriters were disturbed by the prospect and the Committee of Lloyd's was actually told by one of its members – a non-marine underwriter – that unless the business was given up he would retire from underwriting.

But a number of non-marine underwriters still believed that insurance against war damage on land was a legitimate reasonable venture and continued to act on that belief. The Committee of Lloyd's had no right to stop them. Compulsion was impossible. Whatever was to be done must be done by persuasion and agreement. And the agreement must be universal. It must include not merely all Lloyd's underwriters, marine as well as non-marine, but all the British Insurance Offices and all the foreign Offices – if possible on both sides of the Atlantic. No agreement on that scale had ever been made before and it was to the unprecedented task of bringing it about that the Chairman of Lloyd's applied himself in the summer of 1936.

The Chairman of Lloyd's at that time was Neville Dixey, then in his third term of office, and the skill with which he brought this vital agreement into being must give him permanently a high place on the honourable scroll of Lloyd's chairmen. The bombing, when it came, did in Britain alone more than three thousand million pounds worth of damage; and no company or group of companies, no syndicate or group of syndicates, could have attempted to carry such a burden and survive. The insurance market was never intended to pay claims equivalent to the National Debt of a great Power. The only body that could possibly meet the loss was a body with the right to create money. The Government, which alone had the power of inflation, might do it. But no one else could.

Dixey first raised the question with the Committee of Lloyd's in September 1936 and he was given then authority to open up negotiations with marine and non-marine underwriters, and with the Insurance Offices. It was agreed that a clause should be drafted excluding war risks on land;

R

that every Lloyd's underwriter and every British company should be invited to sign it; that marine underwriters should be asked to confine the land war risks on cargo to forty-eight hours after discharge from the steamer; and that continental companies should be invited, and if necessary pressed, to join the concordat. Life insurances and personal accident insurances were to be left out of the scheme, and property in the United States and Canada, which were then outside bombing range, was also to be omitted. But except for risks in America all the world was to be asked to come into the agreement.

The plan was wholeheartedly approved by the British tariff offices which had always disliked and (so far as they could) eschewed war risks on land; and under the combined pressure of the Chairman of Lloyd's and the General Managers of the great British companies the scheme went through. In October 1936 a meeting of underwriting agents was held at Lloyd's and a resolution was passed to outlaw land war risks except for the forty-eight hours after discharge of cargo from a ship. The British companies had already agreed; foreign companies came in and thenceforward the war exclusion clause was inserted in every non-marine policy insuring property on land. It is still inserted and it is likely to keep its place until the millenium.

That was a great achievement of Dixey's and although he was helped by the general atmosphere of the market, he met with some unexpected and extraordinary difficulties. Lloyd's underwriters, always individualists, are often impatient of guidance and in the very thick of the discussion about bombing, when everybody seemed to be agreed on the exclusion of land war risks, a broker managed to insure a building for £150,000 against bomb-damage. And the building was, of all things, a gasometer in the middle of Sheffield. The companies, told of what had been done, very rightly objected. But when the slip was produced to Dixey he found that part only of the risk had been placed at Lloyd's and the balance had been written by a company. At that moment the agreement had not actually been reached so the business was not a breach of any formal undertaking.

But it was an unhappy omen and later on, while the agreement was in force, an insurance company, that was a party to it from the first, grew impatient and was believed to be on the point of reclaiming its freedom to accept the risks when and where it chose. Happily it was persuaded to remain inside the circle; and from that day to this, so far as is known, every company and underwriter has been content to continue the undertaking, has abstained from writing war risks on land and has been unfeignedly thankful that it signed the pledge and honoured its signature. If any under-writer ever fretted at the loss of his freedom he had only to walk out into Lime Street or stroll round Moorgate and gaze on the desolate blank spaces there. That would restore his faith in the Dixey Agreement of 1936.

But the agreement which served underwriters so well put merchants and owners of property into a difficult situation. The Lloyd's market on which they had previously relied for cover was now closed to them and as things stood at the beginning of 1939 they could do nothing but run their own risk. So far as their plants and buildings were concerned they were helpless but when it came to stock there was something they could do. They could let them run down and so reduce the loss that would be suffered if an enemy bomb fell on them. That was the obvious prudent course for a businessman to take; but from the national point of view it might be disastrous. We were, or we ought to have been, working night and day to prepare for the war, assembling food stocks, importing raw materials, building hundreds of tanks and thousands of planes; and if all this activity was to be hampered by fear that the stocks, when gathered together, would be destroyed by bombs, then before the outbreak of the war the Luftwaffe would have won its first victory.

It was a dangerous position and no one could accuse the British Government of being over-hasty in its action. For two years the gap left by the market's war exclusion clause was unfilled. Not till 4th August 1939, a month before the war started, did the Cabinet take the necessary power to supply the urgent need; and not till 28th August were stockholders able to register under a Government insurance scheme. From 3rd September the private insurance of stocks on land against war risks was prohibited by law. The Government was given a monopoly and (with few exceptions) everyone who sold anything was forced by law to take out cover with the Board of Trade. That was the origin of the Government's Commodity Insurance Scheme which lasted till the end of the war.

Although Lloyd's underwriters were not concerned in this scheme, Lloyd's brokers were concerned very closely indeed. They placed the insurances for their clients with the Government, and by a most sensible arrangement the Corporation of Lloyd's was made an agent to collect the premiums from the brokers and pass the money on to the Board of Trade. So for the first time in its history the Corporation of Lloyd's (as distinct from its Members and Subscribers) was engaged in the business of insur-ance. But without special authority it had no right so to engage. The Lloyd's Act of 1871, which had defined exactly what the Corporation might do, said nothing whatever about its acting as insurance agent, and if it agreed now to act as an agent under the War Risks Insurance Act it would undoubtedly be acting *ultra vires* – a grave prospect. To keep the Corporation clear of sin a special clause was put into the War Insurance Act 1939 to this effect:

> The objects of the body incorporated by Lloyd's Act 1871 by the name of Lloyd's shall include the carrying on of business as agents of the Board of Trade for any purposes of this Act.

So the Corporation of Lloyd's was given its Papal dispensation and could play its part without scruple in the work of insuring against bombs. It is characteristic of the thoroughness of Lloyd's Committee's staff that at a time like the autumn of 1939 it could remember so small a point and have the necessary relief inserted in an Act with which the Corporation of Lloyd's was not primarily concerned.

Two years later another Act – the War Damage Act – was passed into law and once again Lloyd's played its part in the administration. The 1939 Act had been confined to commodities for sale and gave no cover for buildings, furniture, machinery, and business equipment; and it was that cover that the new Act of 1941 provided. It might be thought a comparatively simple task for a Government after two years' experience of the Commodity Scheme to produce a plan for insuring all these other interests; but in fact the problem gave rise to many perplexities.

Buildings in the new Act were insured direct by the Government which, instead of premiums, charged an extra two shillings in the £ on Schedule A of the income tax. The Inland Revenue levied it for five successive years and so produced altogether a tax of ten shillings in the £ on the value of all the buildings in the country – a smaller charge perhaps than might have been expected. With this side of the business Lloyd's had no connection; but with the insurance of machinery, business equipment, and private chattels, it was most intimately concerned. Brokers collected premiums from their clients and passed them on to the Corporation. The business was enormous and the strain on depleted staffs considerable.

A true understanding of the Act's subtleties was a matter of extreme difficulty and question after question was referred to the decision of the Board of Trade, which was forced to become almost a judicial body delivering as many judgments in a week as a High Court Judge would deliver in a year. The Committee of Lloyd's helped everybody by appointing a member of their Staff to act as an intermediary between Lloyd's brokers and the

Board of Trade. He became in an incredibly short time one of the greatest living authorities on the Act and ran a sort of kindergarten for brokers who sat at his feet daily and had their problems solved for them by question and answer.

These problems were numerous and some of them could only be settled by a first-class judicial mind. A good example of their difficulty is the leading case of the tombstone and the coffin. Was a tombstone, asked one of the brokers, a building or a chattel? If it was a building it would come under Part I of the Act and insurance would be compulsory. If it was a chattel it came under Part II and the insurance was optional. The Board of Trade considered the point and decided that the tombstone was a building. But what of the coffin? Did that go with the stone? No. On the same authority it was a chattel falling under Part II of the Act, so there was no necessity to insure it. The stone and the coffin must go separate ways.

. . . . . . .

These new forms of war insurance were primarily national concerns and Lloyd's interest in them was indirect. But it had its own problems arising from the imminence and outbreak of war, troubles that were unknown in previous wars but called in 1939 for a bold solution. The most important of these was the dollar problem which might (if it had not been energetically handled) have endangered the valuable connections of Lloyd's with the United States.

Ever since Britain went off the gold standard in 1931 most Lloyd's underwriters had left their dollar premiums unconverted in American banks. That freed them from worry about the exchange and made it certain that they would have enough of the right currency to meet claims on their American policies. The system had worked well and given confidence to the Americans. But as the war clouds blew up in 1939 the Americans became anxious about their Lloyd's policies; and brokers in the United States were writing to their correspondents in London questioning the position of their funds if war should break out. In Lloyd's itself the Americans had full confidence and they appreciated the fact that the dollar balances retained by underwriters were sufficient for the payment of their dollar claims. But if war came, if the British Treasury had to find dollars for the purchase of supplies, if the American cash-and-carry law remained unrepealed and everything had to be paid for in dollars before shipment, how long would those balances of underwriters remain untouched? Was it conceivable that the British Government would leave them alone? Was it not most probable that they would be requisitioned, conscripted for national service and changed into sterling that might be useful on the East of the Atlantic but valueless on the West? If that happened, said the American brokers, how will our clients be paid their claims?

It was a penetrating question and as things stood in the spring of 1939 it was not easy to answer. One obvious course was to ask the British Government for an undertaking that no matter what happened in the war underwriters' dollar balances would be sacrosanct. If that request had been made the British Government would probably have consented to it. But an official promise, however serious, would not have satisfied the Americans who might well think that a pledge given by one Cabinet, in the security of peace, would not bind another fighting for the country's survival, in the last extremity of war. If, in such an extremity, it were possible to conscript Lloyd's underwriters' dollar balances they would, so the Americans thought, be conscripted. And while that possibility remained American business men would fight shy of Lloyd's, and underwriters' American business would be in jeopardy. Some way would have to be found for putting the dollar premiums once and for all outside the grasp of the British Treasury. The American broker must be able to tell his clients that no British official, no British subject, no one under the jurisdiction of British law had the power, with or without the consent of underwriters, to divert Lloyd's dollars from the settlement of American claims.

Various schemes were put forward and discussed for the achievement of this purpose including the transfer of a large capital sum from London to trustees of American nationality in New York. But that plan had holes in it and it soon became apparent that American anxiety was most likely to be assuaged if a separate premium trust fund in respect of U.S. dollar premiums was established by every Lloyd's underwriter, such funds to be held in America under the control of an American Trustee. The American Premiums Trust Fund of each underwriter would be begun by paying into it his existing U.S. dollar premiums and it would receive all future dollar premiums to be earmarked for the payment of claims and expenses arising under policies issued by underwriters in U.S. dollars. The U.S. dollar underwriting accounts would be separately audited and underwriters would be able to divide their dollar profits only when profits were disclosed by a separate examination of their dollar underwriting accounts. The essence of the scheme was that all U.S. dollar premiums should be taken right out of the ordinary premium trust fund of each underwriter and paid into a separate fund in America. The principle of individual underwriting and individual liability would not be affected and each underwriter's affairs would remain separate 'each for himself and not one for another'.

It was a revolutionary scheme but in the hectic atmosphere of those days the most conservative minds were open to revolutionary ideas and when the scheme relating to the establishment of Lloyd's American Trust Fund was laid before a meeting of underwriting agents it was received without demur. With the consent of the Treasury and the blessing of the Bank of England the scheme went through. The Instrument constituting the American Trust Fund of each underwriter was drawn up and an American trustee was appointed. Bank balances were transferred and a few days before the outbreak of war in 1939 the machinery began to turn, and it has been turning smoothly ever since.

. . . . . . .

That foundation of Lloyd's American Trust Fund in 1939 is a milestone in Lloyd's history. Exactly one hundred years had then gone by since the great fire at the Royal Exchange – another milestone – had driven subscribers into temporary exile and breathed fresh life into an almost moribund society. The temptation at this point to pause and look back over the century is irresistible.

In 1839 of corporate sense at Lloyd's there had been almost nothing and what there was of it had shown itself mostly in unseemly wrangling. Every subscriber could then transact whatever business he liked, write what he liked, broke what he liked and dispose of his premiums as he chose. Nobody had made a deposit. Nobody was guaranteed. Nobody had his accounts audited. If a subscriber was insolvent he could go on taking premiums and signing policies until his assets were exhausted and until then nobody either knew or cared what he was doing. Should he fail that was his own bad luck, and if his failure meant that other underwriters got more business, then it was a thing to be rejoiced over, not to be lamented. Now in 1939, and indeed for many years before that date, only underwriting members were allowed to accept risks. Every one of them was backed by a deposit and guaranteed, and (under the supervision of the Committee) everyone put his premiums into trust and had his accounts audited once every year. The corporate sense was now so strong that the failure of one underwriter would be regarded as a blow to all, and members were ready to subscribe annually large sums to a central fund for paying the underwriting debts of a defaulting member. Lastly, each underwriter had established a separate Trust Fund in America in respect of insurance business transacted by him in U.S. dollars. They did it on the advice of the Committee and many of them, if the truth must be told, had only a partial understanding of the details that the scheme involved. Lloyd's had travelled in those hundred years a very long way.

. . . . . .

After three years of war another difficult problem arose at Lloyd's over its American business and this time it had to be thrashed out with the United States Government itself. It sprang from the demands of the American Services and it concerned the information sent to Lloyd's in connection with both marine and non-marine business. The authorities at Washington suspected that valuable scraps of information were reaching the enemy through orders sent to the United Kingdom by American brokers, indicating the name and voyages of steamers, the location of factories and even the movements of population in the United States. They were alarmed by what they thought was happening and if their information had been correct they were doubtless right to be alarmed. But their information was incomplete and few of them appreciated the elaborate precautions that were in fact being taken by Lloyd's to prevent leakage.

In time of peace information of ships' movements comes to Lloyd's from its agents all over the world and after being sorted by Lloyd's intelligence staffs it is published both in *Lloyd's List* – a daily newspaper – and in the *Shipping Index* which is the marine underwriter's *vade mecum*. Every marine underwriter keeps a copy of the *Index* in front of him and its pages are thumbed over a hundred times a day. All the news about ships' movements is open both to underwriters and to the general public. But the moment war broke out Lloyd's agents at home and abroad changed their habits and sent their cables not to Lloyd's Building but to the Admiralty. And the Admiralty, at its own discretion, passed the news on to Lloyd's. Of this news nothing was published in *Lloyd's List* (which almost ceased for the time to be a shipping newspaper) and the only place in which it appeared was the *Shipping Index* that continued to give information as before.

But the distribution of this *Index* was drastically changed. Instead of being openly bought and sold its publication was confined to marine underwriters, marine companies and certain Government offices. Every copy was numbered and carried the name of the person to whom it was issued. Every copy when not in use had to be locked up in a secure place. And every copy sent to an underwriter or company had to be returned to the publisher in the evening of the day of issue and burnt. The Government departments which received copies had to destroy them and certify their destruction to Lloyd's. In this way every single copy of the *Index* was accounted for and throughout the war only one went astray. That one was lost while in the possession of a Government department – stolen in a mailbag robbery on a railway.

In fact the security arrangements at Lloyd's were probably the most efficient and the most free from leakage of any in this country or America; but the American military men, knowing little or nothing of these arrangements, were suspicious and uneasy, and in 1942 they announced the most drastic of steps to prevent news of ships' movements reaching Lloyd's from America. Especially were they concerned with orders to insure, cabled by American brokers to London. They forbad any insurance order to be sent abroad which indicated either the ship or the voyage concerned.

In the sphere of non-marine they were equally drastic. They forbad the sending of any information that concerned any project or industrial plant engaged in the war effort and specifically mentioned information despatched for purpose of reinsurance. At that moment practically every factory and warehouse in America could be described as engaged in the war effort and every private house or apartment occupied by a war worker might be and actually was regarded as so engaged. If the veto stood, the result would be that no order for fire or burglary insurance going from the United States to Britain could mention either the name of the insured, the subject-matter of the insurance, or the situation of the building. The ban was absolute and comprehensive. It looked as though Lloyd's connection with America was going to be snapped and a goodwill built up by fifty years of hard work and useful service destroyed at a blow.

The situation was dangerous and Sir Eustace Pulbrook, then Chairman of Lloyd's, accompanied by a member of his Committee and the Principal Clerk, flew to America to negotiate with a committee of soldiers, sailors, and civilians who were acting for the American Government. It was the first time for a hundred and two years that a Chairman of Lloyd's, in his period of office, had travelled abroad on Lloyd's business, but the issue was serious enough to justify any departure from precedent. The whole of Lloyd's American connection, certainly for the period of the war and perhaps for all time, was hanging on a thread; and as soon as he made contact with the American Committee Pulbrook found that his task was going to be extremely difficult. The authorities in Washington had made up their minds that no information should be sent out of the country to enable insurances to be placed in London. The fact that Britain was an ally had no weight with them and for purposes of security she was to be on the same level as Switzerland or Sweden. Information could leak out from anywhere and in Britain (apart from the possibility of leakage) there was the additional danger of invasion which at one swoop might put into enemy hands all the records of every British institution to be used against America as she continued the war.

By this time most Englishmen were confident that their country was safe from invasion. But Americans, not reared in the tradition of the Spanish Armada and Lord Nelson, naturally regarded the English Channel with its poor twenty-one miles of water as an insignificant barrier. They still believed that England was wide open to Hitler's divisions. In that state of mind they would naturally be chary of their secrets being put into the area of danger. What Pulbrook faced, when he first met the American committee and tried to persuade them that information could safely be sent to Britain, was something uncommonly like a brick wall.

The discussions naturally fell into two parts, marine and non-marine; and Pulbrook's case for Lloyd's was much more easy to expound on non-marine than on marine. But for some reason the American Committee stipulated that agreement must be reached on both or neither. If no satisfactory method could be found for marine then the veto would remain on non-marine as well – a decision that put Pulbrook and his colleagues into an embarrassing position. They were in America to represent both sections of the Lloyd's market and they doubted if they would be justified in sacrificing either for the benefit of the other. If they returned to Lloyd's and told the non-marine underwriters that a satisfactory arrangement could have been made for them but was refused because it was tied up with a bad bargain for their marine colleagues, then the non-marine market (which got a larger proportion of its premium income from the United States than the marine market) would have felt a natural grievance. On the other hand if Pulbrook accepted an unsafe plan for marine in order to give reasonable terms to non-marine the complaints from the marine section would have been equally loud and equally reasonable.

Pulbrook's first success in the negotiations came when the Americans agreed to cut the string between the two types of business and consented to consider information about fire and accident, even if the discussions broke down on voyages and cargoes. It was a very proper concession but until it was made Pulbrook's team had some anxious doubts and discussions on where the line of their duty lay.

In non-marine insurance the American ban including 'activities directly or indirectly connected with the war effort' forbad the sending of information about the nature of a business, its location, its output, and the rate of its activity. On the other hand the amount to be insured, the period of the insurance, the name of any American insurance company interested and the construction of the building might all be sent. An underwriter could be told that he was insuring a fireproof building, but he must not be told whether it made steel girders or firelighters and whether it was in New York or San Francisco. The problem was to give underwriters enough information without breaking this rule.

It was solved by setting up a bureau in New York to which American brokers would send all their non-marine orders for Lloyd's. The bureau would be managed by Lloyd's men sent over for the purpose. It would receive full information from the American brokers, permitted as well as non-permitted; it would select all the permitted particulars, cabling them to London, and file all the non-permitted information at its premises in New York. The London broker on receiving the cable would, without knowing where the risk was situated or what the nature of its industry was, place the risk with underwriters who were equally in the dark. A skeleton covering note identifying these risks by a reference number would be sent from London, not to the American broker but to the underwriters' bureau in New York; and the bureau, marrying the skeleton covering note with the full information on its files, would send a full covering note to the American broker from whom it had received the order. The result was that the risk was placed in London without disclosure of a single fact that might in any conceivable situation be of help to the Germans.

The problem of the marine underwriters was solved in the same way and with the same machinery. The American broker would send to the bureau in New York full information about a voyage to be insured – the ship's name, the nature of the cargo and the voyage. None of that information was allowed to go out of the United States. It was all non-permitted. It was filed away in the bureau's New York office and when the order to insure was cabled to the London broker the bureau substituted for it a few numbers. They were not code numbers and they did not give away either the steamer's name or the voyage or the cargo. But they did enable the marine underwriters at Lloyd's to keep some check on the size of their lines and so avoid being committed to excessive liabilities in a single bottom. It was a most ingenious scheme, and although the underwriters were almost blindfold the results of this most unorthodox underwriting were satisfactory. Above all, the ties between Lloyd's and the United States were not broken.

The successful issue of these difficult negotiations in New York and Washington was the crowning glory of Pulbrook's career; and this is perhaps a fitting place to speak of the great work that he did for Lloyd's. He was elected to the Committee of Lloyd's in 1920 and became Chairman for the first time in 1926, the youngest man (it is believed) ever to be elected to that office. From that time onwards, whether he willed it or not, he was the dominating personality in every Committee on which he sat. The successful development of the audit and the adaptation of the original formula to the changing conditions between 1925 and 1950 were largely due to him and the great service he performed as Chairman of the Audit Sub-Committee. But his greatest hour came in 1940 when he began perhaps the most brilliant series of chairmanships in the history of Lloyd's. From 1940 until 1946 he was Chairman uninterruptedly, and in 1943 the bye-laws were altered specially to make the continuation of his Chairmanship possible. A man of great character, great kindness and great activity, his worth to Lloyd's throughout the war was beyond price. To one member of Lloyd's, who was fortunate enough to sit under him on the Committee in four of the troubled war years, few things could be more welcome than this opportunity of paying a tribute to his memory. He died in 1953.

# 13

## LLOYD'S HOUSING PROBLEMS

*Overcrowding an old problem – Alternative premises to Royal Exchange considered – Committee's mistakes – Staff growing – Policy signing – Captains' Room – Proposed abolition resisted – New Policy Signing system – Offer of space from London Assurance declined – Captains' Room proposal revived – Defeated – Committee resign – Effects of the defeat – East India Avenue site – Kylsant – Sturge's negotiations – Building approved and built – Overcrowding after 1945 – Another new building approved*

---

AT FIRST SIGHT a record of the various premises in which Lloyd's has been housed might not seem an important feature of its history. Whether the underwriters met in Tower Street, Lombard Street, Pope's Head Alley, Cornhill or Leadenhall Street mattered much no doubt to the men who happened to be alive at the time of the various occupations, but in a story that covers nearly three centuries of activity the precise locations at different dates might be considered at best of only secondary interest. That would be a wrong view. In fact they are of interest and of importance. The removals from place to place and (between the removals) the perpetual devices to make the same amount of space provide more accommodation, indicate closely enough the flow and ebb of prosperity. And – what is more – they have influenced both the character of Lloyd's and (at times) the measures taken by the Committee to enforce the strength of a Lloyd's policy.

A partial analogy may perhaps be found in the history of two public schools. Between 1870 and 1890 two schools in the City of London, looking for more space, moved off from their ancient premises – Charterhouse to Godalming and St Paul's to West Kensington. Both changed their characters with the move and both took new and different shapes from the sites to which they went. At Lloyd's, over a long period, the same kind of change has resulted from its moves. Its history shows the same effect of

243

environment working on character and anyone who wants to understand the modern Lloyd's must bear that connection in mind.

When the handful of underwriters, who then made up Lloyd's, moved in 1774 to the Royal Exchange, the unaccustomed space in their new home may have seemed to them like heaven; and doubtless they expected to enjoy the feeling for many years to come. But their complacency was killed by the accession of new subscribers who flocked in during the French wars, and by 1810 the rooms (though two new ones had been added) were crowded beyond comfort and almost beyond endurance. The whole accommodation was desperately inadequate for a market of over two thousand men, and from the descriptions that have been handed down to us the place must at times have looked like a modern tube station in the rush hour. When peace returned the problem was solved temporarily by the decline of business and by a fall of some sixty per cent in the number of subscribers; and for a quarter of a century until the Great Fire of 1838 we hear very little about the need for more room.

After the Great Fire and the return of Lloyd's to the Royal Exchange things were different. With splendid courage the Committee had taken extra space in the new building to provide the Merchants' Room, but within a few years that room had to be given up, not because it was a failure but because the area was needed for more immediate purposes. That was about eighty years before Lloyd's moved from the Royal Exchange to Leadenhall Street and in that eighty-year period the pressure was so constant that there were at least nine or ten suggestions of trekking to new premises – some seriously considered, some toyed with and quickly dismissed, but all of them pointing the way to what actually happened in 1928.

The first suggestion came in an offer from the Government. The Treasury was prepared to let the land on which the Customs and Excise Buildings stood – an area of 15,900 square feet for a ground rent of £6,000 a year. The Committee of Lloyd's were attracted, but were afraid that the expense of building would be too high and refused the offer. Then the South Sea House at the top of Threadneedle Street – the house which had been occupied by Lloyd's after the fire – was reported for sale, but that offer too was refused, perhaps because underwriters had memories of their exile not happy enough to tempt them back to the building.

After another interval of nineteen years a rather mysterious offer of 'premises for the Corporation in Drapers Gardens' came before the Committee and was summarily turned down; and nine years later a building site where the Wesleyan Centenary Hall then stood was considered and also rejected. In April 1891 there is an extraordinary note in the Committee's minutes that the Mansion House was reported to be for sale. But whether there was any truth in the rumour, whether the City Fathers really thought of evicting their Lord Mayor, and whether the Corporation of Lloyd's would seriously have considered building a new home for themselves on that venerable site the minutes do not say. The report that had reached the Committee was probably no more than a piece of gossip brought to Lloyd's by some enterprising estate agent anxious to be first with the news whether true or false.

A very different proposal had come before the Committee eleven years before – in 1880. It was long considered, and, if it had not been discussed in public with an astonishing lack of discretion, it might have brought Lloyd's to Leadenhall Street nearly fifty years before its appointed time. A plot of leasehold land was offered to Lloyd's at the corner of Leadenhall Street and Gracechurch Street, separated by only a few yards from the present site of Lloyd's; and the Committee – as well they might – liked it and thought it a very good pitch. But at that time Lloyd's had still an outside Chairman. There was no Deputy Chairman to act during his frequent periods of absence. That out-of-date old-fashioned arrangement no doubt made it difficult for the Committee to take responsibility in such an important matter as building a new home. There was no one now to galvanize a hesitant Committee into effective action as Angerstein had galvanized the Committee of 1774, and failing a resolute leader the problem was handled in a way that could lead only to one result.

First the Committee issued a circular to members and then they called an extraordinary general meeting to consider the purchase of the Leadenhall Street corner, making it quite clear to the meeting that they were not asking for full authority but merely seeking permission to continue their enquiries. Within a few hours it must have been known to most people in the City, including every prospective buyer of the land, that Lloyd's was after it. A certain amount of criticism of the scheme was made at the meeting, and the Committee declared again before it broke up that all they wanted was to have the question aired. They renewed their promises to do nothing in a hurry.

The Committee did nothing in a hurry. They waited five months and then called another general meeting. With renewed assurances that the members were not being asked to agree to a purchase they suggested a vote merely to strengthen their hands in the negotiations. If they had spoken of a vote to strengthen the hands of other people who wanted the land they would perhaps have been nearer the mark. A month later they held a ballot to decide, not whether the land should be bought, but whether members' subscriptions at Lloyd's should be raised if the new premises were secured. They got a majority vote in agreement but not a majority large enough to be conclusive.

All this open discussion must have been known throughout the City, and in the intervals of their general meetings and ballots the Committee haggled with the owners of the land over the price that would be paid if a majority of members at a subsequent meeting agreed (*a*) to the removal from the Royal Exchange, and (*b*) to the purchase price asked. It is not surprising that the owners grew tired of the negotiations and decided to let the land to the sitting tenants on a building lease. All that Lloyd's had done was to stimulate these tenants and probably drive them into paying more than they would otherwise have agreed to pay in rent. On the other side of the picture the Gresham Committee (which managed the Royal Exchange) was openly told that Lloyd's anticipated a large increase in the rent for the same area of space when their lease at the Royal Exchange ran out. It looks as though the 1880 Committee of Lloyd's were a collection of incompetent bunglers, and forty-three years later if their successors had handled the purchase of the Leadenhall Street site as it had been handled in 1880, it is most unlikely that Lloyd's would be where it is today. Perhaps it is more than a coincidence that within a few months of the Leadenhall Street negotiations breaking down Lloyd's decided for the future to have annually elected Deputy Chairmen who could give a lead to the Committee when the Chairman himself was not available.

What was probably the last suggestion for a new site received by the Committee before the First World War was made in 1907, when a real estate company offered land in Great Winchester Street. Apparently the idea of moving to that part of the City was not pursued and the search for new premises seems by this time to have been given up. But that did not mean that the housing problem was any less acute. On the contrary it was becoming more urgent every year. The Committee's staff was growing and went up in eight years from 100 to 170. Fresh fire and accident business was always coming to Lloyd's, and every non-marine underwriter starting a fresh syndicate, every broker's clerk who left his firm's marine department to deal with their new-fangled non-marine insurances, increased the number of risks written and the number of policies signed. Everything stimulated the demand for more space. Indeed it was the

Sir Eustace Fulbrook, Chairman of Lloyd's, 1926, 1940–6, and 1948; from a painting by David Jagger, R.O.I., in the Chairman's Room at Lloyd's.

difficulty of signing policies that brought the matter of extra premises to a head and it was a suggestion put forward by brokers for changing the system of policy signing that forced the Committee to come to grips with the problem.

To call the old method of signing policies at Lloyd's a system is really to pay it a compliment that it did not deserve. Often it was more like a free fight. It had probably never been altered since the slip came into universal use at Lloyd's, and the fact that it continued as long as it did without bringing the Lloyd's policy into disrepute is one of the minor mysteries in the history of underwriting.

The procedure was as follows. A broker's senior clerk placing a risk showed it to underwriters on a slip of paper, which contained all the essential details and was initialled by perhaps fifty different underwriters acting for fifty to a hundred different syndicates. When he had placed the risk and taken the slip back to the office the senior clerk had finished with it and passed it over to the firm's policy department, which transcribed the details on to a stamped policy, to serve as a legal document that would carry the names of all the underwriters concerned in the risk. The un-signed policy, together with the slip, was handed over to a junior clerk whose job it was to collect the appropriate signatures at the different underwriters' boxes, take the partially signed policies back to the broker's office every evening, and bring them back again to the Room, day after day, until the signatures were completed – a harassing, thankless and some-times heartbreaking task.

The fun started at the point of the policy reaching the Room for signa-ture. The actual signing was done by the junior clerks of underwriters and their method was to take the policies as the brokers' junior clerks left them, bang rubber stamps on them, scribble a few words in ink, make the necessary notes of what they had done in the syndicates' books, and finally hurl the policies into a wire basket for the brokers' boys to collect them in due course. Somewhere in the course of this hurried business they were supposed to check the wording of the policies, but more often than not the check was no more than a lick and a polish. It was a crude way of doing important business, but so long as the clerk had to sign only fifty or sixty policies a day the method may have worked – not well but not intolerably badly. As business grew, however, and the more active syndicates were signing not fifty but three or four hundred policies a day it became chaotic. The brokers' clerks (surely the most unhappy lads since the days of the boy chimney-sweeps) swarmed and struggled round

s

the signing boxes, searching for their policies in the wire baskets, grabbing them when found and carrying them along to other boxes until the process of signing was complete – a process that on a large policy might not be completed for weeks. Then the policy left the Room for good, made its last journey to the broker's office, and was there despatched to the assured who had been awaiting it perhaps for weeks – sometimes even for months.

The delay was bad but the condition of the document itself was often worse. Passed from hand to hand in one loose scrum after another, opened hurriedly by fifty different signing clerks all working at top speed, thumped and hammered by a hundred different rubber stamps, thumbed and turned over by numberless brokers' clerks as they dug their own policies out of the muddle in the wire baskets, it would sometimes emerge from its ordeal as dirty, torn, and ragged, as a shirt from the worst of England's post-war laundries. Occasionally its state was so bad that it had to be destroyed and another document signed in its place, but too often it was sent into the stream of the world's commerce bedraggled and disreputable – a sorry advertisement for the greatest marine insurance market in the world.

This policy-signing scandal was the immediate reason for the demand for more space; and it set in train the discussions which finally took Lloyd's from Cornhill to Leadenhall Street. In 1913 a number of brokers laid before the Committee a scheme for signing policies in a more efficient manner and the Committee appointed a joint sub-committee to investigate the problem. The sub-committee quickly realized that the policy troubles were closely connected with the lack of space and that no reform could be achieved unless more room were provided. A signing scheme that had been put forward was thought to be good but it was unworkable in the number of square feet that the Committee could provide for it.

What was to be done? Every inch of space was already crowded. The Corporation's own staff was working under impossible conditions. The Gresham Committee at that particular moment had no additional room to spare, and for some reason there was no suggestion (as there had been a few years before) of moving lock, stock and barrel to a new site. But there was one possibility or rather a hint of a possibility which seemed to provide the only hope. The Committee of Lloyd's (it was said) might decide to close the Captains' Room and consecrate to the serious business of policy-signing the space that had for so many years been given over to eating and drinking – for the Captains' Room had long since ceased to be a place for

captains and had become a restaurant for members, subscribers, and substitutes. With no foreknowledge of the storm that he was unleashing,
somebody, to provide space for policy-signing, proposed the abolition of
the restaurant. The battle of the Captains' Room – by far the most violent
dispute at Lloyd's within living memory – had begun. Seven years were
to pass before it was ended.

At the start of the action few people realized that a battle had started.
Nothing had happened except that the Committee had been advised by a
representative sub-committee to make what seemed a comparatively
unimportant change, and had agreed to make it. A larger meeting was
called. The proposal for shutting the Captains' Room was laid before it
and with only one dissentient it was approved. The scheme it appeared
was as good as through and the decision practically taken. The catering
firm that managed the Captains' Room and supplied the food and drink,
was given notice to quit. Plans were in the air for building somewhere on
the roof of the Royal Exchange a new room in which members would be
able to lunch; and if the plans for opening this new room were a good deal
less definite than the decision to close the old one, there was seemingly no
unrest among members that could not be settled by the device of appointing another sub-committee.

But things in fact were not so comfortable as on the surface they
appeared to be. Within a few weeks of the decision being made to close
the Captains' Room, a strong underground resistance movement was
started – led by a well-known member, John Povah. Povah, the son of a
vicar of Pepys' old church in the City, and himself a sea captain before he
took to underwriting, was one of the recognized characters of Lloyd's at a
time when interesting characters were more common in the place than,
unhappily, they are today. He was a skilful operator in the overdue
market; he had an almost passionate interest in the history of Lloyd's; and
to interfere with the old Captains' Room seemed to him like tampering
with the Ark of the Covenant.

If the Captains' Room was to be sacrilegiously threatened he would
never be a consenting party and even at this late hour he would do his best
to avert the tragedy. He drew up a petition or rather a protest to the
Committee, took it round for signature and got one hundred and fifty-
seven people to sign it – a remarkable performance that was probably
more of a tribute to Povah's personality than a considered expression of
the signatories' opinion. But it was enough. It served. And in June 1914
the Chairman of Lloyd's announced that in face of this opposition the

scheme for abolishing the Captains' Room could not go on. Some other way of dealing with the policy problem must be found, and a plan proposed by a well-known broker (details of which have not survived) was to be considered instead. Povah had won the first round of his fight.

During the First World War a truce was called between the two armies and the scheme for abolishing the Captains' Room was stopped. But that did not mean that the problem of finding more space for signing policies in reasonable time and in good physical condition had become less urgent. On the contrary, the enormous influx of new business – war risks at sea and bombing risks on land – aggravated the difficulties, and as more men joined the services the increasing lack of staff made it even more desirable to reform the old clumsy system of policy-signing which was now in danger of a complete breakdown. The first year of the war was not a time when either brokers or underwriters were anxious to take on new duties, but one Lloyd's broker found leisure enough to work out a solution and by doing so produced a permanent and vital change in the organization of Lloyd's business. He was Sir Walter Hargreaves, a member of the Committee of Lloyd's and a man of great ability which he devoted during two wars to the service of the British Government and the interests of the insurance market. His plan for policy-signing went far beyond anything that had been proposed before that time. It cut through and abolished the old system and substituted for it a separate office which would do for Lloyd's underwriters in one operation the work that from the beginning of time every man had done separately for himself.

On the morning of the 27th of October 1915, Hargreaves outlined his plan to the Committee of Lloyd's and a sub-committee was at once appointed. In the afternoon of the same day the sub-committee held its first meeting and (subject to the approval of the brokers' and underwriters' associations) approved it. A week later it was accepted by the Committee of Lloyd's. And the Lloyd's Policy Signing Office (then called the Bureau) was well on its way to foundation – a good example of the speed at which things can be done in a highly individualistic society when nobody insists on riding his own hobby horse to the last jump.

The passage of the scheme was greatly helped by the care with which Hargreaves had worked out the details before bringing it to the Committee. He produced it in such a form that it could be put into action almost at a moment's notice. It would be tedious to recite the details in full but the scheme in effect was to turn the signing of policies into a separate business, to take it away altogether from the underwriters' boxes, and to hand it over to a staff of specialists whose whole time would be spent in checking the documents and attaching the appropriate signatures – none of them acting for a particular underwriter but all for the whole underwriting body. The essence of Lloyd's underwriting, which is the individual liability of each man for himself, was not affected. But in future when a clerk put Janson's name or Heath's or Boulton's on to a policy he would do it not as Janson's or Heath's or Boulton's employee but as the employee of the Policy Signing Office – an organization that belonged to all the underwriters in common and had been authorized by them all to act as their agent for the signing of their names.

In his original memorandum Hargreaves made it clear that he was proposing no permanent change. He was concerned only with the duration of the war to relieve the wartime strain and to enable female labour to take the place of the male clerks as they were drafted into the fighting services. That was the limit of his intentions. But the emergency measures of war tend to become the standard measures of peace; and the Policy Signing Office has been no exception to that law. It is still with us. Most of its employees are girls and it is a fair guess that so long as Lloyd's exists the Policy Signing Office will be in existence too. One might wish that all the other devices affecting our lives, which outlived the two wars, were as useful and unobjectionable today as the Policy Signing Office at Lloyd's. Its service to underwriters and brokers has been invaluable, and without it the machinery of Lloyd's would long ago have broken down. Apart from signing policies quickly and neatly it has relieved overburdened underwriters (particularly in the non-marine market) of much work that otherwise they would have had to do themselves. And more than once it has helped the Committee of Lloyd's to maintain the security of a Lloyd's policy by enforcing rules accepted by underwriters in the common interest of the market. Its path has not always been easy and it has sometimes clashed with the more ardent individualists among underwriters, but the great value of the work it does cannot be questioned and it is only right to record in this story of Lloyd's the debt of gratitude that succeeding generations owe and always will owe to the Policy Signing Office and to Walter Hargreaves its originator.

The office opened for business on the 1st of March 1916. For the first eight years of its life underwriters could use it or not as they liked, and to begin with some of them preferred not to join. In its early working, too, there were a certain number of troubles – some of them rather curious. An elderly and high-minded underwriter, much too old for military

service but anxious to help the country in wartime, volunteered to join
the checking staff at the Policy Signing Office and assist them in their
work. It was a worthy gesture but misunderstood, for it produced a strong
protest from other underwriters who objected to one of their competitors
gaining, as an unpaid clerk, information about other people's underwriting that might afterwards prove profitable to him in his own underwriting business. The volunteer had to give up his good work and stick to
underwriting. There was, too, a secession and a split between marine and
non-marine, the non-marine underwriters breaking away and starting an
organization of their own – in the same building as the marine but on the
other side of a narrow passage – doing the same kind of work in very
much the same way but holding no communication with the rival sect
across the way. It was rather like the Scottish Church after the great disruption and in due time, like the two halves of the church, the two sections
of underwriters came together again with the happiest results. Eight years
after the Bureau was begun it was taken over by the Committee of Lloyd's.
It became a department of Lloyd's Corporation and for reasons that
belong to a later chapter in this book the use of the Bureau was made
compulsory for all syndicates, marine and non-marine alike.

.    .    .    .    .    .

Another episode and a rather strange one that happened during the
First World War and had a very considerable influence on the housing
troubles of Lloyd's must be dealt with at this point. The London Assurance
(one of the two insurance companies that survived the South Sea Bubble)
had occupied a large part of the Royal Exchange in which it had its headquarters; but in 1917, needing more room to stretch itself, it decided to put
up a building of its own in King William Street, leaving in the Royal
Exchange only its marine underwriting staff. That would mean that three
large rooms in the Royal Exchange would be available for someone else.
Lloyd's was obviously a possible tenant and a thirty-two years lease was
offered by the London Assurance to the Committee of Lloyd's at a rent of
£5,000 a year plus a premium of £60,000. Those extra rooms would
have gone a long way to solve the immediate problem of Lloyd's. But the
cost was estimated at £12,000 a year and in July 1917 the Committee,
unable to make up their minds, postponed their decision for three months.
Then came another urgent message. It was reported that other would-be
tenants were after the rooms and it was an open secret that they were the
Royal Exchange Assurance, also tenants of the Gresham Committee, who

would like a chance of getting the extra accommodation. If Lloyd's wanted the rooms they must say so quickly for there would be no third chance. Did they want them? The Committee decided that they did not and the Royal Exchange Assurance moved in.

Considering the stress that the Committee had for years been laying on the need for more space, they made perhaps a strange decision when they refused this offer; and their reasons for making it are obscure. Perhaps they realized that the Royal Exchange had ceased to be a satisfactory permanent home for the Society even if the extra accommodation were obtained. Perhaps the arrangement of the space was inconvenient. Perhaps the cost which looks reasonable enough now seemed then to be excessive. Perhaps the war which was at that moment going through one of its blackest phases had shaken their nerve. But whatever the reason, the Committee after taking three months to think the matter over turned the offer down. It should be stated as emphatically as possible that the responsibility for that decision rested entirely on the members of the Committee. They had had ample time to discuss the proposal and they made the choice with their eyes open. But years afterwards there was – indeed there still is – a belief at Lloyd's that one person, without consulting the Committee, rejected the proposal off his own bat; and his reputation has suffered not a little in consequence. But there is nothing in the Committee's minutes to substantiate that belief. The blame, if blame there is, must be shared by the twelve men who were then in charge of the Society's affairs.

. . . . . .

The demand for abolishing the Captains' Room had been based originally on the need for space for signing policies. Before the end of the 1914 war the establishment of a Policy Signing Office in a building on the other side of Cornhill had destroyed that argument for good and it might have been thought that the Captains' Room was safe from the pre-war threat of abolition. But whatever relief the change in signing had brought about was more than outweighed by the general increase in business and in particular by the need of more room for the Committee's clerks, many of whom were working under very bad conditions. And the Chairman of Lloyd's in 1920 was the redoubtable Sidney Boulton. He had argued strongly before the war that the Captains' Room should be taken over and at one of the meetings in 1914 he had spoken with characteristic bluntness of 'hindering the progress of the Room because some of us are too lazy to go out to lunch', a fair comment perhaps but scarcely a tactful way of winning over the opposition. On any subject to which he applied his mind Boulton knew exactly what he thought and in the matter of the Captains' Room he had no doubt whatever. It must go.

Disregarding a promise given in 1914 by his predecessor in the Chair he refrained from calling a General Meeting, and instead consulted privately a few users of the Captains' Room to whom he made it clear that he wanted to take over the space for business purposes. As soon as that decision was noised abroad there came a requisition from the necessary number of members for an Extraordinary General Meeting; and an Extraordinary General Meeting – extraordinary not only in the technical but in the everyday sense of the word – was held in November 1920.

On the day of the meeting by an unfortunate chance Boulton was away ill. His doctor forbad him to come to the City and he was forced to leave the management of the meeting to his Deputy Chairman, St Quintin. St Quintin was one of the most charming men that ever came to Lloyd's but he was not a Sidney Boulton, and it is quite likely that he personally did not like Boulton's proposals. Anyhow it was clear from the first that on the morning of that November day there were very few places in this world that St Quintin would not have preferred to the Chairman's seat which he was in fact occupying. He made no effort to put the Committee's case for abolishing the Captains' Room but straight away called on the requisitioners to state their views. In the biggest battle of his life he began by handing the initiative over to the enemy, and from the moment that happened the opposition swept everything in front of it, with John Povah riding at the head of his troops and cheering them into action.

In his earlier speeches Captain Povah had approached the subject through the stomach, pleading with the Committee not to interfere with what he called the creature comforts of members. The debates indeed that took place before the war might be accurately described as creature comforts versus more business. But in this last meeting Povah took a higher line, stressed eloquently the motif of Edward Lloyd, our pious Founder, appealed to his memory, invoked his shade and gave him at least one sentence too magnificent not to be quoted:

> The spirit of Edward Lloyd our Founder is in the bar of the Captains' Room – may it rest there for ever.

If the spirit of Edward Lloyd has undeed remained in touch with the world since he died in 1713, he must have been surprised by many things said about him at one time and another, but surely nothing can have astonished or depressed him more than Povah's declaration that he was going to live *in saecula saeculorum* in the ill-lighted rat-ridden evil-smelling room in which the Captains' Room Bar was then placed.

Whatever Edward Lloyd's spirit thought about Povah's statement, the meeting liked it enormously and applauded it with enthusiasm. His peroration also had a tremendous effect. Whipping up his supporters with one last burst of eloquence Povah implored the members in words which he believed were familiar to all:

> In the world's broad field of battle,
>   In the bivouac of life,
> Be not like dumb, driven cattle!
>   Be a hero in the strife!

That was a cruel blow at the members of the Committee who were present at the meeting, for by this time, through no fault of their own, some of them were beginning to look uncommonly like dumb-driven cattle themselves. They made a half-hearted attempt to get another sub-committee appointed but the suggestion was still-born and useless, and, when Povah finally put his motion disapproving of the course indicated by the Committee and calling on the Committee to desist from dealing with the Captains' Room, he got a majority so large that it was unnecessary to count the votes.

Technically that motion was not a vote of censure but there was undoubtedly an element of censure in it and soon after it was passed the members of the Committee did a thing that had been done only once before in the history of Lloyd's – they resigned *en bloc*. But with one exception they submitted themselves at the poll again and at that poll a remarkable thing happened – a thing that surely did credit to the good sense of the members of Lloyd's. They re-elected almost all the members of the old Committee and handed back the management of Lloyd's to the men whom they had so exuberantly criticized at the General Meeting. They had had their day out. They had got what they wanted. The Captains' Room was safe. And they were not going to overdo their victory by parting with leaders whom they knew and (despite the episode of the Captains' Room) trusted. The affair blew over leaving no bitterness and was summed up in the language of the Admiralty Division as a collision between s.s. *St Quintin* and s.s. *Povah* – s.s. *St Quintin* held to blame but successfully pleaded compulsory pilotage.

The quarrel over the Captains' Room is for two reasons a landmark in Lloyd's history – first because it forced the departure from the Royal Exchange to Leadenhall Street and second because it was the last fling of the old Lloyd's, the Lloyd's that septuagenarians today remember with advantages and look back on with nostalgic affection.

To take the second point first. It is difficult, if not impossible, to imagine in the present atmosphere of Lloyd's a row blowing up and being fought out quite in the way that the Captains' Room row blew up and was fought out in 1920. The Povah-Boulton clash was almost a family squabble fought in a family setting. The total membership of Lloyd's was then less than seven hundred; of the active members there were probably not more than one hundred, and most of them were people of middle or advanced age who had known each other, man and boy, for the greater part of their lives. Whether they liked each other or not, they had for each other something like a family feeling. They competed in business perhaps more violently than the underwriters do now, they sat cheek by jowl on far fewer committees and sub-committees, they made fewer agreements with each other in their underwriting affairs; but for all that, in the rank and file of members, the tie of a common membership was stronger and more impelling than it is today.

Now there is a membership of more than four thousand and of these possibly seven hundred are engaged in everyday business round and about the Room. The average age of active members must be very much lower than it was forty years ago. The old school tie is more generally worn. The University Appointment Boards have heard of Lloyd's and now they often direct the feet of their young graduates to its gates. The Corporation has a staff in London of over two thousand men and women and so probably have the largest firms of brokers. But the snug atmosphere of the old room in the Royal Exchange, warmed by an open fire in the winter and cooled by a block of ice in the summer, has for the older men at any rate disappeared. It would scarcely be inaccurate to say that the present Lloyd's is to the Lloyd's of fifty years ago what a great cathedral is to a village church. Some people prefer the old atmosphere but the change is inevitable and there is nothing to be done about it. There is no good in a cathedral pretending that it is a village church.

The other point about the Captains' Room quarrel – that it forced the removal from the Royal Exchange to Leadenhall Street – could easily be over-emphasized. A move was in any case almost certain and at some time – Captains' Room or no Captains' Room – it would have had to be made.

But the defeat of the Committee at the General Meeting did hurry the move along and lead to serious enquiries (which might otherwise have been delayed for years) being started while a site in the East India Avenue, Leadenhall Street, was still to be had. If the Committee had secured the Captains' Room for its own use Lloyd's would still have moved, but not so soon, and in the interval the Leadenhall Street site would have been bought by somebody else. It was the Captains' Room revolt that determined not the move itself but its time and its destination.

Two months after the Captains' Room meeting, the Principal Clerk, whose working time at the moment was largely given to cramming an impossibly large number of clerks into an impossibly small amount of space, presented to the Committee a memorandum declaring that Lloyd's must move. He surveyed the sites in the City that were known or believed to be purchasable and even considered the possibility of reconstructing the building of the Royal Exchange to provide the necessary room there. But tinkering with the Royal Exchange was surely out of the question. It would have needed the consent of the Royal Exchange Assurance, the agreement of the Gresham Committee, and a special Act of Parliament altering the will of Sir Thomas Gresham who died in 1579. And even if Lloyd's were successful at all these points – a most improbable assumption – the results could scarcely be satisfactory.

A new site had to be found and here there were some seven possibilities ranging from Gresham Street in the west to Crutched Friars in the east. One plan was to take the whole of Leadenhall Market which the City Corporation was thinking of selling. Another was to buy one of two sites near the Monument and another to move to the north end of London Bridge, which was in some ways the most attractive spot in the whole City of London. But the place that won the day was East India Avenue – the site until 1859 of the home of the East India Company. It might give the requisite area and, though it was cut in two by an avenue which traversed it, there was no right of way and the avenue could be built over – as it actually was – swallowed up and engulfed in the new building that Lloyd's raised. Somewhere through the present building there runs the line of the old road that joined Leadenhall Street to Leadenhall Market and at each end of it stood a gate that was shut every night. That nightly performance made it possible to build on it – the only case perhaps since the Fire of London of a road in the City disappearing.

The site itself is historic. British India was governed from it for two centuries. Clive, Hastings and Sullivan, who knew it like their own homes, fought out some of their bitterest quarrels there; and for years Charles Lamb, as a humble clerk, travelled to and from it every day of the week. Froude, the historian, once said that whoever knows the biographies of the Russell family knows the history of England for three centuries. Whoever knows the biography of East India House knows the history of India for two.

When the East India Company was wound up, a company called the East India House Estate Company bought the land and built some very Victorian offices on it. About thirty per cent of the Company's capital was held by the Brassey family and at some time about 1910 the Brasseys wanted either to reduce their interest or to dispose of it altogether. At that moment, if the Committee had had the necessary determination, they could probably have bought it with little difficulty and at a comparatively low price. But the opportunity passed and the land went on a ninety-nine years' lease to a real property company, which owned several big office blocks in the neighbourhood and realized that if Lloyd's moved house to Leadenhall Street the rental value of all those other buildings would be raised. It was greatly to the advantage of the real estate company to get Lloyd's interested and its very shrewd managing director (knowing of underwriters' need for space) may well have had Lloyd's in mind when he made his ninety-nine years' deal.

Ten days after the deal was completed the First World War broke out and the real property company must have had some uncomfortable moments about its last peace-time purchase. But after five years of war the buildings were undamaged and were in fact far more valuable than they had been in 1914. Already if Lloyd's Committee wanted the land the price had gone up against them. And a new complication had been added – a complication that was to make the purchase by Lloyd's a good deal more difficult than it need have been, to delay arrangements for some twelve months and to strain the patience of Lloyd's Chairman in 1923 almost to breaking-point. The complication was Lord Kylsant. Kylsant, that tragic figure who was then at the height of his power as Chairman of the Royal Mail Group of Shipping Companies, had used part of his company's wartime profit in buying a half-interest in the East India site from the leaseholders. His dreams of greatness, like Kubla Khan's, had always included a stately new building to house himself and his followers. For fifteen years he had had his eye on East India Avenue and in 1918 he secured a footing there. Henceforth he had as much control over the disposal of the land as the real property company, which could do nothing except with his consent. And *vice versa* the company could if it so desired prevent Kylsant from doing what he wanted. The agreement between him and the company might have been designed purposely to produce a stalemate and it very nearly did.

If Kylsant had known his own mind with a little more certainty things would not have been so difficult. But he kept wavering. He was forever blowing hot and cold, now wanting this arrangement and now the other, changing his plan almost as often as some men change their shirts. Sometimes he was for selling all the land and sometimes for not selling any. Sometimes he wanted to part with the back and keep the front for himself and at others he could not bear either to part with the front or to give Lloyd's a decent access to the back. He was a source of great trouble to his associates in the transaction, and long before the deal with Lloyd's was settled the Managing Director of the real estate company was, in his own words, fed up with him. And so before long was the Chairman of Lloyd's who had even more at stake. He was convinced that Lloyd's future was closely concerned in the purchase of East India Avenue and he was determined to get it. But month after month he could make no progress in what he himself called the long and weary struggle.

The Chairman in 1922 and 1923 was Arthur Lloyd Sturge. He came from one of the Quaker families that have played so great a part in the history of Birmingham, and he possessed the qualities that have brought many members of the Society of Friends to wealth and eminence. At Lloyd's he had started in the same firm of brokers as Cuthbert Heath; and when he deserted the broking side of Lloyd's he became first a capable marine underwriter and then one of the pioneers of the new non-marine market, originating the householders' comprehensive policy which is now a familiar document over most of the world. When he was elected Chairman at the end of 1921 he brought to the office great determination and great patience, and he surprised himself by the remarkable capacity he developed for carrying on negotiations in the unfamiliar sphere of real estate. He believed that former committees had handled the question of premises too timidly and been far too much inclined to turn down everything that was offered. Land in the City was getting more and more scarce and Lloyd's could not afford (he said) to 'go on turning things down'. Somehow or other Kylsant must be made to sell a part of the East India Avenue and on that spot a new building for Lloyd's must be raised.

All through the year 1922 the shilly-shallying continued and the real estate company grew so angry with Kylsant that they threatened to make a claim on him for £50 a week until he could finally make up his mind. What their legal rights were is not clear but they declared that they were losing £100 a week themselves, and the fact that they spoke of imposing on their fellow-owner what amounted to a fine showed that their patience was wearing very thin. It was not indeed till well on in the year 1923 that the ice began to crack and serious proposals could be discussed.

In June of 1923 Sturge over the lunch-table had a long private meeting with Kylsant and made some apparent progress. In July Kylsant changed his mind for the last time. In August Lloyd's were offered 44,000 square feet of the land at the back of the site (the land on which the Underwriting Room was built), a passage through to Leadenhall Street and a frontage of 60 feet to provide a dignified entrance. The price asked was £545,000. On the 29th August 1923, Lloyd's Committee (subject to the agreement of Lloyd's members) made a counter-offer of £500,000, and after another two months of discussion between Kylsant and the real estate company the counter-offer was accepted. In December the proposal was submitted to a General Meeting and soon afterwards Lloyd's was the owner of one of the largest and finest sites in the City of London – committed to a new building that would cost with the land not less than £1,000,000. It was a far cry from the time only six years back when an extra charge of £12,000 a year for accommodation was thought to be prohibitive.

The meeting of 1923 at which the members gave their approval to the building scheme was in extraordinary contrast to the Captains' Room meeting of 1921. Now there was no opposition, no passionate speech-making, no quotations from Longfellow, no appeal to the spirit of Edward Lloyd. Everything was harmony and enthusiasm. Such discussion as there was concerned itself with details and when the vote was taken it was overwhelmingly favourable. Not one hand was raised against the proposal and at the close of business a resolution was passed that Sturge should be presented with the Lloyd's Gold Medal – the highest honour that the members can bestow. Whether the meeting knew of the endless patience Sturge had shown and the succession of disappointments that he had taken in his stride, is doubtful. But they did know that he had solved their housing problems for them, that the underwriting boxes, then cram-med into ten thousand feet, would in future have sixteen thousand feet, and that the site had been secured for £12 10s. 0d. a foot while land a few hundred yards away was valued at nearly £50 a foot. They were delighted. In their innocence they believed that the comfort of Lloyd's would be secured for another century and if they and Sturge were both mistaken on that head no blame falls on them, for no one could foresee the enormous changes that were to take place in the next thirty years.

Indeed if they had foreseen the growth that lay ahead and the great development of the future they would have been more eager even than they were, to secure the new building, for it was by chance to prove not only useful in itself but an admirable jumping-off ground for later movement. The purchase of East India Avenue was one of the best strokes of business the Corporation of Lloyd's ever did and Sturge, whose patience and skill made the business possible, must in this matter be placed as high as Angerstein who captured the lease at the Royal Exchange a century and a half before.

.    .    .    .    .    .    .

Before the move to Leadenhall Street members of the Committee staff had swarmed several times and established colonies at various points north and south of Cornhill. By 1923 there were ten of these settlements at work at different addresses in the City signing policies, keeping account-books and looking after the shipping index. And one of the objects in erecting the new building was to bring the groups together again under one parental roof. But the days of comfort in the new building were comparatively short. In March 1928 King George V opened the new building and three years later, in 1931, the then Chairman of Lloyd's was negotiating to buy the Royal Mail Building adjacent to Lloyd's which had been erected about the same time as Lloyd's own building. In the financial blizzard of 1931 the Royal Mail Empire had collapsed, its assets had been split up, and a buyer was wanted for the Kylsant office block. The obvious purchaser was the Corporation of Lloyd's, but five years passed before the building actually changed hands. Then in 1936 it was bought by Lloyd's for £800,000 and the whole property – the Lloyd's Building and the Royal Mail Building – came into one ownership and under one management. Lloyd's were now freeholders of one of the largest blocks of land in the City of London.

Royal Mail House was bought to provide room for future expansion, and just as the men of 1844 and the men of 1923 believed that they had secured space for many years to come, so did the men of 1936 consider the housing problem of the future to be solved. But again demand caught up with supply and soon after the Second World War ended the Principal Clerk was busy once more trying to force a pint and a half into a pint pot. The number of members was constantly rising, the turnover of business was constantly growing; and apart from the increase in turnover and in the premium income everything connected with the place was becoming more complex. In the non-marine market, at any rate, the technique of underwriting was far more intricate than it had been in 1919, and both marine and non-marine men needed more seats for themselves and their clerks. The days when a man and a boy could between them do the whole work of an underwriting syndicate were over.

Underwriters, too, wanted a great deal more help than they used to need from the staff of the Committee and that change involved frequent additions to the number of men and women employed by the Corporation and housed in the building. Many underwriters were relying more and more on the services of the Policy-Signing Office, whose function had broadened out far beyond the original bounds within which it had simply signed policies and returned particulars of them to underwriters' book-keepers. Underwriters had been helped by the Committee in making the banking arrangements which enabled them to offer overseas clients policies expressed in their own currency, and that development in itself called for the assistance and advice of a fairly large number of clerks employed directly by the Corporation. The American connections of underwriters hinged on negotiations carried out for them in Washington, New York and Chicago, and whenever a Government inside or outside the Commonwealth threatened British insurers with another dose of restrictive legislation it was the Committee and its staff that had to take up arms for underwriters. The underwriters' own associations, too, which looked after their purely underwriting problems grew every year in importance and needed more office space. All these changes, numerous and rapid as they were, came about not imperceptibly indeed but without their cumulative effect being noticed by the general run of members; and it is only when one looks back over the period and ticks them off one by one that one realizes the nature of the revolution that had taken place in thirty years, and sees Lloyd's as an organization vastly different from what it was when His Majesty King George V opened the new building in 1928.

In March 1921 the then Principal Clerk had written his memorandum to the Chairman setting out the housing troubles with which he was encumbered and stressing the need for more space. In 1948 his successor sat down to perform exactly the same task. The Principal Clerk was different. The Chairman was different. The wording of the memorandum was different. But the problem and its solution were the same. Space was too short and somehow new premises must be acquired. How were they

The scene in the Underwriting Room as the Queen was replying to an address of welcome on November 6, 1952, when with the Duke of Edinburgh she visited Lloyd's to lay the foundation stone of the New Building in Lime Street; from the painting by Terence Cuneo.

to be got? Should Lloyd's take over the whole of the Royal Mail Building (much of which was under lease to tenants) for its own use and submit the two buildings to a surgical operation which would make the two into one? Should it put up a gallery and get more space by a gamble with the appearance of the Underwriting Room? Or should it go nap on the future, buy a bombed site that faced it on the other side of Lime Street, and put up a new building there? All three possibilities were discussed in the Principal Clerk's memorandum and at a General Meeting in 1950 it was actually agreed to adopt the idea of a gallery which would run round the Underwriting Room and provide a quantity of seating space. But the idea was abandoned and later in 1950 the Committee decided, with no little courage, to go nap and buy the bombed site.

The freehold of that site belonged to several different owners but the lease of most (if not the whole) of the land was held by the same real estate company that had sold the East India Avenue to Lloyd's in 1923. In 1950 the Committee 'after long and complicated negotiations' made a provisional agreement with the company for a ninety-nine years' lease, and a General Meeting authorized it to 'proceed with such further negotiations and to make such financial provisions or other arrangements and to execute such agreements or other documents as the Committee think fit'. That was perhaps the boldest step ever taken by a General Meeting at Lloyd's and the most remarkable sign of confidence in their Committee that the members have ever given.

After the agreement to take a ninety-nine years' lease from the real estate company had been signed the position was this: The land still belonged to the original owners but was, by agreement, to be let to the real estate company and sub-let by the company to the Corporation of Lloyd's. Whatever building was erected would remain in Lloyd's possession only for ninety-nine years, and at the end of that period would either revert to the freeholders or be the subject of a new and no doubt more onerous lease. Why should not Lloyd's, already freeholder on the West side of Lime Street, try to become freeholder on the East side too? Why not buy the bombed land outright? The attempt was made. Negotiations were opened and successfully carried through and in due course the Corporation of Lloyd's secured the freehold at a cost of about £900,000. Subject to the rights of the real estate company, they became absolute owners of three acres in the heart of the City of London. Within thirty years the Society which had never before owned a yard of land anywhere in London had become the largest private freeholder in the City.

T

# 14

## THE FAILURE OF HARRISON

*Danger of audit being outwitted by fraud – Harrison – Motor hire purchase – Guaranteeing bills – Heavy losses – Financed by more guaranteed bills – Cheque dishonoured – Chairman intervenes – Committee's action – Meeting of Underwriters – Agreement to pay Harrison's losses – Policy signed – Formula for payment – Amount borne by underwriters and Corporation – Law action against Corporation – Criticism of Boulton unjustified – Wilcox case thirty years later*

---

To EXAGGERATE THE IMPORTANCE to Lloyd's of the underwriting audit is almost impossible. When it was introduced it was the greatest reform ever attempted within the Lloyd's system. It has conditioned all the other reforms made at Lloyd's in the past forty years and it is the keystone round which the structure of Lloyd's security is now built. But reformers who have looked forward, as Heath, Boulton and their associates looked forward in 1907, to some great change, and have worked long and hard to bring it about, are apt, when the goal has actually been reached, to expect too much from it. Sometimes there is disappointment and even cynicism at the reform's results. After the British Reform Act of 1832 had been passed into law there were in the country three different ways of looking at it – the way of the die-hard who knew that it was Britain's final disaster, the way of the Whigs who believed that it satisfactorily fixed the liberties of Britain for all time, and the way of the radicals who soon came to think that it had done nothing for them at all.

When the members of Lloyd's accepted the audit in 1908 they were on their little stage passing their own Reform Bill; and, unanimous though the decision had been, there were certainly still some die-hards who expected disaster. There were Whigs who believed that no other reform would ever be needed and there were a few far-sighted men who had worked hard to bring the audit into existence, but realized that it was not the last word in reform. Cuthbert Heath was one of these men and Sidney

Boulton was another. Boulton had long had schemes in his head for radical changes in the liability of a Lloyd's policy, and Heath in May 1909 wrote to the Committee a letter or memorandum declaring that (despite the audit) failures among underwriters might still occur. They would not be so numerous as in the past and probably not so large. But the possibility had not been completely eliminated by the audit and from time to time failures must be expected.

When he wrote that letter Heath may have had in mind the danger of deliberate fraud. He may have seen that the audit took for granted a certain elementary standard of honesty in all the underwriting agents – honesty strong enough at any rate to prevent them from diddling their auditors and extracting a worthless certificate of solvency by concealment or active misrepresentation of fact. He must have remembered Burnand and the tricks that he had played, and it may have struck him that the audit by itself would not have forestalled either Burnand's dishonesty or his unscrupulous devices. And what Burnand had done in the past Heath may have realized that others might do in the future.

If those were his calculations he was not far wrong, for within fifteen years of the audit coming into operation two cases of dishonesty occurred, both of them the result of financial gambling and dishonest book-keeping after the First World War. One of them was comparatively unimportant and involved no loss except to the members of a single syndicate; but the other was so widespread as to require the co-operation of all underwriting members of Lloyd's to set it right. That second failure was the famous Harrison case. If it had been timidly handled it might seriously have disturbed the credit of Lloyd's; but in the final issue it not only revealed the strength of Lloyd's but led to fresh beneficial reforms along the lines that some reformers were advocating at the time the audit was introduced. The tradition of the Harrison case still lives but the details are growing blurred, for the story has never been told in detail. Younger men have for the most part only a vague idea of what Harrison did and of the permanent effect the episode had on Lloyd's. If only for their instruction the tale of his folly and collapse should be recorded now.

. . . . . .

Harrison was a comparatively young man who became a member of Lloyd's in the year 1917. In addition to a brokerage business, which he controlled, he had an underwriting agency and a syndicate of five names of which he himself was not one. He wrote a mixed account – marine, general non-marine, and motor – and his estimate of his own abilities was inclined to outrange their true worth. He was never at any time, or in any department of his business, a good underwriter and even if he had run straight and confined himself to legitimate risks he was not a man likely to make large profits for his names or secure for himself a leading position in the market. Even before the transactions that brought him down were exposed, he was known to be in minor trouble and he had been subjected by the Committee to certain additional audits which are reserved for underwriting accounts believed to require special attention from the authorities.

But what really led him astray was his motor account. It was unprofitable in itself, as more than one motor account at that time was, and (what was much worse) it brought him into touch with people outside Lloyd's, of whom some were a good deal cleverer than he was and some at least had learned from experience to recognize – when they saw one – a pigeon ready for the plucking. About one of these gentlemen, when enquiries were made after the smash, the advice received was 'Don't touch him unless you are wearing gloves and then only with a barge-pole'. By quick stages Harrison was led by the nose from stupidity to weakness, from weakness to dishonesty and from dishonesty to crime.

The circumstances were these. After the First World War there came upon the motor industry a burst of hire-purchase business which was necessary to enable mass-produced cars to be sold in the quantities that mass-production requires. Finance companies – at least thirty in number – were formed in England to buy cars from the makers or dealers, and hire them out on easy purchase terms to the men who would ultimately own them, the companies drawing on the hirers for payment in bills of appropriate length. The business prudently conducted was surprisingly profitable. Defaults among hirers were fewer than might have been expected, and when anyone made a default in his payments the hire-purchase company (which was the legal owner of the car) was covered at least to the extent of its second-hand value.

The company to keep itself supplied with working capital would take the bills to a discount house and so make a comparatively small amount of cash cover a considerable turnover. For that reason it was essential to the running of the business that bills drawn on hirers should be such as financial houses would readily accept. But sometimes discounters were shy of this new type of paper and their coyness turned the thoughts of an enterprising finance company to credit insurance. Nothing, it was felt, would improve the value of a bill more satisfactorily than a good insurance policy guaranteeing the credit of the drawee. At first the financiers seemed to have placed the risk with insurance companies, but when they discovered that there was a small but cheaper market at Lloyd's, they began to favour certain Lloyd's underwriters, of whom the busiest, the least inquisitive and the most dashing was Harrison.

In the year 1921 Harrison was brought into touch with a hire-purchase concern called the Industrial Guarantee Corporation and the day on which he started doing business with that company was the beginning of his downfall. Its original capital was two pounds and although two years later the available capital was said to be £2,000, it never at any moment had means to justify any large financial transaction. But its turnover was soon running into millions.

Harrison, whether he made enquiries about the company or not, trusted it and in the space of two years, for a premium of a little over £20,000, he guaranteed absolutely more than £2,000,000 of its bills, putting that enormous amount of money into circulation on the credit of five or six not very wealthy underwriters.

If Harrison had confined himself to the ordinary type of hire-purchase that structure of paper credit would never have been built up. But he was so ignorant or so careless that he did not distinguish between bills backed by cars already in the possession of the final purchaser and bills on cars waiting to be sold by the dealers. The first type of bill is clearly a much better proposition than the second. For one thing, the risk is far more widely spread and, for another, the car can be followed up and when necessary the security on it can be enforced by a sale. But when bills are drawn in respect of cars that have not yet found a buyer, the stock of unsold cars may increase and become unsaleable, and the guarantor may before long discover that he is financing the whole output of an unpopular model turned out by an inefficient factory to be a drug on the market. It is one thing to cover a car that is already sold and a very different thing to put your money on a range of cars that no one is ever likely to buy. The distinction, though not apparently clear to Harrison, was not overlooked by some of the gentlemen who lived with one foot in the car market and the other in finance and (to quote the words of a High Court Judge) it seemed to some of them, when they were told of Harrison's activities, that 'this was just a favourable opportunity for a fraud to be very easily committed'.

The man who was said – not very correctly – to have dealt Harrison his death-blow was a Swede living in London named Holsteinson, a man interested commercially in taxicabs and charabancs. Why he had come to England and how long he had been here is a mystery, for very little was known in this country about his antecedents. He spoke freely of his Swedish relations and the wealth of his family, but when the smash came and enquiries were made of a British Consul in Sweden, it turned out that Holsteinson's father was himself in the taxi-cab business and was assessed for income-tax at £500 per annum. In London Holsteinson grafted on to the family tradition of cab-owning a successful line of his own, his technique being to invent a number of imaginary cabs and charabancs, give them equally imaginary engine and chassis numbers, get bills drawn on the strength of their security, insure the bills with Harrison and then discount them with the help of Harrison's policy. In due course the bills would be either renewed or dishonoured and at a moment convenient to himself Holsteinson left the country – never so far as is known to be seen in London again.

It seems to have been in the early part of 1923 that Harrison learned from his associates of Holsteinson's character and was told that the Holsteinson bills would produce for him a loss of about £17,000. Compared with the deficiency that was piled up in the next nine months that is not a large figure and if Harrison's syndicate had been in a healthy condition the loss might have been borne, not indeed without discomfort but without disaster. But neither Harrison's own finance nor his syndicate was in a healthy state and to find £17,000 by honest means was beyond his power.

In addition to his deals with the Swede, Harrison was deeply committed with at least two English car manufacturing companies who, being short of capital, had run their business with the help of bills discounted on the strength of Harrison's policy. By one of them – the Angus-Sanderson Company – Harrison was given a debenture for a very large sum which he hawked unsuccessfully round the market with inflated stories of its value. It was also said that he had agreed to put money in a timber business in Manchester and being unable to find ready cash had given more bills backed by his own policies. He had helped his Names to pass the Lloyd's audit by backing bills which they themselves had insured and a private overdraft of his own was secured in the same way. Even before the Holsteinson thunderbolt fell he must have known that his position was bad. Holsteinson's collapse was the crowning catastrophe.

At one time in 1923 he and two of his Names were invited by some of their associates to a luncheon-party at the Langham Hotel – surely the unhappiest meal ever taken in that place so famous for its wedding-breakfasts – and there they were informed by representatives of the Industrial Guarantee Corporation of the blow that had hit them. One of Harrison's Names declared afterwards that at that lunch he and one other person pleaded with Harrison to go straight to the Chairman of Lloyd's, make a clean breast of the whole business and tell him exactly what had happened. But Harrison refused. If he breathed a word (he said) the Chairman would put a stop to his underwriting. And that was a disaster he could not face.

He was undoubtedly right when he said he would be stopped by the Chairman. His account most certainly would have been closed at once and that was an unpleasant thought to a man approaching middle-age who had adopted underwriting as his career. That consideration alone would have been enough to deter a weak man of Harrison's type. But Harrison had a far graver reason for holding his tongue, a reason that may have been unknown to the men with whom he was lunching, a reason that might make any risk however desperate, any device however dishonest, preferable to confession. The truth was that Harrison had not merely been keeping the Committee of Lloyd's in the dark about his credit underwriting. He had been perpetrating a deliberate fraud upon them. He had run in double harness two sets of books, of which one was shown to the auditors and the other, recording his credit transactions, was secret and undisclosed. The auditors' certificate, without which he could not trade, had been got by a trick and his credit difficulties could not be revealed to the Chairman without the fraud being admitted.

Among Harrison's advisers and associates there was another school of thought that recommended him to show a bold face to Lloyd's, to the discount brokers and to the world, to brave things out and to settle Holsteinson's bills with cash raised by more of this insured paper. There were always accommodators to be found who for a consideration would accept bills for any amount, and Harrison could turn bad bills into good and make the poorest accommodator's name acceptable by the issue of a policy. The bills would all be declared on the policy and nobody need know that they were mere accommodation paper. Harrison accepted that advice and eight or nine business men were found ready and willing to accommodate for a small fee. The stream of new paper went on running in stronger force than ever. All through the summer it continued and in the early autumn the managing director of one of the finance companies, though he knew about Harrison's difficulties, went on circulating the bills among men of standing and men of straw alike up to and possibly after the moment of final collapse. It is always said that a hunted fox in the middle of a run will stop to bite off a chicken's head as he passes through a farmyard, and Harrison and some of his friends seem to have had the same mentality.

At the beginning of October 1923, when Harrison was still playing his disastrous game, the audit sub-committee were watching his account and insisting on more money being paid into the Names' trust funds. The money (obtained through bills guaranteed by the Names themselves) was duly paid in, but the reports still were that the marine figures were bad and the non-marine worse. Two of the Names in fact wanted to give up marine underwriting as unprofitable – a fact that throws a very curious light on their ignorance of their own position. In the first week of October 1923 came the smash. A cheque of Harrison's was dishonoured. The Chairman of Lloyd's sent for Harrison and told him that his underwriting accounts must be inspected again immediately and although Harrison agreed to produce them – we can imagine with what feelings – the auditor reported next day that access to the books had been refused him. There was another meeting between Harrison and the Chairman, in which Harrison admitted that the affairs of his syndicate were in a hopeless state. A few days later the Chairman learned that the total number of guarantees outstanding could not be less than £200,000.

Lloyd's and its Committee were to receive a certain amount of criticism before the Harrison case was ended and most of it – particularly such as came from the judicial bench – was off the point and unreasonable. But at this distance of time it does appear that the Committee were open to one legitimate criticism and even now the answer to it is not clear. The astonishing feature of Harrison's business was the speed at which his difficulties grew. Between the time he launched out in his dealings with the Industrial Guarantee Corporation and the time when he confessed to the Chairman only two years had passed. Each week the commitments grew, fresh bills were put into circulation, and one man after another was added to the list of claimants who held bills and policies, often for genuine consideration. If the escapade had been discovered in March instead of in October the trouble and the scandal would have been much less serious than they actually turned out to be; and it remains a remarkable fact that through all these months the Committee of Lloyd's knew nothing of what was happening. They were uncomfortable about Harrison's general under-writing account and were watching it with special care. One of the members of Lloyd's Committee was chairman of a finance company which had been discounting some of the Harrison bills, and there was at least one other channel along which the news would naturally flow to the Committee.

For months bills insured by Harrison had been smelling and some had changed hands at a discount of sixty per cent. Even after Harrison had disclosed his plight to the Chairman of Lloyd's, after the Committee had begun their enquiries into the scandal, bills of a nominal value of £10,000 were sold by someone to a man who was described as a book-maker and moneylender. He paid £4,500 for them, and the gentleman who arranged the sale was said to have received for his services a commission of £2,000, leaving a sum of £3,500 as the net proceeds. Whether there is an established market in London for paper of this sort, and (if there is) who are its constituent members, is a mystery. But it is pretty clear that a good many people had known what was happening and had had at least an inkling of the tricks Harrison was playing; and the Committee might surely have known of the business long before they actually did, and have taken the appropriate action.

But if the Committee were open to criticism for what they failed to do before October, they certainly cannot be accused of apathy or neglect from the beginning of that month onwards. Immediately after the scandal had been unearthed they spent a few days of rapid intense investigations and mastered the complicated story well enough to be able to call a meeting of underwriting agents, lay the facts before them, and get their backing for a salvage scheme. The meeting took place on the 11th October, eight days after Harrison's confession, and was probably the first full meeting ever presided over by a Chairman of Lloyd's to discuss the affairs of a defaulting underwriter.

The Chairman at the time was Sturge and he explained to his fellow underwriting agents how the trouble had arisen, told them that the deficiency on the bills' account would certainly be over £100,000, would probably be £200,000 and might quite possibly be £300,000. All these estimates proved ultimately to be under the mark, but it is surprising that in a few hectic days Sturge and his assistants could have unravelled the skein far enough to get within £80,000 of the final figure. Having given the facts as he then knew them, Sturge made what was really an historic statement. 'If we do not pay these bills', he said, 'the name of Lloyd's will be seriously injured and will never recover during our lifetime.' Never before had the members of Lloyd's been told by their Chairman that they must pay the claim of a defaulting underwriter. Never had a Chairman's moral authority (for of legal authority in this matter he had none) been so directly, so firmly, so openly exercised. These are the facts, he said, and this is my proposal. I have no power to enforce it. But it is your duty and your interest to do what I ask. He invited them then and there to guarantee £200,000 to pay Harrison's debts on the bills.

In the discussion that followed Sturge's speech no one questioned his main thesis that the debts must be met, but there was some disagreement about method. Sturge had suggested that the £200,000 could be subscribed by all underwriters, marine and non-marine, in proportion to their premium incomes; and at that point the meeting began to deviate (as meetings are apt to do) into byways. A marine underwriter thought that as this was a non-marine loss it should be met entirely by non-marine underwriters. Another thought it premature to discuss the provisions of funds in this way until more was known about the deficiency and how large it would be. Another considered that the broker who had introduced the business to Harrison should be forced to make a special contribution. Another demanded that credit insurance should at that meeting and for all future time be barred. Another suggested that only a general agreement to foot the bill ought at that moment to be asked for and that a special committee should be formed to deal with the apportionment of the loss.

But Sturge would have none of these things. He had in full measure the Quaker gift of concentrating on essentials, and he saw that the essential need then was for speed. It was not enough merely to make a decision in principle. That might involve long delay in the discussion of details. Here and now the necessary money must be promised and the meeting must not only agree to the general proposition of accepting liability for the payment of all honest claims, but must specifically guarantee the funds with which to pay them. There must be no delay, no room for drawn-out arguments. The £200,000 must then and there be offered to the Committee of Lloyd's for immediate distribution.

In his admirable conduct of the meeting Sturge would take nothing less than that, and thanks to his clear-sighted leadership the motion which was put was carried unanimously. It was not a very formal or even a completely grammatical motion, and a competent lawyer, if he had so desired, could probably have driven a coach-and-four straight through it. But it served its purpose and before the underwriting agents separated they had agreed to bear the burden for themselves and their Names in proportion to their premium incomes. Within a few days a slip for £200,000 had been initialled and the Committee were in funds.

So the guarantee of the debts arising from Harrison's credit underwriting was agreed by the other underwriting agents. For reasons that may have been connected with taxation, the guarantee was put into the form of an insurance contract. A premium of 2s. 6d. per cent was paid by the Corporation to the underwriters for writing a risk that was known to be a loss before it was written. A slip was initialled and a policy signed. The original policy is still in existence – a document of no little significance which, even if it is never exhibited, should be kept permanently in the Corporation's archives. It has indeed a twofold interest. It is the first outward and visible sign of the sense of corporate responsibility which marks the modern Lloyd's. And it is probably the only policy in the history of underwriting in which has appeared the signature of every Lloyd's syndicate and every person underwriting for himself alone. In that respect it is unique.

Large underwriters, medium-sized underwriters, small underwriters, and tiny underwriters – so tiny some of them as scarcely to be underwriters at all – put their names to the policy for their share of the £200,000; and as the shares were fixed in proportion to premium incomes an inquisitive-minded member could have seen exactly what share of the total premium income of Lloyd's came his way and how much went to his competitors. Altogether the document carried the signatures of two hundred and forty-four syndicates and underwriters trading for themselves, some of which must surely have seen the light of day only on the rarest occasions.

The largest subscription of any syndicate was £10,269, and from that figure it is clear that over five per cent of the whole premium of Lloyd's went at that time into the coffers of one concern. The smallest subscription was for eightpence. The underwriter who accepted that eight-pennyworth of liability was an aged member and in 1923 the Father of Lloyd's. The annual premium income of his account (if we work backwards from his line on this policy) must have been less than one-six-millionth part of the Lloyd's total. His premium income must have been about £3 a year. By the time he had settled his claims and met his working expenses the net profit on the account cannot have been large. But when a total loss was claimed on the Harrison guarantee policy he paid up his eightpence like a man.

The gathering at which the agreement to meet Harrison's losses was obtained was a meeting of underwriting agents only and the payment to which it consented was to be made entirely by underwriters. Brokers were not to be asked for contributions. But the Brokers' Association held its own meeting to discuss what should be done and strangely enough, though their business connections were to be preserved for them at the underwriters' expense, the brokers at the Association's meeting do not seem to have been in favour of Sturge's scheme. The majority wanted to have credit insurance forbidden at Lloyd's in future and they called for a declaration from the Committee that the claims on Harrison's syndicates should be paid excepting – and the exception was vital – all claims on financial guarantee policies.

They actually proposed that on these financial guarantee policies the Committee should disclaim all responsibility. Apparently they were content to allow a default of some £300,000 to occur on Lloyd's policies, satisfied that neither the reputation of Lloyd's nor their own business as brokers would suffer in consequence. It may be that when the meeting was held most of the brokers did not appreciate the full facts or understand the service that the underwriting agents were prepared to carry out at their own expense. Two of the largest firms of brokers dissociated themselves from the decision of the brokers' meeting and perhaps they knew more of what was at stake than the smaller brokers. But, whatever the reason may be, the queer fact remains that the underwriters who would have to do the paying wanted to pay, and the brokers who would be protected at someone else's charge were doubtful of the wisdom of paying at all.

Lloyd's Committee rightly took no notice of the Brokers' Association's advice and (the undertaking to pay being completed) a special joint sub-committee was appointed to investigate the claims and divide the money between them. Over a period of weeks or months the Committee met almost daily, disentangling the complicated web that Harrison had spun, moving through a maze of bills, debentures, bankruptcies and receiverships, weighing the merits of the different claims, honest, semi-honest, and worthless, and managing somehow to reach a logical conclusion at the end of their labours.

A prominent member of this sub-committee was Charles Wright, the historian of Lloyd's, whose work of authorship may have been started during the turmoil. The book was finished not very long after the scandal but in it he gave only one short paragraph to Harrison and his ill-deeds. It is a pity that he had to be so sparing in his treatment of the episode, for he knew as much of the affair as anybody, and a record from his pen would not only have been of great interest but would have made this present chapter unnecessary. Perhaps in the circumstances he could not deal more fully than he did with Harrison. Certainly he could not have done what must be done now – he could not have recorded the great value of the service that he and his fellow-members of the special committee did for Lloyd's. They worked like Trojans. They were faced with a mass of transactions that ran by degrees from what was completely honourable to what was blatantly criminal, reaching at the lowest point a Scotsman who was already in prison for fraud. All they could do was to apply the broad principle that all honest losses should be paid, while all losses from fraudulent and speculative deals should be refused.

Attempts were made to express that principle in exact language but the sub-committee soon discovered that it could not be done, and Wright proposed a very broad formula which served throughout the enquiry as the Committee's guiding light. This was the wording:

> The Committee favour a settlement on the basis of paying such portion of the claim as in their view represents the amount of money originally found by the holders of these bills but the Committee reserving the power to refuse claims altogether or to pay only such portions as they deem equitable.

The Committee in fact was to decide each case on its own merits in the light of natural justice, and they did it so successfully that at the end there was comparatively little dissatisfaction among the claimants and at least one firm of very high standing wrote to the Committee in June 1925 to thank them for the fair and generous treatment they had received.

It should be emphasized at this point that the sub-committee concerned itself only with Harrison's credit business – the business which had escaped the audit by the fraud of the secret ledgers. The genuine account which had been laid before the auditors had been bad and unprofitable, but all claims on it were settled and all creditors paid without voluntary contribution, either from the Corporation of Lloyd's or from the body of underwriters. The premium trust fund, together with the deposits and the customary guarantee policies, provided money enough to wind up the underwriting and leave no deficiency. With all that side of Harrison's business the normal machinery of Lloyd's was able to deal, and in difficult circumstances its effectiveness was satisfactorily proved. The special sub-committee had nothing to do with it, confining itself to the credit underwriting which Harrison had dishonestly concealed.

The claims made on the special committee came from all sorts and conditions of men, managers of insurance companies and joint-stock banks, merchant banking houses, discount houses and private discounters, and some accommodators whose suffering would have wrung the Committee's heartstrings if it had not been known that they made a profession of accepting bills they knew they could never meet. Perhaps the most remarkable thing was that a well-known millionaire had, in perfect good faith, discounted, either just before or just after the smash, bills of a face value of £37,000. He received from the Committee the full amount he claimed, reduced only by a reduction from seven to three per cent in his rate of interest. Another claimant, for whom one feels a great respect, was a gentleman with a German name who was offered an *ex gratia* payment and would not take it. Instead he brought and lost an action against Harrison's Names. After the action the sub-committee renewed its offer of an *ex gratia* payment and he refused it a second time. Whoever he was, and whatever his business, he seems to have been one of the few people outside Lloyd's who came out of the affair with reputation and dignity unimpaired.

When the accounts of the credit insurance business were finally closed they showed that the special committee had disbursed a net sum of £367,787, for not one penny of which had the Corporation of Lloyd's or Harrison's fellow-underwriters had any legal liability. Everything that was done, every pound that was paid, was *ex gratia* and both work and money had been expended only to protect the good name of Lloyd's and save honest claimants from a loss on a Lloyd's policy. But where exactly did the money come from? It came mainly from the following sources:

£200,000   subscribed by Lloyd's underwriters in accordance with the resolution at the meeting of agents.

£100,000   contributed by the Corporation of Lloyd's from its own resources.

£88,468   from what was known as the Mutual Fund – a fund which non-marine underwriters had been voluntarily accumulating for some years. The chief interest in the Fund today is that it helped to pay Harrison's debts in 1924 and was the prototype of the much larger central guarantee fund created in 1925 which has been in existence ever since.

When all payments to the policy-holders had been made there remained of the money subscribed a surplus of a little more than £20,000 – roughly five per cent of the total. Considering the uncertain and perplexing circumstances in which the estimate of the losses was made, the Committee could well be congratulated on a very creditable piece of budgeting.

  .  .  .  .  .  .

For the Corporation of Lloyd's the climax of the Harrison case was not the payment of the last claim on the policy but an action at law in which the Corporation itself was the defendant.[1] The action was brought by the Industrial Guarantee Corporation in respect of a number of bills drawn by the Corporation and insured by Harrison's credit policy. The plaintiffs averred that the Corporation of Lloyd's had given them 'warranties and undertakings' to pay itself the claims on Lloyd's policies if the underwriters failed. The underwriters had failed. The Corporation of Lloyd's refused to pay in full. Therefore it had committed a breach of its undertakings and should be forced to pay up. There was a further plea that the audit had not been efficiently carried out, but the plea on which the plaintiff's case in fact rested was the claim that Lloyd's – not the underwriters but the Corporation – had promised to make good Harrison's deficiency.

*Prima facie* that was an extraordinary statement. Everybody who knew anything of business as carried on in the City of London understood that a Lloyd's policy was a contract between the assured and the underwriters named on it. The better-informed people realized that underwriters submitted themselves regularly to a certain discipline arranged by the Committee for the protection of the insuring public; but had anyone ever suggested that a disappointed policy-holder (if an underwriter failed) had legal recourse against the Corporation? According to the plaintiffs it was the Corporation of Lloyd's itself that had not merely made the suggestion but had advertised it to obtain more premium income for its members.

The argument for this revolutionary claim was founded on a lecture which had been delivered nearly three years before by Sidney Boulton at the Chartered Insurance Institute. It was called *The Story of Lloyd's* and it was a very good lecture – so good indeed that at least one person in Boulton's audience still remembers it clearly more than thirty years after it was delivered. It led – like many a lecture on Lloyd's composed and uttered by lesser men since Boulton's day – through the history of Lloyd's to the Society's present activities and its present system of security. It spoke (as everybody does speak) of 'Lloyd's Premium Income' and it contained this sentence:

It has justly been said that in its present organization Lloyd's has

[1] Lloyd's List L.R. Vol. 19, p. 78.

solved the problem of combining individual energy, enterprise and initiative with the collective security of a corporate body.

It was on that rock that the Industrial Guarantee Corporation built its case against the Corporation of Lloyd's.

If the lecture had been allowed to remain a lecture pure and simple, carrying the authority of only one man, then no one, not even the most desperate plaintiff, would have attached any legal value to it. But by an unhappy chance the Committee of Lloyd's in 1921 decided to reprint the lecture as a pamphlet for circulation among people enquiring about the working of Lloyd's; and this decision to publish was minuted with the rather unfortunate phrase 'for propaganda purposes'.

So we get this combination of facts: Boulton declaring that a Lloyd's policy has a collective security; the Committee of Lloyd's adopting Boulton's phrase; and the phrase itself with the Committee's *imprimatur* on it being circulated for the avowed purpose of encouraging the public to take out Lloyd's policies. That, said the Industrial Guarantee Corporation, was enough to establish contractual relations between the Corporation of Lloyd's and anyone who insured with Lloyd's after he had read the pamphlet. The managing director of the Industrial Guarantee Corporation had read the pamphlet, and the Corporation of Lloyd's was therefore legally responsible for the consequences of Harrison's default.

If the plaintiffs' argument had been accepted by the judge; if it had been established as good law that the reprint of a lecture intended primarily to entertain an audience was tantamount to a binding contract with all the world and his wife; if it could be examined, analysed and interpreted with the meticulous regard for language that is given to the construction of a charitable trust deed, then the result might have been embarrassing for a good many people besides Lloyd's.

To a layman the whole thing appears almost ludicrous but the judge took the argument seriously and said that if he had been forced to decide the point he would have found it a matter of great difficulty. But he never did decide it. Instead he found against the plaintiffs on other grounds. He confessed in his judgment that he had thought so poorly of the Industrial Guarantee Corporation and its behaviour that he had very nearly stopped the case without calling on the defendants, not because he was satisfied about the law but because the claim in itself was based on a train of dishonesty. He found that the Industrial Guarantee Corporation had not been induced to insure at Lloyd's by Boulton's lecture; that the suggestion of

Sidney Boulton, Chairman of Lloyd's, 1920–1.

their being influenced by it was an afterthought in their manoeuvres; and that if they had never read it they would still have done exactly what they in fact did. Their purpose in insuring was to enable Harrison to continue despite his insolvency and to conceal the state of his finances from the Committee. They had been throwing dust deliberately into the eyes of Lloyd's Committee and in this action they were trying to make the Committee pay the dustman's bill.[1]

Indeed, in the light of the evidence given before him, the judge could not have believed the plaintiffs' claim to be anything but dishonest; and the wonder is not that the claim failed but that it should ever have been brought into court. The chief witness for the plaintiffs was a Colonel Temple who was shocked by the deceit played on him in the *Story of Lloyd's*. He had taken the trouble, he explained, to enquire about the security of a Lloyd's policy from a firm of Lloyd's brokers and had received from them a copy of the pamphlet. It was that pamphlet which had dispelled any doubts he might have had and satisfied him that the whole funds of the Corporation of Lloyd's lay behind the liability of the underwriters on the policy. If his company had not been led into that belief by Boulton's lecture they would never have accepted Harrison's policy as a backing for their bills. Everything done was done on the strength of that lecture.

But, unfortunately for Colonel Temple, Boulton's lecture had been delivered on the 21st November 1921 and Sir John Simon, who was Counsel for Lloyd's, had with him in court bills insured by Harrison's policy which the plaintiffs had discounted months before that date – a chronological fact that was something of a facer for Colonel Temple. Altogether his cross-examination was a discomforting ordeal and the mental processes of the Industrial Guarantee Corporation, when they carried on the business, were laid bare beyond question. Here is an extract from the cross-examination:

*Sir John Simon:* You understood it to be a representation of Lloyd's that if you insured with a man who you knew to be on the rocks you would have £30,000,000 to pay the debt?

*Temple:* I do not admit that I knew him to be on the rocks.

*Sir John Simon:* Did not Harrison tell you before you even joined the company that he had been badly let down and he wanted to avoid revealing his position to the Committee?

[1] These are not precisely his Lordship's words.

U

*Temple:* He told me that he had been badly let down and that out of the funds he had at his disposal he could not meet the bills and his only method of meeting these bills was to draw upon the guarantee and the deposit he had at Lloyd's.

*Sir John Simon:* You were informed by the Committee in October 1923 that Harrison had been keeping two sets of books?

*Temple:* Yes.

*Sir John Simon:* And after this you carry through a transaction by which Mr M. drew a cheque for £37,000 and became the acceptor of fifty-two bills of which every one was dishonoured?

*Temple:* Certainly not. The transaction could never be done after Harrison had gone down. It was done on the guarantee of Harrison's policy.

*Sir John Simon:* All these fifty-two cases are included in your claim in this action.

*Temple:* I expect so. Yes.

The case against the Industrial Guarantee Corporation was indeed overwhelming and the action did little or no harm to Lloyd's. The facts were published almost all the world over and later on, when Harrison was brought up at the Mansion House on a charge of conversion, the New York *Journal of Commerce* reported the proceedings – surely the first time that that serious-minded paper ever concerned itself with the proceedings of an English police-court. Here and there people hostile to Lloyd's tried to discredit it by attacks based on Harrison's failure, but it was generally recognized that the audit (where it was allowed to function) had been effective and that Lloyd's underwriters had voluntarily, even eagerly, paid the debts that arose from Harrison's frauds. There is nothing to show that anyone was ever deterred from taking out a Lloyd's policy by the publicity given to this escapade of folly and crime.

. . . . . .

There was, however, one man who suffered and suffered undeservedly from the case – Sidney Boulton. Boulton (who had retired before Harrison's doings were known) was a devoted son of Lloyd's. Despite his faults, which were undeniable, he had done it great service, and the thought that his own words had been used as a weapon against the Society which meant so much to him was very galling. To some extent it overshadowed the last years of his life and his unhappiness was not lessened by the thought that the judge who tried the action had treated him personally with unfairness.

What Boulton had said in his lecture, though severely criticised in His Lordship's judgment, was a perfectly proper thing to say. He spoke first of the £30,000,000 as 'the premium income of Lloyd's' and in saying that he used a phrase which was then and is still in common use; which was then and is still perfectly understood; which neither then nor now could lead any person of ordinary knowledge and intelligence to overrate the strength of a Lloyd's policy. But the judge solemnly pointed out that Boulton's statement was inaccurate, that all premiums were paid to individual underwriters, not to the Corporation, and that Lloyd's had neither £30,000,000 of premium income a year nor thirty pence. That animadversion was a masterpiece of pedantry. If when you speak of Lloyd's you always mean the Corporation of Lloyd's, then Boulton was obviously wrong. But if you mean (as in nine cases out of ten you do) the body of men doing business in the Room, then he was perfectly correct and the judge's criticism was – with great respect – ridiculous. It is neither incorrect nor careless nor misleading to speak of Lloyd's premium income.

The other judicial criticism turned on the words 'collective security' that Boulton had used in his lecture. The judge was very severe with him on that head. But one would have expected that a lawyer so precise in his language as to resent the phrase 'Lloyd's premium income' would have been careful to maintain a high standard of accuracy himself; and that before trouncing Boulton for what he said, he would have quoted Boulton's words correctly. But that is exactly what the judge did not do. Boulton had spoken of 'collective security of a corporate body' and the judge without calling attention to what he was doing translated these words into the phrase 'corporate liability' which is not the same thing. Security and liability are not synonymous. To appreciate that you have only to think of cases in which the word security can properly and appropriately be used without indication of legal liability. For example a trader has security in the goodwill of his customers. They have no legal liability to continue buying his wares but the probability of their doing so is the most valuable security in the trader's possession. That is a fair analogy to what Boulton called the collective security of Lloyd's.

The value of that collective security was never more dramatically proved than it was in the Harrison case. Claims were paid by underwriters on policies of which they had known nothing, on which they had no shadow of legal liability, for which they had never received a penny of premium, on which if they had been so minded they could have turned their backs and passed by on the other side. But for all that they subscribed from their own moneys nearly £400,000 to pay the claims. They indemnified every claimant to the extent that his claim was thought to be fair. They paid out great sums on bills that were put into circulation when Harrison was known by the drawer to be on the rocks. They even paid people who had tried and failed to extract money from the Corporation by process of law. If ever the principle of collective security was followed, underwriters followed it in the Harrison scandal, and in doing that they did a great deal to enhance the good name of Lloyd's. No, no! That will not do. It is inaccurate. Let us say, rather, that they did a great deal to enhance the good name of certain persons trading as underwriting members of the establishment or Society generally known as Lloyd's.

It may be thought that the argument in the preceding paragraphs is unnecessarily laboured, but it is only right that the action of the Committee and of Sidney Boulton should be properly understood. Boulton's reputation suffered a good deal from the *Story of Lloyd's*, and even today many who remember the incident believe that he let the side down. The criticism, spoken and implied, that he had to endure was to a man of his temperament a very bitter draught and the taste of it remained with him till his death. Now after more than thirty years it must be pointed out that Boulton's lecture in the circumstances of its delivery was a reasonable statement; that what he said in the lecture was different from what Mr Justice Bailhache said that he said; and that if a mistake was made it was made not by him but by the Committee (of which he was not a member) when they decided to turn his lecture into a pamphlet.

·　·　·　·　·　·

Thirty years after the Harrison scandal was settled and done with Lloyd's had to deal with another case of dishonesty that caused the Committee a good deal of trouble and ended up in a criminal trial. In 1954 the Committee were told that a man called Wilcox, who had been in business for some years as broker and underwriting agent, was in difficulties. According to the chartered accountant who audited the books of Wilcox's syndicate neither Wilcox nor his Names had in their trust funds assets enough to carry them through the audit, the extent of their deficiency being estimated at a considerable figure.

A firm of accountants was at once instructed by the Committee to examine Wilcox's books and after some months of hard work they had a remarkable story to tell. The true deficiency was much greater than had been supposed and – what was worse – there was reason to believe that the underwriting books had been manipulated fraudulently over a period of some years. The size of the premium income had been concealed. Claims had been camouflaged. The trust fund had been tapped. Non-existent profits had been distributed. The Committee of Lloyd's had been misled into believing that audit requirements were satisfied by men of whom some – though they did not know it themselves – were in fact insolvent. So wide indeed was the gap between the true state of affairs and the audited figures, that grave doubts arose about the honesty of the chartered accountant who had been signing the annual certificates and enabling Wilcox to continue his career as an underwriting agent.

As the examination of the books continued, these doubts became certainties, and the remarkable fact was established that a fraudulent under-writer had for years been conspiring with a fraudulent chartered accoun-tant. That two birds, each so rare in his own surroundings, should chance to come together was extraordinary. The odds against such a thing happen-ing must be very long indeed. But happen it did, and the issue of the union was a conspiracy which managed temporarily to defeat the Lloyd's audit.

From the first there was never a moment's doubt that all creditors would be paid in full. No one who had been insured by the members of Wilcox's syndicate would lose by it. Funds at the disposal of the Com-mittee were employed, and it was even decided that in the special circum-stances of the case Wilcox's Names themselves should be relieved of their normal underwriting liability and have the whole of their debts discharged for them. But the question remained what was to be done with Wilcox and his accomplice. Should they be allowed to go scot free or should they be prosecuted and suffer whatever punishment a judge at the Old Bailey might think appropriate to their crime? The natural inclination of a Committee faced with this decision would be to avoid publicity. But in this case the Committee of Lloyd's, with some courage, decided to have the linen washed in public, feeling no doubt that the two men could not be allowed to go unpunished. One of the two pleaded guilty and the other not guilty; and after a long and exhausting trial both received heavy sentences. It was an unpleasant affair but it proved again the determination of Lloyd's members that no Lloyd's policy-holder should ever lose by the insolvency or misconduct of a Lloyd's underwriter.

# 15

## HARRISON'S AFTERMATH
## AND THE BATTLE OF CREDIT INSURANCE

*Dispute over credit insurance – Remarkable proposals – Heath's belief in credit insurance – Sturge v Heath – Danger of law-suit – Compromise banning direct credit insurance – Business turned over to a Company – Its prosperity – New clause to be printed on Lloyd's policies – New duty given to Policy Signing Office – Changes in Lloyd's in twenty years*

---

THE HARRISON DISCLOSURES when they were first made naturally shocked everyone who cared for the good name and future of Lloyd's and a very strong feeling sprang up not only against Harrison himself but against the whole business of credit insurance which had caused all the trouble. Those whose memories went back twenty years recalled the Burnand folly in the same field. And, apart altogether from Harrison's mad ventures, the members of the Committee knew that once quite recently a Lloyd's policy for £12,000 had been signed by one name only guaranteeing the solvency of the Law Car & General Insurance Company which subsequently failed. This credit insurance business (many members felt) was altogether too explosive to be handled. It must be abolished and outlawed. And the sooner that happened the better for everybody. At one of its earliest meetings the special sub-committee, whose terms of reference might be thought to exclude such general considerations, passed a resolution dealing drastically with the future of this type of underwriting. They recommended to the Committee of Lloyd's that in future underwriters' deposits should not be available for credit risks.

The Committee adopted the suggestion and amplified it. They called another meeting at which Sturge told the underwriting agents that everybody had agreed to pay his proportion of the £200,000, but in consideration of this payment the Committee had given an undertaking that 'appropriate steps would be taken to prevent the recurrence of such a disaster'. He was going to explain at that meeting what the steps were.

The Committee, he said, were resolved that:

1. In future they would not audit any account that contained financial guarantee business.
2. All policies should be signed at the Policy Signing Office and stamped there.
3. All policies should bear a statement that the securities and guarantees held by Lloyd's are not available for guarantee business.

If one looks back in cold blood on these proposals without remembering the circumstances in which they were made they appear simply astonishing. Not only did they run counter to the tradition of Lloyd's but they flouted the existing trust deeds and contradicted one of the Acts of Parliament under which the Society was then and still is constituted. The Lloyd's Act of 1871, it will be remembered, confined the activities of Lloyd's to marine insurance but the Act of 1911 extended them to cover non-marine. And that Act of 1911, throughout its sections, carefully included guarantee insurance as one of those activities. In seven different places it spoke of guarantees as permissible and at one place it contained the following words:

> The objects of the Society are hereby extended to include the carrying out of the business of insurance of every description including guarantee business.

Not only does guarantee insurance come within the comprehensive phrase 'business of every description' but to avoid any uncertainty it is expressly included – the only form of non-marine insurance that is specially mentioned from beginning to end of the Act. It almost looks as though the men who drafted the Act set more store by credit insurance than by all the other forms of non-marine business put together. And now the Committee goes on an entirely different tack. Where Parliament says so emphatically 'Thou shalt' the Committee followed the example of Gilbert's Chancery draftsman who put everything right by reading the word 'not' into an Act of Parliament.

They were proposing, too (and this is scarcely less remarkable), to limit the purposes for which underwriters' deposits had been originally put up. And that surely must have been *ultra vires*. For future members some such change might well be practicable. Undertakings could be asked from them before election that would bar them from accepting credit risks except on terms approved by the Committee. But members already elected were in a very different position. Their deposits had been in trust for years and most, if not all of the deeds, named private persons as the trustees. The purposes for which the deposit had been made were set out in detail and there was no doubt that non-marine deposits were available for claims on credit insurance policies. And here was the Committee of Lloyd's resolving by a stroke of the pen, with or without the consent of the trustees and certainly without any order of the Court, to alter the deeds and restrict the uses to which the funds could be put. There is no record of any legal opinion being taken by the Committee and as the full report of the proceedings at the meeting of agents is not now available we cannot know whether the point was taken at the meeting itself. But there was certainly some opposition and the meeting was adjourned 'to enable those present to consider the Committee's suggestions'.

By the light of pure reason the Committee's proposals must be judged to be wrong, but in the light reflected from the Harrison scandal they can easily be understood. Not only had the Committee themselves been horrified by what had been going on behind their backs, but among the body of members they had found the same indignation and the same determination to prevent such a thing happening again. Without serious difficulty they had persuaded members to subscribe the £200,000, but against that promise to pay they had themselves given a promise to make such a scandal impossible in the future. They were convinced that credit insurance could not be checked in time by any audit formula devisable by man, and risks that could not be satisfactorily audited were risks that must not be written. The meeting of agents (the Committee anticipated) would recognize that plain fact and support them without legal hairsplitting in the very simple reforms that they now proposed.

But they had over-estimated their influence with the underwriting agents. Opposition showed itself at the meeting and it was serious enough to make the Committee of Lloyd's postpone their reforms and pass the matter over to a sub-committee, made up of non-marine underwriters, which could with some authority thrash out the difficulties and negotiate with the opposition.

Of that Committee of non-marine underwriters one member still survives and happily he possesses one of the most tenacious memories that God ever bestowed on mortal man. The details are still clearly in his head and he recalls the division of opinion among his fellow-members who were at once reluctant to sacrifice their underwriting freedom, fearful of the damage this dangerous type of risk might do in the hands of a second Harrison, and anxious not to deny their support to Cuthbert Heath, the father of their market. For Heath was not only the founder of modern non-marine insurance at Lloyd's. He was in England, at any rate, the father of credit insurance and he believed passionately not only that it was a legitimate business but that it was one of the bright hopes in the future of international trade. To the day of his death he maintained that belief with increasing vigour, and some people were inclined at times to think that he was in danger of becoming a man with an *idée fixe* attaching far too much importance to his pet panacea of credit insurance.

To that criticism of Heath an answer comes from the most vigorous of his competitors, Sir Frank Nixon. Sir Frank was the head of the Export Credits Guarantee Department which was started by the British Government between the two wars to do the work that Heath wanted to see done by Lloyd's. And this is what Sir Frank Nixon says of him:

> The supremacy of the Bill of Exchange which lasted over a hundred years has been a little diminished. War, nationalism, and the general feeling of insecurity have made it difficult for the Bill of Exchange in the twentieth century to fulfil the same role that it did in the nineteenth. Just as it took a genius to invent a Bill of Exchange, so it required another genius to devise and launch the instrument which might not supplant but supplement the Bill in this brave new and insecure age. I believe that that instrument is the credit insurance policy. I believe that the genius who launched it was Cuthbert Heath.

That tribute to Heath and his credit insurance policy was paid nearly twenty years after his death but it gives the clue to Heath's feelings in 1923 when the Committee launched their head-on attack on credit insurance. He saw Lloyd's with the ball at its feet, able to play a leading part in a new and most valuable department of insurance and throwing the opportunity away at the order of a Committee panic-stricken, as he believed, by the crime of one man which would never be repeated. That in itself was bad enough but when the deed was done without legal warrant and in defiance of the Charter of Lloyd's the situation was intolerable and he was ready to fight the Committee.

It was unfortunate that the two protagonists in this dispute were Sturge and Heath. Both had done great work for Lloyd's but their temperaments did not permit them to work easily together. The clash between them was severe and sharp. Sturge, backed by the Committee of Lloyd's, decided to exclude credit insurance from the audit and in the annual instructions to auditors he inserted a paragraph forbidding them to audit a credit insurance account. Every year these instructions are submitted to the Board of

Trade for its approval and usually they go through without difficulty. But this time Heath intervened. He took legal advice which must have confirmed his opinion that the Committee was acting *ultra vires*, and a solicitor acting for him told the Committee of Lloyd's flatly that if the Board of Trade adopted the alterations in the audit instructions Heath would apply for an injunction to prevent them from doing so.

The position, therefore, was that a dispute between the Committee of Lloyd's on one side and the most distinguished member of Lloyd's on the other was going to be brought into the open, and fought out in a court of law over the body of the Government department which was responsible for the legal management of the Society. It was an unpleasant prospect. The leaders on the two sides temporarily severed diplomatic relations with each other and ceased to be on speaking terms.

The feeling against Heath's attitude was running strongly and it was not confined to the Committee. When the sub-committee dealing with the settlement of claims on Harrison's policies started its work, a prominent Lloyd's broker had actually suggested that no payments to policy-holders should be made until credit insurance had been rendered impossible for the future. That illogical plan, if it had been accepted, would certainly have cleared the decks for a first-class domestic squabble, but it would have done irreparable damage to the credit of Lloyd's and quite rightly it was not well received. Heath, on his side, declared again and again that credit insurance was legitimate if properly conducted, that it ought to be profitable, that its abolition would be bad for Lloyd's and that in any case the Committee had no right to interfere.

Happily the open clash threatened by Heath's solicitor never came about. The instruction to the auditors which was to be the *casus belli* in open court was not pressed, and negotiations by third party continued between the two sides throughout the summer of 1924. A non-marine under-writer, who was at that moment chairman of the Non-Marine Under-writers' Association, was deputed by the Committee of Lloyd's to act as intermediary between them and Heath. It was hoped that one non-marine man speaking to another might be able to discharge a task that members of the Committee were finding impossible. The non-marine underwriter said afterwards that he wore out at least one pair of shoes walking back-wards and forwards between Lloyd's Committee Room and Heath's office. But he was a skilful and tactful negotiator and he broke down the barrier between Heath and the Committee of Lloyd's by a compromise which satisfied the Committee and partially satisfied Heath. The compromise was that credit insurance should be permitted, but only by way of re-insurance. No direct policies must be issued to the public. A merchant wishing to cover the solvency of his customers would not be allowed to bring the risk straight to Lloyd's, but must take it to a company; and the company, if approved by Lloyd's Committee, would be able to re-insure it with Lloyd's underwriters. Lloyd's in future would not be allowed to drink its credit insurance straight from the tap, but might drink if out of an approved filter. For the first time in the history of Lloyd's an official ban was placed on a particular line of business.

The veto (definite as it was) was cast in the form of a voluntary agreement. No consideration was mentioned and the legal force of the undertaking might perhaps have been questioned. But it has stood firm for some thirty years and no attempt has ever been made to evade it. It began in this way:

No underwriter will write *direct* financial guarantee business.

Then it went on to allow re-insurances of companies on condition:

1. That the companies re-insuring should be approved by the Committee of Lloyd's.

2. That prescribed safeguards should be adopted.

3. That policies should be signed and sealed at the Policy Signing Office.

4. (*a*) That guarantees and deposits (other than those specially provided for credit business) should be primarily available for business other than financial guarantee business.

(*b*) That the re-insurance policy should not be utilized for advertisement by the re-insuring company.

For an institution that had lived two hundred and fifty years on the freedom of individual underwriting those conditions were revolutionary enough, but the safeguards referred to in the second condition were more remarkable still.

By those safeguards every broker who placed a credit re-insurance was bound within a fortnight to give full particulars of the risk to the Committee of Lloyd's. Every loss on a policy must be advised to the Committee of Lloyd's immediately it was known. The policy wording must be approved by the Committee. Every underwriter doing credit insurance business must put up £1,000 deposit and if his premium income were more than £2,000 a year he must bring the deposit up to a sum equivalent to half his income. Not more than £500 per name in the syndicate could be accepted on any one firm, company, or individual. In the annual audit any insured bills not met on a due date must be regarded as total losses.

Those were some of the safeguards imposed by the Committee, and to crown the edifice of this security the following words took the place of an arbitration clause:

> Should any dispute arise under this agreement the decision of the Committee of Lloyd's shall be final.

So the Committee dictated the sources from which an underwriter could draw his risks, determined the wording of the policy that he signed, demanded details of every risk that he wrote, fixed the line he might write on any one risk, saw every claim as soon as it was advised, and secured beforehand the right to settle any dispute in their own favour. In the sphere of credit insurance the freedom of Lloyd's underwriting had practically disappeared, and the underwriters' movements were to be almost as closely watched as a prisoner's when he works outside the walls of Dartmoor Gaol.

Rather than cause an open breach at Lloyd's Heath, with all the legal cards in his hands, presented his opponents with all but complete victory and from that moment it was certain that the future of credit insurance could not lie at Lloyd's. The majority of active members were on the Committee's side in the dispute and it is possible that they were right. It may be a fact that this kind of business would not have fitted safely into a scheme of competitive individual underwriting. There are diversities of gifts and it may be that the genius of Lloyd's, with all its advantages in other directions, is not suited to the insurance of bills of exchange.

But the exclusion of credit insurance from Lloyd's did not involve either the end of the business or the abandonment of Heath's interest in it. Frustrated in one market he turned to another and found the companies ready to co-operate with him in keeping the business alive. Six years earlier he had started the Trade Indemnity Company in which he had intended to work the business of credit insurance in conjunction with Lloyd's. Instead, he increased its capital in 1924 and brought several insurance companies in as shareholders. Since then the majority of the directors of the Trade Indemnity Company have been General Managers of tariff offices and the company itself is a prosperous concern with an annual premium income of over £1,000,000 and a yearly issue of policies for more than £600,000,000. The transactions of the British Government which competes with the Trade Indemnity are not quite so large but they are substantial, and the total volume of credit insurance placed in Britain and on the continent of Europe in 1952 was not less than £2,000,000,000. All this is not strictly germane to the history of Lloyd's but it is interesting evidence of the potential business that Lloyd's in defence of its own security abjured and sacrificed in 1924.

• • • • • •

But even if the Committee of Lloyd's were able to forbid direct credit insurance what guarantee had they that no underwriter would ever resort again to Harrison's trick and carry on business as Harrison carried it on under the counter? If the thing had happened once why should it not happen again? What machinery had Lloyd's got to prevent it? The necessary machinery was found in the Policy Signing Office. Originally that office had been what might be called a private side-show – something that underwriters could use if they felt so inclined but (if they preferred to do their own work) could equally well leave alone. It was, in fact, in very much the same position as the Captains' Room. Attendance in the Captains' Room is not compulsory. The Committeemen who manage it do not (like the host in the parable) send their servants into the highways and hedges and compel the guests to come in. And until the Harrison affair the Policy Signing Office was managed on the same principle. There was nothing compulsory about it. But from 1924 onwards it has enjoyed a monopoly of signing policies. Except for a few small policies everything, marine and non-marine alike, is actually signed by it on behalf of underwriters and even the small policies that underwriters are allowed to sign for themselves must carry the Policy Signing Office's seal.

In fact if the seal of the Policy Signing Office is not on a Lloyd's policy then there is something wrong with the policy and a special warning is printed on every policy in these words:

> No policy or other contract dated on or after 1st January 1924 will be recognized by the Committee of Lloyd's as entitling the holder to the benefits of the funds and/or guarantees lodged by the underwriters on the policy or contract as security for their liabilities unless it bears at the foot the seal of Lloyd's Policy Signing Office.

That notice which has now appeared on all Lloyd's policies for more than thirty years is likely to remain there so long as Lloyd's policies are issued and a time may come when its origin and significance have been forgotten. Something of the kind happened in past years over the mysterious letters

S.G. which appeared in the traditional marine policy. Until Wright and Fayle in their *History of Lloyd's* settled the point for good and all, Lloyd's men with a taste for antiquarianism never tired of arguments about their significance. Two centuries from now there may be similar discussions about the meaning of that 1st January 1924 at the head of Lloyd's policy. As the Israelitish children when they looked at the cairn on the banks of Jordan asked their parents: 'What mean ye by these stones?' so underwriters may be asking in 2150: 'What mean ye by this date?' and the right answer will be that the date is January 1924 because Harrison confessed his wrong-doing in October 1923.

The monopoly given to the Policy Signing Office resulted, too, in another change. The Committee of Lloyd's put on to the Manager of the office the responsibility for detecting any credit insurance that might be brought to him for signature. He was given and still has the duty of seeing that every policy is examined to find out if it is a financial guarantee; and if he has any misgivings he must refuse to sign the policy and refer it to a sub-committee which will decide whether it may be signed or no. The Manager of the Policy Signing Office in fact exercises a censorship. He is a watch-dog trained to bark at the first suspicion of credit insurance. His authority in the matter has never been questioned either by brokers or underwriters, all of whom accept it, abide by it, and make no complaints about the loss of their traditional freedom.

Nevertheless, anyone who looks back with even the tiniest scrap of imagination over the sweep of Lloyd's history must surely be struck by these changes of 1924 and the length of the road the Society had covered in a short period of twenty years. In 1904 most underwriters had made deposits and many of them were writing non-marine risks of every kind except life insurance. For writing these risks they had no legal warrant and strictly speaking the policies they signed were not Lloyd's policies at all. But the Committee made no attempt to prevent them. Some underwriters had their accounts audited. Others never allowed an accountant to look at their books. And so far as the Committee were concerned they were at liberty to do exactly what they chose. The Committee made no distinction between the two. When an underwriter failed, as Burnand had failed, on the grand scale the Committee were disturbed and doubtless indignant but they did nothing to protect the assured on the defaulting policies and some even doubted whether the failures of individual underwriters did Lloyd's any injury.

Then came the movement of reform and in 1924, under the leadership of the Committee, the members of Lloyd's were taking on themselves the liability of a fallen fellow-member, accepting drastic limitations on what business they themselves might transact, and agreeing to members of the Corporation's staff censoring the risks they had written to detect breaches of the Committee's rules.

So far had they moved – not merely from the eighteenth-century coffee-house, but from the comparatively modern Lloyd's which they had themselves known, when they started work as office-boys in the early years of the twentieth century.

# 16

## FOREIGN LEGISLATION

*A persistent problem – Slowly recognized at Lloyd's – Nationalism – British requirements from foreigners – Division of assets open to criticism – Weakness of deposits – The ideal plan – Difference between Lloyd's and Companies – Macmillan's scheme – Its weakness – Discussions without decisions – Lloyd's not understood abroad – Difficulty of Lloyd's Clerk to the Committee – His memorandum – Its terms and importance – Neither adopted nor rejected*

---

IF THE GENERAL MANAGER of a composite insurance office were asked to name the most persistent problem that he and his forerunners had struggled with in the last fifty years he would probably answer 'Foreign legislation'. If you were to ask the Chairman of Lloyd's what he and his predecessors had found the hardest nut to crack in the past twenty-five years he would almost certainly give you the same reply. And the problem is not confined to the British offices and Lloyd's. It dogs the steps of every insurance industry which draws part of its income from the other side of national frontiers; and though the form it takes differs with place and circumstance its core is the same for every one who has to handle it. How is he to comply with the regulations of governments other than his own without freezing too much of his assets abroad in deposits and retained premiums?

The problem is obviously more important in this country than anywhere else, for thanks to the size of our insurance business it is connected closely with the national balance of trade. In outline, if not in detail, most of us have begun to understand the problem of the exchanges and learnt to appreciate the value of our invisible exports. But although the dangers of a weak currency are well recognized and the worth of invisible exports is familiar now to every schoolboy above the Upper Fourth, there are surprisingly few people who realize how important a place insurance holds among British exports or how much it does to strengthen the credit side of our ledger. If the facts were understood there would be less easy

A. L. Sturge, Chairman of Lloyd's, 1922–3; from a painting by Sir William Llewellyn, P.R.A., in the Library at Lloyd's.

talk of nationalizing insurance as though the process were as simple and harmless as the purchase of a local gas company. A good insurance connection is almost the ideal export, and our British connection has been built up by centuries of sweat and toil, by skilful underwriting, by vigilance and adaptability, by the accumulation and judicious use of reserves, by generous treatment of policy-holders and by not standing on the letter of the law when one of them presents a *bona fide* borderline claim. It is by giving the best service and by the best employment of their resources that British companies and underwriters have managed to take the hurdles set in their path by overseas governments.

In technical papers read to the Insurance Institute and other learned bodies these overseas obstacles have doubtless been described and discussed, but for some reason very little is said of them in books on insurance aimed at a more general audience. In Wright and Fayle's *History of Lloyd's* the subject is never mentioned. That omission may be explained by the date at which the book was published – 1928 – a year in which Lloyd's underwriters themselves were only beginning to comprehend the difficulties ahead of them. Marine underwriters – and Wright was primarily a marine man – still maintained something of the aloofness characteristic of the nineteenth century and were almost indifferent to the threat from abroad. If a non-marine underwriter spoke to them of legislative difficulties in the way of developing his foreign accounts they would answer in the spirit of the Chief Priest talking to the Iscariot, 'What is that to us? See thou to that.' Marine insurance, they argued, is by its nature international. Merchants and shipowners cannot be prevented from searching out the best market wherever it may be, and so long as Lloyd's underwriters provide them with better rates and better settlement of claims than they can get in their own country they will bring their risks to London.

The non-marine market, more vulnerable than the marine, was less insensitive to the growing danger, but even among the fire and accident underwriters there were some in the 1920's who did not see clearly what great changes were on foot. They did not realize the increasing difficulty they were going to have in playing their competitors in distant lands on their competitors' home ground. A problem that the British offices had recognized early in the century was not seen at Lloyd's as an urgent matter until the 1920's; and the present machinery for dealing with it was not devised until 1938. When the matter was at last tackled seriously it was seen to be more complex for Lloyd's than for the companies. Individual

w

underwriting was more difficult than the company system to fit into the new conditions.

More remarkable than the silence of Wright and Fayle is the reticence of Mr Raynes in his very full *History of British Insurance* published in 1948. The book contains a chapter on Legislation Controlling Insurance Companies but confines its survey to British laws and says little about the more important laws for the control of insurance abroad. Perhaps the subject was thought to be too delicate for open discussion or too complicated for detailed exposition in a single chapter, but to omit it altogether is to leave a significant gap and (incidentally) to deprive British offices of the credit which is their due for maintaining their position abroad in the face of ever-changing difficulties. In a book on Lloyd's a description of work done by the offices would be out of place, but it is not irrelevant to pay a respectful tribute to the skill, patience and enterprise with which they have kept the flag flying overseas in circumstances more difficult than earlier managements ever contemplated or encountered.

It is impossible to discuss foreign insurance legislation without remembering all the time that we live in an era of nationalism, regimentation and protection – influences that colour our politics, our way of living, and our private business. They undoubtedly colour insurance. In many countries there has been continual pressure on the Government to bring in laws that under the guise of security are designed to keep the foreigner out of the home market because he is a foreigner. In Communist states alien insurers are naturally barred, and in other totalitarian polities direct insurance by foreigners is prohibited or made as difficult as possible. But it would be a mistake to regard nationalism and protection as the only motives behind insurance legislation, much of which springs from a reasonable desire to shield an uninformed public from weak insurers whether native or foreign. That in itself is a proper purpose and one that cannot be attacked even by the strongest individualist.

Our own British legislation is a case in point. In 1870 the British Government forbad any life insurance company to issue policies in this country without first depositing £20,000 and the law applied to any foreign office that wanted to start business here. We demanded a deposit from foreigners just as foreign governments now demand a deposit from us; and the deposit must be made here in London. In 1908 a Liberal Government, elected on the issue of Free Trade, passed an Assurance Companies Act that for years controlled the management of fire and personal accident insurance; and in that Act it called for a £20,000 deposit from British and foreigners alike. In 1930 a Labour Government introduced the Road Traffic Act which set up a deposit of £20,000 apiece for companies insuring the third party liability of cars. And foreign companies had to make the deposit if they wanted to trade here – as at least one foreign company did. On the main principle of exacting deposits from foreign companies the British Parliament for years lived in a glass house of its own and could not decently throw stones at its neighbours who called for deposits too.

But whatever the British Government may have done in 1908 or 1930, the principle of forcibly dividing an insurance company's assets into separate national compartments is bad. Insurance ought to be international, and it is against common sense for a country, even if it be rich, to declare that all its risks of fire, death and accident must be borne by its own nationals – or even borne in the first place by its nationals and then sent abroad by re-insurance. It is against common sense, too, to insist on deposits or premiums being forcibly retained in twenty different countries by the same company at the same moment. Whenever a slice is cut off a company's assets and put into a refrigerator in a particular country the company's strength is *pro tanto* reduced, the discharge of its proper functions is made more difficult, and the work of bearing one another's burdens (which is the heart of insurance) is hampered.

The true objection to most modern insurance legislation is this reliance on segregated deposits and retained premiums. They are held in custody for use in a single area and reduce the mobile reserve waiting to be employed in whatever part of the world it may at some unforeseeable moment be needed. In his *History of British Insurance* Mr Raynes quotes a passage from a Toronto newspaper of 1870 written after a great fire which damaged Chicago in 1869. This is what it said:

> What would have become of the sufferers by the Chicago fire if they had had to depend upon the ten Chicago and four Illinois companies that were on the risk? Insurance capital knows no south, no east, no west. Whether the company's home office is in Liverpool, New York, Boston or Hartford, is not in question but is the company able to sell first-class indemnity?

The fixed separation of deposits and premiums and the insistence on having a legally determined number of pounds, dollars, francs or marks permanently in some spot south, north, east, or west of the insurance company's home, are in flat contradiction to the principles of that old

Canadian paper. The insured do not need local deposits. What they do need is to know whether the company is sound at the centre and will be able to get its funds to the scene of a conflagration like the Chicago fire or of any other disaster that may make a sudden call on its resources.

Years ago Lloyd's discovered the weakness of the deposit system and in 1908 fortified it by the audit. And it is an audit or some comparable plan that is the right solution to international solvency. The ideal plan would probably be to have a central international body that insurance offices would be able to join, that would have access to the accounts of its members and would certify their solvency according to agreed standards. Every country that became a party to the scheme would undertake to permit the holders of the certificates to do insurance business within its borders without segregation of reserves and premiums; and merchants and householders would be allowed to make their own choice between this company and that without respect to nationality. That ideal in our divided world looks fantastically Utopian – a flimsy daydream. But when one thinks of the international bodies that have been discussed and even inaugurated since 1945, all of which in some degree involve a sacrifice of sovereignty, the optimist may perhaps cherish his dream and remind himself that with God and common sense most things are possible.

This digression has taken us rather a long way from Lloyd's and its overseas problems and it is time that we return to our proper channel. We may resume with a question. Why has it been more difficult for Lloyd's than it was for the companies to adapt itself to the changing conditions and comply with the demand of modern foreign legislation? The answer lies at the heart of Lloyd's. An insurance company is a person in itself remaining unchanged from the moment of its incorporation to the day of its death (if that day ever arrives). It makes its contracts in its own name, accumulating its own funds and retaining the same identity throughout its life. A man who took out a policy with a company thirty years ago and still retains it is covered by the same party now that covered him when he signed his first proposal form. The liability has lain throughout on the same shoulders. At Lloyd's there is no such continuity. The average span of a member's underwriting career is probably less than twenty years; and if a man who has been insured by a Lloyd's policy for thirty years were to compare his present policy with the first one he received, he might find that only ten names out of a hundred appear on both of them. On the other ninety death in the interval has laid his icy hand. The policy is still a Lloyd's policy but the shoulders that bear the risk are not the same shoulders.

The effect of this difference between Lloyd's and the company system is important when we come to the problem of making deposits abroad. If the law demands from every insurer a deposit of £20,000 in the United States, another £20,000 in Canada and another £20,000 in France, the company wanting to do business in all these countries puts up its £60,000 and treats it as part of its permanent investment funds, looking forward to an indefinite number of years during which it will have the right to trade on the strength of these deposits. But a Lloyd's underwriter whose expectation of underwriting life is only fifteen or twenty years would think and think again before he parted with such large sums for such a short period of business. Even if he could afford to make the deposits at all it would not be common sense for him to tie up so much for so little. A private person does not readily put up £60,000 for a lease of twenty years.

When the English Assurance Companies Bill was being discussed in 1908 and called for a deposit of £20,000 from every new insurer, Lloyd's solved the difficulty by getting its audit accepted by Parliament as an alternative to a deposit. That arrangement has worked satisfactorily for nearly fifty years, and as foreign and Commonwealth governments one after another have demanded deposits inside their own frontiers, the Committee of Lloyd's has tried to make with them the same arrangement that they made with the British Government in 1908. But here they have come into collision with the spirit of nationalism and their attempts have not been completely successful. In fact it became clear during the 1920's that either deposits of some kind would have to be made or a great volume of foreign fire and accident business, actual and potential, might have to be sacrificed.

But how were the deposits to be made? Except on a very limited scale they could not be made by individual underwriters. The Corporation of Lloyd's had no power to make them out of the corporate funds and anyhow the funds were wanted for other purposes. The individual could do nothing. The Corporation could do nothing. Clearly if funds were to be provided for deposits abroad some third party would have to be brought into existence, a body whose sole purpose would be to look after this new side of the business of underwriting, a body supplied with enough capital to carry out the work satisfactorily, a body in close touch with underwriters' needs and wishes, a body in which the Committee of Lloyd's would have the controlling power. The idea like most new ideas at Lloyd's was not popular at first, but like most good ideas it slowly won its way into favour and like most ideas that have brought about reforms it was considerably knocked about before it took its ultimate shape.

In the year 1925 there was a broker at Lloyd's named Macmillan who had had his early training in a North Country office. He was a specialist in certain types of fire insurance and was much concerned about the future of foreign fire business at Lloyd's. His whole career had been given up to non-marine insurance and knowing probably very little about marine broking or underwriting he was free from the inhibitions and prejudices of marine underwriters, many of whom disliked the new-fangled notions of truckling to foreign governments for the sake of an overseas connection.

Macmillan conceived the idea of a new insurance company, which would co-operate with Lloyd's underwriters, make the necessary deposits and issue policies in foreign currencies. It was to have no shareholders except Lloyd's underwriters. The making of profit would be a subsidiary interest. But it would comply with the regulations of overseas governments exactly as though it were a normal insurance office trading on ordinary lines for its own profit and advancement. It was to have a nominal capital of £5,000,000, of which ten or twenty per cent would be called up, and it would employ the bulk of its capital in making such deposits as would enable it to do business openly in foreign countries. Foreign assured would receive the company's policy. When they had claims they would be paid by the company's cheque. If a claim were disputed the company would accept service and appear as defendant in the local court. Between Lloyd's underwriters and the policy-holders there would be no direct contact. Only the company would be visible.

But behind this company façade the underwriters would still be in control. How was that to be done? Simply by arranging that every risk which fell within this scheme should first be written by Lloyd's underwriters and afterwards be insured again by the company. The method was straightforward enough. A broker with a risk to place would take it to Lloyd's and do it in the traditional way, getting a line here and a line there until it was complete. In the normal routine of broking the next step would be to send a covering note to the assured advising him that he was insured at Lloyd's.

Under Macmillan's plan the next step would be for the broker to place the risk again – this time with the company, the company being advised that the risk had already been reinsured with underwriters whose names would be mentioned. The company would agree automatically. The broker would advise his client that he had placed the risk with the company. The company would in due course receive the premium and pay it over to the underwriters who had reinsured it.

The whole scheme turned on the device of putting the reinsurance before the original and then using a company policy, that would be within the foreign law, in place of the Lloyd's policy (kept in the background) which would have been outside the law. Everything would be above-board, legal and honest. The overseas assured would understand the machinery and be satisfied that he still had in effect the security and advantages of a Lloyd's policy plus (for what it was worth) the local deposit. The governments would know that their regulations had been obeyed and the security they demanded provided. Whether the overseas vested insurance interests would have taken this new competition lying down is another matter.

As things turned out that last query never had to be answered, for the scheme did not appeal either to the brokers or to the underwriters or to the Committee. The brokers were apprehensive of a company – even an *ad hoc* company – coming between their clients and themselves. The underwriters had fears of the same kind and wondered perhaps what would happen to them if something ever went wrong with the company. The Committee disliked the underlying suggestion that individual underwriting had had to throw up the sponge. And everybody suspected the thin end of the wedge. The scheme moreover had one immediate and damaging weakness. It was not to apply to America. In America different States wanted not merely a fixed deposit from foreign insurers but the retention of premiums inside their own borders, to assure a constant supply of funds ready for the payment of claims. And the provision of that type of security would be beyond the scope of the company. As the greater part of Lloyd's non-marine foreign business lay in the United States and was growing in importance, relatively and proportionately, every year, the omission of America would have left a wide gap in Macmillan's plan and reduced its value by at least fifty per cent. To solve the problem of foreign insurance without taking America into account was like arranging a wedding without providing a bride.

For these reasons the scheme fell through, but for all that it served its purpose at Lloyd's because it gave a jolt and applied the spur to people's minds. It helped to familiarize underwriters with the idea of a united effort to solve the problem, and directed their thoughts to the solution (which proved to be the right one) of a new organization divorced from the ordinary business of underwriting and concerned only with this one subject. There is no doubt that in this matter the minds of Lloyd's men needed at that time all the jolting and the spurring that they could get. It is easy enough at this distance of time to speak critically of things that happened thirty years ago; and if one is inclined to criticise what appeared to be the apathy of underwriters, one must always remember how new and intractable was this problem of fitting individual underwriting into the pattern of international insurance. One must remember, too, how many difficulties seemingly more urgent than foreign legislation were at that time claiming the attention of the Committee. There was the new building and there was the Harrison scandal, both pressing and immediate, both absorbing the energy of the leaders of Lloyd's. While they remained unsettled it is not surprising that other problems – particularly if they were stubborn and contentious – should be pushed to the back of the queue.

The matter of foreign legislation was not indeed left without discussion. It was constantly brought up but usually on points of detail rather than on general principle. It is probably true to say that never in the history of Lloyd's was a matter of such importance more frequently debated, more reluctantly faced, more constantly postponed. Those who remember the history of Tudor England need not be reminded of Queen Elizabeth's tactics in the vital matter of her marriage. She would talk about it interminably and up to a point allow her subjects to talk about it too. She would ask advice from her ministers and hold out hopes to this suitor and to that. But always at the finish she would escape in a cloud of words from making any decision – remaining right up to her death, as a razzled old woman of seventy, a fair virgin in maiden meditation fancy free. She had discovered the great principle that if in any particular matter you want to do nothing the best thing is to make long unintelligible speeches about it and then adjourn the debate.

The men who suffered most at Lloyd's from the Committee's policy of postponement were the enthusiasts who believed that delay was jeopardizing the whole future of non-marine insurance, and those members of the Corporation's staff who had to deal with new legislation piecemeal, as and when they got wind of new laws and ordinances contemplated or in force in various parts of the world. Lloyd's, unlike the companies, had no local representatives to tell them in good time that fresh restrictions were in the offing. To keep in touch with politics and administrations was not one of the traditional duties of Lloyd's agents, and unless a broker heard from a foreign correspondent that something was likely to happen, the first news at Lloyd's would often be of a public announcement that a new Act had come into force laying fresh burdens on insurers from overseas. In nine cases out of ten the Act would by that time have been drafted by someone who thought only in terms of companies and had no notion of how Lloyd's did its business or of how impossible it was for underwriters to comply with regulations designed only to suit the company system. The result often was a discrimination against Lloyd's arising not from a set purpose but from ignorance of the facts.

Indeed the ignorance about Lloyd's was sometimes amazing. Even as late as 1926 and in the State of New York, which through its insurance department had taken considerable trouble to understand Lloyd's organization, two judges tried an action that involved both underwriters and the Corporation. After hearing all the available evidence the judges decided that the Corporation of Lloyd's was the treasurer for Lloyd's underwriters and on that ground they based their judgment that the Corporation's funds were liable for underwriters' claims. If a thing like that could happen in New York anything was possible in less enlightened courts and less intelligent parliaments; and it is not surprising that underwriters and the staff of the Corporation found it difficult to comply with or even to understand legislation drafted in such ignorance.

When news arrived, as it regularly did, of fresh legislation designed or passed in overseas countries, it was the duty of officials of the Corporation to study it, guess at its meaning, resolve (as best they could) its ambiguities, calculate its probable effect on Lloyd's business and make appropriate reports and recommendations to the Chairman and Committee. Thirty years ago there was not, as there is now, a department of the Corporation staff that devoted its whole time to foreign legislation, and senior officials busy with general administration and other special problems had to find time for dealing with the foreign troubles one by one as they came in. Very often the officials were in a difficult situation. They were pressed by brokers whose interests were likely to be affected by the new laws. They themselves realized the importance of doing something quickly to keep the Lloyd's flag flying overseas. But they had no general principles to guide them and it was not as easy as it might have been to get clear specific instructions from a Committee which had no settled convictions. Some of the Committee's members were prepared to go a long way in adapting the mechanism of Lloyd's to the new conditions. Others disliked the whole business and wanted Lloyd's to resist the new demands, and others (who were perhaps in the majority) found it impossible to make up their minds either way. In all this the Committee represented accurately enough the flow and ebb of opinion in the general body of members. But they did not reach a central principle and until that had been done it was difficult to achieve sound conclusions on specific cases.

· · · · · ·

When Heath revised and re-invigorated the old non-marine market at Lloyd's he was not only bringing back a competitor to the Companies' fire and accident department. He was also challenging one system of insurance with another – the company with the individual. And the contrast between the two is sharp and important.

The General Manager of a company is the head of a great organization. He has his assistant managers and his departmental managers, each of whom in his own sphere is the underwriter. He has a great staff of clerks and inspectors and a net-work of branch offices, subsidiary companies, and agents, all of whom are ultimately under his management. His hand controls a great machine and the purpose to which the machine is geared is the accumulation of premium income at profitable rates. If the manager of a branch office is not doing his work efficiently; if he is not bringing in as much premium as he should; if he appears to be losing old policy holders and not securing others to replace them; then the General Manager can, if he thinks fit, remove him from his post and put in his place someone who is likely to be more satisfactory. By right of his office the Company General Manager can stimulate and direct the flow of business that comes to the company's headquarters.

The Lloyd's underwriter is in a different position. He sits in his place at Lloyd's and has no staff under his control except the few clerks who work beside him and a few more at his office (if he has one) where his under-writing books are kept. There is no one to whom he can say 'you are not bringing in enough business', no one whose duty it is to forage for him and feed him with new orders. He depends entirely on the brokers (who are not his employees) and, even if he is associated with a firm of brokers, the connection will not usually be strong enough to give him the control of the business. Certainly he will not be able to send instructions abroad that this, that, or the other type of insurance is to be cultivated for the underwriter's benefit. He is dependent on the energy and enterprise of the brokers – who are his clients, not his servants. He can help them by giving them the kind of market they need and by adapting his policy to their requirements; but he can do no more. If the brokers were inefficient and did not bring in the business there would be nothing the underwriter could do about it and ultimately his business and the brokers would wither away.

On the other side of the account the system of individual underwriters has advantages that the highly organized company usually cannot enjoy. The freedom, the elasticity, the quickness in adjustment that a business which is controlled by one man only possesses, are of inestimable benefit. A market made up of such one-man businesses, and supported by skilful and energetic firms of brokers, should find it easier to keep pace with the times and anticipate changing conditions than the best equipped organization stemming out from a central authority. But the strange thing is that no body of men working on a large scale has ever been able to develop these advantages except one, the Society of Lloyd's Underwriters. The reason why Lloyd's has succeeded in doing what no one else has ever done might be a matter for debate but, whatever the reason may be, the fact is indisputable. Lloyd's is *sui generis*.

Internationally this uniqueness of Lloyd's is sometimes a source of difficulty and confusion. The system is not generally understood or its working appreciated abroad. The government of a distinct country decides to regulate the insurance done inside its frontiers and sets out to prepare a bill or an ordinance determining who may, or who may not, give insurance cover to its nationals. It takes the best available advice, produces a draft which appears to meet its needs, and passes the draft into law. But the draftsmen and the government alike have been thinking in terms of companies and have cut their cloth to a suit which will fit the companies only. They have produced a uniform into which some of the troops cannot be squeezed. The result has often been unsatisfactory and misunderstandings about the technique of individual underwriting have been the source of many difficulties in insurance legislation.

At Lloyd's, debate without action went on for years, and the Clerk to the Committee, who had to deal with the new foreign laws as they were drafted, found his difficulties as great as ever. His duty in this matter, as he saw it, was to act as gadfly-in-ordinary to the Committee – an embarrassing position. But he did the best he could and in 1929 he drafted a memorandum which put the facts squarely before the Committee, indicating at least one way of solving the problem. It was a very able statement and for two years it was the starting point for most of the discussions and debates that flowed between the Committee and the general body of members.

The memorandum began by setting out the requirements that were commonly insisted upon by foreign governments and suggested a possible method of meeting them. The principal requirements were:

1. Provision of a deposit;
2. Acceptance of service;
3. Payment of tax.

If some of these conditions could be fulfilled then (the memorandum argued) the difficulties of Lloyd's would in certain cases at any rate be greatly eased. But the problem was how to fulfil them. Governments would have to agree to accept deposits covering not Lloyd's as Lloyd's, but all the underwriting members of Lloyd's. A much closer representation of Lloyd's underwriters in foreign countries would be necessary, and somehow money for the deposits would have to be found.

It was common ground that in dealing with foreign governments non-marine underwriters at any rate ought to act as a single unit, that they must all agree to be bound by the same regulations, and that in every country in which deposits were made they must appoint someone to be their ambassador. He would be their envoy to treat with the local authorities on the one hand and on the other to make certain that official regulations were respected by all the underwriters at Lloyd's. That was clear from the beginning and later on as things developed it was seen that (whatever scheme were adopted) it must be arranged and controlled by the Committee of Lloyd's itself – the only body that had the necessary prestige for dealing with foreign governments, the only body that was likely to keep everybody in step at the London end.

The plan suggested to the Committee covered all these points and was designed on bold lines. Its effect on opinion at Lloyd's was great and in many ways it anticipated the shape of things that emerged when the final decision was taken. In his memorandum the Clerk to the Committee proposed that in any country where legal recognition was sought Lloyd's should open a registration office which would keep track of the business done, would arrange the payment of taxes as they fell due, would be authorized to accept service on underwriters' behalf, and generally would superintend the relations between underwriters and the government. In fact registration offices have been appointed in most of the countries where Lloyd's (since the memorandum was written) has complied with local legislation and the functions of the offices are those indicated in 1929 by the Clerk to the Committee.

In words, but not in writing, the Clerk to the Committee, treading very warily, suggested that a finance company should be formed separate from the underwriting business. It would be separate, too, from the ordinary work of the Corporation but it would be under the Corporation's control and charged with the sole duty of providing deposits abroad. Like all the other suggestions in the memorandum, this scheme of a separate finance company anticipated in their essence the changes which the Committee of Lloyd's actually proposed and carried a few years later. In some important details the changes differed from the proposals of the memorandum but they were details only. The frame was the same.

In 1929 the ideas that permeated the memorandum were thought to be too contentious for immediate action and they were not adopted. But neither were they rejected. They lay on the table. The seed had been sown and in seven years' time it bore fruit. There is, in fact, no doubt that the memorandum fixed the essentials of reform and accustomed the minds of members to the possibility of great changes hitherto regarded as alien to the genius of Lloyd's.

# 17

## FOREIGN LEGISLATION
## AND ADDITIONAL SECURITIES LTD

*Trouble in Illinois – The law not being observed – American politics – Support for Lloyd's – The name assumed by American concerns – Demand for deposit of funds in the State – Brokers privately put up funds 1933 – Further demands 1936 – Underwriters put up funds – Committee's difficulties – Opinion still divided – Resolve taken –Meeting of Non-Marine Underwriters – Additional Securities Ltd proposed and adopted – Finance Company – Its capital structure and history*

WHAT MAY BE REGARDED as the turning point in the discussions over foreign legislation came in the year 1933. The incident that forced the issue took place in America in the State of Illinois. For some years underwriters had had an unusually close connection with Illinois, and in 1927 an Act had been passed which enabled them to be licensed and officially authorized them to do business in the State. Several syndicates had taken advantage of the new law. It suited underwriters and it suited the insured public in the State. Underwriters were able to provide the public with cover not obtainable from the local companies, and although they roused – as they were bound to do – a certain antagonism amongst established insurers, they had a considerable backing from bankers, brokers, and other business men who appreciated the service that Lloyd's was able to give them.

But the Act of 1927 had been unhappily worded and it is probably true that the letter of the law was not and could not be precisely observed either by underwriters or by the local insurance companies. That fact troubled the very conscientious mind of the official who was then the State Director of Insurance. Indeed it troubled him so much that he drafted and tried to force through the legislature a bill reforming the system of control over insurance as carried on both by companies and by underwriters. His efforts created some stir in Chicago and Springfield and for three or four years there was turmoil in the insurance life of the State. And Lloyd's – as a local lawyer put it – was at the centre of the turmoil.

For years the centre of that turmoil was a remarkably uncomfortable spot. And even on the periphery the discomfort was considerable. The main whirlpool was made up of a number of minor whirlpools. Almost all the insurance companies doing business in Illinois were caught up in one or other of them; and politicians, calculating the chances of the next election, either stood on the bank watching the movement of the waters or dabbled a foot in one or other of the eddies. To the ordinary English-man American politics will always be more than half obscure, and State politics almost completely obscure; and it would be rash indeed to attempt a detailed narrative of what went on between or inside the parties at any given moment in the life of any American State. But it is clear that in the nineteen-thirties the tug and thrust of rival parties in Illinois was unusually strong. The State had a Democratic governor and a Democratic majority in the legislature. But the Democratic Party was itself divided into sections that did not love each other; and the Director of Insurance being not a Democrat but a Republican was in a difficult position.

He was very far from being a puppet of the politicians. He wanted to be fair to everybody; but he had been advised by the Attorney General that the law was not being observed, and his mind could not rest at ease while a law which affected his department of the administration was persistently broken either by companies or by underwriters. He made one effort after another to get an amending Act through the House of Representatives and the Senate; and it was only when he failed in his first attempt that he began to put severe pressure on Lloyd's underwriters. He believed that the existing law was unsatisfactory and one of his objects in harrying Lloyd's (if that is not too strong a term) was to call attention publicly to the need for fresh legislation. For four or five years he pegged away at his task. Insurance interests were pressing him this way and that, and behind his back they were lobbying the Senators and the Representatives. That was the atmosphere in which Lloyd's non-marine underwriters were doing business in Illinois in 1933. It was a difficult time but (for all the difficulties) there is no evidence that underwriters ever played politics themselves. Indeed when a hint was thrown out to them that they were handicapped by employing a Republican as their lawyer they took no notice of it and stuck to their old adviser.

One fact which should be remarked in all the comings and goings of those years is that no responsible person seems ever to have questioned the security of what we know as a Lloyd's policy. The attacks on Lloyd's underwriters did not take the form of saying 'These men are unsafe', or 'These men do not understand their business'. On the contrary the implication usually was that they were too good at their business, that they could give cover which local companies could not touch and were able to select their risks so cleverly that they quoted cheaper rates than their competitors and still made a profit for themselves. The Association of Insurance Brokers in Illinois testified to the good service that their clients got from Lloyd's underwriters. The bankers, because they got at Lloyd's the best possible terms, were in general strongly pro-Lloyd's. But the official complaint against underwriters was not that they got an advantage from quoting cheaper. It was that they did not keep inside Illinois the funds that they should be keeping and so got a flying start against the companies who did.

There is another point that we need to bear in mind in considering the opposition that Lloyd's faced in America in the nineteen-thirties. In America the word Lloyd's is familiar enough, but by itself it does not mean what it means in England. If you want an American to understand you when you speak of Lloyd's you had better say Lloyd's of London. That will distinguish it from the concerns which under the name of Lloyd's do insurance business inside the United States, concerns which have nothing to do with the London Lloyd's, which are not exactly companies but are certainly very different from the Society whose name they have taken. They must years ago have found that the word Lloyd's was a passport to public favour and they assumed it without regard or reference to the name's true owner. As 'the merchant to secure his treasure conveys it in a borrowed name', so these associations (in 1953 there were at least twenty of them trading in the United States) reflect the goodwill that Lloyd's of London have achieved. They have neither the backing of unlimited liability nor many of the other safeguards that Lloyd's of London has in its long and adventurous life built up by trial, error and experiment. But to many American minds the difference between the men with the borrowed name and the name's legitimate owner is not always clear.

The word Lloyd's in fact has become almost a generic term in America, signifying not a place of business but a special method of carrying on insurance. And in the Illinois Code, drafted in 1935, it is undoubtedly so used. The Code speaks of:

Partnerships incorporated associations individuals or associations of individuals known and operating as Lloyd's.

Sir Percy MacKinnon, Chairman of Lloyd's, 1925, 1927–8, and 1932–3; from a drawing by G. F. Bird.

It declares that:

> no partnerships associations individuals or aggregations of individuals known and operating as Lloyd's shall be permitted to organize as Lloyd's for the purpose of transacting insurance business . . .

And that:

> domestic Lloyd's associations shall be required to keep and maintain in this State . . .

Organized as Lloyd's. Domestic Lloyd's associations. These phrases have nothing to do with Lloyd's of London. The word had almost ceased to be a noun. It had become an adjective signifying a technique different from that of an ordinary insurance company. And the superintendents of insurance, who understood the difference between the real and the imitation Lloyd's, were inclined to misgivings about some of the imitations – misgivings from which the reputation of the original article might undoubtedly suffer.

In the year 1933, when the whirlpool in Illinois was beginning to boil, it happened that two Lloyd's men, representatives of firms which were both brokers and underwriting agents, visited America on their own business. They were both interested in Illinois and they were concerned by the line that the Director's mind seemed to be taking. It was clear to them that the standing of Lloyd's in the State might be in danger, that the licence to underwrite might be withdrawn, that the advantages, direct and indirect, of being licensed in Illinois might be lost for ever. They had an interview with the Director and they decided that the only way to save the situation was to make a deposit of funds and make it quickly. What was needed was immediate agreement. At the earliest possible moment the Director must be given a promise that money would be placed in a local bank and left there so long as underwriters continued to hold a licence. But where was the money to come from and on whose authority were they to give the promise? There was no existing fund to which they could apply for the necessary dollars. On the question of making deposits, both the Committee of Lloyd's and the main body of members were divided in their opinion. And in any case they themselves were not in Chicago as representatives of the Committee. They were there on their own affairs and the only people they could bind were their own firms and any others whose consent could be obtained by cable.

But much was at stake and rather than lose their connection in the State they decided that the right course was to by-pass the Committee of Lloyd's

x

and put the money up privately. They cabled to their firms at home in that sense and they received back authority to guarantee $250,000, which was enough to satisfy the Director. That sum was made up of contributions from six firms of Lloyd's brokers and almost before the Committee of Lloyd's knew what was happening the arrangements had been made. Foreign currency had been deposited in a foreign bank – not by the Committee or the Corporation, not by underwriters, but by half a dozen brokerage firms protecting their own interests and securing their own connection.

That rather dramatic episode of 1933 solved the immediate problem of underwriters and saved the Illinois licence; but it did not settle the turmoil and it did not carry anybody into smooth water. The discussions and the lobbyings went on as before and the State soon called on underwriters to double the amount of the deposit. That increase was arranged, the money being provided as before by private interests; but within three years underwriters were faced a third time with the possibility of being refused the renewal of their licence unless a much larger deposit was provided. The figure required had now risen to five times the original sum. The date for that particular renewal of the licence was 1st July 1936, and the Director (before he granted the renewal) wanted an undertaking that the additional money would be provided promptly.

On the evening of the 25th June, six days before zero hour, no decision had been taken at Lloyd's. But on the morning of the 26th, non-marine underwriters attended a meeting at which they were told the facts by the Chairman of their association and they agreed, then and there, to put up an extra $750,000. The money was to be provided by a loan from an English bank secured by Lloyd's policies and carrying interest at two and a half per cent. In those spacious days there was no dollar gap, no sterling area, no restriction on transfer of funds, no necessity to go cap in hand to the Treasury or the Bank of England. And in the first fortnight of July the dollars were delivered. The Director of Insurance was satisfied.

Meanwhile what were the Committee of Lloyd's doing? Naturally they were advised of every step that was taken by underwriters and naturally they took a very close interest in the run of events. But to the negotiations with the Illinois government and to the decisions taken by the brokers and underwriters they were not a party. They had been told about the deposit and the loan, but when their advice was sought by the brokers and underwriters and the opportunity given them to supply the funds they could only answer with a refusal.

In this the Committee were certainly not to blame. Their legal powers to use Corporation funds for these deposits were at least questionable, and through no fault of their own they had never been able to bring the general body of members into a comprehensive scheme which could be put forward as an alternative to the brokers' solution. On the other hand they had no right to interfere with members' conduct of their own affairs, and even if they had wanted to intervene in this case they could not have taken any effective action. They cannot have felt happy about what was going on, for they saw – as they could not but see – that something like a minor revolution was taking place without their backing or consent. Vital decisions (which ought to be made only by the Committee) were being taken by private members, and changes, likely for good or ill to affect the whole future of Lloyd's, were in progress while the Committee stood aside and waited on events. There was no question of the Committee being defied by the Members. It was simply that one section of underwriters felt bound to advance more quickly than the rest, while the Committee, who had to represent all sections of the community, could not move forward until they were fortified by a clear majority.

Although opinion in the Room was divided on the main question of making deposits, there was on some points a fairly general agreement. They were negative points but they were important. It was, for example, agreed that it was undesirable for private members to continue making their own arrangements for deposits. That might result in Lloyd's speaking to foreign governments in two voices, each of which contradicted the other. It was agreed that there were objections against anybody – Committee or underwriters – putting up deposits with money borrowed from a bank. And it was agreed (even if the premium trust deed permitted it) that to earmark premiums in trust by taking the deposit money out of current premiums would be a bad arrangement. On these three matters some people felt more strongly than others, but if a general meeting of Members had been consulted there would have been a decisive majority on all three.

But the arrangement that had been made in Illinois quite clearly broke two of the principles and came very near to breaking the third. A private arrangement had been made by a few syndicates with a foreign government. That broke principle number one. Of the deposits made in Illinois, the largest came from an ordinary bank loan for the repayment of which private members had made themselves responsible. That broke principle number two. And in respect of this same deposit, the private members who had made themselves responsible were guaranteed by an ordinary Lloyd's policy on which (if a claim should ever arise) the trust funds of the subscribing underwriters would be fully liable. If that did not directly involve the use of premiums in trust it did bring them potentially into the scheme. It might without casuistry be regarded as a breach of principle number three. The situation in fact was extremely delicate. One half of Lloyd's had run ahead of the other. It was as though two horses had been pulling a dog-cart tandem and the leader, breaking the traces, had galloped off and left the dog-cart stranded on the highway.

It was in June 1936 that the arrangements made by Lloyd's non-marine underwriters in Illinois had been completed. It was in December of the same year that the Committee of Lloyd's finally took charge and with the consent of members set up an official organization to deal with the problem of deposits wherever they might be required. How far the second of these incidents resulted from the first it is impossible to determine. *Post hoc* and *propter hoc* are often difficult to separate. They are Siamese twins. Sometimes they can be divided by a surgical operation and sometimes they cannot; and the relationship between the drama in Illinois and the final decision of the Committee in London is one of the cases that defy the surgeon. Whether the Committee in fact made up its mind to take action because of what had happened in Chicago or whether under the general pressure of events it would in any case have worked out its own scheme – that is a hypothetical matter on which every man is entitled to his own opinion. *Propter hoc* is debatable. *Post hoc* is beyond dispute.

Almost exactly six months after the non-marine syndicates had made their deposits Dixey, then Chairman of Lloyd's for the third time, called a meeting of non-marine underwriting agents and laid before it, not the old arguments, which had been debated at so many previous meetings, but the final decision of the Committee to arrange deposits abroad. He said:

> Earlier in the year the Committee came to the definite decision that they were no longer opposed in principle to the making of deposits abroad subject to proper safeguards and provisions. Following upon that decision we received a great many demands and requests that we should endeavour to propound some method whereby the money could be found without making too severe a demand upon underwriters or in any way weakening the audit. The scheme before you is an attempt to meet the situation.

After that introduction Dixey described the Committee's plan for creating a financial company whose sole task would be to raise and supply funds for use abroad – a financial company to be owned by the members and controlled by the Committee of Lloyd's, a company that would draw its revenue from underwriters' premium incomes but would not impinge on their trust funds. It was to be a company whose financial strength would normally increase with every year that passed, able to cope with any demands likely to be made on it so long as the underwriting business of Lloyd's continued to need its help. That speech of Dixey's marked the beginning of a new company – Additional Securities Limited – which finally settled the controversy between 'deposits' and 'no deposits' and has now been working satisfactorily for twenty years. And the really remarkable thing about the meeting at which it was inaugurated was this: after ten years of divided counsels and unbroken indecision the resolution to adopt Dixey's scheme was carried without a single dissentient. The financial corporation suggested by the Clerk to the Committee in 1929 was accepted unanimously in 1936 and was an accomplished fact by 1937.

. . . . . . .

It has been remarked before that at most of the critical moments in its life Lloyd's seems to have had the protection of an unusually efficient guardian angel. Perhaps the angel's most important service has been to provide the right man in the right place at the right moment; and in 1936, when the work of shaping the new finance company was to be undertaken, he was certainly at the top of his form. He had ready at hand two men who were perfectly suited to set about the task and work out the details. One was a member of the Committee, a future Chairman of Lloyd's, who possessed a very constructive mind and an inborn gift for finance; while the other was an ex-Chairman, a man of uncanny judgment, with a genius for detail and almost incredible skill in separating wheat from chaff. Together – with the help of the Clerk to the Committee and the Chief Accountant – they worked out and licked into shape perhaps the most difficult scheme that any Committee of Lloyd's had ever devised. It was not at first sight a task especially well-suited to men who had spent their working lives in underwriting and broking, but they performed it so successfully that an expert in company finance who was asked to criticise the final draft told the Committee that it was highly ingenious and contained so far as he could see no weakness.

. . . . . . .

It was clear that the new finance company, if it were to solve the problem of deposits, must have command of large sums of money not only then but always. It was clear that the money must be found inside Lloyd's and not by an appeal to the outside investor. It was clear that the scheme would have to be carried through by persuasion, not by compulsion. It was clear that, however much members might be influenced by a desire to do the right thing for Lloyd's, they could not be expected to invest over one million pounds in the new company without seeing a reasonable prospect of dividends or interest on their capital outlay. And from all this it was clear that the finance company must be a profit-making concern.

But where was the profit to come from? The only obvious source was interest on the funds that it would invest either at home or abroad. That is the source which provides dividends for any investment company which trades for profit, has its own shareholders and receives its own quotations on the Stock Exchange. But between the ordinary investment trust and this venture of Lloyd's there was a vital difference. The trust company's funds are employed by its directors solely with an eye to satisfactory dividends and capital appreciation. The whole field of investment is wide open to it and if it is skilfully managed it can be reasonably certain of receiving dividends large enough to cover expenses and pass on its own dividends to its own shareholders. The reason for its existence is that it has better opportunities for investment than the private capitalist and can get better use for his money than he could hope to find for himself. If it cannot do that it has no excuse for surviving; and one of the most success- ful of recent investment companies was bitterly attacked at its inception by many stockbrokers and journalists who believed (wrongly) that it would not be able to invest its money profitably enough to pay satisfactory dividends.

Trust companies to be successful must be able to get a comparatively high rate of interest – a good deal higher than the ordinary investor can achieve with safety – and that is exactly what the new finance company of Lloyd's could not do. The whole field of investment was not open to it. Its money must follow not the rate of interest but the needs of under- writers, and its investments would have to be made (irrespective of the return to be had on them) in the countries where the underwriters needed at any particular moment to make a deposit. Its rate of interest on these deposits was certain to be low and even the free money that was not invested abroad must be kept reasonably liquid, which meant that the return on it would be small. At that moment the Chamberlain policy of cheap money was in full swing; the gross yield on dated British Government stock was about three per cent; and the new finance company could not expect even that rate on its invested funds. In its first normal year it actually made (net) less than two per cent and that was not a figure on which as a profit-making concern it would cut much of a dash. Clearly some source of revenue other than interest on capital would have to be found.

The planners of Additional Securities found the new source of revenue in the same device that had served Lloyd's so well before. They proposed an annual levy on premium income – not this time a levy of half per cent but a levy of one quarter per cent, not this time a levy on the whole income of Lloyd's but a levy on the income of non-marine underwriters only. That was the foundation stone and when Dixey explained the scheme to the meeting of non-marine underwriting agents he told them:

> The levy is the heart and kernel of the whole scheme. If you are prepared to agree to that, then the rest of the proposals fits into it like a jigsaw puzzle. If you don't, then the whole scheme breaks down.

The underwriting agents, before whom the proposal was laid, agreed to accept it. They took upon themselves and their Names the burden of the levy, and every year since 1st January 1937 all non-marine underwriters have parted with a quarter per cent of their premium income to Additional Securities Limited. Not all the Names understood in 1937 what was happening or even knew that they were being committed to payment of another levy. Their underwriting agents undertook the payment on their behalf much as godparents undertake obligations on behalf of an infant at his baptism. But the vow made by the agents for their Names has been kept – kept indeed a good deal better than some of the promises made at the font. No one for whom the undertaking was given in 1936 has ever failed in his payments. The members who have been elected since 1936 are in a different position. They, too, have paid every year but they had before their election given an undertaking to pay the levy annually and their own signature is attached to that promise. Theirs was baptism at a riper age.

In 1937 the levy was expected to produce £40,000 a year and in the first year it actually produced £42,535. Fifteen years later it produced over £200,000. The total realized from the levy in the first sixteen years was over one and a half million pounds, contributed alike by underwriters who stood to gain from foreign deposits and by underwriters who never took a foreign risk and got no personal advantage from Additional Securities.

On the strength of the levy the Committee were able to borrow for Additional Securities at three per cent, and at that rate a million pounds of notes was issued at par, redeemable by a sinking fund that was to repay the whole issue in thirty years. All the notes were taken up by members of Lloyd's. They are not dealt in on the Stock Exchange and there is no quoted price for them, but they must have kept their value pretty well. In 1940, for reasons connected with taxation, they were converted into redeemable preference shares entitled to a three per cent dividend and were redeemed at the rate of £100,000 a year. By the end of the year 1955 the issue had disappeared.

The forecast of the Company's future made by its originators in 1936 was accurate enough except that the whole scale has expanded. The then Committee of Lloyd's looked forward to an income of forty thousand pounds a year from the levy. It is now about a quarter of a million. The authorized ordinary capital has proved to be inadequate and has had to be increased, while a new loan stock of £250,000 has also been issued. The gross profit before taxation and payment of interest, which was £50,982 in the Company's first year, was £269,507 in 1952.

Those are very satisfactory figures but much of the increase in revenue has been offset by taxation. In 1937 the Company paid income tax at five shillings in the pound, plus a comparatively small sum for the National Defence Contribution which was introduced by Chamberlain to pay for our rearmament. In 1953 the Company paid nine shillings in the pound income tax amounting to £117,000, plus excess profits levy of nearly £25,000 and a profits tax of £9,000. Altogether between 1937 and 1953 taxation cost the Company nearly a million pounds, but in spite of that enormous unexpected drain on its revenue it has more than fulfilled the financial expectations of its founders.

In the light of this remarkable success the temptation to moralize over Additional Securities is irresistible. When the Company was first suggested nobody really liked it. Nobody was anxious to buy the three per cent notes. Most people hated the levy of a quarter per cent and if any of the more powerful syndicates had refused to come into the scheme the scheme itself would immediately have miscarried. Even if a number of smaller syndicates had stood out the working of the scheme might have been extremely awkward and perhaps impossible. Unanimity was essential and not without difficulty unanimity was attained. Without compulsion – for the Committee had no right to compel – the plan was accepted by every-one. Once they were convinced that foreign deposits were necessary to the prosperity of Lloyd's, once they were persuaded by Dixey that Additional Securities provided the best method of arranging the deposits, the members shouldered the burden and have carried it ever since without criticism or grumbling. It is the old story. The loyalty of its members is the strength of Lloyd's.

# 18

## MOTOR AND AVIATION INSURANCE

*Exchange difficulties – Narrow outlook of nineteenth-century underwriters – The pre-eminence of sterling – Changed conditions in twentieth century – Policies signed in foreign currencies – Blocked currencies – Freak insurances – Aviation insurance early difficulties – Rationalization and combination with companies – New technique – Capacity of the market – Motor insurance – Early difficulties at Lloyd's – Departures from Lloyd's traditions – Comparatively little foreign business – Companies' large premium income*

---

THE OBSTACLES IN THE PATH of overseas insurance that were described in the last chapter arose, all of them, from legislation. For a long time this difficulty was the only one that hampered underwriters and fire managers in the conduct of their foreign business. But within the last thirty years another kind of barrier has appeared – the barrier of currency and exchange. To everybody engaged in international trade the problem of the exchange is difficult and troublesome enough. But to Lloyd's underwriters it has been a worse nuisance than to most men either in or out of the insurance industry, partly because of the Lloyd's system of individual underwriting and partly because of the peculiar position in which (by circumstance and tradition) the old-fashioned Lloyd's underwriter plied his trade.

It is a commonplace thing to say of Lloyd's that when it ceases to be competitive it ceases to be Lloyd's; and in the light of that truism it may seem contradictory to add that until recently Lloyd's underwriters were a sheltered and protected race of men. Nevertheless it is true. The old marine underwriter, though he had to fight hard for his bread and butter, had almost one duty only – to know the right rate for a risk. There was little else that he was called on to know, little other skill that it was necessary for him to cultivate. In general he need have no great interest in the world at large. He never had to go out into the highways and byways to collect his business. Like Milton's fugitive and cloistered virtue, he never sallied out to meet his adversary. That was the broker's duty, not the under-writer's. It was the broker who stood between the underwriter and the cold world; the broker who foraged for him and found business for him; the broker who shielded him from bad debts and paid him his premiums whether the assured had paid up or not. Every premium the underwriter received was due from the broker in sterling. Every claim was paid in sterling. All the exchanges of the world might go wrong without causing very much anxiety to the man sitting in the underwriting boxes at Lloyd's. Shielded and protected in this way, the old-fashioned underwriter was to the last degree a specialist, rewarded (sometimes very handsomely rewarded) for the technical knowledge which enabled him to run risks beyond the capacity of most businessmen to carry. But, by way of com-pensation for running great risks, he was insulated from many of the worries and responsibilities that other men had to carry as part of their daily burden.

The result of this insulation was that a marine underwriter, if he was not by nature of an enquiring mind, could go through life without collecting any store of general knowledge or following any broader interests than the seaworthiness of hulls, the damageability of cargo and the relative skill of various sea-captains. And some of the mistakes of administration made at Lloyd's in the nineteenth century may be attributed in part at least to the narrow outlook of most of the nineteenth-century under-writers who constituted its Committee. In the twentieth century that reproach has been removed. The present-day underwriter (if a respectful compliment may be paid him) is usually much more broadminded, much better equipped as a man of business, than his predecessors of earlier generations.

This widening of the underwriter's outlook is due partly to changes in the technique of marine underwriting and in part to the stern discipline of post-war economics. When sterling ruled the world's banking it was simple enough for a Lloyd's underwriter to neglect all questions of exchange and currency and go on the simple principle of receiving all premiums in pounds and paying all claims in pounds. But the moment sterling lost its Victorian pre-eminence foreign clients began to ask for different treatment. They were no longer satisfied with the prospects of being paid their claims in sterling. They began to ask for settlement on their own ground in their own currency, and it was on their own ground that the underwriter (if he wanted to retain their business) had to meet them. Henceforth he must know something about foreign banking and foreign exchanges and in the last twenty-five years he has been learning a good deal.

Now he is accepting liability and keeping accounts in many different currencies; and at one time in 1937, for Chinese risks alone, policies were being signed at Lloyd's in no less than twenty-eight varieties of dollars and taels. They ranged from Canton silver dollars and Canton national dollars to Tientsin taels, Tientsin dollars, and Tsingtao dollars. Altogether within the last thirty years Lloyd's underwriters (who fifty years ago knew nothing but sterling) have issued policies in more than a hundred and fifty foreign currencies – in American and Canadian dollars, in francs, marks, kroner, Siamese ticals, and Peruvian soles, but never (so far as is known) in Russian roubles. This diversity of currencies must have thrown considerable strain on Lloyd's Policy Signing Office, but the managers of that most remarkable department (to which Lloyd's underwriters owe a good deal more than some of them realize) modestly give the credit to others. 'How accountants', one of them writes, 'sorted out the premiums and paid the claims I cannot understand, but no doubt Lloyd's as usual were able to deal with yet another difficult problem to the satisfaction of all concerned.' Whoever it is that deserves the credit, it is certain that foreign currency business has come to stay, and for this amongst other reasons underwriters need today to be far more men of the world than their forerunners were in 1890. No longer can they be a body of narrow specialists working within the shelter of a closed fortress.

If all currencies were convertible this diversity – once the proper machinery had been established – would not be a serious obstacle in the way of Lloyd's business; but in a world of blocked accounts and controlled exchanges it is sometimes an almost insuperable barrier; and there are still countries with exchanges so difficult that brokers and underwriters have to handle with great caution the orders that come from them. When Britain's economic condition was at its lowest ebb the main problem was how to be certain of buying the foreign currency for payment of claims; but as sterling recovered the difficulty shifted and the problem became not how to pay claims abroad but how to bring premiums home. That trouble has not yet been entirely solved; and if international trade is ever checked by another bad crisis and governments everywhere try to protect their currencies by re-imposing tighter controls over exchange, then the difficulty of keeping both premiums and claims on the move may be revived.

The non-marine underwriters at Lloyd's needed from the first to have a somewhat wider outlook than the old marine underwriter of the nineteenth century, and it is probably true to say that they have always been more closely in touch with the outside world. Their business was never restricted as the marine was to a comparatively small number of industries. They knew that to build up a profitable connection they would constantly have to supply merchants and manufacturers with novel forms of cover. Their function (as they recognized) was to find out what risks different trades had to incur, and then, if a policy to insure them was possible, to devise one. It was of no use for them to sit at their boxes and wait for people to send their fire insurance business along. They must be something more than fire experts. They must be jacks-of-all-trades willing to learn something about anybody's business; to weigh his risks intelligently and, having weighed, to cover them. That was how Heath established not only himself but the non-marine market at Lloyd's, and from the earliest days every non-marine underwriter knew that his future depended on the Heath tradition being maintained. It was so in 1900 and *mutatis mutandis* it is so today. The result has been that the non-marine habit of mind differs from the old-fashioned underwriting outlook almost as much as chalk differs from cheese. And the change has undoubtedly been a tonic to the vigour and enterprise of Lloyd's.

The enterprising spirit of underwriters is evident in all the new types of insurance (many of them producing a large volume of premiums) that have originated in the non-marine market. But it is most easily illustrated by some of the curious out-of-the-way risks that have at one time and another been placed in the Room; and unless some reference were made to them our picture of the modern Lloyd's would not be complete. Some of these risks have not been altogether popular with the Committees of Lloyd's; and the publicity given to such ventures as the insurance against twins has never been welcomed by the authorities. In fact it irritates them.

Few things are more repugnant to responsible Lloyd's men than the idea which has sometimes got around that underwriters live on their freak risks. Of course they never have and they never will. But freak risks have had their value nevertheless and to condemn them wholesale would be a mistake. They have accustomed men's minds to the truth that Lloyd's is the freest insurance market in the world, that leading underwriters have very receptive minds, that Lloyd's is the best place to go to if you want cover which is a little out of the ordinary, and that a risk which is uninsurable at Lloyd's is in nine cases out of ten uninsurable anywhere. If some of the freak risks have been open to criticism for lack of dignity, let us remember that in this world it is possible – in fact it is very easy – to be over-dignified. Dignity carried too far is a paralysing influence. Nothing in this world is more dignified than a mummy.

A few examples of insurances actually placed at Lloyd's may give a picture of some of the unusual risks with which underwriters have been able to cope. They are trivial in themselves but they show how underwriters get the reputation of being able to cover anything. Here are a few:

The owner of twenty-nine flats and private dwelling-houses in London and Brighton believed that if one of his tenants committed suicide or was murdered on the premises, prospective tenants would be shy of them and the value of his property would consequently suffer. He told a broker of his anxiety and for a premium of three per cent he secured a policy to pay a total loss in the event of a murder and/or (no broker can ever make out a slip without at least once saying 'and/or') suicide taking place on the insured premises.

A newspaper or group of newspapers ran a Derby Day competition with prizes for anybody who guessed right the first three horses in the race plus the number of people who travelled to Tattenham Corner station at Epsom. The chance of anyone winning that prize seemed negligible but a premium of £10 per cent was paid by the newspapers to cover themselves against the risk of having to pay.

In 1936 Walt Disney's film character Mickey Mouse had his eighth birthday, and a cable from Hollywood was advertised in the British Press telling any boy or girl who was born on 28th September 1928 that he or she could get a cake for nothing by sending a post card to Walt Disney Mickey Mouse Ltd at an address in London. The organization must have been afraid of the advertisement being too successful, and the demand for cakes too great, for it took out an insurance at a cost of £5 and got a policy expressed in the solemn language of a practised policy draftsman:

> This insurance is to pay 10*d*. per child in respect of each child in excess of the first 2,000 children claiming a cake from the insured in answer to a cablegram as per copy attached hereto which is to be taken and read as forming part of this policy to be inserted in newspapers issued in the United Kingdom excluding Ireland. This insurance is only to cover claims received by the insured during the period of one week commencing on 28th September 1936, and ending on the 4th day of October 1936, both days inclusive.

Another queer risk from the film industry carried a premium of £50 in full:

To pay the sum of £2,500 to any woman who gives birth to quin-
tuplets and £1,250 to any woman who gives birth to quadruplets
during the nine months subsequent to their seeing the film called *The
Country Doctor* provided they are patrons of the . . . cinemas and can
produce a half-ticket as evidence that they have seen the film in any of
the above-mentioned cinemas in Great Britain, Scotland, Northern
Ireland and Channel Islands. Subject to a doctor's certificate that the
children live forty-eight hours. This policy is to indemnify the . . .
Picture Corporation against all claims they may be called upon to pay
under the above wording.

But the strangest of all the freak policies ever placed at Lloyd's concerned the Loch Ness Monster:

To pay a loss of £20,000 in the event of the Loch Ness Monster being
delivered alive at Olympia on or before 25th January 1934.

The premium for the risk was £80, and it is difficult to believe that any
underwriter, either at Lloyd's or anywhere else, ever got a premium more
wildly out of proportion to the risk run.

Transactions such as these are of course the side-shows of insurance,
valuable in their way and sometimes entertaining, but not the serious
work of the industry. It is time for us to leave the sideshows and return to
the main building. In the serious branches of the business, what advance
has Lloyd's made in the past fifty years and what new kinds of insurance
has it developed?

. . . . . .

Most of the experiments undertaken have naturally been made by non-
marine underwriters. But one of the most interesting, and for the future
perhaps the most important, lies in the field of aviation, which has produced
a market made up almost equally of marine and non-marine syndicates,
competing with each other and sharing risks without regard to their
official classification.

Marine syndicates have always been allowed by the Committee to
write a certain amount of non-marine business and the premiums in their
returns to the Committee come under the rather strange title of Incidental
Non-Marine. The volume of premiums taken under that head is limited
by regulation and has to be included in a separate category. But aviation
business – the insurance of planes and airborne cargo – can be written
freely by both types of underwriter. When an air risk is taken by a marine

syndicate the premium is classified as marine. When it is taken by a non-marine syndicate or by a syndicate specializing entirely in air risks the premium is non-marine. For the purpose of insurance at Lloyd's aviation is everyone's business and the organization of the market is for that reason unique at Lloyd's. Thanks to the freedom wisely accorded by the Committee it has been able to keep pace with the sensational growth of flying, and its present capacity is far beyond what anyone could have expected even thirty years ago.

The birth of aviation insurance may be put at some time in the year 1911. In that year pioneers in aviation were carrying out experiments on Salisbury Plain and in other convenient places. Though the planes themselves were then uninsurable, the planes' owners had been coming to Lloyd's to cover their third-party liability which was rather an unknown quantity. There were no proper aerodromes. Planes landed where they could and sometimes they did damage to farming property. After a forced landing crowds of spectators might tread down growing crops, the cost of which would be the basis of a claim against the pilot. Third-party cover of that kind was all that underwriters in 1911 were willing to give. But next year they grew bolder and in July 1912, when military trials were held on Salisbury Plain, a non-marine syndicate at Lloyd's agreed to cover a number of aircraft booked to take part in the competition. Unfortunately the weather was bad, the crashes were numerous, and the loss on the policies heavy – so heavy indeed that the underwriter of the syndicate decided to give up the insurance of aeroplanes completely. No one else was ready to take up the experiment where he dropped it, and the infant market died almost before it was born.

The First World War put an end to all civil aviation and until 1919 the demand for insurance cover lapsed. But the return of peace set underwriters' minds thinking again about the possibilities of this new form of travel, and several syndicates decided to try their hands at insuring planes. Generally they were not successful. Even after the First World War there was comparatively little flying and what flying there was did not produce enough business to feed a competitive market with an adequate premium income. Companies as well as Lloyd's underwriters were hungry and nobody was satisfied.

In any case it would not have been easy to make a profit out of the business, for flying was then at best half-organized; arrangements for repair work were inadequate, and in proportion to their inadequacy the expense of carrying out the repairs was increased. One plane flying over

Africa made a forced landing in what looked like a good clearing thick with long grass – but the grass was deceptive. It hid a mass of anthills which destroyed the undercarriage. The nearest road was a hundred miles away and the plane had to be dismantled and carried piecemeal by porters for the full hundred miles. It reached the road at the beginning of the rainy season and the machine had to be stored there until the arrival of better weather. The only place large enough to take the plane was a pit under the local gallows; and there the pieces remained for several months. When finally they reached the base they proved to be damaged by three separate causes – the anthills, the trees against which the parts were bumped on their hundred-mile journey, and the damp under the gallows. They were useless; and underwriters on top of the expenses had to pay a total loss on the plane. Experience of that kind, falling on a market too big for the available business, made life difficult for aviation underwriting and in order to keep premiums up and reduce working costs aviation underwriters began to think of amalgamation.

In this indeed they were following the fashion of the day. Anyone whose memory goes back to the years that followed the first war will remember a word that has since gone out of fashion but was then on every tongue – the word rationalization. If an industry was not doing well, if its working expenses were too high and its products too dear, if the competition of its rivals was too keen for its comfort and its dividends too low for its shareholders, then the right thing to do was to rationalize. Now the word has had its day. It has ceased to be and its place in the jargon of economics knows it no more. But thirty years ago no journalist who knew his business would write an article on British industry without mentioning it at least once and usually with lively approbation. Not many of the folk who used the word knew what it meant; but the general idea was that everybody should amalgamate with everybody else and thus secure a more scientific, a more efficient, and a more prosperous management.

Stimulated by that prevailing fashion, some Lloyd's underwriters and companies who were interested in aviation insurance decided to do a little rationalizing between themselves. They made up their minds to join hands, share a common sustenance, and take fixed proportions of the profit or loss. It was the first and so far the last venture shared in this way between underwriters and companies, and it produced a form of policy never known before or since. The policy issued by the 'group', as the amalgamation was called, was in three separate parts. The first part set out the terms of the risk; the second was a flysheet containing the signatures of

v

Lloyd's underwriters; and the third another flysheet carrying the signatures
of the companies. Even by the group itself that form of policy has long
been given up, but historically the episode is interesting because it shows
how close to each other in their day-to-day underwriting Lloyd's underwriters and the companies can get; and if things had worked out differently
the habit of joint underwriting and of issuing jointly signed policies might
have spread beyond the limits of aviation. In fact it never did and that is
probably a good thing for Lloyd's.

In 1929 a Lloyd's broker writing in the Air Annual of the British
Empire said that the group enjoyed something approaching a monopoly
of aviation underwriting; and when his article was written that was doubtless true. By joining forces a few underwriters and a few companies had
almost if not quite collared the market. But the 1930's were a period of
great activity and growth in aviation, and it soon became impossible for
one group, however strong, to supply all the cover that was needed. Several
companies which were not members of the group started an organization
of their own, and at Lloyd's other underwriters, both marine and non-
marine, wanted to begin writing air risks as soon as the right moment
seemed to have come. Large syndicates were started to write nothing but
aviation risks. They were made up of Names that already wrote other types
of insurance at Lloyd's and formed fresh combinations for aviation only.

The underwriters of these specialist syndicates developed a technique
that had long been familiar to companies but was not generally employed
at Lloyd's; and it raised at one time a certain amount of discussion and
misgiving. The underwriters would first arrange reinsurance contracts
with marine and non-marine syndicates in the Room, and with these
treaties behind them they would write very large lines – much larger lines
than they meant to retain – passing on to their reinsurers the greater part
of the risk they had accepted. The theory behind the scheme was that
aviation insurance was a highly technical business understood only by the
underwriters who had made a special study of it. Surely the sensible
course for the underwriters who did not specialize would be to leave
themselves in the specialists' hands and, through the channel of these
reinsurance treaties, to get their share of the aviation income which came
to the Room. The system has had some odd consequences and a Name,
who is in an aviation syndicate as well as a marine syndicate, may reinsure
himself as a Name in one syndicate for most of the liability that he is going
to accept as a Name in another. Once a trail of reinsurance has been
started nobody can say exactly where it is going to end.

In the last ten years the aviation market has opened out and widened a good deal. The specialists' syndicates still hold the predominant place in the insurance of planes themselves, but marine underwriters are writing them too and not merely by reinsurance. There are indeed few, if any, underwriters at Lloyd's today who are not in some degree interested in the aviation business, and considering how young the business is, the value that can be covered on a single plane is astonishing. Probably large planes are covered themselves for half a million pounds. They carry a number of passengers almost all of whom have insured their lives for considerable sums. They often carry quantities of diamonds, precious metals, and securities, all of which are insured; and it is possible to cover in the market as much as £3,000,000 on a single consignment of valuables borne by one plane. Underwriters must at times be running more than £3,000,000 on one trip – a remarkable concentration of value and a good illustration of how Lloyd's and the British companies can keep pace with the most rapidly growing industry. Aviation has probably developed more quickly than any other form of transport in the world's history, and despite all the new hazards that it has introduced, the London insurance market has always been able to give it full cover.

. . . . . .

It has been said that the greatest single impetus ever given to the insurance industry came when the internal combustion engine was invented and brought into use. Aviation insurance is only one of the minor products of the invention, and remarkable as its growth has been, it is dwarfed by the astonishing figures of the companies' motor departments. Before the First World War the motor premium figures were not published but they must have been trifling. In 1931 (when the Board of Trade returns first separated motor statistics from those of other departments) the companies had an income from motors of more than £32,000,000. By 1948 the income had risen to £70,000,000 and by 1950 to £102,000,000. The companies' fire departments, after three centuries of active enterprise and two centuries of continuous growth, had an income in 1950 of only £168,000,000; so that in less than fifty years motors had built up a business equal in size to nearly two-thirds of what fire had accumulated in three hundred years. That comparison, of course, involves no criticism of the fire underwriter and does not necessarily carry any compliments to the motor underwriter. But it is a sidelight on the vast and awful revolution in man's life which started when he found out how to explode petroleum inside a steel cylinder.

In the field of motor insurance Lloyd's were pioneers. A syndicate of some size introduced about the year 1904 a comprehensive policy for cars and a scale of premiums based on the simple plan of charging a pound for every unit of horse-power – which as a rough-and-ready guide was not a bad shot at the appropriate rate. How well the scheme did is not known, but another underwriter who wrote for himself had already launched out on a more ambitious scheme. There was enough business to be had and his account grew far too quickly. He was not a very methodical person; he had little or no organization; and his venture did not succeed. He had gone into it without realizing that motor insurance calls for machinery of its own and that the lines on which Lloyd's underwriters had carried on their business hitherto would need to be drastically altered for this new type of insurance. He did not see that some organization would have to be devised specially for the handling of claims, or that the repair of damaged cars and the demands of third parties called for a new technique, different from the old methods of claims settling.

The old-fashioned Lloyd's system of dealing with claims had been devised for marine underwriting, and with some modifications it served well enough for more than a century – from the time when Lloyd's agencies were founded by John Bennett, during the Napoleonic wars, right down to our own day. The plan was to have agents ready to survey damaged ships and cargo at all the chief ports of the world. Merchants and shipowners who were insured at Lloyd's were instructed to call in an agent whenever there was trouble, to obtain from the agent a report and forward it to London. In London the papers would be submitted to the underwriters concerned and on the evidence of the papers alone the claim would be either settled or declined.

With a few changes, such as the substitution of assessors for Lloyd's Agents, that method served the ordinary non-marine underwriter as well as the marine, but it did not at all suit the motor underwriter. A car was much too mobile for an organization of that kind. It could travel in a day from London to Edinburgh and at any spot on the journey it might be damaged – twenty miles perhaps from the nearest town and hundreds of miles from Lloyd's. There were no Lloyd's Agents to help the driver and there might be a long delay before the underwriter, sitting in his box at Lloyd's, could give instructions to someone to look at the car and arrange for its repair. But there is no man on earth so impatient as the motorist with a damaged car. He wants it repaired not next week, not tomorrow but today; and woe betide any insurer who takes his premium and does not give him the rapid service he wants when he is in trouble. And rapid service was the very thing that the well-meaning but unfortunate underwriter who tried to build up this early motor account could not supply. He had started out inadequately prepared and he paid a heavy penalty for his lack of foresight.

Learning a lesson from that unhappy experience another Lloyd's syndicate, in conjunction with a firm of brokers, had a considerable success by making arrangements with garages all over the country and designating the garages as their 'authorized repairers'. Policy-holders were supplied with lists of these repairing firms and were told that if they had an accident they should make contact with the nearest of them, who would give immediate help and start whatever work was necessary without consulting the underwriters. The scheme in a way was an adaptation of the traditional Lloyd's Agency system and it worked so well that the underwriters got a great deal of business, managed it to the satisfaction of their clients and gave what was probably the quickest service then available. The syndicate was reputed to have made good profits but for some reason it gave up its motor underwriting in 1917, sold the connection to a tariff office which is still managing it nearly forty years after the purchase – not along the authorized repairer lines but as part of its own organization.

The system of authorized repairers was a step in the right direction, but as the ownership of cars grew more common it became apparent that motor underwriters needed their own claim-settling organizations, their own engineers and their own third-party experts. They must have their own representatives up and down the country who could reach an immobilized car quickly and authorize without delay the necessary repairs. The Committee of Lloyd's could not do for these new underwriters what they had done with their network of agencies for the marine. They could not select Lloyd's Agents in every town in Great Britain with power to survey and report, and even if they could have made such appointments they would not have made them. The motor underwriters needed their own machinery and either the various syndicates must co-operate to run a single organization for the whole motor market or each syndicate must develop a separate scheme of its own. And that is what happened.

Underwriting members who wished to write motor risks banded themselves into separate syndicates (mostly large ones) and the managers of each syndicate supplied not only an underwriter to write the risk but claims managers, engineers, and legal experts who were housed outside

Lloyd's building and corresponded direct with brokers and their clients. These men gave their whole time to the arrangement of claims and be- haved in every way like the claims-settling department of an ordinary insurance company. It was a new departure in Lloyd's business but it was made so easily that few people at Lloyd's appreciated the change that was taking place or realized that motor underwriters had departed from the tradition of centuries.

The motor syndicates, too, broke through another Lloyd's tradition that had nothing to do with the settlement of claims. Hitherto every syndicate had been known inside Lloyd's by the name of an individual – Percy Janson, Marten, Heath, Sidney Boulton, Ernest Adams, and so forth – and to the outsider the syndicate that insured him was usually anonymous. It was just a Lloyd's syndicate that his broker had chosen to write a particular risk. Except for motor insurance that arrangement still holds but the motor underwriters have never been content with anonymity or identi- fication by the name of one man. Their taste runs more to high-sounding fancy names. They like a title that catches the eye. They prefer their policies to be branded like a proprietary article, believing doubtless that goodwill is built up more easily if your product is christened with an easily remembered name. So they started calling themselves White Cross, or Red Star, or Paladin, or Primus, or Bell, and by doing so they achieved a kind of direct touch with the insurance public – a touch that the ordinary syndicate had never possessed.

They still were supposed to accept risks only from Lloyd's brokers, but their separate existence was recognized by the public as the existence of other syndicates is not. A merchant or a householder will seldom say 'I am insured with Mr Smith's or Mr Robinson's syndicate'. He says simply 'I am insured at Lloyd's'. But it is quite common for the owner of a car to say 'I am insured with the White Circle or with the Nulli Secundus or with the Blue Arrow'.[1] Sometimes perhaps he does not even understand that he has the benefit of a Lloyd's policy signed by Lloyd's underwriters and protected by all the safeguards that the name Lloyd's provides. At least five named syndicates have at one time or another sold their connec- tion outright to insurance companies that had nothing to do with Lloyd's, and their business has passed permanently into the companies' hemisphere – a thing that never happened with the goodwill of an old-fashioned anonymous syndicate. This naming fashion is an interesting development related to change from the old personal groups to large highly-organized

[1] Fictitious names.

syndicates. The work of the big syndicates has been of great value to Lloyd's in the first half of the twentieth century but it may be hoped that the process will not go too far – that in the Lloyd's market, at any rate, personality will never be subordinated to organization.

The claims-settling machinery that the underwriters have built up for themselves works well and the service it gives to the assured is as good as any in the country. But generally speaking it is confined to Great Britain. The syndicates' business is not international. They cover the home field but they do not maintain their own organization abroad and consequently they do not draw their premium income, as fire and marine syndicates draw theirs, from European countries, from America and from the out-lying parts of the Commonwealth. A few ordinary non-marine syndicates enter into motor contracts abroad chiefly in Canada, France and Australia, but the specialist motor underwriter at Lloyd's is generally speaking a non-migratory bird.

In this respect the motor underwriter is at a disadvantage in comparison with the insurance companies whose network of foreign agencies, foreign branches, and foreign subsidiary companies makes it easier for them to collect business overseas and to give the necessary service. Companies do not invariably find that their foreign motor account abroad is profitable, and many of the motor risks on their books may be accepted less for their own sake than to support the connections of the fire and accident depart-ments. They do not publish separate figures for home and foreign business, and when they have been asked by official Committees for a split-up of their premium income between British and foreign they have always replied that the statistics are not available. But it is clear from their accounts that their overseas branches contribute a very large proportion of the total motor income. An insurance office that has a motor premium income of more than £17,000,000 a year must be doing a very large business abroad and it would not be surprising to learn that most of the composite companies draw seventy or eighty per cent of their motor income from America.

The effect of this difference of policy between Lloyd's underwriters and the companies is seen in the figures published annually by the Board of Trade. For the year 1950 the Government return shows the following result under the heading 'Motor Vehicle insurance business':

British companies £102,708,499

Lloyd's underwriters £4,572,816

These figures do not tell the full story for Lloyd's. They do not include the premiums received by non-marine underwriters from contracts connected with overseas motors direct or by way of re-insurance. These contracts have recently grown in numbers; but the income derived from them cannot be very large. Even if the premiums produced by these contracts were added to the £4,572,816, the difference between Lloyd's and the companies would still be wide.

No adjustment or correction would blunt the edge of the Board of Trade figures and there can be no doubt that the companies, mainly because of their foreign connections, have outstripped Lloyd's in this sphere of insurance. That result has come about not because Lloyd's underwriters (where they operate) cannot compete in premiums, or because the service they give is not as good as the companies. It is due entirely to the fact that from time immemorial companies have been organized in one way and Lloyd's in another, and the companies' type of organization was more easily adapted to foreign motor business when it started years ago.

It is something of a paradox that in fire insurance (where the companies had some three centuries' start on Lloyd's) Lloyd's underwriters, coming into the market as intruding amateurs, developed their business quickly and secured within a few years a considerable share of the divisible cake; but in motor insurance, where they started from scratch, Lloyd's underwriters are getting after fifty years only about one-twenty-fifth of the whole. That discrepancy casts no reflection on Lloyd's. It is the rub of the green and no one is to blame for it.

# 19

## COMPULSORY INSURANCE
## AND A NEW INSURANCE ACT

*Growing danger of uninsured car drivers – Road Traffic Act 1930 – Compulsory insurance – Right to insure third party risk restricted to certain Companies and Lloyd's – Weaknesses in the scheme – Deposits not enough – Increased competition for motor business – Company failures – Public's discontent – Government Committee (1936) appointed to report – Lloyd's evidence on advantages of audit – Accepted by Committee in principle – New Insurance Act 1946 – Essence of audit principle applied to companies*

---

APART FROM ITS DIRECT IMPORTANCE in the scheme of insurance, motor business within the past twenty-five years has had, through a chain of fortuitous events, a considerable indirect influence on British insurance law. In the days when ownership of motor vehicles was a privilege confined to rich people it did not matter very much to a man or a woman injured in a car accident whether the motorist was insured or not. The owner was almost always worth powder and shot, and when the driver was held to be negligent he would have enough money to pay for the damage from his own pocket if he had been bold enough to run his own third-party risk.

But with the advent of the mass-produced car the habit of motoring spread from the rich to the comfortably off and from the comfortably off to the hard up. Second-hand cars and motor cycles, particularly if they were not noticeably roadworthy, could be had for a few pounds. The roads carried cars and cycles driven by impecunious adults and irresponsible youngsters who were not bound to be insured and (if they were uninsured) would certainly not be able to pay even moderate damages to the victim of their bad driving. The result was that an injured man (however good his case) had to find out before going to law whether the driver had the means to pay, and to decide as best he could whether it was worth while to pursue the defendant into the courts. If the victim decided wrongly he

335

would find himself the winner of the action but uncompensated and poorer by the amount of his own costs.

Public feeling which naturally sympathized with the pedestrian rather than with the motorist was very properly aroused, and in 1930 the Labour Government brought in the first Road Traffic Bill in the history of British legislation. It dealt with the whole duty of motorists, established penalties for dangerous driving and for driving under the influence of drink, fixed the limits of a vehicle's speed in crowded areas and made it illegal to use a motor vehicle on the road unless the third-party risk for personal injury was covered by insurance. Henceforth the ordinary motorist must be insured or run the risk of going to jail for three months.

That was all to the good but if the public was to be adequately protected Parliament must see to it that the motorist's insurance was a serious genuine transaction, not merely an arrangement to comply with the working of the law. And at that moment motor insurance was as little controlled by law as was marine. There was nothing to prevent anybody, with or without means, from signing a marine policy for any amount. And there was nothing to prevent him or anybody else from signing a motor policy in the same way though he may not have had a spare penny to satisfy a third-party claim after an accident. As motor insurance had not been dealt with in the 1909 Insurance Companies Act, the field was open to every Tom, Dick or Harry capable of signing his name to a document. Theoretically it would have been possible for the owner of one motor cycle to be insured by the owner of another cycle, and as a *quid pro quo* to give the other owner a policy signed by himself. That obviously would not do. To prevent it from happening the Bill restricted the right of underwriting motor risks to certain companies and underwriters, and the Government took upon itself the duty of making sure that the companies and underwriters would be strong enough to meet their liabilities. That was only logical. For many years the Government had protected the holder of the life insurance policies and for twenty years it had protected the holders of fire policies. In neither case was the insurance obligatory, but the Government had nevertheless thought it right to hold the ring and see fair play between the assurer and assured. Now that it was making motor insurance compulsory, saying to the motoring public 'You must insure', how much more was it the Government's duty to make certain that the insurers would have the financial strength to fulfil their obligations.

Unfortunately in drafting the Bill the Government made two serious mistakes, either of which might have been avoided if the advice of Lloyd's had been taken. The Committee of Lloyd's could have pointed out the danger that the Government was running at two points. The first danger-ous mistake was to describe the insurance companies that were permitted to cover third party risks as 'authorized' – a most unhappy word which Lloyd's years ago had deliberately avoided. It was once proposed to the Committee of Lloyd's that insurance brokers subscribing to Lloyd's and entitled to do business there should be called 'authorized Lloyd's brokers' and the Committee refused to agree. Lloyd's brokers are certainly per-mitted by Lloyd's to do what other insurance brokers are not and in a narrow sense the word 'authorized' might fit them. But it is a word of far-reaching suggestion, giving the impression of agency, even indicating some guarantee of supervision by a higher authority and on those grounds it was very wisely rejected. There never was at any time such a person as an 'authorized Lloyd's broker'.

But the Government when it drafted the Road Traffic Bill was more rash than Lloyd's. It attached the epithet 'authorized' to any company or underwriter who complied with the requirements of the Act, and it led car owners to believe either that the Government in some way was behind the companies or that it had satisfied itself of their solvency and reliability – a most regrettable notion to put into general circulation. The Govern-ment was neither behind the companies nor satisfied of their solvency. It accepted no responsibility and exercised no day to day supervision. But to be styled 'authorized' must have been worth a great deal of money to a company soliciting business from an uninstructed public.

The second mistake in the Bill (and the more serious one) was its reliance on the old principle of deposits – an inadequate principle that Lloyd's had seen to be inadequate when it adopted the audit system more than twenty years before. But the Government in 1930 was more than twenty years behind the times and (in spite of the demonstrable success of the Lloyd's audit) it could not break away from its old moorings and appreciate the inadequacy of fixed insurance deposits. To safeguard the citizen, whom it was forcing to take out a policy, it stipulated only that a company doing motor business should put up a fixed deposit and make annual returns to the Board of Trade. The returns were of comparatively little value and the deposit was uniform – a mere £15,000 whatever the risks run and whatever the size of the premium income. A company that had a small premium income, contented itself with a safe quiet account, chose its risks carefully and protected itself against catastrophe with satisfactory reinsurance contracts, put up a deposit of £15,000. The company that liked a dashing policy, aimed at a large premium income, was not selective and wrote fleets, char-à-bancs and other heavy risks without adequate reinsurance, put up the same deposit of £15,000. The whole thing was irrational and indefensible. It was like an architect putting down for an eight-floor office building the same foundation that he used for a four-bedroomed villa.

In terms of logic the principle of deposits and nothing but deposits was clearly wrong. And logic was reinforced by experience. The Assurance Companies Act of 1909, which relied on deposits only, had not achieved security. In twenty-six years fifty insurance companies doing business in Great Britain failed, and by 1930 it was plain as a pikestaff that the 1909 Act (and the principles it embodied) did not solve the problem of how to safeguard a company's policy-holders. To demand a named deposit at a company's birth and on the strength of that deposit to give it *carte blanche*, allowing it to write as much as it liked, grow to any size that it liked, bowl away as merrily as it liked until the day of its admitted insolvency – that had been proved a failure. Lloyd's had learnt the lesson even before 1910, but in 1930 the Government had not learnt it, and the Road Traffic Act following precedent made the same mistake as its predecessors with even worse results.

One of the consequences of the Act was a considerable increase in competition among the companies for this particular type of business. Now that insurance was compulsory, optimists looked forward to a great new demand for cover and on the strength of their £15,000 deposits they went for the business with both hands. But motor underwriting, standardized though it sometimes appears to be, calls for at least as much skill and caution as any other kind of insurance. A man who plunges recklessly in motor business is as certain to find himself in trouble as any other type of underwriter who plays the same game. And very soon after the Road Traffic Act came into force troubles gathered round some of the more dashing companies. Several companies failed within a few years of their receiving the title 'authorized' and most of their failures came from the bad results of the motor departments. In one almost tragic case the motor losses of a composite company not only exhausted the departmental funds but swallowed a considerable part of the life assets as well. In any circumstances these failures would have raised a scandal but here the scandal was sharpened because insurance was compulsory and the Government had given the impression that the companies were officially approved. There was much criticism and after one of the failures a financial paper wondered 'what these authorized insurers buy one half so worthless as the stuff they sell'.

So great was the public discontent at these failures that in 1936 the Government appointed a committee to consider 'in the light of provisions relating to compulsory insurance against third party risks' what changes if any were desirable in the existing law; and as Lloyd's motor under-writers were authorized insurers Lloyd's was represented on the Committee and invited to give its own evidence. Its position differed from that of the companies because the motor underwriters at Lloyd's had not made a deposit with the Board of Trade but had gained their title on the strength of the Lloyd's audit. That fact gave the Committee of Lloyd's a freedom to criticise which no other body enjoyed, and Eustace Pulbrook, who put the Lloyd's case, was probably the most effective of all the witnesses who appeared before the Departmental Committee. He demolished the case for deposits and explained in detail the working of the Lloyd's audit. He persuaded his hearers that the right policy was to extend to the companies not a replica of the Lloyd's audit but a like system, suited to the companies' conditions, which would act for them as the audit acted for underwriters and keep an annual check on their results and solvency. In his evidence Pulbrook described the audit as 'setting up a standard of security' which insurers must attain and prove annually that they have not fallen below it. That was Pulbrook's remedy for the companies' troubles and the Departmental Committee when it framed its report adopted his argument almost in his own language. It recommended that:

> Every insurer should be required to comply with standards of solvency to be prescribed by the Board of Trade ... the standards should be severe but not more or less severe than the standards already voluntarily adopted by the majority of insurers. ... Every insurer should be required to demonstrate to the satisfaction of the Board of Trade not only that he is solvent but that the security offered to his policy-holders is such that the danger of his becoming insolvent is so small as to be negligible.

There we have the heart and purpose of the Lloyd's audit and the Departmental Committee, which included a number of insurance company managers, was unanimously recommending its application to the companies.

For ten years the report of the Departmental Committee lay in a pigeon-hole while matters of greater urgency claimed the attention of Parliament.

But in the first year of peace the Labour Government produced a new Insurance Companies Act in which they adopted broadly the Committee's advice. By that Act Lloyd's itself was very little affected. It was, however, placed under a statutory duty to return every year to the Board of Trade a global summary of the extent and character of the business done by underwriters. And ever since 1947 the total figures of Lloyd's premiums and claims have been published in the Board of Trade Insurance Blue Book – an interesting innovation from which no one is a penny the worse and on the other hand no one seems to be very much the better. It is an oblation to the great god Publicity and not much more. But the companies for the first time in their history had to comply with a standard of solvency set up by the Act and power was given to the Courts of Law to wind up a company which failed to reach the standard. To continue in business undisturbed an insurance company must be able to pay its debts and under the 1946 Act it is deemed unable to pay them if its assets do not exceed its liabilities by:

(*a*) £50,000 or,

(*b*) one-tenth of its premium income in its last financial year

whichever is the greater of the two. That test is first cousin to the Lloyd's audit, not so elaborate, not (as one may surmise) quite so effective but sprung from the same stock, aimed at the same end and based on the same principle.

So the history of the audit system is this. In 1908, after years of discussion, Lloyd's adopts and frames its machinery. In 1909 Parliament recognizes its value so far as individual underwriting is concerned. In 1946 its worth has been proved by the experience of thirty-eight years and the principle is by statute extended to the companies.

At the end of those thirty-eight years the men who first conceived and designed the audit were all dead. Today Heath, Boulton, White, Luscombe are only names. And of others who came before them not even the name survives. But this book will have served its turn if it helps to keep alive the memory of what we owe to them.

# 20

## THE MEMBERS' DEBT TO THE SOCIETY

*The personality of Lloyd's – Loyalty of members and Corporation staff – Its value to Lloyd's – Birth of the 'Society' – 1811–71 – The Corporation's functions – Manifold activities – Incalculable value to Underwriters – Examples – Size of Corporation of Lloyd's staff – A great landowner – Versatility of staff – Debt to Hozier – Corporation's income – Corporate income and Underwriters' premium income compared*

---

MUCH HAS BEEN SAID in this book about the underwriting members and the subscribers of Lloyd's and much about the members of its Committee. Their good and ill fortune, their quarrels, their successes and sometimes their mistakes have been described in detail. And usually the spotlight has been turned on to the individual figures – the actors who have played their part in one generation and another, and contributed their quota to the making of Lloyd's history.

On the other hand the Society of Lloyd's itself (which provides the stage and sets the scenery for the performers) has perhaps not had its fair share of the limelight; and before the curtain falls the rays should be turned for a moment in its direction. Of course it is made up of individuals and its work at every stage has been affected by the quality of its membership, but it has a personality of its own, a character without which the work that has been done by it would not have been possible. To emphasize the importance of Lloyd's the Society is simple enough, but to describe intelligibly the fascination it holds for people who spend their working lives under its protection and its discipline – that is far from easy.

Every society, whatever its purpose, whether it is famous or obscure, humble or exalted, so long as it engages the loyalty of its members will have an individuality of its own. Man by man, the members will differ from each other as far as the tropics differ from the arctic. Some will be quarrelsome, some peaceable; some greedy, some altruistic; some wrong-headed, some prudent; but if they share with each other this one common loyalty they produce what the philosophers call a synthesis. From their diversity the society develops a unity. It becomes an amalgam of all the conflicting qualities of its members. It harmonizes them and develops into a personality in its own right.

It may be thought ridiculous to use such high-falutin' language as this about a heterogeneous collection of men when the only apparent bond between them is the profit motive. All of them have come to Lloyd's with the purpose of making a living and in the hope of laying up a competence before they die. It may be reasonable enough to describe the members of a church or a religious society or a political party as knit together into a single unit by a common loyalty; but is it not ridiculous to think in these terms of a collection of struggling moneymakers whose job in life is to compete with each other and with the rest of the world for the largest slice of a particular cake?

To speak of such a place as though it were anything but a material organization does indeed sound far-fetched; but it is not as silly as it sounds. Although the necessity of making a livelihood is the motive that brings the working members and subscribers together in Lloyd's, their feeling for Lloyd's is not simply materialistic. Most of the active members are ready to make for the common good sacrifices from which in their own lifetime they know they cannot gain any material advantage. There is a tradition, which they recognize and honour, that when the Chairman, whoever he may be, asks them to do something for Lloyd's, they are under a moral obligation to do their best to help him; and whatever his request may be it is seldom that a Chairman asks in vain for a member's assistance. At a general meeting, in which a matter of importance has to be determined, there may be discussion and there may be criticism, but anyone who is at all sensitive to atmosphere is almost always conscious of a common purpose in the meeting and an overriding desire to do what is best not for one or another section of the market but for the Society as a whole.

And that feeling is not confined to members and subscribers. It is no less strong in the men who compose the Corporation's staff. In the business of underwriting they have no monetary interest and materially it is of no consequence to them whether underwriters are making profits or sustaining losses, getting business or losing it. But among the members of its staff the Society has often found some of the most devoted friends it has ever had, men whose enthusiasm has lain in their work and whose leisure time has been spent in the study of Lloyd's history. They have found their greatest happiness in thinking and talking about Lloyd's and they have

A broker's slip of 1951, covering cotton imports into the United Kingdom for £2,500,000, part of a total risk of £5,000,000.

dug into old records to trace the footsteps of Edward Lloyd during his lifetime because they have regarded him as the Society's founder. They have written their own stories of episodes in the Society's history and collected every scrap of information they could find about it in old and contemporary newspapers. They have quite unmistakably felt the fascination of the place and made it one of the main interests in their lives. The material for this book could not have been collected without the generous help of members of the staff, given not as a tedious duty but in a spirit of loyalty and affection for the Society.

The value of this loyalty in the members, subscribers and staff must always be remembered as we go over the Society's history. Without it the Chairmen and Committees would at times have been helpless, and Lloyd's (if it had survived) would be a pale shadow of the great institution that it is today. With this in mind we may embark on a short summary (based mainly on episodes described in earlier chapters) of the work that the Society *qua* Society has done and is doing for Lloyd's.

The date of the Corporation's birth is certain. It was the day in 1871 when Queen Victoria gave her assent to the first Lloyd's Act. But the Act did not claim to be creating a new body. On the contrary, it recognized in its first paragraph that Lloyd's had 'long existed as a Society in the City of London' and that the purpose of Parliament was merely to incorporate a body which was already ancient. It gave no date for the Society's beginning and if one attempts to fix its birthday there is room for wide difference of opinion on the right answer. Of two or three dates any one might with almost equal propriety be accepted as correct, and which one you choose is a matter for your own preference. The romanticist might select the moment when Edward Lloyd first opened the doors of his coffee-house in Tower Street, but to use the word Society to describe the stray collection of customers who dropped in to drink coffee in 1688 seems to be rather a misuse of language. One might apply the word to the shop in Lombard Street and particularly to the place as it was when the war of Jenkins' ear broke out in 1739. And unquestionably Lloyd's was a Society after the new Lloyd's moved to Pope's Head Alley. It was every inch a Society when the frequenters in 1774 moved to the Royal Exchange and by paying their first subscriptions recognized their mutual relations with each other.

The relationship though real was fluid and informal till 1811, but in that year the vital trust deed was signed and from then on the Society had its own written constitution – embryonic and inadequate but for all that a constitution. Already for a long time the place had been controlled by the will of the subscribers, and the duty of satisfying their needs had been recognized by an elected committee. But in 1811 the subscribers admitted (within narrow limits) their duty of obedience to the Committee, and formally accepted the liability as well as the privilege of belonging to a single body. Out of its 269 years of life Lloyd's can fairly be called a Society for 250 and for convenience it will in this chapter be called 'Society' both before and after the incorporation of 1871.

The Act of 1871 defined the Society's object as being:

1.  The carrying on of marine insurance by its members.
2.  The collection, publication, and diffusion of intelligence with respect to shipping.
3.  The protection of the interests of members in respect of shipping, cargoes and freight.

That three-pointed definition has since been widened, but with a few alterations it represents well enough the essential functions of the Society at most stages of its history. Originally its work was to provide space in which the business of marine insurance might be carried on, and that always has been and always will be its primary task. Four walls round them and a roof over their heads are the first essentials for a market of underwriters. The second object quickly followed the first, as Lloyd and his successors, realizing the value of a good intelligence service, began to collect, publish, and diffuse news about ships' movements. After an unsuccessful attempt at journalism Lloyd's established its own newspaper in or about 1734. The first two of the three objects were now being pursued.

The third object was to protect the interest of underwriters, and a good many years passed after the foundation of the Society before that pursuit was started. There may have been moments in the first half of the eighteenth century when the Society took up arms against the attacks of outsiders, but there is no specific evidence that it ever did so until the first Committee was elected in 1772. Indeed without a Committee to act for the Society it is difficult to see how any effective action could be taken, but once the Committee had been installed it took up the duty of protecting underwriters' interests with almost embarrassing enthusiasm. As early as 1779, after the case of the *Mills* frigate had been decided, when shipowners and merchants were in active revolt against it, the Society led by its Committee put up a united front and very successfully protected what it regarded as the interests of underwriters.

Under the leadership of its first Secretary it started the great network of Agencies at home and abroad whose purpose *inter alia* was to protect underwriters from being swindled by fraudulent claims of merchants or shipowners. The peccadilloes of sea captains were exposed, the short-comings of the Admiralty were brought to the notice of their Lordships, and gallantry in the Royal Navy was encouraged by the gifts of swords and silverware to successful commanders. For many years, in fact, those matters took up more of the Committee's attention than any other topic, and so the third of the Society's objects – the protection of underwriters' interests – became for a time, if not for ever, its main purpose. When they elected a Committee to find new premises in 1772 the subscribers provided themselves with the best friend they ever had. From then onwards they have had someone to fight their battles for them – battles sometimes against dishonest policy-holders, sometimes against hostile politicians, sometimes against the unfriendly intentions of foreign governments, and sometimes against the weakness and folly of underwriters themselves.

Both in the handling of news and in the protection of underwriters' interest the work has widened enormously with the growing complexity of business. The Society now has its own printing machinery and its own compositors and readers. It still publishes a daily newspaper – the second oldest of all the existing metropolitan journals – and in addition it prints and supplies to underwriters and insurance companies a daily *Index* showing the current voyage and the latest report of more than twelve thousand vessels. The *Index* lies on the desk of every marine company underwriter as well as at Lloyd's, and it is perhaps the most valuable tool in his bag. The Society publishes, too, an Almanack stuffed with facts about navigation and most of the things that every young sailor ought to know. It prints every year a pocket diary which was started only in 1934 and is now so popular that more than a hundred thousand copies are sold every year. It produces law reports that are regularly quoted in the English and Scots courts, a loading list that is used widely by shipping firms, confidential reference books that supply the records of British and foreign owners and (to be quite up to date) another confidential record of civil aviation. Altogether the Society's publications that are of interest to people outside and inside Lloyd's number about twenty – some daily, some weekly, some yearly, and some issued at intervals during the twelve months.

If the work of the Society in handling news and information has widened out and grown, so too has its brother, the protection of underwriters' interests. A hundred years ago the main part of the Society's work for the protection of underwriters lay in maintaining agencies and in detecting any fraudulent activity that might inflate claims or create false ones out of nothing. If an owner scuttled an over-insured vessel, or a merchant with the help of forged documents shipped a cargo of old bricks, and having insured the bricks as ingots saw to it that the boat never reached its destination, then the Society would act for underwriters, collect the necessary evidence and lend a hand in the prosecution of the criminal. If an alteration in the wording of a policy thought to be injurious to the underwriters were proposed, it would be the Society's task to organize resistance and to maintain a united front against the proposal. In all such matters the body of underwriters looked to the Society as their friend and champion.

Today things are different. The Society still appoints and controls its Agents, but underwriters have their own organization to look after matters of common underwriting interest and except in very rare cases they do not need the Society's help and do not invoke it. They have their own committees for this, that, and the other purpose (some critically-minded people are inclined to think that they have too many and tend rather to become committee-bound) and they can carry on perfectly well with underwriting affairs without constantly running for help to the Society and demanding its assistance. But many problems, which now affect underwriters closely and would be difficult or impossible for an organization of underwriters to tackle, did not exist a century ago. In these problems the help of the Society has been and still is invaluable. Without its intervention they could never have been solved and if they had not been solved the growth of Lloyd's would undoubtedly have been checked.

From previous chapters of this book two or three particular examples may be chosen to illustrate the value to underwriters of the Society's organization and leadership. The first is the Policy Signing Office which revolutionized the system of signing policies at Lloyd's. *Prima facie* that may seem an invention of minor importance but in fact it was very important indeed. The number of policies that are now sent in daily by Lloyd's brokers for signature could never have been signed by the old nineteenth-century method, and unless policies can be signed at a reasonable speed Lloyd's underwriters would sooner or later have to go out of business. Even if it had been possible under the old system to sign all the policies that have to be signed today, their condition at the end of the operation would have got worse and worse. Many policies carrying the names of a large number of syndicates would have gone out into the world looking like the tattered regimental colours one sees hanging in cathedrals to commemorate the valour of a British regiment at the battle of Talavera.

The second example of what the Society has done for underwriters and brokers is Additional Securities – the Company which more than anything else has preserved and developed the foreign connections of Lloyd's. Without help from the Society and its employees no underwriter, no group of underwriters, could have devised the scheme of Additional Securities, arranged its finances or managed its operations. A trained and efficient staff was needed to work out the complicated details of its capital and as conditions change from year to year a competent staff is needed to make the best use of the Company's resources. Exactly what difference it would have made to Lloyd's if the Company had never been started is a matter of conjecture, but it is a safe guess that the overseas activities of underwriters would have been greatly restricted and their total premium income would be far smaller than it is today.

A third example of work done by the Society for underwriters and brokers is the American Trust Fund, which maintained Lloyd's ties with America during the 1939 war and saved for the nation a dollar income of high value. The scheme was complicated to design and not less complicated to work, and no group of individuals, however gifted or powerful, could have attempted either task unless it had had behind it experienced administrators and an adaptable machine. If every underwriter at Lloyd's had been another Angerstein or another Heath, and there had been no Society ready and able to help them, the underwriters could never in the face of the emergency of 1939 have taken the steps necessary for the protection of their business. Indeed if the Society in 1939 had been what it was in 1910; if the staff had been so little used to large administration, so inexperienced in finance and banking; or if the Committee of Lloyd's itself had been made up entirely of the old-fashioned specialized marine underwriters, then the task of launching the American Trust Fund in 1939 would have been impossible. The Fund, started so hurriedly on the very eve of war, is still at work – an integral part of Lloyd's, and as brokers and underwriters pay their premiums into it and their claims out they should remember the debt they owe to the Society itself and to the men (working in the Society's service) who framed and started it.

But great as is the debt that we owe to the Society for the Policy Office, for Additional Securites and for the American Trust Fund, its most valuable work has been the yearly audit and the various reforms that have sprung from its institution. If it is agreed (as agreed it must be) that the beginning of the audit system was a turning point in Lloyd's history and that without it the very survival of Lloyd's would have been in doubt, then it is impossible to overstate the debt still owed by every one who makes his living at Lloyd's to the Society which carried the reform through. Looking back on that great event of 1908 we can see what a revolution was involved in it. Here was a body of individualists, all of them traditionally jealous for their rights; all resentful of any infringement of their independence. Some of them had for years argued almost violently against this innovation and were still, as it seemed, ready to oppose it in every possible way. And yet after one meeting, one appeal from the leaders of the Society, the individualists bow their necks to the yoke and accept without a murmur the new discipline. They could not tell what the results of this audit would be or estimate its effect on their own business, but they submitted to the advice of the Society's Committee and entrusted to its staff the duty of a yearly supervision of their underwriting figures. That momentous step could not have been taken unless the general body of Members had been conscious of deep loyalty to the Society, of a firm confidence in its management, and of a faith in the staff which was to administer the audit under the Committee's direction for the rest of time. The audit secured Lloyd's. The Society made the audit possible.

·     ·     ·     ·     ·     ·

Forty years before the audit was introduced, the revolution it involved could not have taken place. It would have been impossible not only because the members of Lloyd's would have refused their consent to it but because the Society was not equipped to perform its share of the audit work. For a long time the staff provided for the Society was inadequate and poorly paid. The Secretary in 1851 formally complained that he had not clerks enough to do his work properly and was reluctantly given two more to bring him up to strength. In 1854 the salary of the Secretary himself was only £500 a year and the clerks were all underpaid. By 1871 the Secretary's staff had risen to twenty-five clerks, while the waiters, doorkeepers and messengers numbered sixteen – total number of employees forty-four. In 1954 there were one thousand, four hundred and fifty men and women on the list of clerical staff and six hundred men and women employed as waiters, cleaners, engineers and printers.

. . . . . .

Financially the Society in the old days was always solvent, usually comfortable, but never rich. For a long time it had constant difficulty in collecting members' subscriptions but it does not seem ever to have been in the red; and in the year 1870 it had 'in the three per cent consolidated annuities standing in the names of four persons being trustees for the Society' a capital stock of £48,000. For a Society of such eminence with such unknown possibilities of calls upon its resources that was not a very large fortune, but during the next forty years the funds rose substantially and in 1910 the capital balance amounted to £176,000. That was a useful figure but still not big enough for the calls that were to be made upon it within the next twenty years. It stood at about that level till the close of the First World War and then it began to shoot ahead. In 1923, when it contributed £100,000 to the payment of Harrison's deplorable losses and cash was needed for the new building, it had a capital balance of over half a million pounds and was able to subscribe for all the ordinary shares of Lloyd's Building Limited. A few years later the Society took its share in the purchase of the Royal Mail Building and later still, in 1951, it secured the freehold of the new site in Lime Street and became one of the largest landowners in the City of London. By the time the new building on this site has been completed the value of the land and buildings in which the Society has a controlling interest will probably amount to about £8,500,000 – a remarkable achievement for a non-profit making concern which was forced rather reluctantly to go into the property market only thirty years ago.

The extension of the Society's interest has naturally involved not merely an increase in the numbers of the staff but a staff of different qualities from those that were adequate in the nineteenth century. Then it was enough if the Society's servants understood the movement of shipping and knew enough of accountancy to keep a not very elaborate set of books. Now they need to have many other accomplishments. They need to understand the management of office property and some of them by this time are expert at the business, knowing enough about the building trade to be able to talk to architects in their own language. Some of them are competent lawyers. Some know a great deal about foreign banking and certain fields of international relations. Some understand the publishing business and could tell you how to run a printing works. Some could go into the catering business at a moment's notice and even in that tough trade not be marked down as greenhorns. All this development sheds great credit not only on the staff itself but on those who picked it and organized it in the past – most of all on that fascinating person Colonel Hozier. In Hozier's career there were things that could not be called admirable, but their effect on Lloyd's has long since evaporated. The good things he did have survived and perhaps the best of them all is the change he brought about in the capacity and efficiency of the Society's staff.

Exactly how efficient the staff was in 1872 no one can say, but the Secretary who retired in that year had been a square peg in a round hole and the men who worked for him probably took their colour from their chief. Hozier was a very different person. He was a man of great energy and knew a good man when he saw him. He was not always easy to work for or to satisfy and tradition says that he was inclined to overdrive his assistants. But they were a good assortment and thanks, no doubt, to his restless imagination the senior members of the staff seem never to have drifted (as they so easily might have done) into a kind of Civil Service mentality. Many if not most of the older men who worked for the Society in the revolutionary years between 1905 and 1930 were Hozier-picked and Hozier-trained and as they retired they passed on to their successors the good qualities that he had seen and fostered in them. Without men of the right calibre to advise, plan, and execute, neither the aims of Heath, Boulton and Sturge, nor the reforms of the years between 1939 and 1953 could have been realized. And much of the credit for this happy combination goes to Hozier. If he had done nothing else for Lloyd's, his work for the staff would give him a place in Lloyd's history.

.  .  .  .  .  .

The Society's income is derived from various sources, more than half of it from subscriptions which in recent years have produced annually more than half a million pounds. Entrance fees (carried to capital account) vary in their yield with the eagerness of the public to become underwriting members, and in the years that have followed the Second World War they have been on the upgrade. The most productive year was 1954 and it was then a matter for speculation whether the number of candidates could continue at so high a level. A good many people believed that high taxation would check the influx of new members and it did seem likely that surtax payers, weighing the danger of unlimited liability against the profits of underwriting after the Inland Revenue had had its way with them, might decide that the game was not worth the candle. But there were countervailing influences and it may be that taxation has helped to increase, not to diminish, the number of candidates. The income that a Name hopes to derive from his underwriting does not end when he retires from active business; and at a time when saving of the old-fashioned sort is made impossible by income and surtax, an alternative method of providing for old age and retirement has its attraction for men of means. This hope of an additional income that will continue to the end of life has certainly had something to do with the steady influx of candidates in the years since 1945.

The connection between the Society and the underwriting members is so close, and their fortunes are so intimately bound together, that one would expect the growth and prosperity of underwriting to be reflected in the capital resources of the Society. But there is really no reason why the premium income of Lloyd's and the capital wealth of the Society should correspond exactly. All sorts of disturbing factors are at work to prevent it – the ups and downs of trade which affect the premium incomes, changes made by the Committee of Lloyd's in subscriptions and entrance fees, and such comparatively small things as the profit or loss made by the Society on its publications – these things, great and small, help to make it unlikely that the premium income of Lloyd's underwriters and the financial strength of the Society will, over a long period, march step by step. That would be too much to expect. But in fact the results are surprisingly close.

The Society's capital balance is ascertainable, no doubt, for many years back but the premium income of underwriters has been known only for some forty years. A comparison of the two figures – Society's capital and underwriters' premium income – cannot be made for any year before 1913. Here in juxtaposition are the figures of 1913 and the figures forty years later of 1953:

|  | 1913 £ | 1953 £ | Increase £ |
|---|---|---|---|
| Premium Income | 12,861,000 | 225,567,000 | 212,706,000 |
| Society's Capital | 184,000 | 2,489,000 | 2,305,000 |

On these figures the premium income of underwriters in forty years was multiplied about seventeen times and the capital balance of the Society about thirteen times. It looks as though the partnership between the Society and the underwriting membership is not merely prosperous but equitable.

# 21

## PAST, PRESENT AND FUTURE

*Generations and changes – Membership numbers – Mutual help of marine and non-marine – Actual underwriters and Names – Composition of membership – Paths to success – Younger Names – Less fear of the dangers of underwriting – Value of audit to Names – An old man's misgivings – Aggregate of Underwriting profits – Attraction to young men – Its dangers – Loyalty and self-interest – The great men of Lloyd's – Responsibility of rising generation*

---

EIGHTY YEARS AGO Walter Bagehot speaking not of commerce but of politics said that the change which, above all others, produces change is the change from one generation to another. Every generation has its own outlook and none sees things quite in the same light that lighted its predecessors. But the generations usually succeed each other in silence and one does not push another away with a single violent shove. It takes over gradually – so gradually that we scarcely perceive what is happening; and except when we look back, count the numbers of the dead, note the ages of the living and deliberately set the ideas of today beside those in fashion forty years ago, we may forget that the generation we used to know is in the grave – with its conventions, axioms, and beliefs, buried alongside it.

In the smoothness of the change from one generation to the next Bagehot seemed to find an important element working for stability. But, sometimes (he noted) the rhythm changes suddenly. Then instead of a slow almost imperceptible movement we get a sharp jolt. Things happen quickly and the least observant person realizes that he is watching the death of one generation and the birth of another. Bagehot's short life was spent in green pastures and beside still waters, and he actually saw the sudden visible end of a generation in the death of Lord Palmerston – an event that we, who are accustomed to stormier weather, can contemplate without an increase in our blood pressure. We have had experiences far more impressive and far more violent than any Bagehot knew. In the memory of men still middle-aged, two generations have died tragically and two have had a painful birth. Even in our everyday language we recognize the sharp divisions in our lives drawn by 1914 and 1939, and it is commonplace for us to speak of the pre-war, the post-war, and the between-the-wars generations. May there be no more additions to our vocabulary.

Like most other institutions the world over, Lloyd's has felt the impact of the two World Wars and the violent changes that they brought. It will carry the marks of them forever. It would be futile to speculate on what Lloyd's or what anything else would have been like today if there had been no Anglo-German War; but we can be certain that even if the last forty years had been years of peace, changes of great importance would have taken place at Lloyd's. Even before 1914 we can detect at Lloyd's that sudden jolt between one generation and the next which Bagehot detected in the English political life of 1865. New generations were born in the 1880's, when Heath wrote his first fire risk, and in 1908 when the audit was introduced and the efforts of the Lloyd's reformers achieved success. They were generations with a new outlook, a wider ambition, and a greater sense of corporate responsibility. Almost one might say that a new Lloyd's came into existence. Since then the generations have succeeded each other quickly and all the time the tempo has risen. Taken together the changes add up to a revolution; and as every revolution begets new problems to be solved and new difficulties to be overcome, an attempt may be made here to recall some of the problems, some of the difficulties, that Lloyd's has encountered in recent years and to assess some of the possibilities of the future.

.  .  .  .  .  .  .

The figures of premium income set out in the last chapter indicate the astonishing growth of Lloyd's underwriting in the past forty years and the figures of membership tell the same story. In 1913 the number of underwriting members was 631. In 1953 it was 3,603. In 1956 it is 4,177. In one post-war year alone 368 new members were elected – and that figure of 368 was more than half the total number on the list of underwriting members forty-one years before. For this remarkable increase in membership and in premium income the first reason is undoubtedly the development of non-marine business. A comparatively new market brought with it a great mass of new premiums. It lengthened the arm of the Lloyd's broker and all over the world made the name of Lloyd's familiar to people who hitherto had scarcely heard of it.

We cannot gauge the effect of these new non-marine connections on the marine market or estimate the amount of fresh business they have brought to marine underwriters, but it is reasonable to suppose that the new grist has not all gone into the non-marine mill. In the early days of non-marine most of the business came to underwriters from firms whose marine risks had previously been placed at Lloyd's. They were the firms with whom Lloyd's brokers had long been in contact over marine business, and to them the brokers naturally spoke first about the new developments in the market when Heath and his successors started on this new venture. The firms became Lloyd's first non-marine clients, but as the non-marine market grew stronger and began to stand on its own feet the reverse movement set in and the assistance between the two markets became mutual. Brokers coming into touch with new clients over fire and accident business would not remain silent about the possibilities of Lloyd's as a marine market, and there must have been many times when an overseas insurance broker, who had come to Lloyd's originally for non-marine cover, was successfully invited to bring his marine risks to the same place. When Lloyd's underwriters took to non-marine business they were widening their scope and (as has been remarked before) insurance does best when it advances on a broad front. It is indeed certain that every kind of underwriter at Lloyd's has gained from the birth and growth of non-marine insurance. At one time or another there are mutual complaints, and some rivalry, between marine and non-marine, but every underwriter knows in his heart that the well-being of Lloyd's is indivisible and that the progress of one section advances the prosperity of the other. And vice versa.

Of the men who make up the greatly increased membership of Lloyd's a few are active underwriters and these men are the spearhead of the market. They accept and refuse the risks that brokers offer. They control syndicates, determine policy and by their good or bad judgment produce, year by year, a profit or a loss. But they are key men and in the list of underwriting members they are very much in the minority. The great majority of members are Names – men who not being deterred by the thought of unlimited liability have entrusted their fortunes to an active underwriting agent and agreed, for better or for worse, to abide by the results of his underwriting. On paper that seems a bold step to take and the fact that three or four hundred men are willing and eager to take it every year is a strong proof of the place Lloyd's holds in the estimation of the business world.

Who are these men that in such large numbers decide to become Names in Lloyd's syndicates? They must be men of some means, but where do they come from? What other occupations and professions do they follow and what turns their thoughts to Lloyd's? They are elected at almost all ages from twenty-one to seventy, but what is the average age and the average period of their membership? There is no cut-and-dried answer to these questions, and that is a pity. A complete and correct statement, if it went back far enough, might be very valuable to students of Lloyd's history, and would certainly throw light on changes that have taken place in the make-up and functions of Lloyd's in the last hundred years. It might, too, illuminate some of the problems of the present time.

Traditionally, Lloyd's membership is drawn mainly from merchants, bankers, traders, underwriters and insurance brokers. In the Trust Deed of 1811 those were the occupations specifically catalogued, but the deed surprisingly says nothing of shipowners whom one would have expected to be rather prominent among the frequenters of the coffee-house. They are not mentioned in the Deed. In the twentieth century shipowners are pretty well represented in the list of members but at the beginning of the nineteenth they were apparently too few to be classified. Indeed it seems fairly certain that Lloyd's is drawing its members today from a much wider area than it touched a century ago. It includes now those merchants, bankers and traders that the Trust Deed talked about in 1811, but there are also among its names politicians from both Houses of Parliament. There are manufacturers, soldiers, lawyers, airmen, accountants, farmers and medical men. There are men domiciled and doing business in various parts of the Commonwealth who (if they ever come to Lloyd's) can come only on rare occasions and at long intervals. And there is a substantial number of men who work as clerks in the offices of insurance brokers – men who by a strange paradox are employees in the sphere of brokerage and principals in the sphere of underwriting. Above all there are far more young men among the Names now than there were fifty years ago.

As a consequence, presumably of the much wider appeal now made by Lloyd's, its membership has changed greatly, not only in size and quality but in age. What has happened at Lloyd's is the opposite of what has happened and is happening in the general population of the country. In the general population (as everybody knows) the average age is rising all the time. There are fewer young people and more old – less in the twenties and more in the seventies and eighties. The economists worry themselves about what is happening and the doctors recognize it by adding to the

English language the new deplorable word 'geriatrist', which means a specialist looking after a lot of old people, who might be better left alone to end their lives without the interference of modern science. At Lloyd's things are different. There are as many old men as there ever were on the list of members, but the young men are far more numerous than they used to be, and it is probably the fact today that (for the first time in the records of Lloyd's membership) the under-forties outnumber the over-forties. It is worth while to consider the reasons for this change and how it has come about.

There have always been a certain number of men at Lloyd's fortunate enough to be elected underwriting members soon after they come of age. Some of them – Heath and Sturge for example – were sons of well-to-do fathers who were not themselves connected with Lloyd's but chose underwriting as their sons' careers and supplied them with the necessary capital. Such men in the old days were comparatively few in number. Others were the sons of prosperous underwriters, often coming from old Lloyd's families, descendants of men who were underwriters and brokers in the early days of the nineteenth century. These young men had been earmarked for Lloyd's in their boyhood and when they came of age they naturally became underwriting members to carry on in the traditional way the family business. They had the Lloyd's tradition in their blood and most of them made admirable members.

But among the great underwriters of the past these men were in a minority. It was more common for men without inherited means to serve a long apprenticeship, either at an underwriting box or in a broker's office, working hard and putting up with a great deal of drudgery, often indifferently paid but (if they had the right stuff in them) warmed all the time by the hope of becoming underwriting members themselves before they died. The prize was always hanging in front of them and, to the clerk of ability and perseverance, if he could reach it at the end of the race, it was worth years of patient service. An underwriter's deputy or second deputy might be helped by a grateful employer to put up his deposit and join the syndicate he had served as a clerk for fifteen or twenty years. The struggling broker might save enough of his income every year to provide him at last with the necessary capital and give him sufficient confidence in his own position to submit himself for election and become a member of an established syndicate.

That was a normal pilgrimage and many of the ablest underwriters in the history of Lloyd's have gone on it. Sidney Boulton was the son of a ship surveyor. He started his working life as a junior clerk in the Salvage Association and came reluctantly to Lloyd's after a few years on a yearly salary of £40. William Hoade, who was regarded by some of his contemporaries as the most skilful voyage underwriter of all time, started as a clerk at an underwriter's box and won his membership of Lloyd's purely by his own ability. Meacock, who became one of the successful early non-marine underwriters, was an underwriter's bookkeeper until middle-age.

To reach the heights of underwriting as these men did and to become the appointed agent of a large syndicate, either marine or non-marine, is a guerdon still given only to a few. Everywhere the gate is strait and the way narrow that leads to eminence and power, and to that rule Lloyd's is no exception. But the road to membership, the path that leads a man to join a syndicate in which he will be a Name and probably remain a Name until the end of his life – that path is broader and shorter than it was. The decision to apply for membership is apparently not the formidable step now that it used to be, and both young and middle-aged alike seem to take it without the searching of heart that once preceded it.

That change of attitude can be illustrated by the record of two men, one born in 1844 and the other in 1884. Both of them spent their working lives as Lloyd's brokers. Both started with little capital. Both became underwriting members. But they were divided by forty years of time and because of those forty years their careers as Names were almost as different as they could be. The elder of the two became a broker when he was in the twenties and built up a small but prosperous business which maintained his family and himself until his death in 1910. He had some well-to-do relations, one of whom offered, when he was a comparatively young man, to supply him with the capital necessary for him to become an underwriting member. The young man refused the offer, not because he had no ambition to become a member but because he thought the risk of underwriting to be greater than he, as a struggling broker, could prudently undertake. He refused the offer and worked away at his own business, saving money and educating his children, but eschewing all thought of membership until the youngest of his sons was old enough to earn his own living. Then, using his own savings, he put his name forward and when he was in the middle fifties started an underwriting career which lasted for a little more than ten years.

When he died his place in the syndicate was taken by a young man of twenty-six, who was at that moment in very much the same position that the older man had been in forty years before. He, too, was in the twenties and he, too, was a Lloyd's broker. His capital like the older man's was small, but like the older man he had friends or relations who would help him with the required funds. They offered their help and unlike the older man he did not hesitate to accept. He applied for membership before he was thirty and took the place in the syndicate made vacant by the older man's death. Since then he has had over forty years of successful underwriting.

Looking back over the years we can see that both these men did the right thing. The man born in 1844 was right to refuse membership when he was young. The man born in 1884 was wise to accept it. And he was one of the first of a very long list of young men who have since then made the same decision that he made, launching out on their career as Names while they were still in their twenties. And what lies behind the change? Why has a thing that was dangerous or imprudent eighty years ago become safe enough to be reasonably prudent today? Well, all roads at Lloyd's lead to the audit and it is the audit that gives us part at least of the answer to these questions.

Now that the accounts are audited every year and are certified to be up to the Committee's appointed standard it is a much safer thing to be a Name in an underwriting syndicate than it was before 1908. To suggest that being a Name is at any time a completely safe adventure would be ridiculous. You cannot accept unlimited liability without running the risk of losses. You cannot entrust to somebody other than yourself the power of committing you to your last penny without a danger, however faint, that the man you choose will either in ability or in character prove unworthy of your trust. Some underwriting agents will always be better than others and the advice that Charles Wright gave thirty years ago to the man who thought of becoming a Name still holds good. He said simply 'Choose well your agent' – an admirable maxim. An unskilled agent can still lose money for you. A dishonest agent (if you should be so extraordinarily unlucky as to pick one) may still land you in Carey Street. But thanks to the audit the chance of losing money on a considerable scale is much smaller than it used to be, and the possibility of losing everything far more remote. Adopted for the protection of policy-holders, the audit for nearly fifty years has been the Names' sheet-anchor.

·     ·     ·     ·     ·

Before the audit was introduced, in the years when Lloyd's was moving painfully towards a conception of corporate responsibility and people were holding interminable debates about this, that and the other plan for

'The Underwriting Room at Lloyd's', Terence Cuneo's painting of 1949.

achieving it, the stock argument against any common action was the danger of putting all underwriters, good and bad alike, on to the same level of security. The greatest protection against reckless underwriting (so the argument ran) lay in the broker's knowledge of the market. It was part of his duty – perhaps the most important part – to keep his eyes open for weak spots and to fight shy of any underwriter who was plunging or writing too dangerous an account. An underwriter suspected by brokers of sailing too near the rocks would be sent to Coventry by all responsible firms and have either to mend his ways or to retire from business, and so the danger spot in the market would disappear. But if the doctrine of corporate responsibility was accepted and a bad underwriter's claims (if and when he failed) were certain to be settled for him by his fellow underwriters, then brokers would go on doing business with him and he would remain indefinitely a source of trouble and perhaps disaster.

That was the argument. It was never very convincing and it has been proved unsound. The general standard of caution in underwriting has not fallen. Reckless trading has not been encouraged. On the contrary, the credit of a Lloyd's policy has risen to a point never reached before and the general level of prosperity among underwriters is probably higher than it ever was.

But though the fears of the old diehards have turned out to be bogeys and the strength of the Lloyd's community has been enormously increased in the last forty years, the improvement of status has brought with it a change – to call it a danger would be an exaggeration – more subtle than anything the diehards prophesied, too tenuous perhaps to be recognized by any except the older members as they look back and check their memories of the past against their view of the present. Old men forget and old men embroider. When they compare the world as they used to know it with the world as it is today, they are notoriously wrong-headed and unreliable; and any old man who thinks that Lloyd's was better organized in 1900 than it is now must be a dotard or a fool. But his misgivings, such as they are, may be given an occasional airing, and if they are in fact all moonshine so much the better for everybody and no harm will have been done by allowing them at least one appearance in public.

The misgivings in the old man's mind are not very easy to express but they are connected with the great increase in membership that has taken place since the end of the last war. Let us recall the fact that in 1945 the number of underwriting members was 1,960, and in 1956 – eleven years afterwards – it was 4,177. That is an increase of 2,217 – by far the greatest

AA

rise in numbers that has ever been known at Lloyd's in any period. And it is a net increase. To find out how many were elected in that time, we should have to add the number of deaths and retirements and the final result would probably be something between 2,500 and 3,000 elections in eleven years.

In some ways that eleven-year period was not an altogether easy time at Lloyd's and the Committees since the war have had problems to handle perhaps as tough as any that ever confronted their predecessors. Underwriters, too, from time to time have had their own crosses to carry. But in the essential matter of making a profit and avoiding a loss it is probably correct to say that the business of underwriting has been less difficult than it normally is. The good work done by previous generations in establishing the reputation of Lloyd's has been bearing fruit. World-wide inflation (deplorable as it is) has swollen the premium income, and a rising premium income widens the scope of an underwriter's choice, and makes it easier for him to refuse inferior or underpaid risks and so to improve the average quality of his account. Even if the average quality of the risks does not improve but remains the same, an increase in the volume of premiums obviously produces in good years an increase of profits and swells the sum available for distribution among the Names.

What the net underwriting profits of Lloyd's Names are nobody (except the Inland Revenue from whom no secrets are hid) has ever known; but it seems reasonable to assume that the average net profit in good years is not less than eight per cent of the premium income. And taking that percentage as our basic assumption we should find that just before the last war the combined net profits of Lloyd's Names were about £2,700,000 and in 1953 they were about £17,500,000. These figures (and this must be emphasized) do not claim to be correct or anything like correct. They may be too low and they may be too high, but they do indicate that – apart from taxation and the fall in the value of the pound – the ordinary Name of today is better off than his forerunners of even twenty years ago.

.    .    .    .    .    .

Of the underwriting profits made at Lloyd's it must be remembered that a very large proportion goes to the Names – to the men who are underwriters not by profession but by investment. The Names do not select the risks to be written or control the policy of a syndicate. They entrust themselves for good or ill to a professional underwriter. He carries on the business for them and they are bound to honour his commitments. To a young man whose means justify him in taking on the risks of underwriting membership the attraction of becoming a Name when times are good is obvious. If he gets a place in a well-run profitable syndicate – a syndicate that has had built up for it in the past a lasting goodwill – he will, without paying a penny of purchase price, be securing something like a partnership in an established firm. To speak of a partnership in connection with Lloyd's underwriting is not legally accurate, for in Lloyd's underwriting there is no such thing. But for explanatory purposes the analogy between a syndicate and a partnership is close enough and, subject always to the incidence of liability, a name in the syndicate may practically, though not legally, be regarded as a sleeping partner in an insurance business. He runs unlimited liability, does no work, shares the profit and bears his proportion of the losses.

How attractive then for a young man must be the prospect of joining a syndicate that is managed by a successful underwriting agent, is fortified by an established connection, and is making a regular profit for its members. All these good things are there to be enjoyed by him if he has the necessary means available, is ready to accept unlimited liability, can secure election to underwriting membership and is offered a place in a syndicate of the right kind.

But how is he to be elected and how to pick the right syndicate? If he has no inherited connections with Lloyd's he will (if he is well advised) seek either a position of employment in a firm of brokers or – what is more difficult to come by – a job with an underwriter and a seat at his box. He will then be able to look round for himself, find out which syndicate is the most suitable for him to join, ascertain whether the syndicate's agent will accept him as a Name and finally take the step that is going to mean so much to him in his business career. After he has worked in an office or at an underwriting box for five years he will be regarded by the Committee of Lloyd's as a Lloyd's man; and since it is easier for a Lloyd's man than for an outsider to be elected, he will find the path to membership smoother than he would have found it if he had not first spent a few years of apprenticeship. When he does submit himself for election as a Lloyd's man he will have to put up his deposit, declare his means, have the limits of his premium income fixed, and agree to various undertakings that every candidate for membership has to give. But as a Lloyd's man he will have to give an extra undertaking. He must declare that he intends to make

Lloyd's his vocation and promise that if ever, for any reason, he ceases to work at Lloyd's he will submit himself to the Committee and acknowledge the Committee's right to terminate his membership.

All this is well enough. It is a good thing for Lloyd's that it should be attractive to young men of ambition and energy, and there is no doubt that the prospect of becoming an underwriting member and getting a place in a syndicate has brought many youngsters of the right kind to work in brokers' offices. That must have helped to secure the future of Lloyd's. But there is a danger. A young man who starts working as a broker ought to fix his mind from the first on becoming as good a broker as he can be. He should concentrate on earning a living from his work as a broker and not concern himself too much with the profits he hopes to make, as a quasi sleeping partner, out of his underwriting. He should regard himself, not his underwriting agent, as the architect of his fortunes. Like any other institution, Lloyd's needs men who give themselves entirely to their life's work – single-minded men determined to stand on their own feet and to be content (if nothing more is to be had) with the rewards of their own industry.

It is impossible to say how many young men come to Lloyd's because of the prospect of becoming a Name, how many think of their day-to-day employment in a broker's office or at an underwriting box as a sort of back door to membership of a syndicate. But the temptation is undoubtedly there, and it is difficult to believe that men who come in this spirit and with this motive predominant in their minds can add much to the strength of Lloyd's. If they join a Lloyd's firm simply to join a syndicate later on; if they remain at Lloyd's simply because they have given the vocational undertaking, then the probability is that they will be drones. And too many drones are a weakness in the hive.

The best antidote to this weakness (if it exists) would be to instil – if it be possible – into every newcomer a sense of what he and every other member of Lloyd's owe to the Corporation of Lloyd's and to the men who have made it what it is. Let him be taught something of Lloyd's history. Let him appreciate the difficulties that have had to be overcome, the risks that have had to be taken, the sacrifices that have had to be made. The more he knows of what has happened in the past, the more proud he should be of his membership – not proud in a social snobbish way, but with a feeling that he has inherited by good fortune a place made for him by the sweat and toil and enterprise of twelve generations before him. He will then, if he has the right stuff in him, realize that it is for him to show his appreciation and gratitude by doing everything he can to improve and strengthen his inheritance.

In these hurried days the writings of Edmund Burke are much less often read or quoted than they were sixty years ago – which may be thought a pity. But when Charles Wright, who was both in disposition and in politics an old-fashioned Whig, was composing his history of Lloyd's he not only quoted Burke but gave him the last word. The final sentence of Wright's *History of Lloyd's* comes from Burke; and Wright quoted it because it expressed in Burke's flowery language Wright's view of a Lloyd's man's duty to Lloyd's. This is it:

> If we are conscious of our station and glow with zeal to fill our places as becomes our situation and ourselves we ought to elevate our minds to the greatness of the trust to which the order of Providence has called us.

That quotation is precedent enough to justify here another quotation from the same pen. One of Burke's favourite principles was that every generation is a trustee for posterity. It has received an inheritance from its predecessors, which it is no more entitled to mar or squander than the man who holds a life interest in a family estate is entitled to dissipate the capital.

> I cannot conceive (said Burke) how any man can have brought himself to a pitch of presumption to consider his country as nothing but carte blanche upon which he may scribble whatever he pleases. *Spartam nactus es hanc exorna.*

You have inherited Sparta. Treat it properly. You were not born to its citizenship merely to enjoy its advantages. If we substitute Lloyd's for Sparta, then Burke gives us in that quotation exactly the moral we want for the young men now coming forward to assume the duties and enjoy the benefits of membership.

But at Lloyd's the threads of self-interest and of loyalty to Society are tightly interwoven, and if either of the threads had been broken in the last hundred years there might have been no Lloyd's left for the young men to inherit today. For the Society to be healthy and vigorous both threads are essential, and no one can study its history or understand its working without realizing how much every member owes to the corporate enthusiasm of its leaders, both in the past and in the present. Nothing damages a man's reputation at Lloyd's so much as a suspicion that he thinks only of his own pocket, and nothing so surely gains for him the respect of his fellow-members as a belief that he will in any circumstances put the general good before his own immediate interest. Both threads are vital. But Lloyd's is at its best when the loyalty thread is at its strongest. Is it too fanciful to hope that all the young men at Lloyd's will grasp that fact and make it a guiding principle of their careers?

. . . . . .

Looking back now over the past two hundred and seventy years and thinking of the men who have worked at Lloyd's, especially of the men who have at different times been its leaders, shaped its policy and helped it on its path to greatness, whose are the names that we most readily recall? If we had to draw up a list of a select few to whom we of the mid-twentieth century owe the most, whom should we put in it?

In the infancy of the place one name only is familiar to us – the name of Edward Lloyd himself. But he is a little like the founder of Rome – less a historical figure than a patronymic hero. Without Edward Lloyd's enterprise the particular coffee-house he founded could not have grown into a market or evolved into the modern Lloyd's. But when we have said that about him there is scarcely another tribute that we can pay. Nor do any of the men who followed him stand out as shining figures until the eighteenth century was three-quarters gone. There may have been great men in the earlier years but if there were their memory has not survived, and none claims our hero-worship until John Julius Angerstein makes his entrance in 1774. Of his ability, of his services to Lloyd's, of the value of the underwriting tradition that he started there is no doubt; and whether or not he deserves the title Father of Lloyd's (which is perpetuated below his portrait in the Royal Exchange) he must certainly have a place in our hagiography.

Contemporary with Angerstein there were several noteworthy underwriters who must have done a great deal to establish the reputation of Lloyd's during the Napoleonic Wars. The wooden-legged Brook Watson, who was Chairman from 1797 to 1806, was from his connections, if not from his underwriting (of which we know little), a most useful member of the Lloyd's community. He was a prominent figure in public life, Lord Mayor of London, Member of Parliament for the City and Commissary General to the British Army. So distinguished indeed was his career that his eminence at Lloyd's was overshadowed by his other achievements; and the Dictionary of National Biography says nothing of his connection with underwriting or of the fact that he was Chairman of Lloyd's Committee. His prestige and his host of acquaintances in the political world must have been very helpful to the development of Lloyd's, but we scarcely know enough about his work to give him a place in our list of great Lloyd's men.

Besides Angerstein, the one man of that period who must without question be given a place on our roll of honour was not an underwriter at all. He was an employee of the Society – John Bennett, Junior, the first Secretary of the Committee of Lloyd's, appointed in 1804 when he was twenty-six years old. He was a master of the Coffee-House and remained Secretary until his death in 1834. He was the founder of the modern intelligence service of Lloyd's and if one believes that the Society's pre-eminence was built on its shipping news, then young Bennett in an order of merit and service will not be far from the top.

After the monopoly was abolished by Parliament in 1824 Lloyd's went into the doldrums for a long period and great men were very scarce. The only man who might have a chance of honourable mention is G. R. Robinson, the Chairman at the time of the fire in 1839, who pulled Lloyd's together and helped the subscribers to turn disaster into something like triumph. To assess his work accurately on the information we possess would not be an easy task; but there is no doubt that in the years between 1839 and 1850 Lloyd's, which had seemed to be slowly dying, renewed its vitality and recovered its enterprise. And as Robinson was at the helm throughout that period, history must give him the major part of the credit for what happened. If all the credit goes to him it would scarcely be too high praise to call him in the 1840's the saviour of Lloyd's. He gets a place.

Twenty years further on we come to Colonel Hozier who became Secretary on 1st April 1874 and remained Secretary until 1906. Like John Bennett, Junior, he was an employee of the Society, not a member. But like Bennett he played a part at Lloyd's such as few members or subscribers ever played. The work he did for the Intelligence Service and his energy in founding signal stations would alone be enough to give him a high place of honour; but he did more than that. He reformed the administrative side of the Corporation and provided an efficient organization that was to be of the greatest value to the generation that succeeded him. Hozier certainly gets a place on our list.

We have come now to times within the memory of men still living and the task of choosing names for our roll of honour becomes more delicate. Personal feelings begin to colour and perhaps to distort judgments. But there can be no doubt that during the last eighty years Lloyd's has been unusually rich in men who claim our admiration and gratitude today.

366 Lloyd's of London

Unless there had been such men the enormous advance and progress that have taken place in our time would have been impossible, and from the full records that lie open to us it is not too difficult a task to name them. We may have our own preferences and prejudices but the record stands.

First there is Cuthbert Heath whose foresight and imagination not only created the modern non-marine market at Lloyd's but transformed for companies, as well as for Lloyd's, every kind of insurance except marine, life and motors. Every time a non-marine risk is written at Lloyd's, every time a loss of profits risk or burglary risk is accepted by a company, every time a company or the British Government insures a merchant against his bad debts, then the underwriting genius of Heath is recognized. In addition to all this, he was the first man to introduce a working audit at Lloyd's and that all-important service will remain for ever amongst his memorials. There can be no doubt about Heath's place in our roll of honour.

Then there was Sidney Boulton, that impulsive, generous-hearted, contentious figure forever challenging opposition, often in the thick of a dispute with his fellow members, sometimes mistaken but always passionately devoted to Lloyd's. If Heath invented the audit it was Boulton with his drive and energy who persuaded first the Committee and then the body of members to accept it. And that by itself would justify us in placing him on our list. Arthur Sturge, too, both for the determination with which he handled the Harrison troubles after the scandal became known and for the foresight and patience with which he secured for Lloyd's the site in Leadenhall Street, must always be honoured. The move from the Royal Exchange in 1928 was scarcely less important to the Society than the move to the Royal Exchange in 1774 and if Angerstein's name lives in Lloyd's history because he took the subscribers to the Royal Exchange, Sturge's name should surely live for taking the members away from it a hundred and fifty years later.

Lastly, is it too soon to include in our list one more recent name – Eustace Pulbrook? His death is too recent for us to appraise exactly the value of his services, but for six years of war and anxiety he was its Chairman and leader, faced almost daily with new problems for solution and never going wrong in his judgments. Pulbrook's crowning service was his visit to America in 1942, when his genius for negotiation broke down what was apparently a brick wall and saved for Lloyd's its connection with the United States which has meant so much to it for more than fifty years.

These are a few of the great names at Lloyd's. If one were called upon to place them in order of merit for the work they did for Lloyd's – an invidious task – one must surely head the order with Heath and perhaps put second John Bennett, Junior, who was elected Secretary in 1804. The tasks undertaken by the two men were very different, but Bennett's work on the shipping intelligence kept a purely marine Lloyd's going through the nineteenth century and Heath's practical genius made possible the blending of marine and non-marine which has brought Lloyd's to its pre-eminence in the twentieth. The first place in Lloyd's history must go to Heath. Bennett for second place is a personal choice and more disputable.

.     .     .     .     .     .

It is right that the names of these leaders of the past should not be for-gotten – that newcomers to Lloyd's should be made familiar with them and understand at least in outline what they have done for us. Anyone who learns the lesson correctly will see that the survival, let alone the growth, of Lloyd's has never been automatic. It has always been the result of the work done by Lloyd's men themselves. It has been achieved by great effort, often made in the face of heavy odds and against the hopes and fears of men who were well placed to judge of Lloyd's future. When the restriction on marine insurance was abolished in 1824, and for years after-wards, neutral observers wrote Lloyd's off as obsolete or derided it as an anachronism. They believed that even in marine insurance individual underwriting must either disappear or limp along as a historical curiosity. The idea that individual underwriters would ever establish among them-selves a great market for other risks than marine they laughed to scorn.

Nor has that disbelief in Lloyd's future always been confined to out-siders. Lloyd's men themselves have sometimes been sceptics. Not very many years ago an old underwriter told a young man, who was just starting out on a career at Lloyd's, that he was backing the wrong horse and had better look elsewhere for his livelihood. Fortunately both for himself and for Lloyd's the young man was deaf to the old pessimist, went on with his plan and became a leader of the market. But at times the chances against Lloyd's have looked overwhelming and, in truth, there were crises in its history at which one wrong step might have meant its end.

That the end never came; that Lloyd's remains the only place in the world in which individual underwriting is practised on a great scale; that it still thrives; that it is larger and more prosperous than ever before – all this is due to the great men who led it in the past and to the rank and file who upheld and supported them. The ordinary men who had the courage to back their own judgment at their own risk, who did not aspire to leadership but when their opinion was sought preferred the well-being of the Society to their own immediate interests – these men share with Heath, Angerstein, Bennett, Hozier, Boulton, and the other men of mark, the credit for the present greatness of Lloyd's. On their successors in the rising generation its future greatness depends.

The New Building, showing part of the 1928 Building; another impression from
Lime Street by Sidney R. Jones (October, 1956).

# INDEX

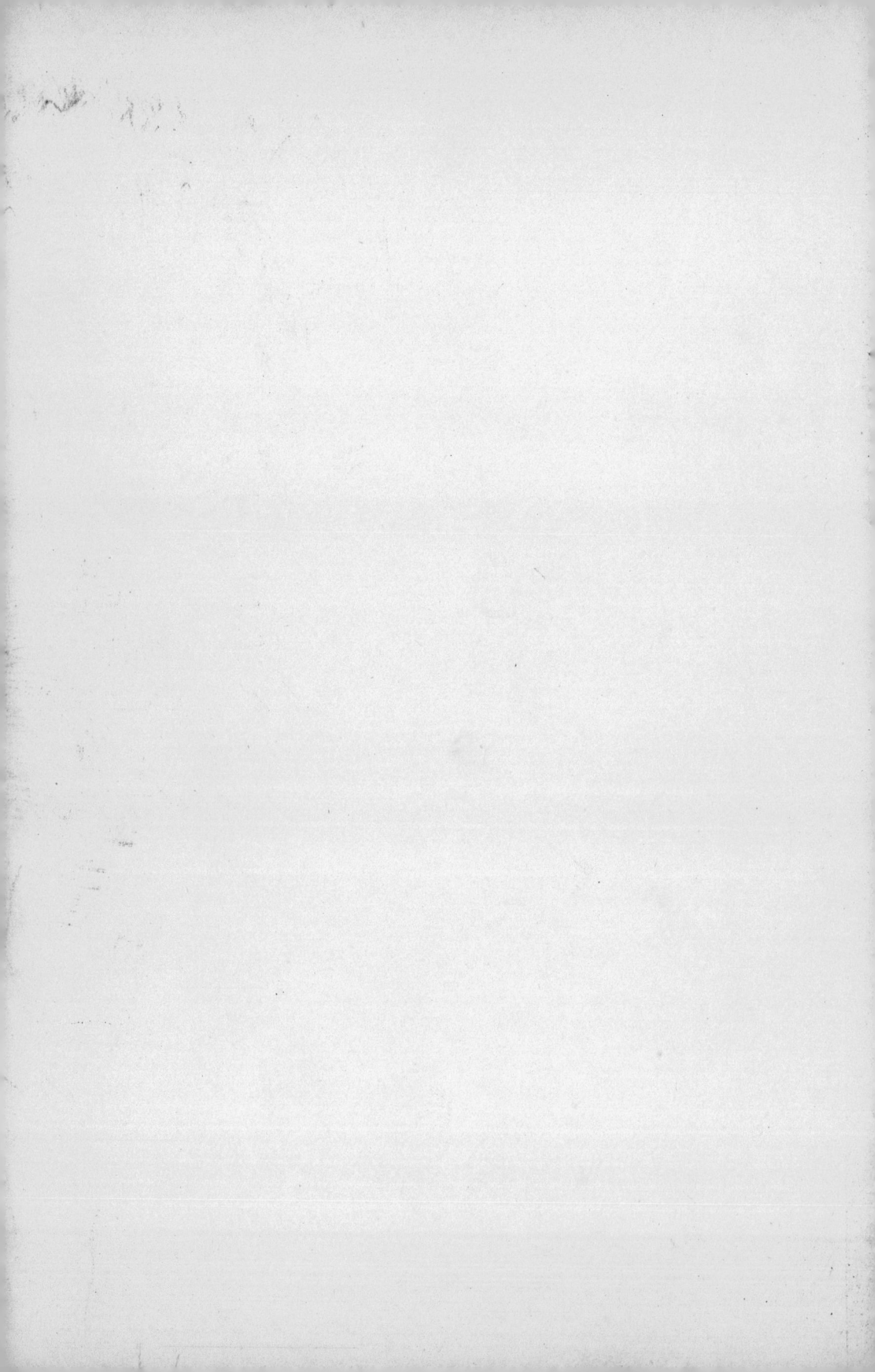